Looking for the Proletariat

Historical Materialism Book Series

The Historical Materialism Book Series is a major publishing initiative of the radical left. The capitalist crisis of the twenty-first century has been met by a resurgence of interest in critical Marxist theory. At the same time, the publishing institutions committed to Marxism have contracted markedly since the high point of the 1970s. The Historical Materialism Book Series is dedicated to addressing this situation by making available important works of Marxist theory. The aim of the series is to publish important theoretical contributions as the basis for vigorous intellectual debate and exchange on the left.

The peer-reviewed series publishes original monographs, translated texts, and reprints of classics across the bounds of academic disciplinary agendas and across the divisions of the left. The series is particularly concerned to encourage the internationalization of Marxist debate and aims to translate significant studies from beyond the English-speaking world.

For a full list of titles in the Historical Materialism Book Series available in paperback from Haymarket Books, visit:
www.haymarketbooks.org/category/hm-series

Looking for the Proletariat

*Socialisme ou Barbarie and
the Problem of Worker Writing*

By
Stephen Hastings-King

Haymarket Books
Chicago, IL

First published in 2014 by Brill Academic Publishers, The Netherlands
© 2014 Koninklijke Brill NV, Leiden, The Netherlands

Published in paperback in 2015 by
Haymarket Books
P.O. Box 180165
Chicago, IL 60618
773-583-7884
www.haymarketbooks.org

ISBN: 978-1-60846-482-1

Trade distribution:
In the US, Consortium Book Sales, www.cbsd.com
In Canada, Publishers Group Canada, www.pgcbooks.ca
In the UK, Turnaround Publisher Services, www.turnaround-uk.com
In all other countries, Publishers Group Worldwide, www.pgw.com

Cover design by Ragina Johnson.

This book was published with the generous support of
Lannan Foundation and the Wallace Global Fund.

Printed in Canada by union labor.

10 9 8 7 6 5 4 3 2 1

Library of Congress Cataloging-in-Publication data is available.

Contents

Acknowledgements   vii

Introduction   1

1 Where Things Start   24

2 Rethinking Revolutionary Theory   72

3 Frame: On Claude Lefort's 'L'Expérience Prolétarienne'   105

4 Working-Class Politics at Renault Billancourt   135

5 Looking for the Working Class   165

6 Reading Daniel Mothé   235

Postface   321
Bibliography   326
Index   337

'Its funny, you know', Russ says, 'but I think it was Charlotte put the look on my face."

'The lady or the city?'

'Definitely the city. I spent years in a studio doing re-creations of big league games. The telegraph bug clacking in the background and blabbermouth Hodges inventing ninety-nine percent of the action. And I'll tell you something scout's honor. I know this sounds farfetched but I used to sit there and dream of doing real baseball from a booth in the Polo Grounds in New York'.

'Real baseball'.

'The thing that happens in the sun'.

Somebody hands you a piece of paper filled with letters and numbers and you have to make a ball game out of it. You create the weather, flesh out the players, you make them sweat and grouse and hitch up their pants, and it is remarkable, thinks Russ, how much earthly disturbance, how much summer and dust the mind can manage to order up from a single Latin letter laying flat.[1]

---

1   Delillo 1997, p. 25.

Acknowledgements

This book is based on my 1999 doctoral dissertation. The research for which would have been impossible without the generosity of The French Ministry of Culture, which provided me with a Bourse Chateaubriand for the academic year 1991–1992 and The Fulbright Program of the U.S.I.A.

While in Paris, I met and interviewed members of Socialisms ou Barbarie. I cannot adequately express my appreciation for their hospitality and willingness to talk: Jean Amory; Helen Arnold; Daniel Blanchard; Pierre Blachier; Jacques Blot; Cornelius Castoriadis; André Charconnet; Sebastien de Diesbach; Jacques Gautrat; Martine Gautrat; Andrée Lyotard; Maurice Kouriez; Alberto Maso; Georges Petit; Jacques Signorelli; Henri Simon; Verdier.

The following people provided me with internal papers from their private collections: Helen Arnold and Daniel Blanchard; Cornelius Castoriadis; Henri Simon; Jacques Signorelli; Verdier. I examined the papers deposited at L'lnstitut Mémoires de l'edition contemporaine (IMEC) in Paris by Jacques Gautrat/Daniel Mothé. I thank Olivier Corpet for his generosity.

Henri Simon went to great lengths to make me feel welcome, introduce me to people and provide me with documents. Even after all this time, I still feel badly that the last parcel got fouled up in the mail, and hope that no harm was done.

Scott Maclemee graciously provided me with documentation and information about the Correspondence group and Kent Worcester information on Johnson Forest. Patrick Fridenson, Dick Howard and Joel Whitebook provided considerable help in the early stages of my research, for which I am grateful. My thanks to my graduate committee – Dominick LaCapra, Steven Kaplan and David Sabean – and to my friends from Cornell, wherever they may be. And to Gerry O'Sullivan, who put me onto Castoriadis in the first place.

This book comes long after the dissertation. My thanks to David Ames Curtis and Clara Gibson Maxwell for their belief in this project from the beginning, and to Gavin Walker for myriad discussions in Philadelphia and afterward that helped keep me connected to this phase of my work even as I was engaged in other things. David Ames Curtis and Kelly Grotke were of immense help in the final stages of preparation. My thanks to the Historical Materialism collective, Sébastien Budgen and David Broder in particular.

Encountering and entering deeply into the work of Cornelius Castoriadis changed me. I had the privilege of getting to know him personally. I dedicate this book to his memory.

Introduction

Socialisme ou Barbarie[1] was one of the most important and influential Marxist groups to emerge after World War II. Centred in Paris around writers like Cornelius Castoriadis, Claude Lefort, Daniel Mothé, Pierre Souyri and Jean-François Lyotard, the group engaged in a sustained, intensive critical interaction with post-war capitalism, politics and culture through the lens of Marx. The group began in 1946 as the Chaulieu-Montal Tendency, part of the Left Opposition in late 1940s Trotskyism. It split to become an independent group in 1949. By its 1967 dissolution, Socialisme ou Barbarie was arguing for the rejection of Marx and Marxism in the name of revolution. The forty issues of the journal *Socialisme ou Barbarie* appearing between 1949 and 1966 conveyed to a significant audience of Left students and intellectuals both the group's vision of socialism as autonomy instituted through direct-democratic worker councils, and their insistence that revolutionary theory must be grounded in a rigorous critical theory of contemporary capitalism.

The group was a central player in debates about Marxism, revolutionary politics and decolonisation that conditioned the 'New Left,' which began to take shape in France during 1957. Innovative political organisations like the collective that published *Arguments* and *L'Internationale Situationniste* were deeply marked by *Socialisme ou Barbarie* and its critique of the USSR and Stalinism, its approach to Marxism and its vision of direct-democratic socialism. Socialisme ou Barbarie was crucial in the debates over the implications of Gaullism for working-class politics that crystallised what later became the *'sociologie du travail'* and was a consistent radical critic of both the Algerian War and the *tiers-mondiste* interpretations of the Front de Libération Nationale that were then fashionable amongst the student and intellectual antiwar movement. The group's radically democratic politics informed the *autogestionnaire* (self-management) intellectual current that flourished in Left industrial politics during the 1960s and 1970s through journals like *Autogestion* and organisations like the CFDT (*Confédération française démocratique du travail*).[2] Diffracted

---

[1] Socialisme ou Barbarie refers both to the group and to the title of the journal they collectively produced. When the name refers to the group, it appears in regular font. When it refers to the journal, it appears in italics.

[2] The journal *Autogestion et socialisme* [*Self-management and Socialism*] was started in 1965 by current and former members of *Socialisme ou Barbarie*, including Yvon Bourdet and Alain Guillerm. Daniel Mothé wrote for the journal in its early period as well. For the centrality of *Socialisme ou Barbarie* as a reference-point in the initial articulation of *Autogestion et*

through the prism of Guy Debord's Situationist art/politics, Socialisme ou Barbarie was also a key influence on the ideology behind the May 1968 student revolt.[3]

Despite all this, Socialisme ou Barbarie remains largely unknown, particularly in the English-speaking world. Its collective work was fragmented by the publication of anthologies undertaken by individuals in the early 1970s.[4] David Ames Curtis translated and published much of Cornelius Castoriadis's work.[5] Other scholars, like Dick Howard, have long drawn attention to that of Claude Lefort.[6] In the United States, the reception accorded to the work by Socialisme ou Barbarie and its members' subsequent writings was largely confined to academic settings. Their trans-disciplinary character seemed to have caused them to fall through the cracks. They were too philosophical for politics, too political for philosophy. In other areas, their reception was confused because the works did not operate from the same assumptions as the 'French theory'

---

socialismes theoretical position, see Bourdet 1963 and 'Les contradictions de la hétérogestion', *Autogestion*, 8, pp. 135–75 and 'Les conditions de possibilité de l'autogestion', *Autogestion*, pp. 9–10.

3   The only systematic expression of a '68 ideology', Daniel Cohn-Bendit's *Obsolete Communism: The Left Wing Alternative* (Cohn-Bendit 1968), was almost entirely plagiarised from *Socialisme ou Barbarie*. In my April 1993 interview, former *Socialisme ou Barbarie* member Alberto Maso (Véga) counted 78 pages in the original French edition that were taken directly from *Socialisme ou Barbarie* articles without attribution, and claimed that the rest was actually written by Danny's brother, Gabriel Cohn-Bendit, a former participant in the group.

4   10/18 published multiple volumes of Castoriadis's *Socialisme ou Barbarie* writings supplemented with other material most of which post-dated *Socialisme ou Barbarie* through the 1970s. Lefort's collection *Elements pour une critique de la bureaucratie*, which appeared in 1971 from Droz (reprinted as Lefort 1979), was the first collection to separate individual contributions from those of the group. These publications were invaluable on their own both for the texts and for the extensive information they provided about Socialisme ou Barbarie. Because they had better distribution than did the journal, they exposed to a wider audience the ideas that Socialisme ou Barbarie had developed. At the same time, they had the effect of making the group appear to be Castoriadis, Lefort and a bunch of other people, to the chagrin of many of the members of the group I spoke with while researching this book. This project tries to treat *Socialisme ou Barbarie* as a collective. Much of it is focused on Daniel Mothé. But the internal documentation that would have enabled a more fleshed-out look at the collective in action mostly pertains to the period after this project stops.

5   See his translations of the three volume set of Castoriadis's *Political and Social Writings* published by the University of Minnesota (Castoriadis 1988). The Agora International bibliographic project cannot be recommended too highly as a resource for people interested in Castoriadis's work: <http://www.agorainternational.org/>.

6   See in particular Howard 1988.

that was then dominant. The situation was different for Lyotard. But his work on the Algerian War, completed while he was part of Socialisme ou Barbarie, was presented to an English-speaking audience in a way that disconnected it from his later writing.[7] The journal *Socialism ou Barbarie* itself has never been translated.[8] An indication of this combination of invisibility and influence can be found in the sense of the tradition of direct-democratic political action particular to the US Occupy movement. Inspired in general by the Spanish 15M and in particular by a call to action from *Adbusters*, the movement has been contextualised within a history of the Situationists.[9] There is little sense of an engagement that goes beyond that to the group that fundamentally shaped Debord's politics.[10] Perhaps this book can play a small role in changing this state of affairs by inspiring interest in both Socialisme ou Barbarie and the later work done by people associated with the group.

As of yet, the political appropriations of Socialisme ou Barbarie have been shaped by the same conflict that tore the group apart: the simultaneous desires to develop a radical critique of contemporary capitalism and remain Marxist. For some, Marxism remains the legitimate language of dissent. But it has been collapsed back into a textual tradition that primarily enables what Piera Aulagnier called a 'rationalisation of alienation.' While it can provide useful heuristics in certain situations, Marxism is now one framework amongst others. As a theoretical framework, it is no longer adequate to comprehend contemporary capitalism or new forms of radical contestation. Its own history has pulverised it as a language of political mobilisation. One of the hopes that animated this project from its beginnings was to present Socialisme ou Barbarie as something other than a merely sophisticated variant of revolutionary Marxism. In the period covered by this book, the group captured something of the collapse of the Marxist Imaginary. What was captured unfolded in

---

7   Lyotard 1993. The fragmenting of Lyotard's work is reflected in the arbitrariness of the book's organisation.
8   Scans of the some issues can be found at the 'Soubscans' project here: <http://soubscan.org/>. As of this writing, pdfs are available for the first 10 issues. Members of Socialisme ou Barbarie collectively edited *Socialisme ou Barbarie, une anthologie* (Simon [ed.] 2010). The press is a tiny operation (http://acratie.over-blog.com/): the text is available by subscription.
9   The call to action can be found here: <http://www.adbusters.org/blogs/adbusters-blog/occupywallstreet.html>. Mackenzie Wark's newer work on the Situationists seems to me to formalise this understanding of a past that links the Occupation to *les Situs*. See Wark 2011.
10 Hastings-King 1999, pp. 26–54.

the heart of the Marxian project. The group itself struggled to come to terms with developments that undermined their own framework.

Some Terminological and Formal Matters

This project involves some terminology borrowed from the philosophical work that Cornelius Castoriadis developed after Socialisme ou Barbarie. I use it operationally so as to organise and clarify phenomena. At times, this approach creates the anachronistic impression that Socialisme ou Barbarie was already using the language that Castoriadis would later fashion, which is not the case. My appropriation and use of that language arises from my work on the group itself and reflects my understanding of its trajectory . For example, the notion of the Marxist Imaginary was inspired by Castoriadis. When I came up with the term in the early 1990s, I had the idea of presenting a full-blown account of it. This ambition resulted in many adventures: relearning the Marxist textual tradition and the ways it shaped and had been shaped by the histories of the main political organisations and of the workers' movement; trying to explain the royalism that links Trotsky's interpretation of Stalin to the gifts offered to the Friend of the Children and Conqueror of Happiness for his 70th birthday; following the echoes of the Bukharin trail to Edgar Morin's puzzling account of imitation show trials in the PCF of the early 1950s. These adventures ran alongside various attempts to generate an account of Socialisme ou Barbarie using the journal in tandem with interviews and internal documents that referred to densities of context that ran well beyond what I had imagined when I arrived in Paris from a place in which deconstruction was confused with a radical politics. The results were endless drafts for potential chapters. Most ended up in boxes. They form the invisible surround for what you are reading. Eventually, I realised that the book itself is a map of a spatially and temporally specific version of the Marxist Imaginary, conditioned by the conventions that obtained while I was making it. The sort of account I initially dreamed of would be a manifold, an open series of other such books, film clips, sound recordings, images and artifacts, memories and experiences. As is the case for any social imaginary formation, the Marxist Imaginary is nothing but versions. Here is another.

From the viewpoint of method, what follows is an alteration between historical sociology and the close readings of texts. The project is split in two. The first part concerns Socialisme ou Barbarie directly; the second concerns the problem of worker writing. The two are intricately intertwined. Each part opens with a sociological frame and moves into engagement with texts. As a function of the differences that separate the space of small Parisian militant groups from that of the Renault factory at Bologne-Billancourt, the results are divergent. The relations to context in the analyses that follow track the situation of Socialisme ou Barbarie. In the earlier chapters, they are central. In the fourth chapter, the group is marginal. The last two strike different balances.

While a more detailed overview is provided in the following sections of this introduction, it is useful to give a schematic version here in order to highlight some of the main thematic and formal features of the book. The first chapter situates Socialisme ou Barbarie in the contest of anti-Stalinist Left politics immediately after World War Two. It uses elements drawn from the work of Pierre Bourdieu to highlight the ways in which the sociological conditions shaped and constrained the group. The departure from Trotskyism put the group in terrain littered with short-lived organizations. The members responded by instituting an internal process of critical engagement with Lenin and Marx that enabled Socialisme ou Barbarie to be an explicit collective self-creation. The chapter stages this early period with that in mind.

Chapters 2 and 3 follow the fleshing-out of a version of the Marxist Imaginary in the pages of *Socialisme ou Barbarie.* The group's analyses of the 1953 East Berlin June Days emphasised worker re-appropriation of the language of revolutionary Marxism, a development that became a template for understanding autonomous worker actions, all of which activated this language to express their opposition to the situations in which they found themselves. It was revolutionary language because they organised in opposition to Communist Party dominated contexts. The re-appropriation also enabled these workers to take over subject positions as revolutionary activists. The ways in which this process worked were shaped fundamentally by conditions at the point of production. The interactions of these factors were performed through direct-democratic forms of collective self-organisation that workers adopted and in the types of demands they generated. Autonomous worker actions enacted a relation to the language of the Marxist tradition that paralleled Socialisme ou Barbarie's own. While the Marxist Imaginary refers to the entire range of socio-cognitive creations instituted in ways shaped by the sedimented history of that tradition, for Socialisme ou Barbarie the language was fundamental, as were the modes of self-organisation enabled by it. In the West, Marxism was the legitimate discourse for framing opposition to capitalism and the range of political options associated with it. Texts and arguments rooted in them play a more prominent role in oppositional politics than they do for dominant ideological positions. The continuities of everyday life are *de facto* arguments for the legitimacy of the dominant order.

As noted above, for Socialisme ou Barbarie the re-appropriation of the language of revolution by workers was shaped by their everyday experience at the point of production. The third chapter frames this understanding and the claim that only workers can know and, by extension, write about, that experience, a claim premised on the group's critique of Leninism. It then outlines the formal characteristics of the type of worker writing Socialisme ou Barbarie valorised. Chapters 2 and 3 are rooted in types of close reading. To the extent that it is an expanded variant of ordinary reading, the exclusion of problematic relations to context follows from close reading. In these chapters, the exclusion is symmetrical with Socialisme ou Barbarie's collective relation to its immediate environment. From that situation, workers are objects of intense interest and political investment. The factory is an Elsewhere. The texts stage workers in the factory as from a distance.

The worker narratives that Socialisme ou Barbarie published in the journal can be read entirely within the interpretive framework of the journal. But the texts the group published, most of which concern the French automobile industry of the mid-1950s, are the only first-person accounts of worker experience in the factories under the industrial Fordism of the period. Most focus on the experience of machinists under pressures of production re-organisation and deskilling as well as production speed-ups. The trade unions could not or would not address such quality of work issues as a function of their integration into collective bargaining. Unlike the collages of strike reports and related analyses also published in *Socialisme ou Barbarie*, these narratives provide a degree of temporal continuity in the staging of shop-floor relations. They describe informal mechanisms whereby workers could mobilise in order to draw attention to quality of work problems. In their use of the language of revolution, they conformed to the pattern described in the analysis of East Berlin. But in these more continuous narratives, autonomous worker actions figure in two directions, one in the context of the group's revolutionary project and another at Billancourt. Separating these registers so they can interact in a more complex manner than would be the case were they treated simply as elements in a narrative of the group's development is one of the tasks that shapes the second half of this book.

Chapter Three introduces the problematic of worker writing, which is the central concern of this book. From this point, Socialisme ou Barbarie itself as an ongoing practical elaboration becomes a secondary motif. With Chapter Four, we move into an overview of the sociological contexts that obtained at Renault's Billancourt factory, the main setting for the group's efforts to solicit workers to write. Chapter Five discusses the Detroit-based worker newspaper *Correspondence*, its organisation and outputs. The successor to the Johnson-

Forest Tendency, *Correspondence* was a fundamental interlocutor (and foil) for Socialisme ou Barbarie's collective understanding of the worker newspaper as an organisational tool and source for worker writing. I then discuss the fraught relations between the groups before moving to *Tribune Ouvrière*. While never a worker newspaper in the sense Socialisme ou Barbarie would have preferred, it was nonetheless an important source for information about everyday experience in the French automobile industry in the journal. My reading of *Tribune Ouvrière* goes beyond this frame and treats it as a documentary source.

The final chapter centres on Socialisme ou Barbarie member Jacques Gautrat, who wrote a series of narratives about his experience at Billancourt for the journal between late 1956 and early 1957 under the name Daniel Mothé. It positions Mothé as inside and outside, a pseudonym and an identity, as a Socialisme ou Barbarie member (Mothé) and a worker at Renault (Gautrat). Mothé was the group's Worker and his texts the main exemplars of the sort of worker writing its members hoped to gather. But what these narratives track is a disinvestment in the language of revolutionary Marxism on the part of workers. The position of Mothé's narratives in *Socialisme ou Barbarie* reconfigures what is documented as unfolding amongst the worker avant-garde in the Abstract Factory at the heart of the Marxist Imaginary. At the same time, positioning these narratives with reference to Gautrat's experiences at Billancourt makes the descriptions particular. These two possibilities alternate in an interesting manner: the book does not treat this as a problem and makes no attempt to 'solve' it.

Mothé provides glimpses of a disinvestment in the Marxist Imaginary that plays out in the socially instituted relations to the language of revolution that enabled autonomous worker mobilisations at Billancourt. From an analytic viewpoint, describing a disruption in the relation of the instituted to the instituting is a problem, one of bringing clarity to registers of social being that are invisible but which are no less fundamental for that. The register of the instituting involves affective, cognitive and social relations to the language of the Marxist Imaginary.[11] There is a problem of how to talk about the instituting at

---

11   Throughout what follows you will also find the notion of a social-imaginary signification. Castoriadis refers to a signification as 'skeins of referrals', provisional nodes in dense networks of associations. In this, the notion is analytical, but it indicates something of ways of living through, of projecting a version of the present and vision of the future predicated on ideas of a politically, ethically and personally more desirable future. Significations are instituted, to the extent that they are condensed expressions of a collective history, and instituting to the extent that these expressions shape cognitive and affective styles, that is, patterns of investment and projection.

all, one that is compounded by the fact that the withdrawal of consent did not affect all relations to the language. By 1957, Marxism was primarily an organisational ideology, a language used by political parties (for example) to speak to and about themselves. At these registers, the production of the language was not interrupted. Mothé describes a history without events. This seems characteristic of the death of a social-imaginary formation. Those invested in it, who inhabit the world shaped by it, would have great difficulty processing the disintegration of their own frame of reference. Those outside are unlikely to capture such granular phenomena.

In the last chapter, I refer to disinvestment as the breakdown of language games. This is not theorised in *Socialisme ou Barbarie*. In early 1957, the group saw itself atop the crest of a mounting wave of proletarian revolutionary activity, and took the events in Hungary (and the ensuing Soviets suppression) as massive confirmations of their assumptions concerning new revolutionary activity and direct-democratic forms of self-organisation. The group also found itself with a larger audience than it had previously enjoyed both in terms of readership and those who attended the group's public meetings. They were not looking for what Mothé described. Neither, for that matter, was Mothé.

The project ends with this analysis. I confronted the problem of managing length, and this choice provided a solution. The end-point leaves open the questions that follow from the worker disinvestment in the basis for the Marxist Imaginary captured in Mothé's texts. It stops before the Audin affair and Algerian War began the transformation of the Parisian Left, typically characterised as the transition from 'Old' to 'New' Left. This shift hinged on the mobilisation of new social groups (students, intellectuals) and created a context that made of the working class a construction that could be classified as imaginary in a quite different sense, an abstract function operative in the texts that introduced these actors to the legitimate language of oppositional politics. The implications of this transition were occulted in a transfer of political energy.

In the 1964 essay 'Marxism and Revolutionary Theory', Castoriadis wrote that conditions had reached such a pass that one could either be a Marxist or a revolutionary.[12] The question posed here is whether the Marxist Imaginary had already been pulverised by its own history as early as 1957. Because the group's trajectory performs and articulates that crisis on another level, the implications of this early moment would have been domesticated had this book integrated them into an episode in the narrative of the progressive unfolding of Socialisme ou Barbarie's overall project.

---

12   Castoriadis 1998 [1964].

I write this in 2013, at a time when even a cursory assessment of the fate of the Marxist Imaginary should make it clear that the surviving aspects of the Imaginary are inoperative politically and dated conceptually. Continuing to invest in Marxism as an adequate descriptive or political language is no longer to engage in a form of praxis that may change the world. It is the rearrangement of elements in a curiosity cabinet. The disposition of a militant has been replaced by that of a collector. The rationalisation of alienation is all there is. The collector's organisation and re-organisation of a closed system of discursive elements enables the avoidance of both Marxism's conceptual and political problems and of thinking the possibilities for basic social transformation that continue to be posited in the present. To rethink those possibilities requires an accompanying philosophical transformation: to take up what Castoriadis called 'the project of autonomy'.

We reach this place at the end of the project. Now, we start over.

On the Construction of the Worker

This project is focused on Socialisme ou Barbarie's construction of the worker. A brief rehearsal of the traditional Marxist conception of revolution will help to set up what Socialisme ou Barbarie was trying to do.[13] In *The Communist Manifesto*, Marx and Engels present the idea of a politics of revolution in the context of a conception of a history that moves in stages. The movement from one to the next is dialectical. Each stage takes shape within the previous as its negation. Revolution is the moment of transcendence, one that suppresses some attributes of the previous stage while conserving and transforming others. Each historical stage is the expression of a dominant rationality, a way of shaping and organising information that reflects and reproduces social relations both amongst people and to the natural world. Because each such rationality operates by exclusions, each provides space within itself for the development of other social logics. Bourgeois society grew out of the forms of commercial interactions that took shape largely in towns, in opposition to the dominant, aristocratic rationality that Marx attributes to the feudal period. The French Revolution marked the transition from one stage to the next. Just as capitalism had supplanted feudalism through a process that culminated in revolution, so socialism would supplant capitalism, with the proletariat acting as the transformative agent. Just as bourgeois rationality had constituted itself within and against aristocratic society around notions of

---

13   A version of this narrative can be found in Lefort 1979 [1952].

formal equality, private property and social relations mediated by money, so the proletariat would enact the basis for a rationality rooted in the suppression of private property and the institution of the collective management of production and society. Capitalism produced socialism's conditions of possibility in the context of industrial production. The task of revolutionary politics was to facilitate the recognition of commonalities, which would result in the transition from the working class as a class in-itself to a class for-itself, from workers who happened to occupy similar positions in the production process to a class aware of itself as a class and conscious of its own interests. Industrial production was crucial, not only because it provided the material basis for social reproduction, but also because it was the most advanced expression of bourgeois thinking and technical development. The proletariat was itself a creation of capitalism.

Marx saw in the situation of the working class in capitalist production the condition of the possibility of social revolution. This view leans on a form of double consciousness. To the extent that each worker is a socially functional subject, each is shaped by the dominant Imaginary. But the relations are circumscribed by class position. It follows that the general relation characteristic of workers to the dominant Imaginary would be one of simultaneous inclusion and exclusion. But for Marx it is the confrontation with actual capitalist production that is determinate. When a worker sells his or her labour power for a wage and enters the space of production, that worker encounters the reality that is shaped and concealed by what Marx called ideology. Technological design, the organisation of work and the system of wages are material expressions of the bourgeois subordination of human relations and of an instrumental rationality that operates on a world comprised of objects.

When Marx characterised capitalist production in the '1844 Manuscripts', he juxtaposed it with an ideal-typical image of artisanal production.[14] Craft-based production presupposes workers who possess skill. Its technologies require active kinetic engagement to operate. Work is a social undertaking. The scale of production is small enough to enable workers to know the whole process and understand the disposition of the objects produced. In capitalist production, technologies perform most of the skilled operations. The work is individuated and repetitive. The sense of involvement with a coherent process is fragmented. The scale of production separates workers from the disposition of the commodities that are produced. For Marx, by shattering the workers' primary mode of meaningful interaction with themselves and the material world,

---

14   Marx 1992 [1844].

capitalism takes from them what makes them human. Alienation reduces workers to the status of an object, to an appendage of the machine.

Taken as an ethical argument, alienation is a tendency rather than an accomplishment. By granting workers a degree of space within a production that does not entirely dehumanise them, this view would make of the experience of production the basis for an immanent critique of capitalism. This conception places workers inside and outside, both participants in and capable of making judgments about that system. Such a relation is the basis for the double consciousness that endows the workers with the possibility of mobilising as a class to become the agent of the supersession of capitalism. This viewpoint is close to that adopted by Socialisme ou Barbarie. However, if one takes this description as factual, rather different consequences result.

The image of the relations of production outlined in the earlier Marx is both subjectively oriented and static. In *Capital*, Marx renders dynamic the relations of production by situating them in the networks that are constitutive of capital. These comprise the centrepiece of his model of competitive capitalism. The model links the exploitation of workers in their everyday experience in production to overall system dynamics. The 'organic crises of capital' – the declining rate of profit in particular – drives capitalist firms to maximise exploitation through increasing the speed of work and/or length of the working day. The same pressures are expressed in decreasing wages. Inside production, technological developments enact a logic that equates efficiency with deskilling. Deskilling makes workers interchangeable. Through processes like enclosure, the corrosive effects of capitalist property relations result in a stream of people driven from older forms of rural production to the cities in search of work. The result is an increasing immiseration of the proletariat. Workers organise themselves into trade-unions and struggle to improve their situation. But from this viewpoint, capitalism cannot accommodate their demands. The overall dynamics of capitalism results in a spiralling deterioration in the lives of working people both inside and outside the factories. Revolution would be the explosion of desperate working people already dehumanised by capitalist production.

Amongst more orthodox Marxists of the 1940s–50s, there was a general agreement about this version of Marx. The sociological or historical analysis of concrete relations of production could produce snapshots. A dynamic understanding required a shift into a mode of economic analysis that emphasised the objective forces that shaped capitalism as a system. Dialectical materialism assumed that the capitalism Marx described was shaped by a sort of essence. Capitalism was made over as a closed system in which there was reality, the space governed by these forces, and the accidental, which included everything else. The emphasis on objective forces reduced the working class to a function. Lukacs's definition of class consciousness as the alignment of working-class actions with objective necessity was a blunt statement of an assumption shared by most orthodox Marxist analyses. This corresponds to a miserablist view of workers dehumanised by capitalist relations of production. It is not surprising that this form of Marxian analysis would become dominant with the Third International: it integrates into the centre of revolutionary politics the need for a Vanguard Party. In the Marxian tradition, the violent suppression of the Paris Commune in 1870 triggered a rethinking of revolutionary organisation along military lines. Leninist organisation was a culmination of this process. Lenin's claim that trade unionism is the highest level of political consciousness that workers will aspire to if left to themselves corresponds to the miserablist understanding of the working class.[15]

Socialisme ou Barbarie rejected the orthodox understandings of history, and of the nature of revolutionary political action. Orthodox Marxism understood capitalism as a variant of an object. The laws that Marx isolated were an essence spread out in time. For reasons that we will analyse in the first chapter below, Socialisme ou Barbarie historicised the model that Marx fashioned of mid-nineteenth-century capitalism. What made the model important to begin with was not the isolation of overall system characteristics, but rather the effects of these characteristics on the situation of working people. So if one historicised the model but retained a focus on understanding the situation of workers, one kept to the political heart of Marx's analysis. This enabled the group to argue that the reconfigurations of capitalist organisation, driven by the tendency to concentration, were qualitative changes. To be coherent on Marxian grounds, revolutionary theory had to account for these changes and work to locate and empower forms of revolutionary action symmetrical with them. To do this, Socialisme ou Barbarie adopted a sociologically-oriented approach to the relations of production. The group's construction of the worker as a social-imaginary signification followed from this move. But the

---

15   As an aside, the trade-union movement was one of the great accomplishments of the late nineteenth–early twentieth-century workers' movement. However, from the viewpoint of revolutionary theory, the trade-union movement followed the logic that Eduard Bernstein had elaborated in the debates that split Social Democrats from revolutionaries in Germany just before World War I. If changes in the organisation of capitalism meant that revolution had to be seen as a longer-term prospect, it followed that the trade-union movement should interact with capital on the best possible terms in order to ameliorate the situation of working people in the short run. This marked a definitive split of revolutionary from reformist politics. *Socialisme ou Barbarie* followed this general logic, but reframed it in terms of their theory of bureaucratic capitalism.

turn to the social-historical raised the problem of how theory, embedded by virtue of the class position of the theorist in the rationality that revolutionary action would overturn, could access the germinal forms of the rationality that would be generalised as socialism through the process of revolution. The solution the group settled on was to encourage workers to write about their own experiences at the point of production.

Overview

What you have been reading to this point assumes other features of Socialisme ou Barbarie's project. So we turn to an overview.

Socialisme ou Barbarie began its trajectory as an independent group when the Chaulieu-Montal Tendency split with the Trotskyist Parti Communiste Internationaliste (PCI) in 1949. The Tendency was started in 1946 by Cornelius Castoriadis and Claude Lefort around 'The Russian Question'. Trotsky had argued that the USSR was 'basically socialist' and that the Stalinist bureaucracy was an expression of Stalin's illegitimacy as Lenin's successor. Against this, the CMT developed a quite different analysis, one that took Soviet bureaucracy seriously. The result was a comprehensive theory of bureaucratic capitalism that enabled the Tendency to argue that, from a viewpoint informed by the analysis of the relations of production, the Soviet system was a new form of capitalism. The fusion of party and state created a centralised bureaucratic apparatus that managed Fordist-style production design in the same kind of top-down command-oriented manner as its Western counterparts. But the power of the Party apparatus removed the brakes that limited the exploitation of workers in Western forms of capitalism. It was all the worst features of capitalism made even worse. The early issues of *Socialisme ou Barbarie* are largely taken up with the demolition of associations linking Stalinism to socialism and of the Trotskyist interpretations that claimed as much.

The group linked the nature of the Soviet system to the Leninist vanguard party. Both bureaucratic-capitalist management and the Leninist party separated the *dirigeant* from *exécutants*, those who issue commands from those who carry them out. This division of intellectual labour was the defining characteristic of bureaucratic capitalism in general. In the Leninist context, this separation derived from the same miserabalist notion of the working class that was inscribed in orthodox Marxism. The claim that the Soviet system was not socialist raised the question of what socialism was. From the outset, the group emphasised that worker-collective management of production and its outputs would be the defining criterion. This position was argued by appealing to history: the abolition of private property and the expropriation of capitalists had not by itself resulted in socialism in the USSR, because the problematic nature of the division of intellectual labour was not recognised. The Soviet system enabled revolutionary militants to understand that mistake.

The centrality of worker control to socialism was not a new idea: it was a main slogan in the Russian Revolution, just as the Soviets were to be the instruments that allowed it to be exercised. But the way Socialisme ou Barbarie conceptualised it, particularly after the revolt in East Berlin and French general strikes of the summer 1953, was to elaborate its notion of socialism as direct democracy. Chapter Two provides a detailed reconstruction of the group's analyses of the worker actions of summer 1953. In general, the analyses show a continuum that linked conflicts at the point of production over the organisation and pace of work to the forms adopted by what the group called autonomous worker actions. It is interesting to note that, from the outset, the group focused on the situation of semi-skilled workers and their conflicts with management (be it Party or factory) as involving fundamental questions about the management of work. Skill becomes the implicit centre of the group's vision of worker autonomy and the enabling condition for conflicts at the point of production to issue into the germinal forms of a socialist rationality.

Conceptually, Socialisme ou Barbarie linked autonomous worker actions, their forms of self-organisation and demands, back to everyday experience at the point of production. Central to this linkage was their notion of bureaucratic capitalism. For Socialisme ou Barbarie, bureaucracy designates a process that converges across its manifestations on the separation of the *dirigeant* from *exécutants*. It is an *eidos*, or a form that is best understood as resulting from a phenomenological interrogation. As a form, it provided the group with a device for unifying a considerable range of phenomena. As an analytical device, it was sufficiently abstract to allow the introduction of detail and grain. At the same time, it was a theoretical move that enabled modes of passing from the particular to the general.

Bureaucratic capitalism as a general phenomenon was expressed at the level of concrete relations of production through a fundamental contradiction. In a Western context, Fordist management operated by imposing a rigidly top-down understanding of production on a shifting, complex environment. This tended to individuate workers and exclude them from creative interaction with their work in a manner symmetrical with the design logic of assembly-line technologies. But the imposition of this production design in a complex, shifting environment generated problems and irrationalities, the addressing of which required workers to interact creatively with their work. Without that engagement, production would grind to a halt. But this register lay outside the production design that mediated the viewpoint of management. The result was ongoing confrontation between the top-down command/control structure of capitalist management and quite different conceptions of hierarchy and organisation particular to informal worker collectives. Because, in the main, trade unions had at this time shifted toward collective bargaining, they were unable to address problems connected to the pace and control of work. So in their interactions with the unions, workers confronted a situation parallel to that which they encountered with management. Autonomous worker actions like the East Berlin 'June Days' were positive expressions of the proletarian rejection of bureaucracy. The types of self-organisation and demands asserted the political nature of the conflicts at the point of production and demonstrated the inability of the dominant organisations to accommodate them. Their position outside the dominant order made of them potentially revolutionary actions.

Socialisme ou Barbarie collectively posited the workers who participated in such actions as a new worker avant-garde. Their project developed as part of an ongoing dialogue with it. Many issues of the journal from this period are assemblages of information about, and interpretations of, these actions. The interpretations link the actions together as aspects of an overall revolutionary movement. This movement is then situated with respect to broader characteristics of bureaucratic capitalism on the one hand, and with respect to the group's teleological vision of socialism as direct democracy on the other. As with any revolutionary theory, the idea was to enable workers to take a distance from their immediate concerns and grasp the revolutionary implications of their actions. Between 1953 and 1957, the pages of *Socialisme ou Barbarie* connected many such actions into a mounting wave of revolutionary action: the East Berlin 'June Days'; the 1955 general strikes at Nantes and St. Nazaire; Poland and – especially – Hungary in 1956. They alone on the French Left were looking at these actions. They alone were able to see it.

The superimposition of the schema of bureaucratic capitalism on workers' everyday experience opened space for descriptions of that experience to have a political function independent of the analyses of autonomous worker actions. This led the group to solicit and publish autobiographical accounts of work in contemporary industry. They were written 'from the inside' by workers, based on their everyday experience of production. One explanation for this followed from rejection of the Leninist party. Revolutionary militants could not represent the workers. This entailed the rejection of other forms of representation of working-class experience from the outside, like academic sociology. Workers should represent themselves: this was basic to the notion of direct democracy. Worker writing in a style consistent with speech would give the journal a way to address an audience quite different from that which was addressed in the majority of their articles. The content of the pieces emphasised the commonalities that linked worker experience at the point of production and solicited recognition from the worker-reader. In theory, this made of these texts an instrument to bring about class consciousness. They also resolved the problem of how theorists could overcome their class-positions and access the germinal form of a socialist rationality that was developing through conflicts on the factory floor.

Socialisme ou Barbarie published a range of first-person narratives written by workers that described the conditions of industrial production. These were supplemented with an 'excerpt from the worker press', drawn mostly from the newspaper projects discussed below. Most of these texts are devoted to the automobile industry: the main Renault factory at Boulogne-Billancourt just outside of Paris was the most recurrent setting. Because of the situation within which the group operated, these texts are the only first-hand accounts of work in the automobile industry of this period.[16] The French Communist Party had no interest in such analyses: for them, the working class was the mass of individuals who turned out for Party or CGT actions. Even as they had more consistent contact with working people than did Socialisme ou Barbarie, smaller proletarian-revolutionary groups, like the one that became *Lutte Ouvrière*, never broke out of the self-referential space of Trotskyist discourse. Academic sociology of the time was only beginning to turn to industrial work as an object of analysis. Such works as were produced operated with a detached observer. In this way, the sociology of work paralleled industrial sociology, which was in general an extension of management.

The third chapter is a critical analysis of the project outlined in Claude Lefort's 1952 essay, 'L'expérience prolétarienne', for assembling, publishing and interpreting these worker autobiographies and of the text it takes as the exemplar of worker writing, Paul Romano's 'The American Worker'. Lefort's project is symmetrical with his position on revolutionary organisation, one which was quite close to that outlined below in the context of the American-based Correspondence collective. The task of revolutionary theory is to interpret worker actions and experience with the idea of clarifying their implications. Revolutionary organisation has no independent status, and revolutionary theory should not move from interpretation to suggesting action. This article outlines a phenomenological approach to worker narratives centred on isolating and describing 'the proletarian standpoint'. Like the narratives Lefort takes as examples, the standpoint is productivist, located on the factory floor.

---

16   Fridenson 1986, pp. 530–1.

INTRODUCTION

It consists in the sightlines and forms of motility specific to production, but extends to the experiential frames within which informal collectives of workers, delimited by shop and shift, make work a collectively organised and controlled process and skill a collective attribute. This approach would provide a double frame that would enable access to the rationality central to the institution of socialism: one at the level of specific contents; the other at the level of the social relations that shaped their meanings.

The chapter then turns to a literary analysis of the specific characteristics of 'proletarian documentary literature'. Romano's text is written with a first-person narrator who speaks in the present tense to describe experiences from a shop-floor perspective. The writing remains close to the oral culture of the shop floor. The art of the text lay in the construction of sentences that intertwine the particular and general in a way that opens the experience up to readers while providing a compelling realism effect. The conceptual underpinning of the text is a kind of phenomenology of worker experience in production that legitimates itself with reference to recognitions on the part of the worker who read the galleys. The primary audience for the text is other workers. The function as data emerges through comparative reading.

Socialisme ou Barbarie tried to carry out something like the project Lefort outlined through the worker newspaper project. When the group decided to gather writing from workers beyond the limits of the group and not simply reproduce texts transmitted to it by other militant organisations, as was the case with the Romano piece, they attempted to move beyond the sociological space within which the group operated. They encountered a very different space at Renault's Boulonge-Billancourt factory, the symbol of working-class power for the Parisian Left. The fourth chapter is an overview of the political and professional contexts that obtained at Billancourt.

Tribune Ouvrière was launched in 1954. The collective that produced it was not controlled by Socialisme ou Barbarie, but group member Daniel Mothé participated in it. Insofar as Socialisme ou Barbarie was concerned, the worker newspaper was modelled on the American 'Correspondence' project. The analysis of the project works on the basis of published and internal materials from Socialisme ou Barbarie along with copies of both 'Correspondence' and *Tribune Ouvrière*. 'Correspondence' was the incarnation of the Johnson-Forest Tendency after it split with Trotskyism. Counting among its members C.L.R. James, Raya Dunayevskaya and Grace Lee Boggs, this group was an interlocutor of fundamental importance from the Chaulieu-Montal period. 'Correspondence' was predicated on the idea that workers had withdrawn from the dominant order and were already enacting socialism at the shop-floor level. The job of the worker newspaper was to simply allow workers to 'speak'.

The collective saw writing as an extension of speaking. Workers therefore had a 'natural' style of writing. Intellectuals were inclined to see in that 'natural' style grammatical and other errors. So they had to get out of the way. Socialisme ou Barbarie did not see the same kind of withdrawal from the dominant ideology that their US counterparts did, nor did the group operate in a context that allowed for the same assumptions concerning worker writing. Socialisme ou Barbarie collectively saw working-class culture as dominated. From this, it followed that simply asking workers to write would be asking them to produce imitations of forms of writing understood to be legitimate. There were no contemporary exemplars of writing that remained closely tied to spoken French. So the form would have to be a construction.

Tribune Ouvrière never became the worker newspaper the group hoped it would. But, for other members of the collective that produced it, that was never the point. For them, it was the focus of an experience of militant activity, a way to create contacts amongst workers across shops and to transmit information about conflicts and problems. It is an invaluable source for accounts of the pressures brought to bear on semi-skilled workers in the course of Fordist production and the resulting conflicts over production-speeds, hierarchy and professional autonomy. The articles are written from a variety of styles, only some of which correlated to Socialisme ou Barbarie's understanding of worker writing. These articles detail the role of autonomous worker actions as a feedback-loop connecting the unions (often unwillingly) back to problems that arose in the pace and organisation of work, questions the unions could not coherently address because of the nature of collective bargaining. *Tribune Ouvrière* also contextualises the accounts published of autonomous actions in *Socialisme ou Barbarie* by detailing the problems attending to their mobilisation in heavy industry. Socialisme ou Barbarie's involvement with *Tribune Ouvrière* revealed the specificity of the group's construction of the worker. The project had been set into motion on grounds intuitive for the members of Socialisme ou Barbarie. But the political context at Billancourt filtered writing in ways almost the opposite of those which obtained in the context in which the group operated. The context reduced the sort of writing the group privileged to noise. More broadly, it indicated the class-specific nature of writing as a form of expression. Workers did not write into, or for, the paper. The examples of worker writing the group did publish from *Tribune Ouvrière* were done by political militants. The relations between these aspects of being-worker are explored in the final chapter.

The central character through these analyses is Jacques Gautrat, who wrote for *Socialisme ou Barbarie* as Daniel Mothé. The book ends with an extended analysis of the series of the autobiographical texts he published in the journal across 1956 and 1957. Much of the chapter is a close analysis of Mothé as a figure inside and outside of Socialisme ou Barbarie and as a narrative function in the texts. The texts are deceptively simple. They intertwine accounts of everyday experience with viewpoints on that experience particular to Socialisme ou Barbarie and are written in a language the art of which is to appear virtually artless. The texts themselves describe Mothé's professional life as a machinist in AOC, a limited-run machine-shop that primarily produced prototypes and replacement parts. Most relate failed attempts at political mobilisation to protest a political question (Algeria) or address problems related to the pace and organisation of work. Because of the nature of politics in the factory, when autonomous actions happened, the actors articulated themselves in the language of revolutionary Marxism. This makes of them a unique space of appropriation, one that performed exactly the relation to Marxian language that Socialisme ou Barbarie saw as the natural horizon for autonomous action, but in a particular, curious way. It enacted a relation to the language parallel to that of intellectuals in its sensitivity to contextual variations. In the texts Mothé published about the period immediately following the Hungarian Revolution, the reader can see this space coming undone. Where Socialisme ou Barbarie saw the Hungarian Revolution as a culmination of the mounting wave of working-class revolutionary activity that began soon after Stalin's death, Mothé details a basic crisis in the relation of workers to the language of revolution itself. The fragmentation is all the more interesting in the pages of *Socialisme ou Barbarie* because it lay outside the group's focus and seems to anticipate future problems with the Marxist Imaginary. The argument is that this fragmentation is an initial instance of what will become the crisis of that Imaginary. It provides a way to think about how ideologies come apart. But the situation in which this happens is ambiguous. We defer a conceptual discussion to the postface as the questions are better posed with the grain of these accounts fresh in the reader's mind.

In part, this project is a history of Socialisme ou Barbarie. While it relies primarily on the journal, where internal documents are still available, the project crosses a path made from fragments from the journal, in which pseudonymous narrative functions address the working class in general, to Socialisme ou Barbarie as a small militant group that met biweekly in the second-floor space of 'Le Café Tambour' located in Paris, near the Bastille metro stop. Between 1953 and 1957, the group was comprised of around 20 members, 15 of whom attended meetings regularly. Castoriadis, Lefort and Georges Petit comprised the old guard. The rest had come by 1952 through a variety of routes that will be detailed in the chapters below. The journal's production was the focus of most meetings, and the centre of the group's collective life: writing articles, collective discussion and editing of drafts; decisions about what to publish and when. A slightly different configuration of the group tended to the material aspects of publication: getting the materials selected to the printer, running galleys back and forth, picking up the print run; wrapping and dispatching issues for subscribers along with the supplementary items that may be included each; delivering issues to bookstores. To some Socialisme ou Barbarie members, this pointed to the internal hierarchy that distinguished 'the intellectuals' from the 'ordinary militants'. But as a group, it was the 'ordinary militants' that largely enabled it to operate.

Like any collective, Socialisme ou Barbarie was a network of personal relationships. It was also a web of correspondence amongst members called away from Paris for periods of teaching or other longer-term reasons, and between the collective and other political groups, nationally and internationally.[17] Alongside contacts with other political organisations came publications, the receipt of which were noted at the beginning of meetings. But mostly, Socialisme ou Barbarie was a mesh of ongoing discussions. To present themselves to the public, the group organised a study circle on Lenin (1949). The following year, Castoriadis gave a series of lectures on Marx's *Capital* (1950–1) at what is today *L'Ecole des Hautes Etudes en Sciences Sociales*. Later, Socialisme ou Barbarie periodically held public meetings in the auditorium at *Mutualité* in the 5th arrondissement. Each had a particular decentred format as a function of the restrictions placed on the political activities of non-French citizens, which prevented the group's most eloquent speakers, Castoriadis and Véga, from appearing on stage. Many who attended have noted this format. Even in public, Socialisme ou Barbarie did not work like any other group on the Parisian Left.

Because of the fragmentary nature of the materials available for the period covered in this book, much of what follows is written using the journal as its analytical centre. In the sections devoted to worker writing, I also used copies of 'Correspondence' and *Tribune Ouvrière*. While I was able to use a considerable amount of internal documentation on the life of the group, there is much more of it for the period from 1956 onward. A project that dealt with this later period could pose the question of how to write about a collective

---

[17] After 1956, Socialisme ou Barbarie had cells in other locations, including one quite active on its own terms in the early 1960s in Le Mans. But in the period covered in this project, this is not yet the case. Socialisme ou Barbarie was also actively in contact with other political organisations outside of France that were engaged in parallel projects. Principal among these was the Johnson-Forest Tendency, which later became 'Correspondence'. On this relationship, see Chapter 5 below.

quite differently. This movement back and forth from the journal to the group enables some observations. Socialisme ou Barbarie as a group was not exactly in phase with the journal. The group was more internally diverse, a mosaic of revolutionary-Left political viewpoints. Articles that were published typically involved points of consensus. The journal moves in a linear fashion with subsequent issues presupposing, building on or modifying positions from previous issues. Internally, the group was more diffuse. In an open letter from May 1956, in which Castoriadis threatens to leave, he complains about the lack of internal continuity, with projects taken up and then abandoned, and how individual positions in discussions never seemed to change. The same distance affects even the dates that appear on each issue of the journal: it was not at all given that an issue would appear in print anywhere near the date on its cover. What held Socialisme ou Barbarie together was the group itself as a collective process. The journal is an expression of that process. The analysis undertaken in this book uses the idea of the group as a process to shape the overall approach to the material. But the process as it appears in the journal and internal documentation is not identical with that which went into making it. Something basic has long since slipped away. From this follows a certain ambiguity in each of the sentences below that makes of the group a subject followed by a verb.

But this is not just an intellectual history of the group. I was also interested in *Tribune Ouvrière* and the texts by Socialisme ou Barbarie member Daniel Mothé as accounts of everyday experience in the French automobile industry in the 1950s. It seemed to me that if one is to read these texts, one has to have a good understanding of what Socialisme ou Barbarie was doing at the time in order to account for and open up what information there is about shop-floor experience, both in what conforms to and exceeds their revolutionary project. This required moving through two quite dense contexts, the one in which Socialisme ou Barbarie operated and another, quite different context at Renault's Billancourt factory. This in turn required a combination of methodologies drawn from intellectual history, philosophy and literary theory in some places, sociology and the history of work in others. The hope is that the writing makes of this a seamless whole. The combination of social spaces and methodologies opened up ways to think about the Marxist Imaginary from different angles which would not have been available if the project had remained within a single level of analysis. Socialisme ou Barbarie is important not just for its own production. The open-endedness of the group's relationship to the worker as a signification makes of it a source of information about the nature of work in the early phases of industrial Fordism and, inadvertently, about the process whereby Marxism began to come undone as a language workers could appeal to in order to mobilise themselves. These considerations had an impact on when and how this project ends. The idea was to hold Socialisme ou Barbarie at its point of maximum openness in order to allow the question of whether one can see in Mothé's texts the initial moments of the crisis of the Marxist Imaginary. No-one was looking for that. Not even Socialisme ou Barbarie.

In a sense, the book you are holding is a large fragment of the group's history. This was by design. Because the idea was to use Socialisme ou Barbarie with and against itself to stage something of the crisis of the Marxist Imaginary, I chose to leave questions open for the reader rather than assimilate them back into the seeming inevitability that follows from a continuous narrative of the adventure of an intellectual group from 1949 to 1967. It also followed the fact that the material is quite complex and I could not assume familiarity on the part of readers with either *Socialisme ou Barbarie* or the archival documents. While I am not opposed to following out the rest of the group's history, and it would be possible to do so, given the time and leisure, for now the reader is referred to other sources for an account of this overall narrative. One might first turn to Philippe Gottraux's *Socialisme ou Barbarie: Un engagement politique et intellectual dans la France de l'après-guerre*.[18] Gottraux's book is a historical sociology of the group that covers the whole of its development. While its analytical dimension is hamstrung by the rigidity of its Bourdieu-inspired framework, the basic history is thorough and the biographical material he presents valuable. The book is important in shifting attention to the group as a collective. It had not yet appeared when I wrote the dissertation on which this book is based.

Marcel van der Linden's *Socialisme ou Barbarie: A French Revolutionary Group (1949–1965)*[19] provides English-speaking readers with a clear and concise general history of the group. It brings material from Dutch council communists like Cajo Brendel who attended meetings with the group for certain periods. The addition of contemporary outside perspectives on the life of Socialisme ou Barbarie is most interesting, even as they occupy positions within debates that one would prefer to understand. The account of the 1958 split between Lefort and Castoriadis is invaluable for those familiar with the group. Nicolas Poirier's *Retour sur la notion de l'expérience prolétarienne*[20] covers the same material that can be found in the first part of Chapter Three with the kind of generality

---

18   Gottraux 1997. On Gottraux's book, see Poirier 2011, pp. 7–20 and Escobar 2012.
19   van der Linden 1997, pp. 7–37.
20   Poirier 2011, pp. 164–75.

that comes from making a free-standing piece about a text quite tied to the trajectory of the group.

Of the more recent work on Socialisme ou Barbarie that discusses the period addressed in this book, the closest in terms of inspiration and material analysed is Andrea Gabler's *Die Despotie der Fabrik und der VorSchein der Freiheit. Von 'Socialisme ou Barbarie' gesammelte Zeugnisse aus dem fordistischen Arbeitsalltag*.[21] Gabler undertakes a comprehensive analysis of the worker writing published in *Socialisme ou Barbarie*. It covers several texts not examined below, such as Georges Vivier's *La vie en usine*, which I do not address because the writing did not conform to the conventions of 'proletarian-documentary literature' that organises my analysis. It also includes analyses of Henri Simon's text on work at L'Assurances Générales Vie, which is touched on in passing, and Philippe Guillaume's 1961 text 'Dix semaines en usine', originally published in *Socialisme ou Barbarie* no. 31. Gabler's approach is more sociological than that which I adopted here. Her piece is well worth the reader's attention.

The presentation of Socialisme ou Barbarie tracks the group's particular situation. After the split with the PCI, the group entered a period of isolation. The chapters devoted to this period treat the group largely as if it were its own context. The relation to context changes with the introduction of the worker newspaper project, which entailed crossing from the delimited field of ideological production particular to the revolutionary left, to the very different space of factory-floor politics at Billancourt. Here, Socialisme ou Barbarie was almost vanishingly small. The publication of Mothé's work coincided with an abrupt change in the group's visibility. The last chapter opens onto some of these broader contexts. Because I could not assume familiarity with the texts and because I am using a considerable quantity of archival material that former members of the group were kind enough to give me access to, much of the writing is narrative. The research was done in Paris during 1991–2. I had not planned on returning to the dissertation on which this is based, but the experience has been more interesting and rewarding than I expected. So I am pleased that the opportunity arose thanks to the good offices of Sébastien Budgen and the anonymous readers who found it to be important.

---

21   Gabler 2001, pp. 349–78.

CHAPTER 1

Where Things Start

Imagine that you are in Paris in early 1949. You sit in a café and hold in your hands a copy of the first issue of *Socialisme ou Barbarie*. The cover is printed on heavy paper. It is white with a red horizontal band across the top. '*Socialisme*' appears inside the red horizontal in a black font; '*ou Barbarie*' is just below, smaller, in the white area. A thin red line makes the right lower quadrant of the white area a discrete space within which is arrayed the table of contents. Drawn by some curiosity, you open the journal and begin to read.

In the opening pages of *Socialisme ou Barbarie* no. 1, the group introduces itself. The 'Presentation' appears without an attributed author and is printed in italics. The italics give the piece a sense of unfolding in a meta-space just above the rest of the issue. The introduction tells you that Socialisme ou Barbarie is the name of the journal and the group of revolutionary militants who produced it. The group began within Trotskyism but was lead progressively to distance itself from it because of the latter's 'reformist attitudes (in the deepest sense) with respect to Stalinism combined with an effort to maintain intact the Bolshevik politics from the heroic period in the face of a constantly evolving reality'.[1] It should not be of surprise that the group originated within Trotskyism: some kind of relationship with the movement is more or less inevitable for one who positions him or herself as a revolutionary and comes to understand the problems created by Stalinism. But *Socialisme ou Barbarie* was driven to break with Trotskyism following a logic that would be shared by any worker. Despite being the main organisational expression of anti-Stalinist revolutionary politics, Trotskyism provided no responses to basic questions: What is Russia? What is Stalinism? What are its social bases? What are its economic roots? How to understand the bureaucracy that has dominated Russia since the early 1930s and Eastern Europe since 1945?[2]

The group understands the development and expansion of bureaucracy to be the defining characteristic of contemporary capitalism. Bureaucracy is the fundamental problem: analysing it is the thread they pull.[3] What unifies bureaucracies is the division of intellectual labor that separates the *dirigeant*

---

[1] Socialisme ou Barbarie 1949a, p. 1; English translation in Castoriadis 1988a [1949a] and Curtis (ed.) 1997.
[2] Socialisme ou Barbarie 1949a, pp. 1–2.
[3] Singer, Brian 1979, p. 36.

from the *exécutant*, those who direct from those who carry out directions. Seen in this way, bureaucracy is a command system. The situations which it now occupies make of it a new configuration of power. Those who occupy places within these bureaucracies form a new social class. The actions of this new social class have transformed and will continue to transform both the relations of production and the potentials for revolutionary action.

The 'Presentation' then situates the group and its preoccupations with respect to Marxism. The way this is carried out indicates a combination of immersion in that tradition and iconoclasm with respect to it. The group rejects orthodox Marxism. Given the emphasis on the present, it makes little sense to adopt 'a relationship to Marx like that which Catholic theologians adopt towards scripture'.[4] Marxian analytical frameworks are only useful as long as they illuminate developments in the contemporary world. When they do not, they will be abandoned. The priority is not fidelity to Marx, but to provide a coherent orientation for a revolutionary politics adequate to the post-War world. 'Without development of revolutionary theory, there can be no development of revolutionary action'.[5] The article assumes the prerogative that subtends this relation to Marxism. But the relation is a process, as is the group itself. The journal will be its reflection, a forum for analysis, reflection and debate: 'The discussion will be free within the context of our general conceptions, with the constant hope that they will not become an endless dialogue amongst a few individuals'.[6]

The group addresses the reader and a broader working-class audience simultaneously. *Socialisme ou Barbarie* characterises its project as based on new forms of proletarian revolutionary action, which are linked to the specific nature of worker experience in both the Soviet and Western forms of contemporary capitalism. The project will require extensive analytical and political work. It is presented with a sense of urgency. In 1949, the logic of concentration that both explains and drives the confrontation between imperial blocs appears to be heading toward a third world war. Only a proletarian revolution can stop it. Whence the alternative: socialism or barbarism.[7]

---

4 Socialisme ou Barbarie 1949a, p. 2.
5 Socialisme ou Barbarie 1949a, p. 4.
6 Socialisme ou Barbarie 1949a, p. 6.
7 On the opposition as 'a presently contending alternative', see Curtis 1989.

Imago Mundi

The article entitled 'Socialisme ou Barbarie' is also without an attributed author.[8] The typeset uses the same font that can be found throughout the rest of the journal's content. The reader enters the interior of the group's project and is presented with a map of the world. Its structure and theory of history derive from Marx's *Communist Manifesto*,[9] which is extensively cited in the opening pages of the text. History moves in stages. Each stage is discrete. One stage emerges from within and supplants another.

The history that is presented is that of bureaucratic capitalism. The presentation is divided into two parts, each of which provides a broad outline of the international situation in order to situate and make a frame around SB's conception of the revolutionary project. 'Bourgeoisie and Bureaucracy' outlines a history of Western capitalism. Driven by the logic of concentration, the stage of nationally-based competitive capitalism was supplanted by that of monopoly capitalism between 1880 and 1890. World War I represented the explosion of the monopoly-capitalist political order. As it was for Lenin, Word War I was the political and military result of imperialist competition between national monopoly sectors for access to cheap raw materials for large-scale industry. While the state forms particular to monopoly capitalism broke down as a result of the war, imperialism remained as both the result of concentration and as one of its motors. The main result of World War I was the convergence of monopoly sectors of the economy and the State and a proliferation of bureaucracies that mediated economic activity. In heavy industry, the development of management unfolded along a parallel trajectory. World War II resulted from the inability of the forms of bureaucratic capitalism instituted after the Great Depression to manage capitalist crisis. By 1949 it appeared that the end of the war had been accompanied by a new, more thoroughgoing form of bureaucratic capitalism. But the logic of concentration and imperialism continued to push events forward. The end result is likely to be a third world war.[10]

The second section, 'Proletariat and Bureaucracy', provides an overview of the history of the workers' movement since the nineteenth century, its consolidation through the Second International and its failure from a revolutionary viewpoint. It then turns to the Russian Revolution and provides an indication of the trajectory whereby the revolution gave way to a fusion of party and state. The revolution had expropriated capitalists and abolished private property.

---

8   The piece was published without attribution, but was written by Cornelius Castoriadis.
9   Marx 1988.
10 Castoriadis 1988 [1949a], p. 6.

But rather than issuing in socialism, the result was state control over economic activity. The editorial links this in part to the logic of the Leninist Vanguard Party. The separation of the *dirigeant* from the *exécutant*, those who command from those who carry out the commands, was repeated in the separation of a party of professional revolutionaries from a working class unable to achieve revolutionary consciousness without its intervention in the fusion of party and state. Production was nationalised under the slogan of worker control. Due to acute shortages in skilled labour, worker control entailed an educational process that would enable the workers to assume control at some future point. In the meantime, the party cobbled together a managerial apparatus from the specialists it could locate. The party-state then acted in the name of worker control to institute the same approaches to production found in advanced Western industry, first in its Taylorist then in its Fordist form. The editorial characterises this as the turning point, past which the party-state apparatus began to fully separate from the workers and impose itself as a new ruling stratum. With the 1921 New Economic Plan begins full-blown Soviet bureaucratic capitalism.[11] The Soviet apparatus consolidated its power over the international Communist movement with the Third International and imposed its ideological and organisational models on the Communist Parties. In France, this would become evident with the transformation of the Parti Communiste Français into a mass political party after the 1936 Popular Front. A parallel process unfolded in the trade-union movement, with the Confedération Genérale du Travail acting as the French exemplar.[12]

The editorial claims that the working class of 1949 was aware of this history and had derived from it some fundamental lessons. The older objectives that had been central for the workers' movement throughout the Russian Revolution were no longer viable. This history has shown that the expropriation of capitalists, the abolition of private property through its nationalisation, and all the modes of designating 'worker control' to that point were not adequate to bring about the institution of socialism. The bureaucratisation of the Soviet system engendered new and particularly brutal forms of exploitation of the workers and peasants. The bureaucratisation of Western left-wing parties and trade unions accompanied their integration into the normal operations of the capitalist *status quo*. In both contexts, the political dimensions of bureaucratisation had combined with new managerial and technological developments that rationalised and intensified the exploitation of workers. The lesson

---

11   Castoriadis 1988 [1949a], pp. 23–40.
12   We will leave a closer account of what this means in the French context for Chapter 3 and what follows it.

that the working class had drawn from all this was the need to rethink the meanings of socialism and revolution:

> It must be understood that the expropriation of private capital (by the state or nationalisation) is only the negative half of the proletarian revolution. These measures can have no positive significance if they are separated from the positive half: the direct management of production by the workers. This means that the directing of the economy, from the level of central overall direction to that of businesses, cannot be left to a stratum of specialists, technicians and competent, 'capable people' and other bureaucrats. It must be undertaken by the workers themselves. The dictatorship of the proletariat cannot be merely political; above all it must be an economic dictatorship. Otherwise, it will only become a slogan that conceals the dictatorship of the bureaucracy.[13]

It remained for a new revolutionary movement, one aware of history and able to rearticulate the basic conceptual and political orientations inherited from the past, to elaborate the basis for a new revolutionary project. For Socialisme ou Barbarie, this would centre on direct worker management of production and, by extension, of society.

Where Things Begin: Leaving Trotskyism

The post-war Left was a field of cultural production that in its overall logic conformed to the way Pierre Bourdieu characterised such fields in general:

> One of the most significant properties of the fields of cultural production is that they propose to those who work within them a space of possibilities, if you like, a problematic (objectively given in the form of an ensemble of real or possible positions) which tend to orient their research, even without their being aware of it, by defining the universe of possible questions. This problematic both fixes their enterprise in time and space and makes it relatively independent with respect to direct social and economic determinants. Product of the history of the field itself, this space is marked by the ensemble of intellectual benchmarks, often incarnated in intellectual 'stars' or various 'isms'. These must be mastered, at least in

---

13   Castoriadis 1988 [1949a], p. 48.

practice, in order to participate in the game. Above and beyond all agents, this space functions as a sort of common reference system that situates contemporaries, even when they do not consciously refer to each other, by virtue of their common situation within the same intellectual system.[14]

For Bourdieu, cultural power is at stake in the playing out of the game of position within a given cultural field.[15] Cultural power is the ability to impose one's frame of reference. The logic that informs his analysis has been characterised as legitimist to the extent that it operates with the assumption that power is the goal for all players.[16] While the model is illuminating in several respects, the 'fit' between it and revolutionary political organisations comes at a price. For example, Trotskyism fits into it because of the nature of its relations to the dominant Communist Parties and its mode of argumentation. The price one pays is the reduction of revolution to a rhetorical tactic in a struggle for position within a field of cultural production. Everyone who plays a game assumes that the game itself is legitimate. So, if one takes Bourdieu's modelling seriously, revolutionary political positions that operated within a given field of cultural production placed out of play the field itself and the socio-economic contexts that shape it because they operated within that field at all. Of course, each would assume that the outcomes of play would be improved were they to become dominant.[17]

The post-war French Left was dominated by the PCF. In part to compensate for the disparities that separated the PCF from revolutionary opposition groups, the latter articulated their positions using forms of 'heretical subversion'. Bourdieu generalised the term from Max Weber's notion of cultural reproduction across conflict between bureaucratic priests and charismatic prophets.[18] Heretical subversion relies on a form of argument that collapses ongoing cultural production by dominant positions back onto the texts that comprise their doctrinal and historical core. The appeal to sources is

---

14   Bourdieu 1989, p. 213.
15   Bourdieu 1977 and 1984. For an outline of how one might use Bourdieu's work to think about left-wing politics in particular, see Bourdieu 1980c and 1981. For the notion of the field of cultural distribution in particular, see Bourdieu 1989. The relation of the notion of field to history is elaborated in Bourdieu 1980b.
16   For this critique of Bourdieu with specific reference to class, see Grignon and Passeron, 1989.
17   Gottraux 1997 walks into this trap.
18   See Bourdieu 1991, pp. 127ff. The variant heretical argumentation is taken from Bourdieu 1984.

used to argue that the original messages have been distorted or abandoned. The appeal to history enables the fashioning of counter-histories that demonstrate the arbitrariness of both the dominant position itself and the histories shaped in its image. The use of this approach eliminated the obvious asymmetries separating groups that rarely numbered a hundred members from the PCF, which counted over two million members and won nearly twenty-five percent of the popular vote in the 1947 parliamentary elections. All organisations were rendered as abstract, equivalent, sources of ideological propositions.[19] A correlate of this was that heretical argumentation also reduced political affiliation to the type of commitment particular to small organisations comprised of revolutionary militants.

The Trotskyism of this period conformed particularly well to a model rooted in conflict between a charismatic prophet and bureaucratic priests. Trotsky's personality, eloquence and prestige as a function of his close association with the Russian Revolution made of him a quintessential charismatic prophet. This material, and the political situations that he confronted after his 1928 exile, made heretical argumentation the only logical form with which to advance his claims to be Lenin's legitimate successor. The particularities of his situation made it simple to transpose these claims into the language of revolution. The broader political movement that took shape around him and his writings replicated both his preoccupations and modes of argument.

The thematic content of the texts from the first issue of *Socialisme ou Barbarie* outlined in the sections above show a group still deeply imprinted by its origins as the Chaulieu-Montal Tendency within the Left Opposition of the Fourth International. Trotsky's personal associations set up the centrality of Lenin, the USSR and Stalinism as political and analytical questions in his written work. His particular analyses of Stalin established the link between the latter and the question of bureaucracy. The association of Stalin with bureaucracy that enabled the separation of the 'real' revolution from Stalinism, and the Leninist Vanguard Party from the bureaucracy that supplanted it, was

---

[19] This compensation works in another way quite different from what one would associate with the pattern of heretical argumentation outlined above. By routing critiques of the PCF through Stalinism, it created a sense of distance with respect to it. This distance was also a form of containment that was a condition of possibility for writing oppositional texts in such an asymmetrical context. This chapter recapitulates that sense of distance in its exclusive focus on Socialisme ou Barbarie. When we turn to politics in the Renault factory at Bologne-Billancourt in Chapter 4 as well as in subsequent chapters, this sense of distance will abruptly come undone.

critical for Trotsky's positioning of himself as the keeper of the flame of real revolution. The understanding of the latter as a second proletarian revolution had been staged against the screen of the USSR and Stalinism throughout Trotsky's work. This second revolution was to be its reversal both logically and politically. These registers converged in the centrality of worker control and of the idea of soviets or councils. From this followed the importance of claims to be closer to the workers in the game of position both with respect to other Fourth International tendencies and with respect to the dominant Communist Parties. To position oneself close to the workers was to move along the natural horizon of Marxian discourse and doctrine and to demonstrate a better command of Marxism and a higher level of doctrinal purity – just as Trotsky had done with respect to Stalin. From this follows the curious *mélange* of highly technical language and modes of addressing the working class in texts, the production of which was both a mode of differentiation and a form of militant activity.[20] This move was also figured against the history of Leninism as a movement back to the idea of the Party articulated in the 1902 pamphlet, *What Is To Be Done?*,[21] in which the production of such texts is a form of political action during periods without particular hope for revolution. Their mixed nature follows from the Bolshevik emphasis on maintaining a clear distinction between the inside and the outside of the organisation through clarity of political line. These concerns and the forms of practice that accompanied them structured the particular notion of being revolutionary. The context in which these practices were situated tied together militants and organisation.

By the time the Chaulieu-Montal Tendency split with the Parti Communiste Internationaliste (PCI) in 1949, it had already broken with the Fourth International majority on a number of grounds. CMT had been started in 1946 on the basis of 'The Russian Question'.[22] They rejected Trotsky's interpretation of Stalinism. Their rejection opened questions of what Stalinism was and how it could be explained. CMT developed its collective critique of both Stalinism and the dominant Trotskyist interpretations of it around the category of bureaucracy. The Tendency subsumed Leninist conceptions of political organisation into their critique of bureaucracy. This move opened space for a rethink of the nature of revolutionary organisation and of the proletarian revolution that it would work to bring about. The fashioning of these positions entailed

---

20   In the French context of 1949, it also was a result of the reduction of political affiliation to the compartments particular to small organisations comprised of revolutionary militants.
21   Lenin 1977 [1902].
22   We return to this in the next two sections of this chapter.

an independent return to the sources of the Marxian tradition. The result was a relation to Marx quite unlike that found in Trotsky or in the post-war majority tendencies. But this relation had yet to have any significant impact on the conceptual or linguistic devices used in the initial texts published in *Socialisme ou Barbarie*. And Socialisme ou Barbarie had not yet at all moved from the inherited assumption that the Soviet Union was the *telos* toward which the West was moving, an assumption that derived from the position occupied by the Russian Revolution in the dominant Marxist understanding of the revolutionary tradition.

The 1949 positions outlined by Socialisme ou Barbarie were extensions of those articulated by Chaulieu-Montal. But they are not on their own explanations for the decision to leave the PCI. In the texts collected and published as *In Defence of Marxism*,[23] Trotsky had written that if a second proletarian revolution was not triggered by the Second World War in the USSR, then the basis for revolutionary opposition would then have to be rethought.[24] His assassination in 1940 confronted post-war Trotskyism with a problem. The movement had been fashioned around Trotsky as the main source of political orientation. Without him, there was neither a centre nor a clear source for legitimate theoretical propositions. Majority tendencies within the post-war Fourth International cauterised the problem by creating an orthodoxy based on Trotsky's writings and the form of dialectical materialism that subtended them. Left Opposition tendencies like CMT and the US-based Johnson-Forest Tendency took Trotsky's last writings as their point of departure and began to carry out the project they called for. Because the opposition departed from Trotsky's work, the orthodoxy of the majority necessarily included space for it. Even a demolition of both Trotsky's interpretations of Stalinism and the association that would link him to proletarian revolution, like Lefort's 1948 essay, *Les contradictions de Trotsky*, could be accommodated.[25] The project called for in the last writings requires such a displacement. While these divergent trajectories created moments of awkward co-existence, the Majority Tendencies had neither the power nor interest to exclude the opposition.

By the summer of 1948, the question of whether or not to leave the PCI had been debated within CMT for some time. The transcript of a meeting from

---

23   Trotsky 1942.
24   See 'The Present War and the Fate of Modern Society' in the September 1939 text 'The USSR in War', in Trotsky, 1942.
25   Lefort 1948–9.

May 1948 provides a glimpse of what the members understood to be at stake.[26] The discussion was shaped by a dispute between Castoriadis and Lefort about what the critique of the Leninist Vanguard Party entailed for a new revolutionary organisation.[27] The main positions had been presented as written interventions. This critique linked the separation of a cadre of professional revolutionaries from the masses to the development of the Stalinist state-bureaucracy. Lenin's justification of the party lay in its ability to elaborate perspectives that would allow the masses to transcend attachment to the immediate and attain the class consciousness required for revolutionary action. CMT saw in the separation of the party from the masses that of the separation of *dirigeants* from *exécutants*, which made of the party a bureaucratic organisation. The Soviet system under Stalin was an unfolding of its implications. The critique was straightforward when the object of analysis was the Soviet Union. But its implications for a new revolutionary organisation admitted of several possibilities.[28]

Lefort took from the critique of Leninism the conclusion that any party organisation was the germinal form of the bureaucratic state. A revolutionary organisation should be a 'committee of struggle', the activities of which would be restricted to creating linkages between and commenting upon actions that arise 'from below'. It would have no independent organisational status:

> The essential problem is to fashion ourselves as a revolutionary core.[29] I do not say 'party' intentionally. At present there is no possibility of building a revolutionary party. Chaulieu still believes there is an actual worker avant-garde. But the truth is that the Trotskyists react to certain events without any [corresponding] class reaction.[30]

The 'revolutionary core' would comprise militants who would produce historical and political writing that would empower worker movements. These would be produced while the organisation itself was merging with that movement.

---

26 'Proces verbal de la reunion de Tendance du dimanche 2 mai – extraits', in Castoriadis papers (PCI 2 Item 18).
27 On the trajectory performed by this dispute through the history of Socialisme ou Barbarie, see Poirier 2011 pp. 307–420 and Chollet 2012.
28 The dispute that shaped this 1948 meeting would recur periodically in almost the same terms across the trajectory of Socialisme ou Barbarie until Lefort left the group in 1958.
29 This is a recurrent term for Lefort. It refers to a group of revolutionary militants whose objective is to empower worker movements with the idea of merging into them. The idea is similar to that held by Johnson-Forest. We take up their position in Chapter 5.
30 PV, p. 4.

Connection to, and reliance upon, 'the spontaneity of the masses' was critical, not only in principle, but also because 'in the times of greatest crisis "the farthest flights of theory fall short of the reality of the proletarian revolution"'.[31] This position translated ambivalences concerning the organisational form of the PCI in itself. The ongoing internal problems became adequate grounds for leaving.

Castoriadis rejected these arguments both theoretically and in their pragmatic consequences. He characterised Lefort as someone who, 'basing himself on the spontaneity of the masses, seeks new ways to not build a party'.[32] Rehearsing Lenin's critique of 'tailism', Castoriadis argued: 'To rely only on the spontaneity of the masses is to abstract yourself from society and the way in which revolution itself develops'.[33] This offered two possibilities for political action: immersion in very local situations, or the development of a revolutionary line. The first tends toward incoherence because it dissolves any possibility of a revolutionary line. The second makes the 'committee of struggle' a party that operates behind a different name. Castoriadis counterpoised a notion of revolutionary organisation as a stream of 'continuous propaganda' that 'does not repeat what the workers are doing, but emphasises what the workers could do' by 'placing the revolutionary mission in front of them'. As Lefort pointed out, subtending this notion of organisation is the belief in a kind of dialogue with the worker avant-garde. Without this dialogue, Castoriadis's position is Leninist. With it, perhaps this position is something else. While this may have gone without saying in 1948, the increasing East/West polarisation that accompanied the early phases of the Cold War was squeezing out space for both revolutionary opposition to the PCF and for autonomous worker actions. These latter would demonstrate that there was a worker avant-garde with which dialogue would be possible. If this formation is historically variable, then the status of a revolutionary organisation would vary functionally. Were one to apply Lefort's position to guide a response to that variability, the revolutionary core would go silent during these periods. Applying Castoriadis's position would enable the organisation to continue engaging in propaganda activities

---

31 Typescript of a speech from 2 May, 1948 in Castoriadis papers (PCI 2, Item 17), p. 2. The reference is to the Johnson-Forest Tendency's 1947 *The Invading Socialist Society*.
32 Typescript of a speech from 2 May, 1948 in Castoriadis papers (PCI 2, Item 17), p. 1.
33 Ibid. handwritten addition. *'Tail-ism'* [*khvostism*], *'tail-enders'* – expressions originally coined by Lenin to describe the Economists, who denied the leading role of the party and the importance of theory in the working-class movement; their position implied that the party should trail after the spontaneously developing movement, follow in the tail of events. Lenin 1970 [1903], p. 103, n. 6.

that would reflect its orientation toward dialogue when a change of situation enabled it.

These positions shaped the Tendency's debate. The militants aligned with Lefort advocated a break with the PCI; those aligned with Castoriadis opposed it. The discussion itself rehearsed mostly pragmatic reasons for staying or leaving. Those aligned with Lefort assumed that departure would dissolve the tendency as an organisation. This eliminated concerns about continuity and simplified the question at hand. Those aligned with Castoriadis outlined a series of pragmatic reasons for remaining with the PCI. The internal culture of the PCI often smothered discussion. CMT provided them a space. This was a significant aspect of the tendency's appeal. The cycling through of new militants that resulted from that appeal would be lost were they to leave. The Party provided the basis for contact with other tendencies internationally. This epistolary network included the Johnson-Forest Tendency, which was a fundamental political interlocutor for the Tendency and Socialisme ou Barbarie. The Party provided a base for coalition-building among parallel political organisations.[34] Most importantly, the PCI provided the Tendency the material base for the circulation of texts within the International and the possibility for their distribution beyond the confines of the Party. It was the substructure for political work. The PCI screened the people with whom the Tendency came into contact. In Castoriadis's view, outside that context Lefort's 'committee of struggle' was doomed to become 'a discussion group that would involve people met at random'.[35] A bit later, after apologising for the breach of decorum he was about to commit, Castoriadis pointed to the class composition of the Tendency. It was made up of 'intellectuals and petit-bourgeois'. Outside the Party milieu, its class composition would assert itself and the group would 'wander off on tangents'.[36]

In the spring of 1948, most of those involved with CMT still understood the PCI as a necessary milieu. Practical interaction with it kept a check on the class composition of the group and anchored it in a space that enabled a sense of contact with the working class. The anchoring was largely a social effect which followed from the various networks of which CMT was a part. The milieu also provided orientation for the Tendency's textual production. The Party was the material base for the production and dissemination of texts

---

34 As an example, the transcript mentions, in passing, work being carried out with the *Fédération Anarchiste* at the time.

35 Intervention by Marie Rose, p. 1.

36 These paragraphs are a compressed synopsis of the views expressed in PV, 2 May.

within the organisation, the International and beyond.[37] It also enabled the reception of these texts. Tendency writings made extensive use of the style of heretical argumentation. Such arguments and the rhetoric that accompanies them are turned inward. The result was texts that primarily addressed other militants, but were written as if they addressed the working class directly. In this respect, the revolutionary left was a field of cultural production like one in which 'musician's music' circulates, a space comprised of practitioners whose work largely addresses other practitioners amongst whom virtuosity is valued so long as it operates within certain genre conventions. Musician's music circulates largely without the intermediaries to stratify reception for the benefit of a broader audience by telling their audience that lay beyond the field of practitioners what it is that they like to like and the ways in which they like to like those things. But the assumption that one's work can nonetheless reach a broader audience is operative because it is reinforced socially within the community. This relation is effective so long as the context remains transparent. In other words, just as the rules disappear into a game as it is being played, so, in the medium term, a readership comprised of other militants would disappear. They held together the assumption that the working class was the actual addressee of these texts. This may explain why the mention of CMT's class composition was a breach of decorum. It threatened a disruption of the transparency of context and, by extension, basic assumptions about the way in which the members of CMT were revolutionaries.

The discussion from the spring of 1948 is interspersed with references to squaring the Tendency's political viewpoints with tactical choices made by the PCI Majority. The consensus was that it was not problematic to maintain Party discipline so long as doing so did not conflict with matters of principle. In a 1973 interview, Castoriadis provides an account of Chaulieu-Montal's trajectory through the PCI. He connects the Tendency's decision to leave the PCI with Tito's split from the Comintern in the summer of 1949. The PCI Majority framed the Eastern European countries under Soviet control as capitalist. This resulted in a wholesale misrecognition of what was happening in Yugoslavia. On the basis of that misunderstanding the PCI called for a united front with the Yugoslavian CP. So far as Chaulieu-Montal was collectively concerned, it was a Stalinist organisation.[38] A united front with Stalinists was the final straw.[39]

---

37 This was among the points enumerated by Castoriadis for staying. PV 2 May, pp. 2–3.
38 Castoriadis 1997, pp. 3–4.
39 The statement about Party discipline is drawn from the May 1948 debate cited below. In it, the question of following PCI lines that ran counter to CMT positions was broached. Most

The 'Open Letter to the Militants of the PCI and Fourth International' published in *Socialisme ou Barbarie* no. 1, provides a more detailed account. By the summer of 1949, the sense of imbrications evident in the discussion from the previous spring had been snapped. Where in 1948, the Party had provided the CMT with a material base, social reinforcements and access to a readership, it was now characterised as 'a tiny machine spinning in a void'.[40] The organisation's preoccupation with the ongoing internal problems created by Trotsky's assassination had been exacerbated by the pressure of Cold War polarisation. By the summer of 1949, it precluded everything else. This collapsed CMT back onto itself. The Tendency's political line and its development was now the centre of its collective identity. Because the PCI had become so caught up in its own devolution, it had not developed 'an autonomous ideological base'. It was therefore incapable of any coherent understanding of the contemporary world.[41] This misrecognition of the nature of the Yugoslavian CP was a prime example. It followed directly from an inadequate understanding of the nature of bureaucratic capitalism.[42] The letter presents the break as a consequence of the ideological development of CMT. Juxtaposed with the 1948 debate, the outlines of collective disinvestment in the social milieu that operated under the aegis of the Party emerge as a determining factor in shaping the end of CMT and the beginning of Socialisme ou Barbarie. Political differences with the majority that had remained within tolerable limits became insuperable problems as a result. The recentring of the Tendency on its own political project was an aspect of this. By the end of the letter, the PCI is characterised as a dead thing in a way that calls to mind the break-up of a love affair.[43]

What the letter does not say is that Socialisme ou Barbarie was now moving into political terrain whose history is littered with groups that quickly disappeared because they were unable to fashion ways to develop politically, intellectually and personally. The group defied this history because of the way it approached itself as a collective project. The category of bureaucracy was central to this. The next section provides a closer analysis of it.

---

who mentioned it argued that they were able to act in accordance with discipline without compromising principle. This line did not allow for that.

40   Socialisme ou Barbarie 1949b, p. 91.
41   Socialisme ou Barbarie 1949b, pp. 91–2.
42   Socialisme ou Barbarie 1949b, p. 99.
43   Socialisme ou Barbarie 1949b, pp. 100–1.

The Theory of Bureaucratic Capitalism

Socialisme ou Barbarie used a particular notion of bureaucracy as a regulative idea to shape their assessments of contemporary capitalism and the revolutionary project. Because it is fundamental to understanding Socialisme ou Barbarie, this section steps out of the historical narrative to present an overview. The opening section of this chapter provided a synopsis of the group's staging of the post-war situation as bureaucratic capitalism. This section provides a minimal reminder before turning to the presentation of the group's usage of bureaucracy.

For Socialisme ou Barbarie, contemporary capitalism was a new form of organisation characterised primarily by the proliferation of bureaucracy and transformations in its functions and meanings. These changes described several trajectories. In the Soviet system, the fusion of party and state comprised the central movement. In the West, the fusion of the economy's monopoly sectors with the state resulted in a proliferation of bureaucratic mechanisms for the redistribution of resources and mitigation of the effects of the cyclical nature of capitalism. The second main trajectory emerged from within advanced industrial production, following on the creation of management as the controlling stratum in Fordist-style production. The role and nature of managerial bureaucracy in industrial contexts differed fundamentally from networks of clerks processing orders and generating paperwork described by Balzac or in Melville's *Bartelby the Scrivener*.[44] The new state bureaucracies charged with administering socio-economic planning either by sector (West) or for entire economies (Soviet) also differed in kind from the nineteenth-century Prussian state-bureaucracy that was characterised in Marx's *Critique of the Philosophy of Right* as an epiphenomenon of singular mediocrity and incompetence. In these nineteenth-century manifestations, bureaucracies were restricted to administrative functions separated from the relations of production. From this followed the Marxian categorisation of bureaucracy as a means, a mode of transferring information from one part of the superstructure to another.

As was noted in the previous section, Socialisme ou Barbarie's point of departure for taking up bureaucracy was Trotsky's framing of the 'Russian Question' while the group was still part of the Fourth International. The critique is here split between this section and the beginning of the next. In Socialisme ou Barbarie's general view, Trotsky merely transposed the nineteenth-century Marxian understanding of bureaucracy into the centre of his interpretation of

---

44   Melville 2011.

Stalinism.[45] In that context, bureaucracy was less an analytical category than it was an expression of Stalin's illegitimacy that grafted like a parasite onto the revolution and endlessly repeated its salient characteristic of being illegitimate in the heavy-handed brutality and ineptness that accompanied the rapid expansion of Soviet industry and collectivisation of agriculture across the 1930s.[46] Trotsky's usage fulfilled tactical functions as well in its separation of the revolution proper from its Stalinist 'betrayal' and of Leninist organisation from the state forms created under Stalin. Because Trotsky believed that the second proletarian revolution would sweep away Stalin and his institutional expression, bureaucracy required no further analytical attention.[47]

Socialisme ou Barbarie saw this as wrong. At the conceptual level, the problem can be seen as reflecting the Tendency amongst orthodox Marxists to replace the historically variable characteristics of capitalism as a mode of production with the characteristics of capitalism as a noun. This made capitalism into a temporal object shaped by essential predicates. An essence deploys in time as regularities. Such regularities comprised the underlying dynamics that shaped the capitalism that Marx analysed. Seen retrospectively, these dynamics become objective forces; projected into the future, they become laws. Capitalism becomes immutable and its laws eternal. It is as if Marx's critique of mid-nineteenth century bourgeois political economy had been elevated to the status of prophecy.[48] From this followed the separation of a reality governed by these laws from the accidental. Stalin was understood as an aberration. So the consequences of his rule were epiphenomenal.

Trotsky's framing of the 'Russian Question' and the understanding of Marx that was of a piece with it had been rejected by Chaulieu-Montal Tendency well before they broke with the Fourth International. Following a logic to which we return later in this chapter, Socialisme ou Barbarie would come to position Marx's critical analyses of competitive capitalism as being of fundamental importance but necessarily tied to a particular time and place. This accompanied the group's shift away from economic analysis to focus on concrete relations of production.[49] Bureaucratic capitalism provided the frame

---

45 Lefort 1957, p. 20.
46 The most explicit statement is Trotsky 1941. The same basic ideas can be found throughout Trotsky 1945.
47 This is a recurrent critique of Trotsky in *Socialisme ou Barbarie*. See Lefort 1957, pp. 19–21 and Lefort 1979.
48 This characterisation leans on Part I of Castoriadis 1998 [1964–5].
49 See below on Castoriadis's 1950–1 seminars on Marx's *Capital* for a more detailed presentation of the moves involved with this. This section contains the minimum information required to set up the notion of bureaucracy.

that enabled both general characterisations of these changes as they appeared in post-war capitalist organisation and the analysis of specific relations of contemporary industrial production.

In the post-war world, bureaucracy had become a new social form and the individuals occupying places within it parts of a new social class. For reasons that will become evident below, bureaucracy entailed fundamentally new distributions of power.[50] The Soviet system was the most advanced expression of this new social arrangement. It presented an image of a society dominated by an apparatus that grew out of the fusion of the Bolshevik Party and the state that had been shattered by the deliberate actions of the Party and recomposed around it. Wracked with irrationalities and conflict, the bureaucratic apparatus used systematic terror to hold the system together.[51] In Western capitalist firms, bureaucracy occupied spaces created by the separation of ownership from production. This separation followed on the creation of stock offerings as a way to address the increased capital requirements in large-scale industries. While the bureaucratisation of firms began with monopoly capitalism, it only acquired its paradigmatic configuration with the development of assembly-line based production processes and the introduction of modern forms of management.[52] At the level of Western states, parallel changes in the nature and role of bureaucracy had begun in response to the Great Depression. The expansion of the state had been driven by attempts to mitigate the political and social consequences of the cyclical nature of capitalist activity. The Cold War and the institution of what Dwight Eisenhower would call 'the military-industrial complex' in his farewell speech of 1961 extended this process still further. What Paul Virillio called the 'pure war' of production, logistics and obsolescence as expenditure without the need for events can be understood as the perfected expression of this form of bureaucratic capitalism. Socialisme ou Barbarie defined Western 'state capitalism' or 'fragmented bureaucratic capitalism' around an American prototype. At the same time, Socialisme ou Barbarie saw Western and Soviet forms as linked by an identity at the level of relations of production. In 1949, they appeared to be pushed toward conver-

---

50   Lefort 1979, p. 299.

51   We return to this in detail below in the context of an analysis of Castoriadis's 'The Relations of Production in Russia'. The clearest overall image of the USSR is developed in Lefort 1979 [1956], a remarkable analysis of the XXth Party Congress.

52   These are the defining characteristics of Industrial Fordism. As this project is focused entirely on this from Chapter 3 onward, I defer providing a detailed bibliography. For a good history of management as a social form, see Boltanski 1982.

gence by the same logic of concentration. The early phases of the Cold War made of this a potential cataclysm.[53]

For Socialisme ou Barbarie, bureaucracy was a political and analytical category simultaneously.[54] It intertwined the particular and the general, historical specificity and teleological projection. Because the category had to enable movement from characterisations of the post-war social order in general to the analysis of specific relations of production, the category was necessarily abstract. Bureaucracy was an *eidos* or form. Like the results of any phenomenological investigation, this *eidos* was constructed from a comparative analysis geared around the isolation of commonalities. Its utility was demonstrated through the analyses it structured which were, in turn, positioned in the context of the group's revolutionary project. But it was not itself the subject of extensive independent elaboration. The debate about Socialisme ou Barbarie published in a 1957 issue of the journal, *Arguments*, distinguished the group's usage of the category from a sociology of bureaucracy. Because it was rooted in a kind of phenomenological reduction, Socialisme ou Barbarie's notion of bureaucracy does not account for the range of bureaucratic forms.[55] It neither entails nor excludes extensive analysis of administrative functions or of their internal organisations. The accounts that Socialisme ou Barbarie published about work in an administrative context were quite detailed but focused on how that work was conditioned by the same kinds of separations and conflicts characteristic of relations of production in advanced industry.[56] Socialisme ou Barbarie was not carrying out the sociology of bureaucracy. The group analysed the relations of production in contemporary capitalism shaped by bureaucracy.

Socialisme ou Barbarie's usage of the category designates a process of bureaucratisation that converges on a series of separations.[57] Of these, the most important is the division of labour that separates the *dirigeant* from the *exécutant*, those who command from those who carry out these commands. This separation is repeated within bureaucratic organisations in their hierarchical modes of operation, in the fragmentation of information and in relations between bureaucratic systems and what lies outside of them. In the work published by Socialisme ou Barbarie, the central expression of

---

53   We return to this in more detail in the next section.
54   'The theory of bureaucracy is a theory of revolution' (Lefort 1957, p. 21).
55   See the debates about *Socialisme ou Barbarie*'s conceptions of bureaucracy in *Arguments*, 4. This list derives mostly from that of Edgar Morin's '*Solécisme ou Barbarie*'.
56   Simon 1956.
57   On bureaucratisation as a social dynamic, see Lefort 1979, pp. 299ff.

this separation of the *dirigeant* from the *exécutant* unfolds on the factory floor in the context of advanced industry. In Marxian terminology, this is referred to as the point of production. The introduction of management enabled the acceleration in the development of assembly-line technologies. Taken together, these constituted a wholesale transfer of creativity to management and away from workers. However, in everyday production this transfer was revealed as an ideological desire rather than an accomplishment. This created what Socialisme ou Barbarie referred to as the fundamental contradiction of bureaucratic capitalism.

In an assembly-line dominated, industrial-Fordist context, management relations to production are mediated by process designs that stage it as flows of materials and/or components through a series of work stations. Skilled work is performed by technologies. Workers are individuated and tied to particular stations. Their roles are either to perform repetitive actions or to monitor the machinery. This relation enacts the transfer of creativity to management both directly by way of control over the production process and indirectly by way of technological design. Workers are reduced to atomised, deskilled extensions of the machines. But production in fact does not entirely correspond to production as designed. Problems continually arise that require creative, often improvised action from workers. For Socialisme ou Barbarie, this fundamental contradiction entailed a series of confrontations. Management's top-down, individuated view of work stands against worker collectives that organise themselves informally by shop and shift. Managerial control over production-speed and outputs confronts workers' shared conception in which work is a social undertaking, the pace of which is collectively determined. The understanding of skill as built into technological and production-process designs is opposed by informal collectives within which skill is distributed in such a way as to comprise a collective attribute.

The problems that arise in production and workers' responses to them fall outside managerial conceptions of the process. For Socialisme ou Barbarie, this meant that bureaucratic capitalism presupposes that workers are able to creatively engage with work that is organised to exclude them. Without this engagement, production would grind to a halt. But managerial approaches to production have no way to accommodate this. As a consequence, informal worker collectives are continually activated by and against the production process. These collectives, with their rejection of formal hierarchy and capacities for deliberative action centred on the *bricolage* of capabilities that enables the mobilisation of skill as a collective attribute, comprised the everyday sources of revolutionary potential in their basic, pre-political orientations. This characterisation anticipates some of the types of conflict that Socialisme ou Barbarie will read off from the accounts of worker experience analysed in subsequent chapters: questions of hierarchy, control over the design and pace of work, and autonomy.

To posit the separation of the *dirigeant* from the *exécutant* as the defining feature of bureaucracy is to make of it a command/control system. Control and its correlates in predictability and efficiency are assumed in any extension of bureaucratic rationalisation. But control disappears as a consequence of the bounded rationalities characteristic of bureaucratic systems. The management of a given production process is an administrative objective and the steps devised to meet that objective a means to an end. Much in the way that rules dissolve into the playing of the game they structure, control dissipates into processes or procedures. Like the rules of a game, it surfaces through problems, breakdowns or conflicts. Consider a conflict that might erupt over the reorganisation of a production process. From a viewpoint shaped by Socialisme ou Barbarie, this might be seen as an example of worker struggles to retain a degree of personal and professional autonomy. For an industrial sociologist the same conflict might be seen as an example of social deviance amongst the working class.[58] For management, power and exploitation dissolve into procedural rationality. Many analysts of bureaucratic systems have pointed to this systematic capacity to reduce anything to an administrative objective that can be approached through the extension of neutral procedures to the exclusion of ethical or political considerations.[59]

In system-theoretical terms, a bureaucracy is a social system that operates with an imperative to reduce complexity.[60] These systems are networks of specialised and compartmentalised functions linked by information networks. To be transmitted, information has to be at once processed and fragmented in ways that fit it into the particularities of the system's organisation. This would enable it to move through layers of administrative hierarchy, each of which would be a network of repetitive procedures. These networks would be differentiated not so much in kind as by status. A bureaucracy is in a sense

---

58   See Castoriadis 1988e [1957b].

59   Bauman 2000 provides a particularly forceful presentation of this problem as a central enabling condition of the Holocaust. This neutralisation presupposes the combined effects of a sense of professional identification, compartmentalisation both in terms of information that circulates and in terms of professional role, informal coercion and patterns of authority and information flows (which map one onto the other) in bureaucratic systems.

60   See 'Crises of Crisis Management: Elements of a Political Crisis Theory' in Offe 1985 and Offe 1980.

a map of its environment figured in terms of regularity and predictability. Bureaucratic systems also create maps, both of themselves as systems and of the environments they administer (the territory) that are also figured by the internal protocols of the system itself. They interact with the territory by imposing the map on it. But because the territory is complex and dynamic, this substitution inevitably involves gaps and irrationalities. The more such systems exclude the feedback loops which might link map to territory, the more the actions of these systems tends to generate problems, often to the sides of or around the mapped spaces.

For Claus Offe, in state bureaucracies this cycle triggers *ad hoc* expansions of bureaucratic systems in response to crises which arise when gaps and irrationalities pose problems for system regularities. This in turn generates a new range of crises which generate new *ad hoc* expansions and so on.[61] Socialisme ou Barbarie focused on conditions at the point of production and did not frame bureaucracy as reactive in the same way. Instead bureaucracy imposes maps of production in a rigid manner and attempts to contain the effects of gaps and irrationalities through coercion. This is of a piece with Socialisme ou Barbarie's tendency to duplicate the division of the *dirigeant* from the *executant* with another that placed routinisation on one side and creativity on another. From this followed the understanding of conflicts generated at the point of production as potentially revolutionary. They were outside the dominant system and could not be assimilated by it.[62]

A bureaucracy so understood would tend to eliminate the feedback loops that would enable coherent adjustments. It is impossible to imagine a bureaucratic system that entirely eliminates these loops. But it is not difficult to imagine their restriction to types of information that mirror administrative rationality back at itself. An extreme case would be that of Soviet factories during the 1930s as described by writers like Victor Kravchenko in *I Chose Freedom*, in which an entirely top-down system centred on administering plan objectives to the virtual exclusion of feedback loops in factories creates a hellish situation entirely held together by coercion and violence.[63] At the same time, Socialisme ou Barbarie's view of the history of capitalism acknowledges the

---

61   Offe 1985.

62   In a 1992 interview with *Socialisme ou Barbarie* member Sebastien de Diesbach, he told me a story about writing his 1964 text, 'L'hierarchie et la gestion collective', published in *Socialisme ou Barbarie* nos. 37 and 38, that undercut this opposition. He explained the text by saying he had taken a job in production management. None of them had ever worked in management. They did not understand how it works.

63   Kravchenko 1947, Chapter 13 among many possibilities.

revolutionary capacities of capitalist systems to transform themselves and reshape the entire mode of production as a consequence. If this distinction between routinisation and creativity were absolute, one wonders how such transformations would have been possible.

The conflation of map with territory encapsulates a view of a bureaucratisation that is an expression of bourgeois rationality. By conflating representation with what is represented, it reduces the world to a collection of objects. Interactions among them follow the rules of mechanical causation. These premises can be combined in a schema of unlimited rational mastery.[64] In the conflation of map with territory what emerges is a view of systems that are blind to themselves and only indirectly aware of the wider environments in which they operate. But this is too simple. Perhaps a better way to look at the operation of these systems is to revert to the distinction between the instituted and instituting. Like any social-historical phenomena, bureaucratic systems are both instituting and instituted. The systems are themselves social-historical creations that transform the environments with which they interact. However, the mode of operation common to them is predicated on a near-absolute privileging of the instituted over the instituting. This translates into the metaphor of mapping and the substitution of a world of objects for one that is in process. In contrast, the general modality of self-organisation attributed to worker collectives is one in which the status of the instituting is at parity with the instituted. In the example provided earlier, this parity operates in the play of improvisation and constraint that is implicit in the view of skill as a collective attribute that is set into motion within specific situations.[65] In fact, one does not often find the schema that shapes Socialisme ou Barbarie's notion of bureaucracy presented in this abstract a manner in the journal outside the periodic synthetic presentations of the state of Socialisme ou Barbarie's revolutionary project because any advantage there might be in clarity is offset by giving the impression of self-enclosure. It is more often deployed to shape specific analytical moves in specific contexts. For example,

---

64 See Castoriadis 1998, pp. 172–5. The theme of unlimited extension of rational mastery as a fundamental social-imaginary signification particular to capitalism is a recurrent *motif* throughout Castoriadis's later work.

65 The relation of the instituted to the instituting is one of the main questions entailed by the notion of autonomy in Castoriadis's later work. Direct democracy is posited as the collective form of self-organisation that, in principle, enables the closest approximation of autonomy with respect to this relation. The qualification 'in principle' follows from the open-ended nature of the form, from the possibility of moving away from it via a collective decision. In other words, the fact of direct democracy enables but does guarantee autonomy at the collective level.

it hovers in the background of the group's assessments of economic planning. It is most extensively operative in the descriptions and analyses of social relations and conflicts at the point of production that will be at the forefront of the rest of this book and which served as fundamental points of orientation for the development of Socialisme ou Barbarie's revolutionary project.

'The Relations of Production in Russia'

The stated objective in Castoriadis's 1949 essay, 'The Relations of Production in Russia' is to 'dissolve mystifications' concerning the nature of the USSR. Taken as a whole, the text is a demolition, on Marxist grounds, of claims that the USSR was socialist. Its primary target is Trotsky. Because there was scant information about the economic conditions in the USSR, Castoriadis takes Charles Bettelheim's *La planification soviétique* as a secondary point of departure.[66] Castoriadis regarded Bettelheim as 'almost the only person who defended Stalinism by doing something other than repeating Stalin's speeches'.[67] Bettelheim's data on the distribution of income in Soviet society is reworked to demonstrate the disproportionate role of the bureaucracy and to solidify the claim that it constituted a new class formation. For our purposes, what is particularly useful about the text is the explicitness of its Marxian conceptual framework and its situating of the bureaucracy and the relations of production structured by it in a notion of social totality.

Castoriadis devotes much of the piece to opposing the claim made by Trotsky and others that the capitalist characteristics that persisted in the USSR were restricted to the distribution of income. The relations of production were socialist.[68] In Trotsky, these claims are the correlates of the characterisation of the Stalinist bureaucracy as an epiphenomenon. The initial and most basic counter is that the fusion of the party- and state-apparatus separated from

---

66 Bettelheim 1945; Souvarine 1940, originally published in 1935, and appeared in translation by C.L.R. James in 1940. There is little doubt that it was known, particularly given the assessment of the Stalinist USSR as state capitalist, but it is not referenced in this piece. Kravchenko 1947 sold quite well, only to be followed by the 'Kravchenko Affair'. The text is cited by Castoriadis but is used with caution. Ante Ciliga's *The Russian Enigma* is reviewed by Lefort in 1950 for *Les Temps Modernes*. For an indication of the change in the environment of information compare the presentation of conditions in the USSR below with that in the first part of Lefort 1978.
67 Castoriadis 1973 p. 283. English translation: Castoriadis 1988g [1973].
68 Castoriadis 1988b [1949b], p. 108.

meaningful worker management of production cannot be socialism. Rather, it is what Lenin saw as the ideal toward which monopoly capitalism was already tending in 1917.[69] This raises the central question of how to understand relations of production. Castoriadis argues that Trotsky had been content with hand-waving in the general direction of relations of production in his interpretations of the Soviet system without ever saying what they were, or how they were structured. This hand-waving is of a piece with Trotsky's separation of distribution from production in order to maintain the position that the USSR was socialist insofar as the latter was concerned.[70] To counter this, Castoriadis focuses on the separation itself. His critique is built around a series of citations from Marx's *A Contribution to the Critique of Political Economy* to demonstrate on its own grounds the incoherence of the separation of distribution from production. They are linked aspects of a single overall structure:

> The conclusion which follows from this is, not that production, distribution, exchange and consumption are identical, but that they are links of a single whole, different aspects of one unit. Production is the decisive phase, both with regard to the contradictory aspects of production and with regard to the other phases. The process always starts afresh with production. That exchange and consumption cannot be the decisive elements is obvious; and the same applies to distribution in the sense of distribution of products. Distribution of the factors of production, on the other hand, is itself a phase of production. A distinct mode of production thus determines the specific mode of consumption, distribution, exchange and the *specific relations of these different phases to one another.* Production in *the narrow sense*, however, is in its turn also determined by the other aspects. For example, if the market, or the sphere of exchange, expands, then the volume of production grows and tends to become more differentiated. Production also changes in consequence of changes in distribution, e.g., concentration of capital, different distribution of the population in town and countryside, and the like. Production is, finally, determined by the demands of consumption. There is an interaction between the various aspects. Such interaction takes place in any organic whole.[71]

---

69   Castoriadis 1988b [1949b], p. 117.
70   Castoriadis 1988b, p. 122.
71   Marx 2000 [1859] pp. 427–8.

Material production is an aspect of an overall system, each aspect of which determines and is determined by the others. Among these, production occupies the central, structuring position. It follows that, in principle, any distinction as to the character of one aspect as over and against another does not make sense. One could also say, as Castoriadis does, that making such a separation raises questions about the nature of the system as a whole. If distribution is capitalist and distribution is determined by relations of production, then the relations of production must be capitalist. Conversely, if the relations of production were socialist, then distribution would be as well.[72] Castoriadis then demonstrates with a host of citations that this argument is not particular to Trotsky. Versions of it are repeated in many Third International analyses of the Soviet economic system to defend its socialist character and are all subject to the same critique.

A few pages later, Castoriadis follows with a well-known passage from the 'Preface' to the same text:

> In the social production of their existence, men inevitably enter into definite relations, which are independent of their will, namely relations of production appropriate to a given stage in the development of their material forces of production. The totality of these relations of production constitutes the economic structure of society, the real foundation, on which arises a legal and political superstructure and to which correspond definite forms of social consciousness. The mode of production of material life conditions the general process of social, political and intellectual life. It is not the consciousness of men that determines their existence, but their social existence that determines their consciousness. At a certain stage of development, the material productive forces of society come into conflict with the existing relations of production or – this merely expresses the same thing in legal terms – with the property relations within the framework of which they have operated hitherto. From forms of development of the productive forces these relations turn into their fetters. Then begins an era of social revolution. The changes in the economic foundation lead sooner or later to the transformation of the whole immense superstructure.[73]

---

72 Castoriadis 1988b [1949b], pp. 111ff.
73 Marx 2000 [1859], p. 429.

WHERE THINGS START									49

The base/superstructure distinction is here balanced with an organic totality-style treatment of the production system. In the essay, this move sets up a critique of the juridical formalism that subtends claims regarding the political meaning of nationalisation or state ownership independently of any transformation in the relations of production. The critique is extended with reference to Engels's discussion of the historical tendency of juridical forms to begin as an adequate reflection of the systems they shape and then develop into ideological expressions of the viewpoint and interests of the dominant class.[74] These arguments all return to the centrality of relations of production, a social totality that also justifies Socialisme ou Barbarie's productivist orientation to come. The passages taken from Marx are statements about the interdependence of the phases of material reproduction. They do not refer to dynamics that might shape the behaviour of these relations across time. This conception of interdependency and the hierarchies among them shapes most of the analyses Socialisme ou Barbarie produced across the period covered in this book.

Castoriadis argues that this formulation from Marx should be taken literally: 'The lesson of this text is clear. The relations of production are concrete social relations of man with man, of class with class as they are realised in the constant, daily production and reproduction of material life'.[75] This points to a break with the tendency in Marxian writing to treat the working class as a generality that responds to, and reflects, the arrangement of objective forces. Fleshing out the implications of this position becomes a central preoccupation for the group after 1953. At every point the analysis of the relations of production is frame-contingent. Later in the essay, Castoriadis provides a definition of the relations of production that enables a clear distinction between their capitalist and socialist versions:

1. Relations of production, in general, are defined by the mode of *managing* production (organisation and cooperation of the personal and material goals of production, definition of the goals and methods) and by the mode of *distributing* the social product...[76]
2. The class content of the relations of production is founded upon the initial distribution of the conditions of production (monopolisation of the means of production by a particular class, constant reproduction of this

---

74   Castoriadis 1988b [1949b], pp. 114–16.
75   Castoriadis 1988b, p. 114.
76   Castoriadis 1988b [1949b], p. 125

> monopolisation) and is manifested in the dominant class's management of production and in the distribution of social product in its favour.[77]
>
> 3. From the point of view of the exploited class, the class content is manifested through its reduction to the narrow role of executants and, more generally, through its human alienation and total subordination to the dominant class (...)[78]

The first point uses direct control over the management and the setting of objectives to distinguish capitalist relations of production from socialist ones. The other two distinguish between the *dirigeant* and the *executant* to characterise the relations specific to capitalism. Castoriadis then reverts to the description of competitive capitalism drawn from Marx. In capitalist relations of production, the fundamental relation is that of the employer to worker. The employer controls the conditions of production. The worker sells his or her labour-power for a wage.[79] Ownership of the means of production includes that of the physical space and the technologies, both of which are past or dead labour. Ownership extends to control over the organisation of production and the setting of objectives.[80] Workers who sell their labour power in this context find themselves locked into a situation predicated on exploitation and alienation:

> In conclusion, the inherent exploitation of the capitalist system is based on the fact that the producers do not have the means of production at their disposal either individually (artisanal) or collectively (socialism) and that living labour, instead of dominating dead labour, is dominated by it through the intermediary of the individuals who personify it (capitalists). The relations of production are relations of exploitation under both their aspects, *qua* the organisation of production properly so called and *qua* the organisation of distribution. Living labour is subordinated to dead labour in production proper since its viewpoint is subordinated to that of dead labour and is completely subordinated to the latter. In the organisation of production, the proletariat is entirely dominated by capital and only exists for the latter. He is also exploited in the process of distribution since his sharing in the social product is governed by economic laws (expressed by the employer on the level of consciousness)

---

77 Castoriadis 1988b [1949b], p. 126.
78 Castoriadis 1988b [1949b], pp. 126–7.
79 Castoriadis 1988b [1949b], p. 137.
80 Castoriadis 1988b [1949b], p. 138.

that define his participation not on the basis of the value created through the power of labour, but on the value of this labour-power. These laws, which express the profound tendency of capital accumulation, bring the cost of producing labour-power more and more down to a physical minimum...[81]

To understand the relations of production requires an account of the circuits within which they operate. As noted earlier, what determines the immediate circuit is control or management: the setting of overall objectives that shape the nature of production. Workers who sell their labour power enter into that system. At a more general level, material conditions and social arrangements converge, and are driven by the dynamics and organic crises of capital. For example, insofar as workers are concerned, the falling rate of profit plays out as the ratcheting up of the intensity of exploitation and a diminishing of returns. The polemical character of the text pins its arguments to a fidelity to Marx. This makes it difficult to say whether Castoriadis saw the organic crises of capital and the increasing immiseration of the proletariat as operative on a deep structural level in the capitalism of 1949. When Castoriadis notes that bureaucratic capitalism tends toward a negation of the laws of competitive capitalism, he refers primarily to the elimination of otherwise 'natural' limits on exploitation in Russia. But given the role played by categories like the concentration of capital in other texts of this period, it is reasonable to conclude that he did. This point serves to emphasise the importance of the shifts that Socialisme ou Barbarie was to make over the next two years.

The brief outline of the relations of production under socialism that follows is interesting in its generality.[82] Worker management of production at both the macro and micro levels would necessarily entail basic transformations in the way production is organised and carried out. But compared with what Socialisme ou Barbarie would later stipulate about the content of socialism, it is perfunctory, serving as a counter-example. The main argument proceeds from the relatively detailed outline of conditions under competitive capitalism to an outline of relations of production under Soviet-style bureaucratic capitalism. The scenario is largely the same except that it is now the bureaucracy that occupies the situation of the capitalist. The party bureaucracy now monopolises the means of production and the determination of its organisation and goals. It controls consumption. It has abolished labour markets. Because the Soviet system saw itself as a workers' state there was no need for

---

81 Castoriadis 1988b [1949b], pp. 131–2.
82 See Castoriadis 1973 and 1988g [1973].

unions or the right to strike. By 1940, even the ability to leave one's job had been removed. The basic relations of production are those of advanced capitalist industry. What differentiates them is that any limits on the exploitation of workers present in the West have been eliminated.[83]

Castoriadis notes evidence of worker resistance to this scientifically engineered hell. From a revolutionary viewpoint, however, this resistance is aleatory, limited to pilferage or a sort of 'active indifference'. Dominated by a brutal bureaucratic capitalist order and without hope of relief or organisation, Soviet workers were in a horrific position, one that 'if not offered another way out [...] cannot but bring this class's political and social degradation'. But the suffocation of the workers was also that of the apparatus. Following on the logic of the fundamental contradiction of bureaucratic capitalism, the system as a whole should tend toward collapse. In this context, the plan serves to structure and legitimate this form of exploitation and is itself an ideological document. Because Bettelheim's analysis accepted its premises, it could not help but be an apology for it. It is with some glee, then, that Castoriadis uses it to demonstrate that the apparatus expropriates a significant percentage of what it was understood to be distributing. This is taken as a demonstration of its status as a new type of class formation.[84]

'The Relations of Production in Russia' is an intricate combination of innovation that also enacts a relation to inherited conceptual frames consistent with heretical argumentation within an operative field of cultural production. The assumption behind Bourdieu's model is that, despite whatever might be articulated at the level of content, positions within a given field compete for the cultural power that follows from domination which lay with the ability to structure the reception of cultural objects and, by extension, to impose one's textual canon and interpretive protocols. By extension, breaking with a given field is still a move in the same game. Were this to be universally the case, a consequence would be conservatism with respect to tradition or the canonical materials that comprise its centre that would often be at cross purposes with the claims that might be made using those materials. The handling of Marx and Lenin in 'The Relations of Production in Russia' can be read through this lens: it positions the text within the breakaway from Trotskyism. At roughly the same time, however, Socialisme ou Barbarie was distancing itself from that

---

83   Castoriadis 1988b [1949b], p. 137.
84   See Castoriadis 1988b [1949b], pp. 144ff for Castoriadis's critique of Bettleheim's use of this data as a springboard for an apology for the bureaucratic capitalist order and as an anchor for arbitrary modelling assumptions – for example in the positing of a viable labour market.

context and had initiated an informal process internally so as to enact quite different relations to the canon and enable continued development outside of the previous frame of reference.

On Lenin

Between November 1949 and July 1950, Socialisme ou Barbarie held 16 meetings devoted to reading Lenin. These were 'not educational meetings in the traditional sense, but much more research meetings'. They were attended by a group of perhaps 10–15 people. The participants included four or five members of Socialisme ou Barbarie along with others from *La Gauche Communiste de France*, a successor to the Trotskyist Courant Communiste Internationaliste which Lefort had been part of during World War II. The GCF held itself at a remove from the PCI, and was linked to Socialisme ou Barbarie by personal friendships.[85] They were later joined by people from the Bordiguist *Internationaliste* group. The GCF contingent did not remain. The people from *Internationaliste* did. Participants were given a reading list in advance. Each meeting began with a presentation by Castoriadis. Some of these were prepared, others were extemporised from notes. Each was followed by a series of semi-formal interventions. These were transcribed. The more open discussion which followed was not.

The *précis* published in *Socialisme ou Barbarie* 5/6 summarised the goals for the series:

> The need to study Lenin's work derives, first of all, from the need of the avant-garde to submit its heritage from the past to critical examination. The confusion that currently reigns between Leninism and Stalinism renders this all the more imperative. The fact is that Leninism was the first attempt at a complete response to all the programmatic questions that posed themselves to the revolutionary movement; he was the first to place himself at the level of world revolutionary strategy and tactics; his actions had, from one end to the other, an exemplary character not realised before or since. All this shows that there is no possible

---

[85] Leaving aside the peculiar pattern in French Trotskyist circles in 2012 of resurrecting group names from the past, there seems to be a new CCI. Some very general information about the GCF is available on their website here: <http://fr.internationalism.org/taxonomy/term/114>.

elaboration of a revolutionary programme without a clear balance-sheet on Leninism.[86]

Chaulieu-Montal had done similar collective readings but the lack of documented traces makes it difficult to know how they proceeded.[87] In these meetings, Socialisme ou Barbarie was turning to the central texts of the tradition in order to alter the group's collective relations to that tradition. Castoriadis's introduction to the series makes this quite clear:

> Why study Lenin?
>
> It is a matter of knowing whether there is a continuity in the workers' movement and what that continuity is and our attitude with respect to that continuity. We have to have the courage to get to the bottom of the question and ask: is the weight of the past on the minds of new militants useful or damaging? Perhaps the primary task is a relentless struggle against this famous 'tradition' in the name of which the worst stupidities are maintained despite all appearances and the worst betrayals are committed?
>
> Undoubtedly it is. There is an entire side of the tradition of the workers' movement that weighs very heavily on contemporary proletarian consciousness, and there is an entire host of zombies in worker organisations that justify their status as mouthpieces by referring to this 'tradition'. One can never do enough to liquidate that tradition.
>
> But we must liquidate it rationally in the light of a critical examination and a serious analysis of its content and of the contexts that shaped it. To say that the revolutionary movement must completely liquidate its past presupposes that it knows that past.[88]

The introduction goes on to provide tactical justifications for turning to Lenin: the ubiquity of reference to his work makes an assessment unavoidable, etc.[89]

---

86 Socialisme ou Barbarie 1950, p. 144. I have transcripts of these lectures from Castoriadis's archive. Unfortunately, the set is incomplete. For the present discussion, that the session on imperialism is missing is particularly unfortunate.

87 But see, for example, the short pieces on Hegel's Logic published in Castoriadis 2008 or those on the Russian Question included in Castoriadis 1988.

88 Castoriadis: Presentations on Lenin, 1949–50 (CC Papers, file SB-1B), First Conference, p. 1

89 'Like it or not...the great majority of worker-militants align themselves consciously with Marxism and its most advanced form of practice – Leninism. This is true whether

The central objective was to move beyond acts of 'demystification' that would, in theory, open up the works of Lenin, Marx and Engels in ways that exceed and run counter to their dominant usages. Remaining within these usages would be to treat the works as static and the tradition of which they are part as a closed circuit. Such a move would reduce militant action to textual interpretation. It would place them in a position not unlike writers in contemporary academia who make radical claims with respect to a rationality that they appeal to through their style of explanation and in so doing place that rationality outside the space of critique. The neutral space that situates the reader of such texts is enacted and legitimated through the text's interpretive procedures even as the content of the critique would undermine it. The past and its repetition are like dead weights on the present. One is reduced to substituting the sense of movement that can follow from re-animations and re-arrangements of aspects of that past for political action in the present. The programme outlined above would liquidate[90] this whole conception of tradition and the relations to it that are typically enacted more often than conceptualised. The justification for doing so is an argument from consequences. But this does not entail the simple rejection of the Marxian tradition or of the history from which it derives and which is, in turn, articulated through it:

> Because Leninism is a viewpoint that extends to almost all the problems that the revolutionary movement confronts, these questions are absolutely vital for the proletariat – such as the question of the development of proletarian consciousness, of the party, of the nature of revolution in a developing country, the national question, the nature of imperialism and the response to imperialist war, the nature of the state, of the bourgeois republic and the dictatorship of the proletariat in particular, the role of

---

one is talking about worker-militants under the influence of Stalinism – which endlessly exploits the linkage of Leninism to Marxism – or anti-Stalinist militants; it is impossible to link a contemporary conception of revolutionary ideology and revolutionary programme without clarification of the question of Leninism. This task is all the more urgent given the degeneration of the Bolshevik Party and the historically unprecedented equivocation created by the III International between Leninism and bureaucracy: for some, the fact that Stalinism issued from Leninism constitutes its justification while for the others, this same fact is only the objective demonstration of the bureaucratic character of Leninism'. Ibid., p. 2.

90 Liquidation used in this manner was Trotskyist slang.

unions under capitalism and under worker-control, etc. Can we simply throw out the Leninist approaches to these matters? Of course not.[91]

The elaboration which follows is here quoted at length:

> In other words, a critical appraisal of Lenin poses the more pressing contemporary problems that confront the workers' movement with respect to the revolutionary programme and workers' power. On this, allow me to say a few words about the utility of this work for our group.
>
> What distinguishes us from the other Left groups that are close to us, that is which position themselves in uncompromising struggle against capitalism – bourgeois or bureaucratic – is not the intense desire that we want to show regarding the construction of the theoretical foundations for a revolutionary programme, nor even our orientation toward the construction of an effective revolutionary leadership – on those points, everyone agrees if not in acts then at least in words. What distinguishes us is that we consider the clarification of revolutionary theory to be in vain and the construction of a revolutionary direction impossible without the most detailed possible definition in the present conditions of the revolutionary programme. The elaboration of this programme passes through the analysis of Leninism. The Leninist approach is the only programmatic approach to this day to be coherent, systematic and universal as a whole.
>
> These reasons are for us central. But there are many other reasons that justify taking up Leninism as an object of study. Leninism enables us to study an entire developmental arc, from the constitution of the Bolshevik party and its struggles, to its seizure of power, the responses it gave to problems encountered once it had power and its final degeneration. The party was incontestably revolutionary and proletarian from its introduction of Marxism into a quasi-feudal country: it was brought to power by the most grandiose revolution in history and ended with the instauration of the most modern regime of exploitation. Its development transcended the limits of a national phenomenon to embrace the global workers' movement, not only by its consequences but intellectually. The Third International was founded on Leninist principles and was the first and last real International to this day. Finally, we study Leninism because it is

---

91   Castoriadis: 'Presentations on Lenin', 1949–50 (CC Papers, file SB-1B), First Conference, p. 3.

only through it that one sees the development of practice linked so intimately to the development of theory. The Bolshevik Party was the only one that gave no answer to urgent practical questions without a deep theoretical examination that was not shaped by a desire to harmonise reality with their ideas or their theoretical viewpoints with slogans. To use a literary expression, it is with Leninism that the revolutionary movement reached its classical period, the phase during which the development of theory and practice went harmoniously together and were crowned with results at once magnificent and terrible.[92]

The series will understand Lenin as a kind of template for revolutionaries in his range of engagements and commitments and close consistent relationship between theory and practice. The approach to reading Lenin will be historicising as well. It broaches the question of the party in terms shaped by theoretical justifications and their historical outcomes, both those which were intended and those which were not. The idea is to influence the development of a revolutionary programme that accommodates the situation of workers in contemporary capitalism in a project framed by a vision of socialism that orients it toward the future. The goal is to extract a schema from Lenin that would shape Socialisme ou Barbarie's collective militant practices. This schema would direct the processes of making certain modes of interaction or procedures: the tight linking of theory and practice; an openness of conceptual frames to new forms of social being; continuous interrogation; tireless work. It would take as given the international viewpoint that Leninism played a fundamental role in fashioning. But it would contextualise and so be distanced from the particular choices made by Lenin himself. For example, this engagement with Lenin will again pose the question of revolutionary organisation and the critique of the Vanguard Party and the implications of that critique for the group itself.[93] Framed in this way, the schema is neither imitation nor repetition. Rather, it is a mode of structuring an open-ended activity. If one takes this literally as

---

92 Castoriadis: 'Presentations on Lenin', 1949–50 (CC Papers, file SB–1B), First Conference, p. 4
93 In other words, the revolutionary organisation would not itself perform revolutionary actions as would a cadre of professional revolutionaries that operated in the name of the working class. Ideally, it would work in a symbiotic relation with the worker avant-garde as an aspect of an overarching revolutionary process, in which the organisation would attempt to provide interpretations and clarity and the workers would be the primary actors.

suggesting an approach to the redirection of a working process, it would require internalisation through repetition and time before the schema would disappear into the practices it structured. Perhaps this contributes to explaining the lag that separated such internal statements about leadership from changes in the writing that appeared in *Socialisme ou Barbarie*.

The approach to Lenin that Castoriadis outlines was informed fundamentally by the differences in historical situation. From 1949 the arcs that were in the making for Lenin had become apparent and the consequences of choices that may have been forced by contingent factors had become manifest. This relation to *ex post facto* historical outcomes enables a derivation of 'meaning' or direction. The derivation of sense and implication from the past is an exercise in reading-off patterns from the present. A shuttling back and forth between the two could shape ways of being-revolutionary operative outside the system of constraint and reinforcement particular to the field of cultural production Socialisme ou Barbarie had left behind. The reading of history was central to this operation. Like any such reading of history the group's reading would rest on certain assumptions. Castoriadis makes some of them explicit at the end of the typescript:

> For us there is no serious analysis of history of the workers' movement nor is there any revolutionary perspective outside the following principles:

1. Each phase of the workers' movement is an expression of a phase of the economic development of capitalist society and of the proletariat itself as the essential productive force of modern society.
2. Each phase of the workers' movement also corresponds to a phase of social development in general, in particular to the collapse or reorganisation of the social groups most closely linked to production and to social life in general that is closest to the proletariat.
3. Each phase of the development of the workers' movement is an expression of a step in the development of class consciousness, a new objective experience which poses new tasks for the proletariat across the successes and failures of the movement and at the same time gives them the objectives that enable them to resolve its problems at the levels of consciousness and reality.[94]

---

94 Castoriadis: 'Presentations on Lenin', 1949–50 (CC Papers, file SB-1B), First Conference, pp. 5–6.

These assumptions frame Lenin(ism) as an expression of a particular phase of development in the history of the workers' movement. By foregrounding the relations of the party to forces beyond itself, the approach has Socialisme ou Barbarie's critique of the Vanguard Party built into it. This analytical unit, 'party-workers', is then contextualised by fitting it into an image of the social totality outlined earlier with respect to Marx. This notion of social totality would allow the phase in the history of the workers' movement expressed in the relation of the party to be integrated into a network of determinations that would refer it to the concrete relations of production that obtained at the time. The operation could then be reversed, moving from concrete relations of production outward to forms of revolutionary action. The final step would position these analytical outcomes in the context of a progressive narrative that charts the unfolding of the proletarian revolutionary project. These steps rehearse as a historical method the approach to autonomous worker actions the group will take after Stalin's death.

Unfortunately these seminars survive as a very incomplete series. What remains is comprised largely of handwritten notes and transcripts of discussions. The discussions are interesting due to their range of responses. Each group that attended had read the material and was already familiar with the contexts out of which the texts arose. They are debates on points of interpretation or the political utility of a given move in Castoriadis's presentations. The general character of the discussion shows that there is no sense in which these meetings resolved problems or represented a definite step in any particular direction. There was no 'OK, now that's been sorted...' Rather, they were interpretations that posed questions and initiated or inflected ongoing conversations. They were also, as I argued earlier, aspects of a process centred on developing practical ways to move forward as a revolutionary group outside the milieu of Trotskyism.

The Logic of Concentration and the Cold War

While the reading circle devoted to Lenin was moving through the tradition at one rhythm, the writing and collective editing of articles for publication in the journal moved at another. The articles that appeared in the journal devoted to the international situation from 1949–50 make extensive use of *Imperialism, The Highest Stage of Capitalism*[95] to describe the general dynamic underpinning inter-bloc conflict. The record of the meeting devoted to Lenin's

---

95   Lenin 1977.

pamphlet on imperialism does not survive, but imperialism is the first on a list of major themes to be addressed. In the *Capital* seminars of the following year, Castoriadis frames Lenin's text as 'a description of monopoly capitalism' and not a theory in the sense that Marx had developed for competitive capitalism. In the texts on the international situation, however, the overarching tendency that drives events is concentration.

For Lenin, the process of concentration drove the transition from market to monopoly capitalism:

> If it were necessary to give the briefest possible definition of imperialism we should have to say that imperialism is the monopoly stage of capitalism. Such a definition would include what is most important, for, on the one hand, finance capital is the bank capital of a very few big monopolist banks, merged with the capital of monopolist associations of industrialists; and, on the other hand, the division of the world is the transition from a colonial policy which has extended without hindrance to territories not seized by any capitalist power, to a colonial policy of monopolist possession of the entire globe, which has been completely divided up.

Lenin goes on to enumerate five more basic features of imperialism:

1. The concentration of production and capital has developed to such a high stage that it has created monopolies which play a decisive role in economic life; 2. the merging of bank capital with industrial capital, and the creation, on the basis of this 'finance capital' of a financial oligarchy; 3. the export of capital as distinguished from the export of commodities acquires exceptional importance; 4. the formation of international monopolist associations which share the world amongst themselves, and 5. the territorial division of the whole world among the biggest capitalist powers.[96]

Socialisme ou Barbarie took Lenin's account to be an accurate description of the underlying processes that drove the evolution of monopoly capitalism. Imperialism remained a significant aspect of bureaucratic capitalism as an overall social form in which it was both an expression of the tendency to concentration and a force that was driving that tendency:

---

96   Lenin 1977, p. 700.

> The analysis of the contemporary world situation, presented in this review since its first issue, can be summarised as follows: the fundamental characteristic of the contemporary period is the struggle between the American and Russian blocs for the domination and exploitation of the world. This struggle finds its source in the inexorable necessity that pushes the dominant class in each bloc – the American trusts and the Russian bureaucracy – to increase its profits and power, to assure the exploitation of all of humanity, to secure its domination against all external attack and internal uprising. Since there is little chance that the proletariat can, by a revolution that would head off war, overturn the exploitative regimes of the East and West, it is more than likely that the struggle between the two blocs will culminate in a third world war.[97]

The early phase of the Cold War was a repetition of the logic of imperialism at a higher level of generality. However, the group rejected the dialectical framework into which Lenin placed his description. So while the overall situation could be seen as moving along a single overarching logic, a closer look, as appears in Castoriadis's 1949 essay 'La consolidation temporaire du capitalisme mondial', revealed a more heterodox situation:

A. The year 1948 has demonstrated: on the one hand, the impossibility of any lasting compromise between the American and Russian blocs; on the other hand, it confirmed the division of the world into two closed zones, within which the system of exploitation has achieved a relative consolidation, in the short term.
B. It now appears that absolute confirmation of the inevitability of war cannot be derived from a uniform process leading to total and overt conflict. On the contrary, a phase is now opened of compartmentalisation, with the localised containment of conflict points. Some conflicts may even be eliminated.[98]

The abstract tendency toward inter-bloc war, driven by the logic of capital concentration, translated directly into events at every point. Castoriadis argued that war remained 'unavoidable', even though inter-bloc confrontation had entered a phase of compartmentalisation and localisation of conflict. Any consolidation of position was temporary. Cracks beneath the surface

---

97 Castoriadis 1954a, p. 1.
98 Castoriadis, 1949, p. 22. This is part of a summary of two lectures given by Castoriadis at *Socialisme ou Barbarie* meetings in Febuary, 1949.

would eventually undermine this stability: the result would be acceleration toward war.

These cracks ran along the spaces described in Trotsky's notion of uneven development. The unevenness of economic expansion in 1949 was evident in a number of indices. Castoriadis used OECD data on 1948–9 rates of overall economic expansion and their different rates of diminution by sector, the spatial unevenness of development, and the reduction of international relative to domestic exchange, to argue that aggregate expansion masked deep structural problems.[99] These indices were not secret, and Castoriadis's interpretation of them not eccentric: the U.S. had used the same data, recognised signs of trouble, and tried to respond through the Marshall Plan. Socialisme ou Barbarie read the Marshall Plan as an American effort to address the unevenness of development by aligning the weakened European economies with its own through exchange mechanisms and trade agreements in which European countries were in no position to participate. American planners soon recognised the gap that separated the plan from reality, and responded by setting goals for European economic development over the period 1949–52. These goals would have been totally unrealistic even if Congress had funded them. For Socialisme ou Barbarie, these difficulties indicated that the Marshall Plan was affected by the same problems as other, more totalising state plans. Premised on inaccurate feedback, and incapable of creating mechanisms to compensate for it, the Marshall Plan was elaborated entirely on the basis of projections more reflective of bureaucratic system goals and internal criteria than of the environment it was designed to regulate. Castoriadis concluded that the Marshall Plan could not be more than a temporary palliative. Its limits were already becoming apparent during the first economic quarter of 1949, in signs of an American overproduction crisis and depression. Still in this respect working out of a standard Marxist framework, Castoriadis saw in overproduction evidence of the failure of American efforts at system stabilisation. The only other mechanism available to assure system cohesion was war. Therefore, Castoriadis argued, barring revolution, the failure of the Marshall Plan to counter uneven economic development, and the political crises caused by it, would push Western bureaucratic capitalism into all-out war against the Soviet-dominated bloc, and this sooner rather than later.[100] The Korean

---

99 For this analysis, see Castoriadis, 1949.
100 This summary does not do justice to the complexity of explanations offered for the permanent crisis of decadent Western capitalism all of which are ultimately traceable back to the nature of monopoly and bureaucratic capitalism suggested earlier – the suppression of markets, the artificiality of prices in a monopoly-environment, the use of highly

War seemed to confirm Socialisme ou Barbarie's darkest prognostications. Socialisme ou Barbarie viewed the Korean War as resulting from Western failure to stabilise their economies, and as the inevitable outcome of the American strategy of 'cold war'. This strategy involved the demobilisation of the World War II armed forces as an official acknowledgement of peace. For Socialisme ou Barbarie, demobilisation was a 'calculated risk' designed to buy time adequate for an upgrade of military hardware and strategy in anticipation of nuclear war. The Korean War crumbled this façade of peace, and pushed Socialisme ou Barbarie to the following conclusion:

> The Korean War is, *in its form*, a civil war in the context of a backward country struggling for its national independence. But this is a form the content of which is entirely empty ... the theory of a struggle for 'national independence' is, in this case, the exact homology, in workers' terminology, of the theory of the 'police operation' in bourgeois terminology. In reality, the fact that tiny North Korea and the immense USA have only played such a small role up to now cannot be explained if the former was not, behind the scenes, under the power, and tight control, of Russia.[101]

Given the model outlined earlier, this local conflict-by-proxy between the imperial powers appeared to be the incident that would lead to global war. The revolutionary intervention of the proletariat represented the only way to disrupt this logic. But Cold War political polarisation had eliminated any prospect that working-class revolution would originate in either bloc. Socialisme ou Barbarie analysed the alienation of French workers from trade unions and political parties as a result of their every action having been forced into an international political frame. Worker disaffection combined with trade-union polarisation to prevent any coherent action from taking shape that could have addressed stagnant wages, higher prices and demands for 'wartime' production increases. The French workers were standing by, alienated from politics, unable to envision the future, waiting to see what happened.[102] Socialisme ou Barbarie saw the plight of French workers as emblematic of workers generally. Given this passivity, Socialisme ou Barbarie could do little more than describe what they argued was the withdrawal of the working class from politics and conclude on that basis that at that moment there was no organisation capable

---

rationalised production techniques as a means of cutting cost, which also have the effect of rendering overall production increasingly irrational, etc.

101 Socialisme ou Barbarie 1950a, p. 100. See also Socialisme ou Barbarie 1952.
102 See, for example, Bourt, 1950. On Bourt/Gaspard/Hirzel, see Chapter 5, below.

of stepping in to shift politics or theory onto revolutionary ground. This was the onset of modern barbarism:

> We can...define these two notions. The decadence of the capitalist regime is the period during which the latter enters into a state of permanent crisis, even as it continues to develop the material and human preconditions of a superior order – in other words, even as it continues to develop the premises of socialist revolution. In contrast, the decomposition of this system would begin at the moment when the objective possibilities for the creation of a superior social order disappear...This, precisely, is the possibility of modern barbarism, no longer as a tendency developing constantly within exploiting society, but as a phase of social decomposition, during which the forces of production as well as revolutionary class consciousness undergo profound and lasting regression. Modern barbarism would be the historical period in which the possibility of revolutionary communism would be absent.[103]

However, the Korean War did not result in a third world war. In late 1952, Socialisme ou Barbarie published an article that acknowledged their obvious error in the overstatement of the importance of imperialism and the concentration of capital in their analyses of inter-bloc conflict. The consequences of this error were a 'the-sky-is-falling' reading of Korea and an overestimation of the Western bloc's coherence. Socialisme ou Barbarie explained the latter problem – of the actual incoherence of the Western bloc – by arguing that American domination 'lacked a social base'.[104] In other words, the Americans controlled the Western bloc because they were in a materially advantageous position after World War II that enabled them to forcibly assume a leadership role. The bloc was a creation of force that was held together by force.[105] Socialisme ou Barbarie argued that the lack of a social base was reflected in a basic instability in the American position. Squabbling between the allies over matters of strategy was evidence of this instability. American leadership, exercised through political pressure, was therefore an artificial, superstructural phenomenon. It was not an expression of the contradictions that structured relations between 'social forces', which would have made it 'organic'. Socialisme ou Barbarie developed this 'disunity thesis' in order to explain why world war

---

[103] Castoriadis, 1949, p. 26.
[104] Socialisme ou Barbarie 1950a, p. 100.
[105] This analysis matched point for point the characterisation of the Stalinist state in Castoriadis 1988b that would later be defined as totalitarian in Lefort 1978.

had not happened. It was a rather strange explanation that enabled Socialisme ou Barbarie to move on without drawing any conclusions.[106]

The *Capital* Seminars

Beginning in November 1950 and continuing through June of 1951, Socialisme ou Barbarie held a second series of meetings focused on canonical materials. These took the form of lectures on Marx's *Capital* that Castoriadis delivered at *Le centre d'études économiques*, part of the 6th division of *L'Ecole Pratique des Hautes Etudes*, which later became *L'Ecole des Hautes Etudes en Sciences Sociales*. These seminar length lectures were typed out in their entirety. The series of sixteen moves from a general introduction through an overview of Marxian and bourgeois political economy to a close reading of substantial portions of *Capital*. They are too complex to be summarised here and would be good candidates for separate publication. This section concentrates on the final four lectures, which attempt to 'disengage a philosophical schema' that shaped Marx's work on competitive capitalism and use it to determine whether a comparable theory could be constructed to account for the overall dynamics that shape monopoly or bureaucratic capitalism.

The starting point for this segment of the series is: there is no theory of monopoly or monopoly capitalism in Marx. There are suggestions of how Marx might have proceeded with the project in *Capital* Volume III.[107] But they are no more than suggestions. The question is how one would go about constructing such a theory. The obvious move would be to use a theoretical schema drawn from *Capital* itself. In Castoriadis's view, the abstraction of that schema opens onto a methodological question concerning the conditions under which an analysis of a specific economic form can proceed from the particular to the general. This would enable the passage from description to theory. This question is vexing if one is not content with the production of the sort of metaphysical models favoured by bourgeois economists that substitute for social reality. Castoriadis argues that the main advantage that Marx brings to the critique of bourgeois political economy was that his theory of competitive capitalism as a social system accounted for significant aspects of social reality because it placed the analytical and political questions of class in the foreground.

---

106 See the unsigned editorial 'La situation internationale' in *Socialisme ou Barbarie* no. 11 (Nov–Dec 1952), pp. 55–9.
107 See Marx 1959, Chapter 52, 'Classes'.

Any parallel theoretical account of monopoly or bureaucratic capitalism would have to do the same.

Castoriadis argues that, for Marx, the conditions of possibility for the movement from the particular to the general fundamental to *Capital* followed from the singularly advantageous context in which he worked. Competitive capitalism enabled the assumption that a single firm centred on a single process produced a single commodity. The value and/or price of that commodity was a social function because of the roles played by markets. This made of it a discrete system with more or less standard analytical units, the actions of which were at once individual and social and that operated as a system with the regularities that Marx was able to point out. But the centre of the analysis was not the description of these regularities but their consequences for workers. For Castoriadis, while the model Marx constructed of competitive capitalism involved simplifications and operated at a considerable remove from economic realities, the political core of his analysis was so important that these limitations were secondary problems. The model worked out some of the regularities that the system produced through its functioning in general and which could be seen as conditioning it in turn, and then linked them to the questions of wage labour and exploitation.[108]

The evolution of competitive capitalism was driven by tendencies to concentration both at the levels of capital and the organisation of production (through its horizontal and vertical integrations). Concentration, particularly in the organisation of production, destroyed the laws that enabled its evolution by undermining the assumptions concerning the nature of firms that enabled Marx to generalise. Further, the tendency to concentration did not result in a single type of productive unit that supplanted the type upon which Marx relied. Not all economic sectors concentrated in the same ways. Even within the sectors furthest advanced in these terms, the outcome was not uniform. Monopoly is a theoretical construct. The complete domination of a given sector of production by a single firm is a limit-state. Those sectors characterised by intensive concentration are typically oligopolies, small numbers of firms which operate within national boundaries as *de facto* cartels, particularly insofar as raw materials are concerned. Monopoly would enable the simplifications required for system modelling. Oligopolies do not.

Marxian theories of monopoly had in the main treated it as the aggregation of individual productive units. Seeing monopoly as a combinatorial

---

[108] Centre d'études économiques. Socialisme ou Barbarie, Conférence de M. Chaulieu, 25 May 1951, pp. 8–9. The argument concerning the movement from the particular to the general can be found in the 8 June lecture, pp. 10ff.

phenomenon would enable its disaggregation. This allowed orthodox analysts to claim that the same general laws Marx pointed to in *Capital* continued to function. Castoriadis argues that concentration results in both quantitative and qualitative changes in organisation. To demonstrate what is meant by qualitative change, Castoriadis turns to a series of bourgeois economists, approaching them in the manner of Marx as objects of critique and re-appropriation. Monopoly is not merely the aggregation of smaller productive units. It is also the elimination of markets in their competitive capitalist forms. This basically transforms the nature of value or price. Value is no longer a social function in the same way as it had been for Marx. On the one hand, loosely following Hayek, one could imagine a monopoly that sets prices entirely on the basis of internal bureaucratic criteria. This would make it arbitrary with respect to external factors but comprehensible in terms of power arrangements within the bureaucracy itself. Hayek had argued that, because firms are not transparent to themselves, the history of price is the main index that firms can appeal to in order to assess their own performance. This makes of the history of price the basis for rational activity. Castoriadis mirrors this understanding of bureaucratic system-operation as tending toward irrationality by the elimination of feedback. A second possibility is to see monopoly pricing as based on assessments of demand elasticity. In this case, the monopoly would be oriented toward a space external to itself, but would only derive from demand-elasticity information about its immediate contexts – conditions local to primary materials or the activities of production units integrated within a larger chain, or local to the context in which commodities were offered. In both cases, value is changed from a broadly social function to a description of particular states of affairs. Castoriadis argues that while every particular situation would be amenable to a description, exhaustive description would not be possible. Even if exhaustive description of a particular situation were in principle to be generated, nothing would enable the passage from the particular either temporally or spatially. By the removal of the kinds of social relations that underpinned value in competitive capitalism, monopoly capitalism undercut the basis for movement from the particular to the general that would enable an analysis comparable to what one finds in Marx.[109] The same analytical problems repeat in contexts characterised by the progressive fusion of highly concentrated firms with the state and bureaucratic-capitalist contexts, although in different ways.[110]

---

109   8 June, pp. 12–25.
110   On bureaucratic capitalism, see the seminar of 22 June.

This is not to say that oligopoly behaviour is therefore incomprehensible. Rather, the conclusion is that comprehending their activities is primarily a sociological question. The main Marxian analyses of monopoly capitalism, including Lenin's pamphlet on imperialism, are relegated to the status of descriptions.[111] The problem of generalising on the basis of any series of descriptions of different situations recapitulates that of an exhaustive knowledge of each situation. In other words, once one moves out of competitive capitalism the primacy of economic analysis is undercut. The same gesture historicises the economic analysis of competitive capitalism. Economics operates on the same plane as other forms of social analysis do: its utility is determined situationally. That utility would be shaped by the ability of a particular analysis to illuminate the situation of the workers politically.

As was the case with the meetings devoted to Lenin, the implications of these seminars are not immediately apparent in the texts published by the group.[112] But they do clear the way for the turn in Socialisme ou Barbarie's collective focus on forms of autonomous worker action and their modes of self-organisation after the death of Stalin in 1953. From there, Socialisme ou Barbarie begins to look to council forms as a way of thinking about worker self-organisation and of linking them back to accounts of everyday experience at the factory floor in order to complete the circuit of situating councils as an expression of conflicts in contemporary relations of production. It is at this point that the fundamental contradiction of bureaucratic capitalism moves to the fore as a structuring heuristic.

Where Things Stop

Socialisme ou Barbarie's apocalyptic view of the Korean War coincided with their most difficult period as a group. The delimited field of ideological production from which Socialisme ou Barbarie had emerged was collapsing. The Fourth International imploded in 1952, the most visible effect of the Cold War's political polarisation and its elimination of space from which revolutionary dissent might be articulated. The PCF's 'revolutionary' posture co-opted much of its language. In France, Socialisme ou Barbarie was virtually alone in

---

111 25 May, p. 16. Again, because the session on imperialism from the meetings on Lenin is missing, it is difficult to know whether this conclusion was already present there or if it is something new with these seminars.
112 A text summarising the conclusions was published as Castoriadis 1953 and Castoriadis 1954.

opposing the PCF on Marxist grounds and, behind it, the USSR. But the journal no longer sold much beyond the confines of the group. Claude Lefort later characterised this period as the group's 'desert crossing' of the 'long night of Stalinism'.[113] The period 'cannot be imagined by anyone who was not there'.[114]

Between 1950 and 1953 the group moved into new theoretical territory and away from Trotskyism and the preoccupations of its militants. The indices of the growing distance that separated Socialisme ou Barbarie from Trotskyism included: the group's position on the USSR; its insistence on a close analysis of contemporary capitalism without regard for the past; its insistence on theoretical innovation to accommodate the emergence of new types of political action; its attitude toward the major figures in the history of Marxism; and the increasingly philosophical character of its main texts. These same developments prompted several militants to leave the group, many of whom had followed the group out of the PCI. A particularly difficult loss was that of psychoanalyst Jean Laplanche, who had been important for political and financial reasons during this period.

Raoul was a PCI militant sympathetic with the positions of the Chaulieu-Tendency, but who remained in the Party. He wrote the following letter to Castoriadis in 1954. In it, he complains about the consequences of these shifts and tries to inform Socialisme ou Barbarie of its consequences for what Raoul took to be the journal's core audience:

> I have no intention, for the moment, of talking about the Socialisme ou Barbarie group as it is currently. But simply, and in a few words, I want to talk again about the past. Things happened as they happened. You left when you left and as you left. Is it not useless to go through it again? It probably could not have been otherwise. I want to say two things. 1. When you left surrounded by Laplanche, Lefort, Bailhache, and then, a little later, came back for Bourt, it was impossible to follow you. All the more so because – not all the more so, it is the main reason – when Trotskyism was wrapped up, labelled 'mystifying' and rejected as a movement as pathetic, your journal did not even bother, even for four pages each issue, to follow the uneasiness of those who stayed [in the PCI], and to respond to it at their level and in their way. 2. Knowing a little about your activity, when one reads the journal one gets the impression [that Socialisme ou Barbarie is] a group of Marxist philo-econo-sociologists who leave to history (indeed without asking themselves whether

---
113   Lefort 1974, p. 2.
114   Ibid.

this is a good idea) the task of introducing (by osmosis undoubtedly?) to the class those fundamental discoveries of which the aforementioned journal deems them worthy.[115]

Raoul's basic complaint was that he felt abandoned by Socialisme ou Barbarie because it no longer linked itself directly or indirectly to Trotskyism. He implies that the journal's initial audience was mostly Trotskyist militants like himself who found *Socialisme ou Barbarie* useful ammunition in factional activity. Socialisme ou Barbarie was initially understood as an ultra-left group of Trotskyist heretics. Raoul, for one, would have preferred them to remain that. By becoming something else, something less recognisable, the group had alienated its audience. For Raoul, the group and its journal had abandoned the working class and politics in favor of 'philosophico-economico-sociological' problems, couched in a difficult language used without regard for its reception. Regardless of what one makes of his pronouncements about the working class, Raoul's letter does point to the problem of the language that members of the group used in their writing, the difficulty of which increased as the group's process turned inward. This placed Socialisme ou Barbarie's theoretical project at cross-purposes with its political goals. The next chapters find the group wrestling with this problem.

The polarisation of politics and the shutting down of the discursive space from which Socialisme ou Barbarie might have spoken, the collapse of the delimited field of ideological production from which the group had come and the loss of its initial audience all combined to isolate the group. This isolation and sense of powerlessness was written into the group's analysis of the international scene. As indicated earlier, Socialisme ou Barbarie saw the Korean conflict as the opening round of World War III. This war was the culmination of the logic of imperialism, driven by the abstract tendency of capital concentration. Political polarisation precluded any possible revolutionary intervention by the working class. The onset of World War III confronted each member with the choice: wait around Paris for the inevitable Soviet occupation of France and work to construct clandestine resistance organisations; or leave France for Canada.[116] Two Socialisme ou Barbarie militants left soon thereafter: their departures combined with that of Laplanche and others to reduce Socialisme ou Barbarie to less than a dozen members.

---

115   Castoriadis papers, file SB– 3:6, 'Letter to Castoriadis, 9 February 1954'.
116   Camille and Neron soon found themselves in Canada. This account of their departure comes from a number of interviews, particular with Véga in April, 1992.

One index of the straits into which this plunged the group was the journal. *Socialisme ou Barbarie* had appeared five times during 1948–9. Only three slight issues came out between 1950 and 1952. To make matters worse, as the danger began to pass of the Korean War turning into World War III, Castoriadis and Lefort split over the question of Socialisme ou Barbarie's status as a political organisation.[117] The group ceased to exist for several months.[118]

This bleak period was also one of transition. A gradual influx of new members began when Socialisme ou Barbarie assimilated the '*Internationaliste*' tendency of the Bordigist *Union de Gauches Communistes* (UGC) in 1950. This brought into the group Raymond Hirzel (Bourt, Gaspard), Alberto Maso (Véga), Jacques Signorelli (Garros) and Martine Gautrat. In 1952, Martine's ex-husband Jacques (Daniel Mothé) also joined.[119] Georges Petit, who had attended every meeting since he first heard about the Chaulieu-Montal Tendency during 1947 without joining the group, and who would later manage the journal's circulation, finally became a member in 1951. By the end of 1952, Henri Simon had arrived. Jean-François and Andrée Lyotard, along with Pierre and Mireille Souyri, began their involvement with the group during 1952 as well. Souyri introduced Lyotard to Socialisme ou Barbarie while they were teaching together in Constantine, Algeria.[120] They joined once they returned to Paris and remained active from the places to which their teaching assignments took them.[121] The group was changing at the level of personnel and political background. These new members soon began to shape the new directions taken by Socialisme ou Barbarie's revolutionary project.

---

117   The texts generated during this dispute were published in *Socialisme ou Barbarie* no. 10 (July–August 1952) under the heading '*Discussion sur le parti revolutionnaire*' and included an Introduction (p. 10); '*La direction proletarienne*' (pp. 10–18), signed by Chaulieu; '*Le proletariat et le probleme de la direction revolutionnaire*' (pp. 18–27) signed by Montal.
118   Chebel d'Appollonia 1991, vol. 2, p. 165 n. 172.
119   On Mothé, see Chapter 6.
120   See Lyotard's tribute to Constantine and to Souyri in Lyotard 1988, and in Lyotard 1989.
121   Lefort 1974 p. 4 cites every one of these changes as beginning his disaffection with the group.

CHAPTER 2

Rethinking Revolutionary Theory

Introduction

When a blood vessel burst in the brain of Joseph Stalin, the Conqueror of Happiness and Friend of All Children, on March 5, 1953, late Stalinism's shapelessness and stagnation were transformed into a multivariate crisis. The death of Stalin, the figure around whom Soviet Marxism had been constructed since the 1930s, rendered chaotic the symbolic order. Chaos in the significations that ordered the dominant imaginary interacted with the political fragmentation of Soviet leadership to intensify the fractionalisation of the Party bureaucracy and complicate relations between Moscow and Eastern Europe. This chaos was mirrored institutionally in the collective 'Malenkov interregnum'.

The opening move in Socialisme ou Barbarie's initial reading of the situation in the USSR was not unlike what one could have found in much of the Western press:

> The changes that have emerged in the USSR and its satellites since Stalin's death are important both in themselves and for the comprehension of the bureaucratic regime. The death of the personage who had been for over twenty-five years, for the bureaucracy, the uncontested incarnation of its power and the feared and hated despot over his own class, in posing a formidable problem of succession, would necessarily provoke upheaval amongst the bureaucracy's personnel and threaten to explode the struggles between clans that had previously been repressed by the absolute power of one person. Meanwhile, it is not enough to determine in themselves the changes in internal and external politics. If such changes take place, it is because the objective situation in Russia and its satellites increasingly impose them. Stalin's death undoubtedly facilitated them, by the disappearance of the person who had incarnated the previous leadership, by the rupture of the petrification of teams and politics that characterised the last years of his reign. It [Stalin's death] must have also, once again, accentuated and condensed it [the objective situation] in time to the extent that the new ruling team wants to derive from them all the advantages that may favour its consolidation of power.[1]

---

1 Socialisme ou Barbarie 1953, p. 48.

The conflict between bureaucratic factions over Stalin's successor was an internal struggle for power conditioned by the socioeconomic consequences of late Stalinist 'shapelessness'.[2] The ravages of World War II had been followed by a long autumn of the patriarch which appeared to be replicated in widespread shortages, poverty and the systematic suppression of information necessary to make the economy function rationally. Stalin had represented, in his person, the unity of the system: now that unity was gone. The Party was improvising in an explosive situation, one that could be at any moment exacerbated by the re-emergence of class conflict ('properly social contradictions', in Trotskyist terminology) in the context of weakened bureaucratic control. But the meaning of this could not be understood by simply aligning each bureaucratic clique with a particular social interest or sector, as if now the problems of uneven development were coming home to roost. Rather, understanding it presupposed an account of the nature of Soviet bureaucratic capitalism:

> The '*étatisation*' of the economy, and the concentration of political power that accompanies, are of a piece with a tendency to control all sectors of social life. And the bureaucratic mentality favours the institution of a rigorous discipline on individuals' conduct and thought. The extent to which state control requires violence does not depend in a mechanical fashion upon the structure of the economy, but also on historical factors (the origin of the bureaucracy, the international situation, etc). The Russian bureaucracy came into existence while fabricating its own economic base: terror was a means of imposing class unity, the hostility of all against all, for the profit of the functioning of the whole.[3]

The unity of the Soviet system was directly linked to that of the bureaucracy which had forcibly held it together. The 'Malenkov interregnum'[4] was prompted by the recognition that a rapid compromise between bureaucratic factions was necessary to stabilise the Party apparatus. At stake was the stabilisation of Soviet society itself.[5] From this perspective, the most interesting dimensions of the struggle over succession were its inconsistencies and hesitations. Each revealed or expressed fissures or contradictions that ran through all levels of Soviet society. In domestic affairs, they included: the amnesty of political

---

2 The expression comes from Nove 1992, p. 294.
3 Nove 1992, p. 52.
4 Nove 1992, p. 331.
5 See the excerpt from L. Slepov, 'Collectivity is the Highest Principle of Party Leadership', an editorial in *Pravda*, April 16, 1953. Quoted in Daniels 1993, pp. 246–7.

prisoners; the ending of the anti-Semitic 'doctors' plot' hysteria;[6] the lowering of prices and the purge of the Ukrainian CP.[7] Socialisme ou Barbarie noted the increased complexity of relations between Moscow and Eastern Europe.[8] The same logic explained Soviet foreign policy, particularly its pursuit of *détente* and a face-saving way out of Korea.

But for Socialisme ou Barbarie, the most salient outcomes of the death of Stalin emerged during the summer of 1953 in the form of autonomous worker actions, the East Berlin 'June Days' in particular. The group's initial interpretation situated the Berlin uprising in the context of responses to Stalin's death and, by way of these, to less explosive actions in Czechoslovakia and Hungary. The group's second interpretation aligned it with the August 1953 general strike that shut down France by paralysing communications. This chapter is a critical reconstruction of the second interpretation. By situating these actions with reference to each other, Socialisme ou Barbarie was able to see the emergence of a new form of working-class politics with significant revolutionary potential. The group began to elaborate a revolutionary programme on this basis, a vision or a schema quite innovative and very different from what the group had carried with it beyond the confines of Trotskyism. Because the rest of this book operates within this new schema, and because it informed the writing at each point, we present the whole of it now. But, as you will see, neither of these actions presented this schema, nor does it show up all at once in the pages of *Socialisme ou Barbarie*. East Berlin in particular presented the group with a 'germ' – the basis for a subsequent elaboration that enacts, implies or creates space for it. The programme itself was elaborated through the group's dialogue with the worker avant garde, tracking and extrapolating from its actions. So the following is an extended riff, a variation, a creation of the group.

A defining characteristic of this new form of political action was the reappropriation of direct-democratic worker councils. Worker councils formed within a sequence that moved from wildcat to an unlimited general strike. For Socialisme ou Barbarie, this sequence was a plausible trajectory for moving from worker control over production to that of society as a whole. The demands formulated by the councils linked the actions back to conflicts that unfolded in everyday life at the point of production. Demonstrating these linkages

---

6 This was connected to the deposing of Beria from the head of the GPU. The text of the Central Committee's indictment and the Supreme Court verdict against Beria are reprinted in Daniels 1993, pp. 247–50.
7 See Nove 1992, pp. 331–41.
8 For a recent general account, see Swain and Swain 1993, pp. 77ff.

shifted examples of 'proletarian documentary literature' in the manner of Paul Romano's 'The American Worker' to a central concern. The rest of this book explores the implications of this shift and what it entailed for the group's revolutionary project. Positioning autonomous worker actions with respect to each other opened space for a transformation of 'the content of socialism', a teleological device that could both provide the worker avant garde with a sense of direction and function as the basis for a critical assessment of worker actions both as they had happened and in their revolutionary potential. Symmetrical with this, there was a rethinking of the idea of revolution itself. As Castoriadis put it in 1955:

> Thus, beginning with a critique of the bureaucracy, we have succeeded in formulating a positive conception of the content of socialism; briefly speaking, 'socialism in all its aspects does not signify anything other than worker's management of society', and 'the working class can free itself only by achieving power for itself'. The proletariat can carry out the socialist revolution only if it acts autonomously, i.e., if it finds in itself both the will and the consciousness for the necessary transformation of society. Socialism can be neither the fated result of historical development, a violation of history by a party of supermen, nor still the application of a programme derived from a theory that is true in itself. Rather, it is the unleashing of the free creative activity of the oppressed masses. Such an unleashing of free creative activity is made possible by historical development, and the action of a party based on this theory can facilitate it to a tremendous degree.[9]

The previous chapter traced Socialisme ou Barbarie's trajectory beyond Trotskyism along several lines. The development of the group's particular usage of bureaucracy to characterise the relations of production in contemporary industrial contexts resulted in the basis for a politically-oriented form of sociology in the reading of worker experience. The emergence of these new autonomous actions gave that sociological project a political space. The group fashioned historicising relations to Lenin, Marx and the broader Marxian tradition. From Lenin they abstracted something of a schema or template that could orient a new revolutionary practice. By working through Marx, the group undercut the primacy of economic analysis in a way that opened space for more differentiated combinations of sociological, historical, political and

---

9   Castoriadis 1988, pp. 1–25, originally published in *Socialisme ou Barbarie*, 17 (July–September 1955).

economic interpretations of phenomena in the social world. The links between the various steps in this process of working through relations to tradition and particular outcomes in terms of writing published in the journal were not direct. Yet with the thaw occasioned by Stalin's death and assessments of these new worker actions, the consequences of the earlier movements become evident.

In the readings of Lenin, Castoriadis placed the development of a new revolutionary programme at the centre of their concerns. The critique of the Vanguard Party militated for some kind of interaction between the revolutionary organisation and a worker avant garde, even as the location of it was not obvious at this point. The autonomous actions of the summer of 1953 provided Socialisme ou Barbarie with a plausible worker avant-garde. The sequence of actions that moved from wildcat strikes to a general strike also enabled a conceptualisation of revolution as a process that broke with the militarised understanding that had been central to the Marxian tradition since the Paris Commune.

But more important for the group were what these actions enabled them to move to the centre of their revolutionary project. The central element was direct-democratic worker councils, which were the type of self-organisation undertaken by the workers involved with both actions. In the group's earlier writings, Castoriadis's in particular, a socialist economy was predicated upon control by workers over the outputs of production in addition to its organisation, modes of compensation and so forth. These were presented as general defining conditions of socialism. Councils enabled these to be tied to a specific organisational modality. They arose out of conflicts specific to contemporary industrial organisation that could not be addressed by the managerial and political/trade-union *status quo*. Socialisme ou Barbarie saw them as rejecting trade-union domination of working-class politics in both its command-control form and its fragmenting effects on the working-class rejection of bourgeois forms of hierarchy in general.

The calls for class unity also enabled Socialisme ou Barbarie to read off from them the effects of a kind of practical movement along a range of political options framed by the Marxian tradition. This reading-off made of the worker avant garde a mirror image of revolutionary militants. The Marxist Imaginary was a shared natural horizon: movement with respect to it was the condition of the possibility of any revolutionary action. The dialogue the group saw itself as undertaking presupposed this shared horizon. This explains why the group saw the Berlin 'June Days' as exemplary, as would be the Hungarian Revolution in 1956.

The 'June Days': East Berlin, 16–17 June, 1953

Socialisme ou Barbarie's analyses of the East Berlin uprising of June and the French general strike of August 1953 were spread over *Socialisme ou Barbarie* nos. 12, 13 and 14. The central analyses published in no. 13 under the rubric 'Worker Struggles in 1953' interpret the two strikes together as signalling the emergence of new revolutionary initiatives from the working class that presented new possibilities and problems for revolutionary theory.

Socialisme ou Barbarie's view of the East Berlin uprising was based on the work of Benno Sternberg[10] that was eventually published in 1958 as *La classe ouvrière en Allemagne orientale*. Pierre Naville's introduction to the published version never mentions the author's links to Socialisme ou Barbarie.[11] The manuscript circulated widely in anti-Stalinist left circles for several years prior to its publication, and in these circles, Sternberg's affiliations were well known.[12] *Socialisme ou Barbarie* published two early fragments of his work as one of several case studies on Eastern Europe.[13] Sternberg's account of the uprising, 'Combats ouvriers sur l'avenue Staline', was published in *Les Temps Modernes*.[14] There seems little doubt that Socialisme ou Barbarie comrade Claude Lefort had something to do with its publication. The article constitutes the only analysis of East Berlin to appear in *Les Temps Modernes*, and its analytical framework reflects the views of a minority position relative to the journal's main editorial collective.[15] 'Combats' is divided into two parts, with the revolt

---

10   Sternberg was a Romanian Jew, a sociologist by training, who spent some time in Germany immediately after the war. Sternberg made his way to France by early 1948. He was a member of the Trotskyist PCI for a while and, I believe, left the Party along with Socialisme ou Barbarie. Sternberg published articles in *Socialisme ou Barbarie* under the names Hugo Bell and Benno Sarel; his internal name was Barrois. For an interesting portrait of Sternberg, see Pierre Vidal-Naquet's account of his interactions with *Socialisme ou Barbarie*, 'Souvenirs à bâtons rompus sur Cornelius Castoriadis et "Socialisme ou Barbarie"', *Revue Europèenne des Sciences Sociales; Cahiers Wilfredo Pareto*, no. 86 (December, 1989), pp. 17–26, reprinted as Busino 1989, same pagination.

11   Sarel 1958.

12   See Merleau-Ponty 1964 [1955] which is based almost entirely on Sternberg's manuscript.

13   Bell 1950 and 1951. The other countries extensively analysed in the early numbers of *SB* were Yugoslavia and, to a lesser extent, Czechoslovakia.

14   Sarel 1953.

15   On Lefort's relationship to the TM collective, see Boschetti 1988, especially pp. 231–2. Sternberg's political position was not assimilable by the dominant tendency in the TM collective, gathered around Sartre and de Beauvoir. Boschetti points out that Lefort was only tolerated because of his close relation with his teacher, Merleau-Ponty. The grounds for the clash between Sartre in his 'ultrabolshevik' phase, as Merleau-Ponty called it, and

itself forming a sort of *caesura* between them.[16] A slightly longer, and earlier, account of the aftermath of the 'June days' appeared in *Socialisme ou Barbarie* no. 13, along with an article written by Véga that recapitulated the substance of the 'Combats' and added to it a brief analysis of the strike demands and a critique of Trotskyist press reports.[17]

Sternberg's work on East Germany concentrated primarily on the relationship between the German working class and Stalinism. In particular, he focused on worker resistance to the imposition of Soviet-style social and economic organisation played out in shop-floor-level conflicts. During 1947–8, conflict in the sectors of heavy industry most closely linked to military production involved the Communist Party (SED), trade-unions and factory committees [*comités d'enterprises*] in a struggle for control over production. Later, conflict centred on opposition to the 'Anti-cosmopolitan Campaign' that used insistence on the superiority of Soviet technical literature and Stakhanovite production techniques and the organisation of production as wedges in a broader effort to impose Party control.[18] These conflicts between the Stalinist Party faithful and local workers for political and organisational power in industry did not affect all sectors simultaneously: different industrial sectors were integrated into the plan at different times. However, once a given sector was integrated, the pattern of conflict repeated.

Lefort were clear for some time: see the polemical exchange between Lefort and Sartre around the latter's 'The Communists and Peace'.

16   The dynamics of the revolt proper get a much fuller treatment in Sarel 1958, based in large part on the participant accounts and documents published as Ministère fédéral pour l'unité de l'Allemagne 1954.

17   Véga 1954 and Bell 1954.

18   Stakhanovism refers to the Soviet version of Taylorist 'scientific management' outlined by Frederick Winslow Taylor in his 1911 book *Principles of Scientific Management*. It emphasised that tasks in production needed to be reduced to optimal movements in order to maximise efficiency. Optimisation was determined with the assistance of a science of fatigue in which workers were subjected to the measurements of the time-motion men ('*les chronos*' in French slang). Taylor's work, and the broader current of views on the efficiency and organisation of production of which it is a condensed expression, were fundamental to the development of the whole of assembly-line based production from management to the use of science and measurements as an approach to work in the organisation of the line itself, the centre of industrial Fordism. Taylorist principles were adopted wholesale in Soviet industry. The assumption was that, in a workers' state, the results could not possibly be a rationalised exploitation of the workers. Stakhanov was the Soviet 'hero of production', someone who drove production norms ever higher and, as such, embodied the convergence of Taylorist principles and working people. There are extensive citations on this in subsequent chapters.

Sternberg's articles traced these conflicts in the industrial sectors most directly involved in war production (1949–51) and later, as they affected the construction and building trades (1952–3). *Neues Deutschland*, the Party's official newspaper, was an important source of information. Articles usually argued that the successful implementation of Stakhanovism would speed up socialist construction. The paper published stories of the struggle between Stakhanovite progress and 'backward' local workers and detailed their 'retrograde' patterns of resistance. These conflicts were central because the paper was edited and written by Leninists who saw factories as both theatres of social progress and centres of Party power ('every factory shall be our fortress').[19] This did not, however, mean that their sympathies necessarily lay with the Party. Tensions became explicit in the period leading up to the 'June Days'. It is likely that these same divisions predated them, which simplified the procedure of reading this official source 'against the grain', using techniques familiar to oppositional movements that confront a hegemonic media.

The two long fragments of Sternberg's book manuscript published in *Socialisme ou Barbarie* framed the group's subsequent interpretation of East Berlin. The first reviewed changes in East Germany's relationship to the USSR. Between 1945 and 1947, the Soviets considered East Germany a source of reparations. The earliest Soviet position was that, since socialism was possible in one country, and given the catastrophic damage inflicted by World War II, Germany had a particular obligation to assist in its (re)construction.[20] The integration of East Germany into the Soviet social and economic system began in 1948. In the context of these more general changes, Sternberg tracked the shifting relations between the East German working class and the Communist Party.[21] The outline of how they would play out was established in 1945. Before the Red Army was turned loose on the population, workers hung red flags with hammers and sickles alongside the white flags in front of buildings to welcome it. They set up factory committees that were conceived of as embryonic trade unions,

---

19   On Soviet Stakhanovism and its East German variant, see Siegelbaum 1988. Thanks to Joshua Feinstein for the point on Ulbrecht and Stakhanovism.

20   Bell 1950, p. 2.

21   A very different interpretation of the Berlin uprising follows from this focus, emphasising Soviet ambivalence about retaining Germany: 'In the wake of Stalin's death, dissolution of the DDR was seriously considered. During the spring of 1953, the Soviet Union's collective leadership was keen to reduce international tension in all spheres, and in this context the future viability of the DDR as a socialist state was discussed. Indeed, if the East German workers had not gone on strike in June 1953, forcing the Soviet Union to intervene or face international humiliation, Soviet support for the DDR, already restricted in April, may have continued to decline' (Swain and Swain 1993, pp. 96–7 and 235 n. 46).

and restarted production in some areas under the control of these committees, mistakenly assuming that this was what was meant by Stalinist notions of worker control. Conflicts within the Party were soon set off: the expectations of German KPD members who returned from exile in Moscow were very different from those of the initial 'core of orthodox Stalinists' that formed 'outside and against the spontaneous initiative of the worker avant-garde'.[22] For Sternberg, this was the earliest of a long list of conflicts that revealed the nature of Soviet occupation.[23] The Communist Party was not the type of party imagined by the returning exiles. The type of 'worker control' understood by the Party had nothing in common with the types of political organisation anticipated by those who set up factory committees in 1945.

The second article developed the last point through a series of emblematic conflicts in heavy industry. Between 1946 and 1948, each conflict brought into opposition Stalinist Party cells, trade unions and factory committees. These conflicts unfolded during the early Cold War period, which was also that of the integration of East German heavy industry into the system of Soviet military production. Sternberg's article provided a number of specific examples of conflict and derived a pattern from them. Once a Party cell was established in a factory, it immediately began working to subordinate the trade union to its political direction by co-opting or replacing union functionaries. Sternberg argued that this pattern mirrored the wider experience of the German intelligentsia and its relationship to the Party.[24] Once in control of the union local, the Party and union began to coordinate efforts to circumvent, render ineffective, and finally eliminate the factory committees that had been established during 1946 to signal German commitment to industrial democracy. The pattern was repeated at each organisational level. At each level, mechanisms established by the workers to manage production were transformed into arenas of contestation within which Party activists and workers struggled for control of the

---

22   '[Le premier] nouyau de staliniens "dans la ligne" [s'est donc formé en 1945], en dehors et contre l'initiative spontanée des ouvriers d'avant-garde"' (Bell 1950, p. 4).

23   The article provides several such indicators of Soviet occupation from 1945–6: poverty and material shortages, decreasing birth rates, increasing mortality-rates. Sternberg argues that the situation began to change after 1946 only because the continued extraction of reparations was no longer profitable.

24   The only review I have been able to locate of *La classe ouvrière en Allemagne orientale* criticises Sarel for overemphasising the centrality of conflicts within the factory when discussing the various alliances between the 'old intelligentsia' and the state after 1951, arguing that this confrontation with the regime largely occurred outside the factory and was not of working-class origin. See Duhnke 1959.

enterprise. These conflicts would continue until the Party co-opted, contained or eliminated the forum.

The Party thought that the introduction of Stakhanovite activists and work-brigades, accompanied by substantial organisational and technical modifications, and the methods for calculating production norms linked to output quotas set by the Plan, would initiate the same pattern at another level: a period of conflict; a period of co-optation; a period of consolidation; the elimination of local resistance.[25] However, the close relationship between the brigades and ongoing production processes, and the basic ambiguity of their composition and direction, meant that informal worker resistance could not be entirely eliminated. Outlining a view that fits awkwardly with Sternberg's interpretation in his book on the Soviet Stakhanovite movement of the 1930s, Lawrence Siegelbaum argues that the limited accommodation of contestation was integral to brigade operations.[26] Seigelbaum's view, which owes much to Michael Burawoy, assumes that contestation is a permanent feature of industrial organisation. Contestation functions as a feedback system that links management and production, and as an important mechanism in the continual negotiation of political relations that enables industrial production to function. This view of Stakhanovism integrates it into a more general notion of industrial organisation as a continual, productive conflict/debate. In contrast, Sternberg's position recapitulates that of other *Socialisme ou Barbarie* texts in positing a dichotomy between routinisation and creativity and mapping it onto shop-floor-level conflicts. For Sternberg, on the other hand, the brigades were forms of organisational colonialism continually resisted by workers. Given the framework that he develops, Sternberg's argument would seem sufficiently compelling that, even if one were to concede that the separation is simplistic in other industrial contexts, it would be operative in this situation. We will return to this general question in subsequent chapters in the context of more granular information.[27]

The fragments of Sternberg's longer work published in *Socialisme ou Barbarie* do not address developments after mid-1948. I cannot tell if draft

---

25 Space does not permit an extensive analysis of the creation of a specifically East German Stakhanovite movement, complete with a local Stakhanov via the 1948 Hennecke movement, which was the most extensive effort to carry out such an export in Eastern Europe. See Siegelbaum 1988, p. 306 and more extensively Sarel 1958, pp. 61–84.
26 Seigelbaum 1988.
27 This line, consistent from the original *Socialisme ou Barbarie* editorial, is stated with most analytical clarity (and not without some problems) in Castoriadis 1988a [1949a], pp. 81–125.

versions of *La classe ouvrière* covering the period between 1948 and 1953 were circulated in the group.[28] The 1958 book continues the examination of the confrontations between the Soviet-dominated Stalinist apparatus and local attempts at self-organisation. In general, the Russians saw the factory as a single organic community within the workers' state, which by definition had no need of oppositional organisations like trade unions. Following the same logic, there was no official recognition of discrete working-class interests that were not synonymous with those of the 'workers' state'.[29] Sternberg pursued his investigation of the conflicts between the Party and the workers by looking at the first Five Year Plan, and its reorganisation of production through the use of production quotas and cadences that were set at the state level without regard for the particularities of individual enterprises.[30] Conflicts triggered by new state demands were played out as struggles between the Party and the trade unions and as intensified worker resistance to Stakhanovism.[31] The resistance to Stakhanovism took the form of sabotage, slowdowns, and local work stoppages. By demonstrating the persistence and intensity of this resistance, Sternberg set up his reading of East Berlin as an expression not simply of local tensions, but of much more pervasive problems that centred on the imposition of Stalinism in its concrete, material forms.

For Sternberg, the Berlin uprising could only be understood against this background. The revolt was rooted in the same pattern of conflict. It emerged in a particularly politicised form in Berlin for a number of reasons. After 1952, relations were tense between the highly skilled and autonomous German building trades and Soviet-style production and planning. This longer-term tension was intensified by larger, structural problems like the German eco-

---

28   In the meeting transcripts that I have from the various archive sources, Sternberg's book is not mentioned as having been read by everyone as a group project in the way other texts occasionally were. But its contents were well-known.

29   Bell 1953.

30   See, on this point, 'Vers de nouveaux rapports de production' in Sarel 1958. Siegelbaum 1988 provides a long, detailed account of local norm committees engaged in complex and interactive process of give and take with the production particularities in 1930s USSR. See also Swain and Swain 1993, especially chapters 2 and 5.

31   On the development of the Hennecke movement, which Siegelbaum 1988 cites as 'probably the most developed of such post-war phenomena' (p. 306) and an East German analogue to Stakhanov, see Sarel 1958, pp. 61–84. See also Sarel's 'Classe ouvrière et gestion des usines' in Sarel 1958 on the types of worker resistance to the brigades which turned them into sites of political contestation between them and the Stalinist bureaucracy and the workers. On worker resistance to the integration of the older intelligentsia into the Stalinist apparatus, see pp. 122–4; on the conflict over the first Five-Year Plan, pp. 124–8.

nomic crisis as well as by accidental factors, such as the bungled introduction of the 'New Course' by the SED, the effects of Stalin's death, and international detente.[32] Sternberg's analysis argues that the patterns of worker resistance in the context of the specific situation of the building workers were the most important of these factors in explaining the 'June Days'.[33]

The *Stalinallee* was the East German regime's monument to itself, an enormous, highly visible construction project that gathered together thousands of workers from all parts of the country.[34] That these workers, devoted to constructing a huge monument to Stalin and politicised through endless meetings organised by Party activists and brigades, were at the forefront of the June uprising is an irony worthy of Ambrose Bierce. Sternberg's *Les Temps Modernes* article exploits this irony, treating the building workers and their wildcat strike as both a metaphor for the whole East German situation and an outline of the shape of revolutionary politics to come:

> 1952 was the year of Stalin Avenue – *Stalinallee* – formerly Frankfurterallee. Before the war, it was an opulent avenue of which nothing remains in 1945. Reconstruction began in 1949. But the real *Stalinallee* was born at the beginning of 1952: worksites end-to-end along four kilometers; in all the adjacent streets, teams of factory-workers, in principle voluntary, cleared the ruins; in winter, one worked by electric torchlight. The *Stalinallee* was the pride of the regime, which had made it the centre of East Berlin life and, in a sense, of East German life; press and radio, writers and composers adopted it as a favorite theme. Teams of Party agitators formed discussion groups there that swelled with passers-by, construction site workers, those who cleared sites; tens of thousands of building workers flowed into it. They were needed: they were the centre of interest. Meanwhile, the construction industry ran at a loss and the administration again posed the question of production norms.[35]

---

32 A concise overview of these conjunctural factors can be found in Wolfgang H. Kraus, 'Crisis and Revolt in a Satellite: The East German Case in Retrospect', in London, 1966, pp. 41–66. Other materials consulted on the uprising include, in addition to Swain, Brandt 1955, which uses the same basic set of sources as Sarel 1958 (a heavily edited version of the article) but which suffers from a particularly noxious rightist 'adaptation' by one Charles Wheeler; and Hildebrandt 1983.

33 See also Kraus 1966, pp. 52ff.

34 On the *Stalinallee* and Soviet urbanism, see Castillo 2001, pp. 181–206. On 'socialist realist' architecture in East Germany more broadly, see Castillo 2005.

35 Sarel 1958, pp. 139–40.

The integration of the construction trades into the planned economy began in early 1952, roughly coinciding with the change in scale of the *Stalinallee*. It set off intense conflict. Once again, integration into the planned economy began with the setting of production quotas that could not be met. These quotas created deficits that could only be made up through the introduction of 'superior' Soviet techniques. 'Shock brigades' introduced these new techniques that included the reorganisation of tasks and production speed-ups. Wages were redefined to tie in more directly to production levels. Building workers collectively refused to accept the changes and soon found themselves in conflict with the state. The workers used a variety of grounds to justify their refusal to comply. These ranged from protests over what amounted to wage reductions to public statements that equated rationalisation and deskilling.

For Sternberg, this widespread, informal resistance to the Stalinist reorganisation of work was best expressed in the transformation of brigade meetings into theatres of conflict. Workers often emerged from these meetings with more clearly articulated arguments for resisting reorganisation. Brigade meetings were frequently covered by correspondents from *Neues Deutschland*. Their articles, designed to show the retrograde character of local workers, paradoxically made public and circulated workers' arguments. In the weeks immediately prior to 16–17 June, articles in *Neues Deutschland* on these meetings outlined workers' criticisms of the state's effort to tie wages directly to the new, and largely unreachable, norms in a context of rising prices and material scarcity. These accounts highlighted the awkward position in which brigade leaders were placed by such objections. Brigade leaders were workers themselves, and were also affected by the problems of tools and materials. They might be personally or politically inclined to sympathise with the workers. At the same time, their positions as activists gave them significant material privileges.[36] There were, therefore, limits to how far the brigade leaders' sympathies with the workers opposed to integration could go. For Sternberg's purposes, the accounts of these brigade meetings provided in the Party press were a staging of the larger conflicts he wanted to trace.

The official response to this resistance was usually to publicly condemn it and then convene a meeting. One such meeting, a joint productivity conference gathering together administration workers, union officials and 'activist' workers, convened on 22 February 1953, during which it was decided to cut wages, materials and tools and at the same time to raise production levels. A second conference was held in April to determine how to implement

---

36   A situation exactly parallel to that outlined in Siegelbaum 1988, pp. 77–98.

the decisions of the first. Yet another was held in June.[37] At the same time, a complicated dance involving the apparatus and workers was occurring on the construction sites, closely monitored by the official press. Production levels were raised, temporarily lowered, then 'voluntarily' raised again. The editorial chorus in *Neues Deutschland* glossed this stop-and-start as revealing the machinations of 'backward elements' bent on hindering socialist progress, retrograde carry-overs from the bad old days of class struggle.[38]

Because of its timing, this conflict over the integration of construction into the planned economy was explosive. The political fallout of Stalin's death, internal conflicts in the SED, the easing of war tensions and open ambivalence in Moscow as to East Germany's status all exacerbated tensions created by persistent material and food shortages, rising prices and falling wages. On 9 June, the Politburo issued its 'New Course', an official self-criticism in which the Party acknowledged errors and offered some concessions as recompense. However, these concessions were directed primarily at the middle class and the church.[39] Construction workers had just been hit with what amounted to a salary cut: the 'New Course' did not address this or any other worker grievance. This 'oversight' was a trigger for the action.

This unrest surfaced at the *Stalinallee* for several reasons, having to do with its particular status and the conditions that prevailed there. The project's size made it exceptionally visible, and its political significance made it a particular focus of the Party press and political education/agitation. *Neues Deutschland* devoted extensive coverage to the project and its problems. Because it was a memorial to Stalin, the Party orchestrated an intensive campaign of political education. Marxist discussion circles convened regularly at various locations around the site. This agitation had two key unintended consequences. First, workers were forced to attend the political classes, which provided them with an opportunity to actually read Marx and Lenin, undiluted by the official Party catechism. This was a crucial dimension for Sternberg's reading of the actions he argued that this direct exposure to Marx and Lenin gave the construction-workers access to Marxist categories and a history of class struggle that they would later appropriate to express themselves and to articulate their demands. These same meetings also enabled workers to establish contacts and create

---

37 'Depuis février, semble-t-il, on n'avait pas realisé de grands progres' (Sarel 1958, p. 142).
38 Sarel 1953 p. 676.
39 These concessions included an end to state persecution of the church and the restoration of property confiscated by the state from *emigrés* to West Germany, should they return. They also announced the suspension of food rationing and promised, but did not set, lower food prices.

networks that extended beyond the normal boundaries of production – particular construction sites, work brigades and shifts. Both were necessary preconditions for the 'June action'.

The power of these normal boundaries, and an indication of how unusual was the case of the *Stalinallee*, can be seen by comparing it to Daniel Mothé's 'La grève chez Renault',[40] which appeared in *Socialisme ou Barbarie* no. 13. In this article, Mothé describes a small group of machinists who tried to organise some kind of action in support of the August 1953 *Postes, Téléphone* and *Télégraphe* strike (PTT strike). As the strike was violently opposed by the entire range of trade unions, this mobilisation would have had to happen outside their control. Mothé and his comrades quickly run into the fragmented communicative conditions of modern industrial organisation. This fragmentation was on its own too great a barrier to overcome, and the mobilisation efforts came to nothing. The ability of workers to communicate across the complex divisions of large-scale production is a special situation. It is an important result of militant activity.

The week of 8–14 June was marked by considerable unrest along the *Stalinallee*. During this same week, political division began to emerge within the *Neues Deutschland* coverage. By the end of the week, the paper was publishing accounts of brigade meetings that explicitly sided with the workers against the Party and official-union leaders. On 14 June, the paper published a collection of worker accounts of conditions. The following, rather lengthy excerpt is revealing:

> On 28 May, when, following the official news that 60 percent of the workers had raised their norms, a meeting of the *Stalinallee* brigade leaders and activists took place. This assembly of men, considered by the regime as its best supporters, rejected the majority of the norms on which the government had just decided. The *Stalinallee* Party-Secretary, Muller, had been against the meeting: it had occurred on the initiative of brigade-leader Rocke. 'He's the one who got us into this', said Muller. Brigade-leader Rocke, it seems, had organised the meeting on his own, without the support of any apparatus. He had, in fact, serious reasons to have something against the Party and management. At the beginning of May, his brigade began working on a new construction site. 'I had only just got there when three men from the Party's central leadership, including the time-motion man, came to discuss production norms. I asked them to wait until I had assembled my entire brigade, because half of them

---

40 Mothé 1954.

worked on another street...But the time-motion man told me that my colleagues had just given their approval to raising production levels, and that the site foreman had their signatures in his pocket. I replied that this was a lie, and I was right. This manoeuvre having failed, the 'chrono' declared to me that, at any rate, he only allowed brigades that had agreed to higher production levels to work on the bigger sites: 'Over there, we raised our levels by 6.5 per cent'.[41]

An immediate result of Brigadier Rocke's story was that the workers discovered that there had been lots of problems with the Norm Department. Some of these had even triggered work stoppages. As word of these stoppages became public, the chief of the Berlin CP argued that discipline needed to be stepped up and an example made. The *Neues Deutschland* editorial that accompanied the 14 June 1953 collection of accounts that detailed conditions along the Stalinallee opposed this, arguing:

> The *'chronos'* have lost all contact with the colleagues in the work-sites. They carry themselves with arrogance...The *'chronos'* tell themselves that, thanks to their dangerous schemes, they will be highly rated by management, but they are wrong because an enterprise will never function without the workers...The *'chronos'* should not imagine that they will succeed for long if they act against the interests of the workers.[42]

This is the kind of moment upon which Sternberg relied. The editorial attacked the Party by attacking the *'chronos'*, who walked point on the question of norms. It also revealed the kinds of coercion that they routinely brought to bear on brigade leaders. For example, only brigades that exceeded production levels could get access to the larger and better-paying sites. Often, this pressure forced brigade leaders to act against the interests and desires of the workers. In this case, the brigade leader sided with the workers against the Party primarily because of the clearly duplicitous way in which the Party, represented by the *'chronos'*, treated the workers. For Socialisme ou Barbarie's reading of the situation, what mattered here for analytical purposes was that the workers recognised that their interests diverged from those of the Party, and the fact that the workers' assembly played a prominent role in this recognition. Only once assembled publicly did information surface about similar problems with the *'chronos'* at other sites, such as about limited work stoppages and the threats

---

41 From 'Il est temps à renoncer la baguette', quoted in Sarel 1953, p. 681.
42 Sarel 1953, p. 682.

issued by the Party. In this context, shaped by Soviet notions about how workers should comport themselves in a workers' state, the act of coming together unofficially to share information was already political.

On the afternoon of 8 June, after eight days of inconclusive negotiations, workers from sector 40 of the *Stalinallee* voted to strike and march on the Ministry Building. They stopped work on 16 June and about one hundred workers began to march. By the time they reached the Ministry Building, the march had grown to almost ten thousand people. During the night of 16–17 June, the strike spread quickly, and changed from a limited protest over the imposition of higher production norms and piece-work rates into a general political strike. For Sternberg, this night was a moment of extreme clarity. Popular action shot the gaps created by the incoherence of East German social relations. Faced with a rapidly developing revolutionary situation, the state teetered. That night, power passed from the state onto the streets:

> On 16 and 17 June, the workers, the popular masses, went out into the street and held the power of decision and execution. The break between officialdom and the population was total. For that day at least, the ambiguity characteristic of relations within East German society was erased. That is why it is not possible to trace the image of the 'June Days' using only official sources. To the extent that the masses, in June 1953, made themselves independent, gave themselves their own organisations, no longer expressing themselves by the means – multiple to be sure, but diversionary – offered by official organisations, to that extent it is only possible to approach the truth by relating directly to the actions of masses: what matters, from then on, is that one attend to the testimonies of those who participated in the revolt.[43]

Understanding the nature of the movement, and explaining the speed with which it evolved, were problematic for *ex post facto* analysts not only because both were impossible to reconstruct from official sources.[44] Such actions, by their nature, exceed representation. They are forms of collective doing. Their

---

43   Sarel 1958, p. 157.
44   This would not have surprised *Socialisme ou Barbarie* militants, who would interpret it as analogous to the inability of bureaucratic management in industrial settings to recognise the informal self-organisation of workers, even though the daily operation of the system as a whole relies upon the continued existence and efficient operation of these very collectives. This translates into what Castoriadis called the 'central contradiction of bureaucratic capitalism'.

representation is like an audio recording of an improvisation which captures everything but the improvised part. The revolt itself was, and remained, a hole in the middle of Sternberg's analysis. One might argue that the essential had already been explicated through his analysis of the long-term resistance to the 'bureaucratic colonialism' practiced by Stalinist organisation. Initially, Stalinism was welcomed by the German workers because they saw it as a different type of communism. But these same workers later resisted Stalinism through continual struggles at the point of production. The *Stalinallee* workers were, therefore, typical East German workers. However, without the benefit of the particular conditions that prevailed in the *Stalinallee*, it is doubtful that these workers could have moved from isolated struggles to collective action. What made this action paradigmatic for Socialisme ou Barbarie was its ideological dimension: the turning of Marx against the dominant Marxism evident in the modes of organisation by strike committee and in the demands for substantive worker control over production. By the morning of 17 June, German police and military forces in Soviet armour began moves to suppress the revolt. It had spread overnight to encompass between four and five hundred locations. The strikes continued for some time after the violent clashes in Berlin on 17 June. But they were largely invisible to those outside.

While Sternberg's work lay at the centre of Socialisme ou Barbarie's collective understanding of the Berlin uprising, the group advanced two other, closely linked, readings. The first was published in *Socialisme ou Barbarie* no. 12. Apparently written sometime in June 1953, this reading positioned the 'June Days' in the context of Stalin's death and the succession crisis that followed. The action demonstrated the group's premise that the problems experienced by the Party were necessarily crises, both for the Party itself and for the social system that it held together. The 'June Days' were a direct expression of a general crisis created by disunity in the Party, which was itself the unity of the social system.[45]

Socialisme ou Barbarie's second interpretation was framed as a critical analysis of the coverage of the uprising in the Trotskyist press. This reading tried to unpack the political implications of the demands promulgated by the workers during the night of 16–17 June. This analysis was written later in the summer, in light of the French PTT strike. It works out of a comparative framework that positions the Berlin action against the PTT strike to argue that they, together, signalled a new type of revolutionary politics.[46] To understand this claim, and

---

45 Socialisme ou Barbarie 1953.
46 Véga 1954.

its implications for Socialisme ou Barbarie's revolutionary theory more generally, we turn to their understanding of the French general strike.

The August 1953 French General Strike

During the evening of 5 August 1953, a committee of *Force Ouvrière* militants at a Bordeaux PTT office launched a strike to protest against the Laniel government's attempt to cut public-sector workers' salaries and retirement benefits. Spreading along the PTT communication and transport networks, within days it had become an unlimited general strike involving more than four million workers. The strike shut down the post, telephones, and nearly all public transport. It paralysed the country and cut it off from the outside world. From the outset, French trade-unions (CGT-FO-CFTC) scrambled to contain the action and reassert themselves as necessary mediators between the working class and the state. Despite intense pressure from the government and unions, and internal problems that will be discussed later, the strike held until 21 August. At that time, with the movement already weakening, the unions and the Laniel government cut a deal that simply accelerated the strike's dissipation.

It is surprising that an action of this magnitude had for a long time vanished from the history of the Fourth Republic. One exception was Georgette Elgey's *La République des contradictions 1951–1954*.[47] Her description of a panicking Laniel government and military is tempered by a certain admiration for the strikers. The strike received a more detailed analysis in Jean-François Noël's 1977 monograph,[48] from which most subsequent accounts draw their information.[49] There are several plausible explanations for its disappearance from histories of the Fourth Republic. The 1953 PTT strike was, for the most part, a peaceful action that generated relatively benign demands. Its character is evident when compared with the near-civil war that accompanied the 1955 shipbuilders' strikes at Nantes and St. Nazaire. The PTT strike occurred in isolation. It took place during the annual summer holiday, and generated much sympathy in that it caused little inconvenience. It was also isolated in the sense that it was neither followed by other actions nor evoked by later actions. Not the finest moment in the history of the French trade unions, the August strike was never incorporated into their institutional memories. It came too soon to be appropriated by the reconfigured anti-Stalinist French 'New Left' that emerged

---

47 Elgey 1968, pp. 150–70.
48 Noël 1977.
49 See for example Rioux 1987, pp. 218–23.

during 1957 as a function of the combined impact of the Algerian war and the crisis of Stalinism. While *Socialisme ou Barbarie*'s theoretical positions would deeply influence this 'New Left', it is a measure both of the group's isolation in 1953, and of the selective power of the contexts within which Socialisme ou Barbarie was later appropriated, that its treatment of this strike was also forgotten.

Most of the group's interpretation of the August 1953 strike was elaborated in a series of articles in *Socialisme ou Barbarie* no. 13. A short introduction and chronology was followed by Daniel Faber's article on the PTT strike.[50] Georges Petro detailed how the strike spread along the French railway system.[51] Daniel Mothé, about whom I will have more to say in subsequent chapters, described the response of the Renault workers to the strike in the days after the end of the summer holidays. A short account of strikes amongst the *'bureaux-gares'*, linchpins of the PTT system of mail distribution, was written too late for no. 13, and appeared in the next issue. Taken together, these articles develop the following general points. The August 1953 action was a spontaneous general strike that occurred outside the control of, and against, conventional bureaucratic political and trade-union organisations. It rejected both the existing organisations and the type of politics they practised. Using the example of the collusion between the state and the trade unions to end the strike, Socialisme ou Barbarie demonstrated that all bureaucratic organisations participated – in one way or another – in the same socioeconomic game, and defended the same general interests. Socialisme ou Barbarie's history of the strike tried to portray it as a manifestation of a working-class unity that formed in the period leading up to the action. Trade-union resistance necessarily put them in opposition to worker interests. The PTT strike also provided important lessons on the problems of workers' self-organisation. Socialisme ou Barbarie saw the strike as hampered by the workers' reliance on status-quo ideology. However, the strike's demands, particularly for direct worker control over production, signalled the emergence of a new political terrain. This politics was directly comparable with that which (briefly) emerged during the East Berlin 'June Days'. This section considers the nature of the PTT and the contexts that shaped the August strike.

---

50   I have not been able to identify this writer. Various Socialisme ou Barbarie members indicated that he might have been a PTT worker.

51   Petro was a pen-name used by Georges Petit.

In 1953, the PTT was the most important public-sector operation in France.[52] It was responsible for mail, telegraph and telephone services. The PTT was also involved with banking, which was (and is) associated with the others because of the link between the telegraph and wire transfers.[53] It is best understood as a system of interlocked, specialised distribution networks. Of these, the postal system was the most important, complex and difficult. The post was a bureaucracy set up to move high volumes of specialised material from place to place. The mail moved through a network of distribution centres that were linked together by railroad. The postal and rail systems were, therefore, tightly imbricated: this close relationship was reflected in the way the 1953 strike spread.

By the early 1950s, this system was under pressure. The volume of mail passing through it was steadily increasing. State-budgetary constraints ruled out a redesign of the system, or even an upgrade of existing technology to accommodate the increased volume.[54] The increased volume therefore meant speeding up the pace of circulation – and work – throughout the existing system. The system, in its barest outline, relied heavily on manual labour. Mail was hand sorted, dragged about in large, heavy bags and manually loaded onto trains. These bags were manually offloaded, resorted and delivered. Delivery was usually done by bicycle or on foot, regardless of the weather. Trucks were still not widely used in 1953.[55] The system was essentially the same as it had been fifty years earlier. Several Socialisme ou Barbarie members told me about an article Philippe Guillaume wrote after quitting the OECD in 1958. The article described working as a mail handler at the St. Lazaire station in Paris, loading and offloading 50–100 lb bags of mail to and from trains eight hours per night, the work exacting an enormous physical toll, invisible to the passengers boarding or leaving the same trains.[56]

---

52   An important additional context for understanding the PTT's financial situation that cannot be addressed here is the considerable extent to which it was destroyed in the war, and the costs of rebuilding it. See Noël 1977, pp. 71–2.

53   Noël 1977, Introduction.

54   In relative terms, using 1948 as the reference-point of 100, mail volume in 1954 was 128.3: at the same time the number of employees had dropped from 100 to 96.5. See Noël 1977, pp. 71 ff.

55   Noël 1977, Chapter Two.

56   The article was interpreted in a variety of ways: as a reflection on the conditions under which these workers laboured, beneath the noses of the bourgeois passengers yet invisible to them; as an index of Guillaume's suffering for his decision after the de Gaulle coup of May 1958 to 'go amongst the workers'; as an index of his drinking problem. Unfortunately, I have yet to locate a copy of this article.

In 1953, if one wanted to communicate across distance in France, one used the mail. The telephone system was rather primitive: most calls required an operator to make the appropriate connections. Nonetheless, the volume of telephone calls was also steadily increasing. This placed yet another strain on an already overburdened system. In every PTT sector, the same story obtained: increased traffic pushed the system to its limit and outstripped the capacities of available, largely manual, technology. This pressure resulted in steadily increasing production speeds and steadily deteriorating work conditions. As one example among many, the physical effects of deteriorating work conditions included increased rates of repetitive-motion problems amongst telephone operators. Meanwhile, the same budgetary restrictions that prevented technological upgrades also caused slowdowns in hiring and promotion. Already low wages stagnated.[57]

The PTT's internal problems were linked to, and exacerbated by, the more general stagnation of the French economy, caused in large measure by the Vietnam War.[58] Economic stagnation preoccupied the governments of the early 1950s which were dominated by the right. In 1952, Pinay tried to address the problem by imposing wage and price freezes. In practice, employers observed the wage freeze and ignored the price controls. Not surprisingly, this resulted in a marked decline in the working-class standard of living. After Pinay's resignation, and a prolonged ministerial crisis, the conservative and business-friendly J. Laniel formed a government hobbled by fractured, contentious relations between the parties of the right.[59] Although Laniel considered Pinay and his policies to be old-fashioned, he picked up where Pinay left off, making a renewed effort to use austerity to revive the economy. Unlike Pinay, Laniel actively opposed the programme of social benefits that the PCF had secured for public-sector workers during its tenure as part of the 1947 tripartite government. So Laniel added an attack on social benefits to Pinay's budgetary austerity programme. This guaranteed that his programme would encounter

---

57   See Faber 1954, p. 24.

58   The cost of the war, and its effects on French workers, was a constant theme in *L'Humanité*'s polemics against the governments from 1947 on. 'Vietnam is being fought on the backs of the working class' is a typical slogan.

59   Pinay resigned on 23 December 1952. Rene Mayer's government (7 January–21 May 1953), and particularly the period immediately following his resignation, is referred to here as the prolonged ministerial crisis. The Gaullist Joseph Laniel was appointed on 26 June, and wasted little time before going after the public-sector workers. For a general overview, see Rioux 1987, pp. 202–20. For a detailed account of the French foreign and domestic crises, political paralysis and economic difficulties of the politically fragmented period from 1951–3, with a large focus on ministerial intrigues, see Elgey 1968, pp. 19–191.

opposition. To head off this opposition, Laniel requested 'special powers' from the National Assembly in July 1953. He then waited until most French workers, with the exception of those in the public sector, were on summer holiday, before announcing his programme. It would have cut public-sector social benefits and would have exacerbated already deteriorating conditions in the PTT by suspending any new recruitment, increasing the retirement age, cutting pensions and freezing wages.[60]

The programme triggered an explosion of long-running conflicts within the PTT over attrition[61] and wages.[62] In J-F. Noël's 1977 analysis, these economic factors explained the unified nature of worker action. Noël relied heavily on the strike coverage that appeared in the PCF-owned newspaper *L'Humanité*. To counter *L'Humanité*'s partisan distortions, Noël read a cross-section of the trade-union press. The coverage devoted to the strike in *L'Humanité*, like its coverage of all working-class issues, aimed to reinforce the 'unity' of the PCF-CGT and the working class, usually by referring to the legacy of the 1936 Popular Front.[63] Following his sources faithfully in his assumption that wage issues are naturally political and that the organisations expressed this, Noël explained the strike in terms of long-term, largely economic tensions. That said, Noël is careful to assign the strike's origin an organisational affiliation: it was initiated in Bordeaux by revolutionary-syndicalist militants who were affiliated with the FO for anti-communist reasons.[64]

Socialisme ou Barbarie's account incorporated different assumptions about the nature of working-class politics. Instead of treating solidarity as a quasi-natural outcome of wage disputes, the articles analysed how workers actively constructed a sense of class solidarity. The group also argued that, while long-term economic and organisational tensions within the PTT played important

---

60   The surreal reliance on the idea that austerity is a way to address socioeconomic problems has continued across the entire period that separates the writing of the dissertation on which this book is based to the revamping of this chapter for publication. At this point, in 2012, the cognitive paralysis involved is as much about the slow collapse of the American empire as anything else.

61   See Noël 1977, pp. 75–6 for an account of the programme of attrition – the elimination of highly paid, relatively skilled positions through test results, sackings and the non-replacement of retirees.

62   See Faber 1954, p. 24 for a table of PTT national minimum-salaries according to job-description and -location. While the article does not provide detailed information on the cost of living, it is universally agreed that the wages paid to PTT workers, particularly the less skilled workers involved in distribution-operations, was extremely low.

63   See Chapter 3 on this theme and its functions.

64   Elgey 1968 locates the start of the strike firmly within the FO (Elgley 1968, p. 154).

roles in the strike and its timing, they provided only an abstract explanation for the action. D. Faber argued that, in order to explain the unity of the workers in the face of Laniel's actions, one had to look to the events of the winter of 1952. PTT workers had agitated independently for a united trade-union front to advance their demands for a pay differential to compensate them for handling Christmas-season volume increases. This same movement for trade-union unity was still active in early 1953. Workers organised a large meeting at the Salle Wagram by direct subscription,[65] renewing calls for trade-union unity.[66] At this meeting, representatives of the FO, CFTC and CGT found themselves on the same stage, despite the CGT having categorically refused to meet with the others.[67] Union representatives also found themselves before a room full of PTT workers, whose attendance amounted to a demand that the unions put aside the logic of pluralism and act together to advance common working-class interests. For Faber, this movement was an important precondition for the August 1953 strike. It provided workers with a concrete experience of self-organisation around issues that opposed them to the unions, the PTT and the state. From this experience, Faber argued, PTT workers began to develop a sense of class solidarity and the outline of an autonomous organisation.[68]

Socialisme ou Barbarie's understanding of the strike's tactics also diverged from those of the strike's other interpreters. For Elgey and Noël, the PTT movement was a curious anachronism, a sudden and strange re-emergence of revolutionary-syndicalist traditions comprehensible as an imprint given to the strike by the Bourdeaux FO militants whose agitation sparked it.[69] In contrast, Socialisme ou Barbarie argued that the action should be seen as an active re-appropriation of the general strike as a weapon, in terms and for reasons shaped by the context and conditions of 1953 that, incidentally, involved older

---

65   Direct subscription means that the workers create their own subscription rolls, raised money and coordinated publicity directly, thereby bypassing the unions.
66   The balance of power amongst the trade-unions in the PTT was somewhat atypical. The FO was numerically dominant across the board. The CGT controlled certain sectors by virtue of controlling certain trades, particularly metallurgy in the broadest sense. Amongst the predominantly female telephone operators, the Christian CFTC, which elsewhere was usually in the minority, was dominant.
67   The CGT in particular was not anxious to meet with representatives of FO, not surprising given that the *Force Ouvrière*, financed by the US, split with the PCF-dominated CGT in 1947.
68   Faber 1954, pp. 22–4.
69   See Kriegel 1964, volume 1, pp. 522ff. on the effects of the disastrous 1920 railroad strike on the revolutionary-syndicalist wing of the SFIO. See also Elgey 1968 and Noël 1977.

traditions as such. The strike was an important example of worker self-organisation and an assertion of a new political space.

For the group, the strike itself presented mixed results. It arrayed the ensemble of the French working class against Laniel's programme and prevented its implementation. Massive public support hemmed in Laniel and prevented the government from declaring the strike illegal and requisitioning transportation. Popular support for the strike also made it politically impossible to use the police to intimidate the strikers. Further, the government's nervousness over its inability to end, or even contain, the strike began to escalate into panic as the end of summer holidays approached, bringing with it the prospect of an even bigger, even more politically damaging strike. The trade unions were in a similar situation. Their inability to control the strikers undermined their claims to represent the working class. All sought ways to de-escalate and get in front of the strike, preferably on terms tactically advantageous to themselves. They shared the government's panic about the end of the summer holiday. Recognising that a spreading strike would imperil the government, the FO and CFTC decided that their primary loyalty had to rest with the state. This decision prompted them to conclude agreements with Laniel that undercut the strike.

For Socialisme ou Barbarie, this was a 'trade-union betrayal'. Because of what they saw as limitations in thinking about organisation, the workers were in no position to respond to union actions by 21 August. These facts frame the group's interpretation of the strike. From a revolutionary perspective, the workers gained important experience through the strike. Particularly important were its development outside of union control and its achievement of some concrete, if narrowly defined, political goals. However, the strikers' inability to respond to the 'trade-union betrayal' demonstrated that the workers were still conditioned by the dominant ideology and by the major political and trade-union organisations:

> It was at this moment that the entire working class did not know how to transcend the narrow limits within which the trade-unions had enclosed the strike: the public-sector workers did not openly advance more general demands, and the other workers (the metal-workers in particular) did not recognise in these strikes the struggles of all workers against their oppressors. Meanwhile, despite the great confusion that reigned in the minds of the strikers as to the ultimate objectives and the real possibilities of the movement, no illusions remained about the so-called economically and politically neutral character of the strike. The strikers understood the

political stakes in a struggle that put them against the government, and the oldest workers talked to the young about June 1936.[70]

Socialisme ou Barbarie saw the August 1953 strike therefore as presenting the revolutionary movement – comprised of the worker avant garde (the strikers) and the theoretical work carried on by revolutionary militants that developed in parallel with that avant garde – with new potential and new problems.

Even though the strike had shut France down for two weeks, it proved quite fragile in the end. There were problems of organisation and coordination. By the time the strike collapsed, some workers had begun to address these problems, in a limited way, by forming inter-professional liaison committees. Socialisme ou Barbarie argued that these committees might have formed the core of a new, more comprehensive organisation. Workers also organised subscription campaigns to raise money for their families, who suffered along with them because the unauthorised action had cut them off from union strike funds. Each of these initiatives was important. The main problem that Socialisme ou Barbarie saw was the strike's lack of directly elected strike committees. These committees should have been capable of coordinating strategy; their absence enabled the unions to form their own steering committees, which played a crucial role in ending the action. Socialisme ou Barbarie also argued that the strike limited itself by not moving beyond the syndicalist tactic of '*grève aux bras croisés*'. This was the silent refusal to work: typically the strikers stood at their work stations with their arms folded. Noël describes strikers leaving home each morning to gather near their workplace to look at each other, and thereby assure themselves that something was still happening. The strikers never took their protest to the streets, never organised demonstrations. Street demonstrations would have brought the strike to the public and, thereby, into a more explicitly political realm. In this regard, the French workers were not as radical as their Berlin counterparts.

For Socialisme ou Barbarie, the PTT strike posed several important questions. How should an autonomous strike organise itself? How should it provide itself with continuity? How should it deploy publicly? How might workers (and theorists) think about the importance of momentum? The PTT strike demonstrated that, without some mechanism to assure the continuity of demands and action, strikes become increasingly fragile over time. For Socialisme ou Barbarie, the lack of adequate organisation explained the gap that separated the strike's initial period of spontaneity and its subsequent drift. It also

---

70   Dussart 1954, p. 17.

explained the strikers' lack of clarity as to its goals.[71] The organisation problem prevented the strike from adapting to a shifting, complex situation.

From their earliest articles, *Socialisme ou Barbarie* compared the French and East Berlin strikes. In the latter, workers immediately took their action to the streets. They elected strike committees that provided forums for collective deliberation, from which issued coherent, politically substantive demands. Soviet tanks precluded any longer-term developments. The question of the longer-term adequacy of strikes committees therefore remained unanswerable. From Socialisme ou Barbarie's perspective, the East Berlin action was more advanced, more revolutionary. Articles pointed to the Berlin workers' sophisticated ideological foundation, rooted in their intensive exposure to Marx through the Party-controlled reading circles at the *Stalinallee*. If the building workers were exemplary because they appropriated Marxist categories to articulate their opposition to a state that built itself ideologically on the same basis, the sentiment behind their action was universal. Its universality in the German context was evident in the spread of the action during the evening of 16–17 June. It was universal in the context of Socialisme ou Barbarie's vision of the working class because these Marxist categories underpinned the group's entire project, and ordered their comparative reading of strikes.

East Germany presented a unified political context amenable to *Socialisme ou Barbarie*'s understanding of revolutionary politics. The French political context was far more fragmented. Daniel Mothé's article, 'La grève chez Renault', which we referenced earlier, used the machine shop in which he worked at Renault's Billancourt factory as a microcosm within which was observable the nature and effects of this political fragmentation. The article details the way in which the Billancourt workers received the PTT strike during its last days as they returned from their summer holidays. August 18, 1953 marked the return to work for the less senior metal workers. The *'métallos'* were the largest, most politicised and volatile industrial trade in France, the quintessential worker in left-political mythology. The possibility that they might join in the strike caused panic amongst the government and the trade unions.[72] The PCF-CGT, dominant amongst metalworkers, stood to lose most if these work-

---

71　Ibid.
72　Note 67 gives an indication of the balance of organisational power in the PTT. Obviously, this balance would be upset if the CGT-dominated 'métallos' entered, widened and intensified the strike. The general strike was already considered a threat to state stability. Elgey reports that it worried the military, particularly after negotiations with the strikers collapsed on 15 August. Pierre Mendès-France summed up the official perception of the situation in his famous 'Nous sommes en 1788!' See Elgey 1968, pp. 166–70.

ers joined the strike. At one level, the coverage of the return to work in the PCF's daily newspaper, *L' Humanité*, can be read as playing to the vanity of the '*métallo*' constituency.[73] The paper devoted much of its 18 August reportage to the events at Billancourt. The following day, a short article entitled 'Premiers Débrayages chez Renault ou la rentrée n'était hier que partielle', began with the single voice assessing the situation:

> And us? We got started...Yesterday, Renault re-opened. 10 to 15,000 workers returned from vacation. The phrase was on everyone's lips, the question in everyone's eyes...

The implication is clear: with the return of the Renault metalworkers, the Real Workers had entered the scene. The Real Workers were looking around, trying to figure out the situation. And because the PCF-CGT opposed the PTT strike, the Real Working Class was already acting by not doing anything.

At the same time, *Socialisme ou Barbarie*'s version of the real workers, Mothé's AOC (*Atelier Outillage Centrale*, the limited-run machine shop where Mothé and Hirzel worked) voted to strike. Later that day, a joint CGT-CFTC-FO meeting produced a tract that announced the formation of a unified trade-union front. Trade-union unity had been one of the PTT workers' central demands: here it was occurring at Billancourt, in a political context dominated by the CGT. The strike spread across the plant during 20 August: *L'Humanité* printed another joint tract. According to *L'Humanité*, the entire Billancourt factory was shut down on 21 August. The unity of the working class behind the PCF-CGT banner – the natural order of things from the Party's viewpoint – was achieved and reflected in a 'magnificent meeting' called by the three main unions that afternoon.[74]

Mothé's article can be read as a parody of *L'Humanité*'s coverage of the situation at Billancourt. The article employs transcribed worker conversations. Rather than issuing from the Real Working Class, Mothé puts the conversations in the mouths of scattered groups of younger militant workers who spend the early part of the week of 18 August wandering around the political geography of Billancourt, trying to figure out where the strike was and why nothing was

---

73   In 1953, the CGT controlled 72 percent of the 'métallos'. There is rather extensive literature on the 'métallos' and radial politics. See for example, Kreigel 1980 or Molinari 1991. For a more local case study, concerning shipbuilding in Nantes/St. Nazaire, see Oury 1973.

74   That the paper's coverage was an extension of organisational brinkmanship is by now evident – the themes that are introduced here are developed more fully in my chapter on the politics of Billancourt, below.

being coordinated.[75] Mothé portrays these workers – and himself – as initially quite enthusiastic about returning to work under conditions that bode so well for an extension of the holidays in the form of a strike. Once actually back at work, Mothé and his unnamed comrades walked into the factory with growing dismay. They tried to initiate a work stoppage in solidarity with the PTT strikers. Their efforts were met with an initial enthusiasm that soon dissipated in the face of union hostility and threats of reprisal. The union representatives seemed to patronise Mothé and his friends (and, from Mothé's viewpoint, the workers in general). They also seemed to view the small work stoppage they orchestrated as something of a joke: 'The CGT delegate also showed up excited, like everyone else: "What do you think?", he asked, with conspiratorial winks. What was thought was clear: the vast majority of the shop did not want to go back to work'.[76] By 20 August, however, CGT representatives were openly hostile.

Mothé and his comrades roamed the factory on 18 August, trying to convene meetings between workers during which they might discuss what to do without the interference of the union delegates. Their journey took them around the whole political landscape of Billancourt. They began amongst the highly skilled, relatively autonomous shops of the 'l'Artillerie' (machine repair), where there was some enthusiasm, as there was in the AOC (limited-run machine shop), which voted to stop work. By the time Mothé and his comrades arrived at Department 55 (cutting bars and shock absorbers), they numbered about sixty workers: they were able to force a stoppage of work in the Department by surrounding everyone who tried to keep working. While this was going on, union representatives had withdrawn from the floor, waiting to see what happened. At the centre of each stoppage was a small meeting: the main demand that issued from these meetings was for the convening of a large, central factory meeting by the CGT the next afternoon. The CGT convened a small meeting in the AOC, an obvious ploy to limit the previous day's agitation. The AOC workers voted to continue the strike: groups of workers set off to a different series of semi-skilled Departments; first Department 88 (drive-trains), then Department 31 (body work – *décor de carrosseries*). In Department 31, the AOC workers encountered resistance from both the foremen, who pres-

---

75 Mothé's use of the transcribed speech is thematised in his 'Problèmes d'un journal ouvrier', which I analyse in Chapter 5.
76 'Le délégué cégétiste arrive lui aussi gonflé à bloc, comme tout le monde. "Qu'est-ce que tu en penses" dit-il, en faisant des clins d'oeil complices. Ce qu'on en pense est clair, la grande majorité de l'atelier ne veut pas reprendre le travail' (Mothé 1954, p. 35).

sured the workers under their command to stay at their machines, and from the union delegates:

> At this moment [while in Department 31] an incident occurred that summed up the entire orientation of the trade-unions in this movement. The CGT delegates from our shop came in furious and began to harangue our group, demanding that all workers return to their respective shops. 'You must stay in your shops: the others are big enough to take their responsibilities'. Among the CGT delegates, only 1 of the eighty-eight delegates is furious. He does not understand this position. Where are the delegates from 31?[77]

Mothé's description of these two days at Billancourt provides an overview of the problems faced by workers trying to organise strike actions independently of union control. They began and ended in isolation. The unions moved quickly and efficiently to contain any threat to their positions and exerted tremendous pressure on workers to act only on union command. The quote clearly shows the CGT representatives using these tactics to confine strike initiatives to the shops from which they came.[78] By Wednesday, August 20, Mothé's strike movement had been reduced to small meetings involving workers from adjacent shops.[79] On that day, *L'Humanité* reported on the 'spectacular meeting' of the CGT-FO-CFTC. Mothé reports being puzzled about the meeting and its location outside the factory and not in the immense, and politically significant, areas where the 4CV assembly lines were located. The 'spectacular meeting' did not, therefore, employ the most symbolically loaded areas of the Billancourt political landscape.[80]

The balance of Mothé's article lists other examples of worker-initiative running up against CGT 'sabotage', which undercut autonomous action in support of the PTT workers during the strike's last days. In one shop, an informal meeting was broken up because the organisation of the shop was such that two workers continuing to work meant that all the shop's machinery ran, making as much noise as if everyone was working. Near the end of the article, Mothé reports that a small committee issued a call for action on the part of all metalworkers in the Paris region. Nothing happened. When Mothé arrived at the

---

77   Mothé 1954, p. 37.
78   The methods employed to coerce left dissidents in the trade unions will be discussed in more detail in Chapter 4.
79   Mothé 1954, p. 38.
80   See Fridenson 1979.

factory the next morning, the AOC was working. The CGT delegate told the workers, during a meeting held later in the morning, that: 'the strike committees have been organised for a long time. They are out playing belote. No-one wants them to take an interest in the strike'.[81]

Conclusion

Castoriadis wrote the following assessment of the 1953 actions:

> First of all, it is clear that the ideological obstacles preventing this avant-garde from organising itself and acting have not been eliminated. There are no elements in the objective situation today than there were yesterday that would enable these workers to define a programme for themselves, or to manifest a proletarian form of organisation. Even if a few spontaneous class-actions suddenly appear, the situation not will be greatly modified. Certain questions – for example, the form of organisation, or the direction of struggles and their objectives – would be posed immediately by the facts themselves, although in an initially narrow form. In this atmosphere, the avant-garde will again be sensitised to Marxist thought and ideology, and a fusion could take place between them and militants of revolutionary-Marxist groups.[82]

The East Berlin 'June Days' and the PTT strike are evidence of an emergent worker avant garde, one that is, like most of us, hobbled by entanglements with the dominant ideology and limited in perspective because it is tied to immediate concerns in ways that are shaped by that ideology. These limitations could be overcome practically if more autonomous actions are undertaken. Here there is an assumption either of a kind of contact that runs laterally across the working class or something on the order of the *Zeitgeist*. On the one hand, such contact is the result of political action and not its precondition, just as communication across the fragmented environments of contemporary industrial production is accomplished by militants and not a presupposition for militant action. On the other hand, it is symmetrical with the idea internal to Socialisme ou Barbarie that these actions signalled the beginning of what would become a mounting wave of proletarian action, one that appeared, on

---

81   'Mais il y a longtemps que les Comités de grèves sont organisés, ils jouent à la belote, puisqu'on ne veut pas qu'ils s'occuper de la grève ...' (Mothé 1954, p. 42).
82   Mothé 1954, p. 26.

one level, to culminate in the Hungarian Revolution. A consequence of this ongoing practical movement that would enable a recognition of limits and obstacles on the part of the worker avant garde was an increased contact with the Marxian tradition which would, in turn, transform these actions by transforming the levels of awareness shaping their unfolding. This relationship is, then, a natural horizon that shapes any possibility of revolutionary action. The work of a revolutionary organisation like Socialisme ou Barbarie has a fundamental role to play in encouraging and shaping this interaction. A revolutionary organisation – characterised as a party in the above – can facilitate this overall orientation through the development and dissemination of a vision of socialism. The organisation also had an important role to play in encouraging the worker avant garde to act in a coherent, self-reflexive way to deal with problems of organisation and continuity.

In addition to assessing the overall situation of this emergent worker avant-garde, the group undertook a comparative reading of demands. At the most basic register, when workers decided to act autonomously, they did so in order to gain control over their professional lives. This is expressed in the fact that, given the opportunity, workers organised themselves along direct-democratic lines in the form of strike committees. Seen from a perspective informed by *Socialisme ou Barbarie*, these committees would be a germinal form of worker councils. It is also expressed in the fact that the demands generated in these contexts tended to converge on the general question of hierarchy. For the group, a basic demand for worker management of production lay behind the problem of hierarchy. In order to draw out the revolutionary potential posited by these actions, Socialisme ou Barbarie extended its perspective forward in time. The radical potential of the form of organisation and questions of hierarchy and control could be clarified with reference to a vision of socialism understood as direct democracy instituted by worker councils. This projection gave Socialisme ou Barbarie the basis for a 'revolutionary perspective' in terms with which it tried to evaluate the 'socialist' or 'revolutionary content' of a given action. Within the group, this perspective was framed as an aspect of a dialogue with the worker avant garde and would, presumably, find its way to them in the form of the journal. It would be the central message stuffed in bottles and tossed into the ocean.

The 1953 strikes provided more specific information as well. Both had their origin in conflicts that set workers against trade unions, political organisations and the state. This coincided with the group's theory of bureaucratic capitalism. There was another confirmation at the level of demands. Both strikes occurred in the context of marked increases in the rate of work, or what Marx called intensive exploitation. Particularly in East Berlin, cadence increases were accompanied by attempts to reorganise work, to extend the reach of standardised or rationalised production into semi-skilled and skilled forms of labour. From the viewpoint of the worker, then, rationalisation was about deskilling and the loss of professional identity and/or autonomy, and about its consequences for production rates. Conflicts over production norms are conflicts of its organisation and thus over the control of production. They are political and not merely economic or efficiency issues.

Socialisme ou Barbarie had a parallel view of wage issues. Workers loudly objected to any restructuring of rates because such restructuring usually amounted to pay cuts, whether directly or indirectly. Here the two actions considered were empirically quite different: there was a move to piece rates and other, similar attempts to use wage levels, or to spur increased production output amongst the building trades in East Berlin. These accompanied the introduction of Taylorist organisation into previously autonomous trades. With the PTT, the strike happened in a space of organisational and technological stagnation coupled with increasing volume as a function of failure on the part of the state to invest in infrastructure. These factors packaged wage freezes (*de facto* cuts) in conservative austerity. But for Socialisme ou Barbarie, what was significant about wage demands was that, when workers generated the issue in the context of autonomous actions, they never limited themselves to the economic dimension. They invariably coupled wage demands with demands for increased control over the organisation of work. These demands for control flowed from what Socialisme ou Barbarie saw as the fundamental reality of shop-floor life. Workers experienced production through the mediation of informal worker collectives that practically elaborated a type of hierarchy fundamentally opposed to that embodied in Fordist production design. Understanding these informal collectives was thus a central empirical, political and philosophical issue.

CHAPTER 3

Frame: On Claude Lefort's 'L'Expérience Prolétarienne'

Socialisme ou Barbarie saw a new *'problématique'* for revolutionary theory emerging from the East Berlin uprising and the French general strike of Summer 1953. Central to this new *problématique* was the elaboration of a notion of autonomy. Socialisme ou Barbarie's initial understanding of the term designated strike actions that workers carried out beyond the control of, and in opposition to, the bureaucratic trade unions and political parties that adopted direct-democratic forms of self-organisation. The group connected direct democracy to the potentials continually posited in the course of the conflicts that shape everyday worker experience on the factory floor. Claude Lefort's 1952 essay 'L'experience prolétarienne', outlines the way to understand that experience. For the moment, suffice it to say that the group conceptualised this experience as being shaped by the basic contradiction of bureaucratic capitalism, and as following from the worker response and resistance to its effects. Actions like the East Berlin 'June Days' and the August PTT strike were both expressions of these conflicts and experiences that made linkages explicit. In their modes of self-organisation and the collective formulation of demands, autonomous actions were the 'germ' of revolution 'from below'. The task of revolutionary theory was to comprehend, clarify, and situate this 'germ' by connecting it, on the one hand, back to the everyday experience at the point of production and, on the other, to a vision of revolution and of direct-democratic socialism. The task of revolutionary politics was to make this theoretical project as widely available as possible in order to help the 'worker avant garde' become more self-reflexive on the question of organisation, and more cognisant of the revolutionary implications of their actions.

'L'experience prolétarienne' outlines a project for *Socialisme ou Barbarie* rooted in a vision of the worker and of worker experience that is derived from reading and interpreting 'proletarian-documentary literature'. The project is the temporal inverse of the group's collective approach to autonomous worker actions. In the latter, aspects of autonomous worker actions were linked retrospectively to conflicts that arose in the ordinary experience of production. Lefort proposes a time-forward form of revolutionary political action that presupposes a distinction between manifest and latent dimensions of worker experience and situates the dissemination of a comparative analysis and interpretation of worker narratives as a production of social-imaginary significations that could unify and transform this latent register into the subjective basis of a form of proletarian class consciousness.

Because of Lefort's positions on organisation, for him there was a strict separation between what working people could write about, from 'inside', about their experience at the point of production and what revolutionary militants, who are outside of that experience, could otherwise access. From this follows the centrality of worker-autobiographical narratives. The second part of this chapter considers this source-material directly. Lefort envisioned Socialisme ou Barbarie's primary role in revolutionary politics as consisting of collecting and disseminating a wide range of these narratives, supplemented by comparative analyses and interpretations alongside systemic critiques of contemporary capitalism. But for reasons that will be touched on here, and explored in more detail in Chapter Five, the collection never materialised. Workers simply did not write. The second section examines some of the consequences of this unforeseen limitation. I analyse Paul Romano and Eric Albert's first-person accounts of experience at the point of production as literary constructions that produced a specific 'realism effect' through the use of particular generic and linguistic conventions. By doing this, I hope to introduce a certain instability into the relation, which Socialisme ou Barbarie took as unproblematic, between shop-floor experience and its textual representation.

Claude Lefort's 'L'experience prolétarienne' (1952)

The schema that ordered Socialisme ou Barbarie's conception of revolution relied upon the close examination of working-class experience. This put the group in little-explored territory. Even though traditional Marxism placed the proletariat at the conceptual and political center of its concerns, its treatment of the working class as the embodied expression of abstract economic forces foreclosed close analysis of concrete relations of production. It also evacuated questions of how the proletariat could act as a revolutionary agent by conceiving of revolution as a quasi-automatic result of contradictions that played out at the level of 'objective forces'.[1] French 'human sciences' had not yet begun producing researchers who took the French working class as a legitimate object of study. Through the 1950s, anthropology was dominated on the one hand by research on the 'exotic', and on the other by the conflict between structural anthropology and philosophy over which discipline 'owned' episte-

---

[1] Lefort 1952. Reprinted as Lefort 1979a. Reference here is to Lefort 1979a, p. 74.

mology.² Sociology, for the most part, operated in a zone of inquiry that hovered between politics and the university. While students of Georges Friedman, like Alain Touraine, produced studies of the French working class in modes quite distinct from American-style industrial sociology, it was only with the failure of the workers to oppose the Gaullist Fifth Republic in 1958 that the academic discipline – represented notably by Touraine, Serge Mallet and Michel Crozier – concerned itself with the 'fate' of the French working class.³ Only industrial relations and industrial sociology took the problem of shop-floor experience seriously. However, the field was dominated by American researchers who, in the main, viewed industrial conflict as the social expression of psychological deviance. This epistemological position was the direct recoding of the political worldview particular to the capitalists who employed them.⁴

Even Marx's early writings offered little in the way of a historically specific approach to working-class experience. Lefort argues that this follows from the double image of the proletariat in Marx. The proletariat is a creation of capitalism, positioned at the leading edge of technological and organisational development. It operates simultaneously inside the dominant bourgeois rationality by virtue of its socialisation and outside by virtue of the experience of the reality of exploitation that the dominant rationality legitimates and conceals at once. This unique situation is what enables the proletariat to develop a rationality that goes beyond that of the bourgeoisie and to become the historical agent that brings about socialism. This position is juxtaposed with another in which ruthless exploitation and wholesale alienation have reduced workers to a less-than-human status. Lefort argues that this second image is symmetrical with a notion of revolution as explosion and of a socialism that requires no internal articulations at the level of theory because it would simply replace capitalism 'as a negative to a positive'.⁵ This is the image of the proletariat that came to be dominant in Marx.⁶

---

2   See Dosse 1991.
3   See Touraine 1955. *Arguments* no. 12/13 is an important compilation of texts on 1958 and the French working class. I will return to the interaction of revolutionary politics and the nascent 'sociologie du travail' in Chapter 6.
4   This is not to say that the work of people like Elton Mayo was without utility: see the extensive, critical use made of Mayo in Castoriadis 1988 [1957]. Donald Roy's work, which represented a marginal, more explicitly left/critical variant of industrial sociology, is fundamental to Castoriadis's 1958 text. See pp. 184–8.
5   Lefort 1979a, p. 74.
6   This miserabalist conception of the working class, which emphasises its exploitation to the near exclusion of other aspect of working-class life, is evident in Engels *On the Condition of*

Working against this predominance, Lefort takes up a version of the first but positions it in the specific context of post-1945 capitalism. His approach is conditioned by the assumption that alienation is a tendency rather than an accomplishment. This assumption is rooted in Socialisme ou Barbarie's view of the basic contradiction of bureaucratic capitalism, according to which capitalist managerial ideology and practice tends to exclude workers from creative interaction with their work while, at the same time, that creative interaction is continually required in order to solve myriad problems that arise in the course of production. If workers were completely alienated, not only would revolutionary action be impossible, but capitalist production itself would grind to a halt.[7] Implicit in the use of the concept of bureaucratic capitalism is the more basic claim that modalities of exploitation, conflict and creativity are variable and historically specific. The situation in bureaucratic capitalist enterprises is different from that of enterprises in earlier periods and experience at the point of production is particular not only to this type of organisation, but also to the specific situation of the workers' movement.[8] Even if there were a fully articulated approach to this register of working-class experience in the early Marx, it could serve only as a template. The problems of analysis would still have to be posed again.

'Proletarian Experience' emphasises the radical creativity of the working class and the historically contingent character of that creativity. Following in part from his position on revolutionary organisation, Lefort argues that only workers can know and write about their experience: revolutionary theory must be confined to analysing and interpreting what they write.[9] Using Paul Romano's 'The American Worker' and Eric Albert's 'Témoinage: La vie en usine' as points of departure, Lefort outlines a programme for the investigation of 'the proletarian standpoint' that would isolate and describe the significations that structure proletarian comportment. These analyses would be supplemented with critical accounts of autonomous worker actions which would function as statements of political horizon, and as broadly synthetic analyses of contemporary capitalism. Lefort also imagines the collection of these narratives as the basis for a wide-ranging working-class sociology 'from the

---

the *Working Class in England, 1844* and in the (quite remarkable) analysis of the English working class of 1860 in volume one of *Capital*. By contrast, see, for example, Thompson 1966.
7 Castoriadis 1988 [1949].
8 This refers primarily to the configuration of trade unions and political parties dominant at a given time and the possibilities that may or may not exist for autonomous action. On this, see further on in this section.
9 Lefort 1979a, *passim*.

inside' that would include all aspects of worker interaction with the dominant culture and be centred on the question of whether there was a specific 'mentalité ouvrier' and what it might look like. Worker narratives would be part of an ongoing dialogue between the group and the worker avant garde that was to be the center of Socialisme ou Barbarie's activity as Lefort envisioned it. But it never became the model for the group or the journal because, despite the solicitation for writings which frequently appeared in *Socialisme ou Barbarie* (as well as in related projects like *Tribune Ouvrière*), workers simply did not write.

Lefort's emphasis on second-order descriptions and interpretation follows from his position elaborated in recurrent debates within Socialisme ou Barbarie on 'the organization question'. A point of consensus within the group was the vision of revolution as the culmination of a process whereby the working class, acting autonomously, would consciously assume the direction of production and, by extension, of society. Positioning themselves broadly within the tradition of the general strike, members of SB emphasised the content of socialism rather than the modalities of transition. With this, the group put aside the more militarised conceptions of revolution that emerged within the Marxian tradition in response to the violent suppression of the Paris Commune, which served as the logical basis for Leninism. The move was in significant measure a result of the group's shared preoccupation with the historical fate of Leninism. There was little disagreement over the basic analysis. The Vanguard Party was a military organisation that, in its division between Party and Masses, recapitulated the division of intellectual labour characteristic of bureaucratic capitalism in general which separated *dirigeant* from *exécutant*, thinking from doing, those who conceptualise from those who carry out orders. It was this, and not questions of ownership, that shaped the outcomes of the revolutionary movement. The consequences were apparent in the trajectory taken by the USSR.[10]

While there was agreement about the critique of Leninism, Socialisme ou Barbarie was not of one mind about how best to avoid repetition of the problem of the Vanguard Party in their own activities. Cornelius Castoriadis argued that the group should be an organisation that generates revolutionary theory aimed at empowering the worker avant garde and not be worried about appearing to recapitulate the Leninist split between theorist (those who think) and masses (those who follow instructions). Theory developed in a dialogue with the worker avant garde: it represented a complementary, but not separate, form of activity. Social relations within the organisation could be seen

---

10   See Chapter 1, above.

as a kind of laboratory for revolutionary sociability unfolding in its own, particular register. For Lefort, the problem of bureaucratisation was paramount. Not only was a revolutionary organisation in itself a problem, but theoretical production had to avoid falling into the trap of telling the workers what they were 'really doing'. For Castoriadis, this would make political work impossible because one or another version of this relation was built into the nature of theory itself. 'Proletarian Experience' can be read as Lefort's attempt to address this practical impasse. The project outlined *was* revolutionary action.[11] We will see in the second part of this chapter that this desire to not tell the workers what they are really doing had consequences for the selection of texts that would constitute 'proletarian documentary literature'.

Following Marx, Lefort (and the group more generally) saw the proletariat as a creation of capitalism, positioned at the leading edge of technological and organisational development, simultaneously inside the dominant rationality by virtue of socialisation and outside it by virtue of the experience at the point of production of the realities of exploitation and irrationality that the dominant rationality legitimates and conceals. Conflicts at the point of production would, in theory, make of workers the source of an alternate rationality that might inform socialism – but because they are also participants in the dominant rationality, the elements of this rationality would be fragmentary and workers erratic in their abilities to recognise them. The same problem repeats in an exacerbated form in the theorist, whose capacity to generate theory presupposes certain training and skills that come tied to precisely the rationality that theory works to overthrow. Individual narratives written by workers that detail experience at the point of production provide militants access to these conflicts and the industrial realities that condition them. A phenomenology of these narratives would use a comparative approach based on the idea of the eidetic reduction to produce second-order descriptions of structuring characteristics of worker experience in general. These second-order descriptions would point to the latent content of that experience, disengaging universal substructures with revolutionary political potentials from the contingency of the particular and feeding them back to the worker avant garde through the medium of the journal.

This relation to worker writers, and, by extension, to the worker avant garde comprised revolutionary action in part because, following on the ways in

---

11   See the debate on revolutionary organization published in SB 10 (July–August, 1952): Chaulieu, Pierre, 'La direction prolétarienne', pp. 10–18, and Montal, Claude, 'Le prolétariat et le problème de la direction révolutionnaire', pp. 18–27. The reference here is to Montal's (Lefort) statement: There is no need for a revolutionary organisation at all.

which he was sensitive to the problems of objectifying the working class, Lefort tended not to differentiate within it. This effectively eliminated any space for militant action: there were no tasks to be performed by militants within the working class.[12] One had to be either with the workers, which was good, or to be outside, which was bad. One could either be a worker or a militant, but not both. The generally phenomenological approach to worker narratives was symmetrical with this view: revolutionary militants could gather worker narratives and create interpretations of those narratives as their part of an ongoing dialogue with the worker avant garde. But that role, and the dialogue along with it, would be progressively effaced by the unfolding of the proletariat's capacities to direct, manifested in revolutionary action.

Throughout 'Proletarian Experience', Lefort argues that the analysis of the proletarian standpoint had to be thoroughly historical. It cannot generate transcendental claims or reify worker experience. The results of analysis must account for everyday experience at the point of production in terms of its specific historical determinants. He outlines what is at stake by referring to Marx's theory of social change, using the well-known schema of the transition from feudal to bourgeois domination outlined in *The Communist Manifesto*, and the more elaborated version in *The German Ideology*, as points of departure. Perhaps one reason the revolution will not be televised is that revolution cannot be understood through the analysis of discrete events. Rather, revolution of the sort that replaces one historical form with another is a result of the progressive unfolding of potentials that are being worked out in the previous social-historical formation:[13]

---

12   This point emerges from a reading of the exchange between Lefort and Jean Paul Sartre that resulted in Lefort's departure from *Les Temps Modemes* in 1954. Particularly important is Castoriadis' 'contribution' to the debate which, in the context of a general defence, criticises Lefort on precisely this point. See the first two parts of Sartre's 'Communists and Peace' originally published in TM no. 81, July 1952 and 84–85, November 1952; reprinted in Sartre 1964. Lefort's 'Le marxisme et Sartre' originally in TM no. 89, April 1953 along with Sartre's response, 'Réponse a Claude Lefort'. Lefort's article is reprinted in Lefort 1979; Sartre's in Sartre 1965. Sartre's two essays are translated as Sartre 1968. Castoriadis 1953a is a response to Sartre's attack on Lefort. It was reprinted in Castoriadis 1974 and is translated in Castoriadis 1988, pp. 207–41. See also Merleau-Ponty 1973.

13   This point could be much more fully developed, particularly since it addresses one of the more common charges levelled at Marx(ists) concerning the problem of periodicity and, by extension, of accounting for changes leading up to capitalism. Lefort's arguments can be found in Lefort 1979a, pp. 4–5. See also Lefort 1978, originally published in *Les Temps Modernes* no. 78.

> Marx does not say, but allows to be said, that, from its origin, the bourgeoisie is what it will be, an exploiting class, underprivileged at first to be sure, but possessing from the outset all the traits that its history only developed. The development of the proletariat is entirely different; reduced to its economic function alone, it represents a category that does not yet possess its class-meaning/direction [*sens*], the meaning/direction that constitutes its original comportment, which is, in its definitive form, struggle in all class-specific forms within society against adversarial strata. This is not to say that the role of the class in production should be neglected – on the contrary, we will see that the role workers play in society, and that they are called on to play in making themselves its masters, is directly based on their role as producers – but the essential thing is that this role does not give them any actual power, but only an increasingly strong capacity to direct [production and society].[14]

Lefort's opening line reproduces a problem in Marxism that Socialisme ou Barbarie elsewhere critiqued at length: the treatment of the bourgeoisie as if it were incapable of creativity or transformation.[15] Such a view constructs the bourgeoisie in the image of its rationality and then shifts to the claim that the bourgeoisie was always, in its essence, what it would become once it was dominant. History changed nothing except its position.[16] But Lefort's point does not centre on this schematic analysis of the bourgeoisie and its rise to power; rather, it provides both a backdrop against which he begins to set up the problem of understanding the nature of the working class, an a shorthand way of staging the present as conditioned by bourgeois domination.

Lefort's lines make explicit the assumptions about class formation that run through much of Socialisme ou Barbarie's collective evaluations of autonomous worker actions. As a class in itself, the proletariat occupies a common position in the production process, which sells its labour power for a wage, engages in certain types of conflict at the point of production, and so on. The shift into reflexivity, into a class for itself, is predicated on recognition of what links the people who occupy a common position in the production process and the conflicts that arise there, as well as the interests and political projects that arise from that recognition. In a strict sense, both registers are historical

---

14 Lefort 1952a, pp. 4–5.
15 For the most fully worked out statement of this critique of Marx, see 'L'expérience de l'histoire du mouvement ouvrier' in Castoriadis 1974, translated as 'On the Experience of the History of the Workers' Movement' in Castoriadis 1992.
16 See Castoriadis 1974.

so both forms can be understood as endowed with certain meanings and/or a sense of direction [*sens*].[17] But, following on the logic above, the class initself is circumscribed by its immediate situation. The possibilities for a shift into a class for itself and would be fragmentary and scattered. For Lefort, the transition of the working class into a class for itself hinges on its assimilation of an overarching telos – its 'increasing capacity to direct production'. Both the telos and process of assimilation are conditioned by the types of conflict characteristic of bureaucratic capitalism. So there is a level of directedness that may unfold through everyday experience and conflict and another, linked but not identical, that follows from the same experiences reprocessed through different significations.[18] The relation between these registers echoes Vico's conception of social development, with history understood as a spiral, a circular motion spread out temporally and in principle progressively that allows for both repetition and change. Struggle acquires its meaning relative to an overall (revolutionary) project (here, a synonym for direction), and the overall project is, in turn, continually inflected by particular struggles. The role for revolutionary militants in feeding back descriptions and interpretations of the commonalities that link worker experience, based on the close reading of worker writings, is to facilitate the shift into this kind of collective self-awareness. And in line with his critique of deductivism,[19] Lefort argues that this propels analysis toward close scrutiny of what social-historical conditions shape and inform worker experience, and away from the heady aether of the dialectic.

For revolutionary militants to access this experience, they would need to position themselves 'inside' it, but are prevented from doing so by their social positions. From this follows the centrality of narratives written by working people about their experiences at the point of production. As noted before, what militants can bring to the dialogue that links them to the worker avantgarde (for which worker writers stand in) is the comparative analyses of the narratives that would provide a coherent description of workers' 'spontaneous

---

17   A term taken, along with the problems in translating it, from Merleau-Ponty.
18   The language of social-imaginary significations is taken from the later philosophical work of Cornelius Castoriadis. While it appears throughout this chapter, it operates primarily as a heuristic rather than as an explicit analytic category. Here it refers to the revolutionary project and its reconfiguration of elements of everyday experience in terms shaped by an understanding of socialism as direct democracy.
19   The position that bourgeois thought in general is characterised by an effort to derive reality from the concepts used to think about/order that reality, a position common to Marx, Nietzsche, and others.

comportments' in the context of industrial work, the precondition for apprehension of the 'proletarian standpoint' specific to a particular period. What this phenomenology consists in by now should be clear. It would use comparative readings, informed by revolutionary theory, to isolate and interpret types of conflicts, practices or other patterns that emerge as universal (and politically coherent) from within accounts of proletarian experience. The usage of methods drawn from transcendental phenomenology would be loose, but the assumptions are similar. The reductions as Husserl developed them were a method for isolating universal aspects of meaning attached to a concept from within the shifting terrain of usage. The reductions move through a series of steps of comparing exemplars in order to produce intersubjectively verifiable sets of necessary predicates clustered around a 'determinable x'.[20] But there is a fundamental difference between objects and social groups or processes as objects of knowledge. Phenomenology transposed empirical objects to transcendental objects in a quest for certainty. For Lefort, the goal of comparative reading is the delineation, transformation and (revolutionary) politicisation of what Castoriadis would later term the social-imaginary significations that shape worker experience.

These premises come together in the analysis of what Lefort called a 'reconsideration of the subjective element of class formation'. This issue was crucial in the early Marx but remained underdeveloped because the reduction of history to the play of objective forces rendered it epiphenomenal.[21] For Socialisme ou Barbarie, it was a basic analytic and political matter. Revolution does not simply happen. Revolution is made by people who consciously and collectively assume control over their lives, their surroundings, and the society in which they live. They can only do so on the basis of their experience. Here, experience refers to the explicit content of experience processed through a re-imagining of what is, at the level of the worker narratives at least, their latent political content. A subjectively oriented restatement of the transformation from a class in itself to a class for itself, the re-imagining of this latent dimension provides workers with the fore structure(s) of revolutionary consciousness, the condition(s) of possibility for revolutionary agency. The 'subjective'

---

20   See paragraph 87 of Husserl 1962 for the distinction between the object in itself and the noematic, and on the function of inverted commas in restricting meaning to the noematic.

21   The opening pages of Lefort 1979a expend considerable energy to define and defend this domain from within the Marxist tradition.

therefore had a central place in revolutionary theory.[22] The term 'subjective' is used in a specific sense:

> If it is true that no class can ever be reduced to its economic function alone [...] it is even more so that the proletariat requires an approach that enables one to attend to its subjective development. With some reservations as to the implications of the term, it nonetheless summarizes better than any other the dominant trait of the proletariat. It is subjective in the sense that its comportment is not the simple consequence of the conditions [that objectively shape its] existence, or, more profoundly, the conditions that require of it a constant struggle for transformation. [One cannot define the working class by] constantly distinguishing its short-term fate. [Rather, the] struggle to elucidate the ideological [preconditions] that enable this distinguishing constitutes an experience through which the class constitutes itself.[23]

The subjective designates that which is eliminated by the reduction of the working class to a simple economic category entirely shaped by the position it occupies within industry, the ways in which the workers accommodate their situation and struggle to transform it. For Lefort, the subjective is the domain within which the bases for a working class 'for itself' are practically elaborated. Again, this class for itself is the fore structure of a revolutionary 'for itself' that would institute socialism. The analysis of this subjective domain posed

---

22   SB used phrases like this in a quite different sense than is current largely in interest group-based politics fashionable on American campuses. Its usage has nothing to do with the 'post modern' notion that subject positions are constituted discursively to such an extent that one can simply pick one out that best corresponds to the structure of affect – a variant of shopping in a 'free market' where 'rational actors' calculate their interests and buy (into) a politics off the rack. Such shopping need never call into question the system of distribution that supplies particular options to the exclusion of others, any more than one would be led to think about transnational capitalism by roaming the Gap. For SB, the goal was rather autonomy: the revolutionary project aspired to institute direct democracy, the political form within which autonomy might be operationally possible.

23   The last sentence is quite difficult to translate. It appears to try replacing a more Trotskyist mode of analysing worker struggles in terms of short-term prospects with a more abstract form of interrogation into the political or ideological preconditions that enabled Trotskyism – and others – to assess the 'meaning' of worker struggle. This reflexive, properly philosophical and open-ended mode of interrogation is posited here as the experience through which the class might develop. See Lefort 1952a, p. 6.

a methodological problem of isolating the particular dimensions of everyday experience on the shop floor to be analysed. It also posed a problem of data.

The everyday experience that concerned Socialisme ou Barbarie took place within informal collectives that formed by shop and by shift in modern industry. The collectives are the scenes out of which a given 'spontaneous comportment in the face of industrial work' or horizon structure emerges. The analysis of these collective comportments extends the rethinking of intentionality begun by Merleau-Ponty in *Phenomenology of Perception*, particularly in the section 'The Body as Expression and Speech'.[24] Merleau-Ponty transposed the Husserlian framework directly onto the problem of subjective orientation in the social-historical.[25] For Merleau-Ponty, Husserl's transcendental subject becomes a historically situated, embodied subject that moves through and constitutes a meaningful world. Intentionality, directedness toward/constitution of the world, is mapped onto the body as the source of spatial orientation, and the site upon which cultural meanings are written. This places intentionality between the personal and the social. By the seminars of the mid-1950s, in the context of a more general shift away from subject-centred thinking, Merleau-Ponty made intentionality explicitly social by reworking it through the notion of institution.[26] A subject is instituted in that it articulates itself and its world by way of specific pre-existing forms of rule-governed activity; a subject is instituting in that such an engagement is never simply a passive acceptance but is at once an operationalising of the rules and a creative bringing-into-being of the environment circumscribed by them.[27] The characteristics of what came to count as proletarian documentary literature mirror this in the preference for a sense of an embodied narrator who uses a suitably working-class language in the present tense, capturing sightlines and a sense of movement through the spaces that are staged.

---

24   Merleau-Ponty 1965, Chapter 6.
25   From Merleau-Ponty's viewpoint, Heidegger's effort to push the inquiry about the nature of the copula into a single general question of Being could be viewed as itself an effort to institute a transcendental philosophy of finitude. On how difficult it is to separate what philosophy says from what it does institutionally, see Frangois Dosse 1991 and Descombes 1979. Both detail the consequences of Merleau-Ponty's thinking as opening the field for structuralist anthropology to take over the position formerly occupied by philosophy.
26   The notion of institution as used by Merleau-Ponty derives from a reading of Husserl 1970. See Merleau-Ponty 1970. The seminars on the notion of institution have since been published as Merleau-Ponty 2002 and 1998. See also Howard 1988, p. 167.
27   The notion of rules in relation to particular language games is an important theme explored in Wittgenstein's *Philosophical Investigations*, which could be profitably crossvoiced with Merleau-Ponty's thinking in this regard.

Lefort regarded the working class 'for itself' as a practical creation elaborated on a continual basis through the play of general patterns of assimilation and conflict characteristic of experience at the point of production under bureaucratic capitalism. The notion that the '*sens*' of working-class experience was its 'ever increasing capacity to direct' served as a premise and a sort of filter that enabled Lefort to order experience as an analytic problem. Lefort argues that the particular working class 'for itself' manifests itself as a viewpoint linked directly to particular practices. The notion of practice can be broken into two components: a narrow or immanent level and another, implicit level that unifies practices and gives them a direction. At the more immanent level, it refers to the actual working at a machine, the repertoire of motions and decisions required to perform a given task. This immanent level is situated in a larger ensemble of social relations and practices that socially and informally regulate, inform and organise both relations among workers and the performance of work. These practices shape the deployment of skill as a collective attribute, the pace of work and so forth. This same register of practice shapes relations between workers and the representatives of factory management: foremen, time-motion men (chronos), and industrial organisation generally.[28] Central to the acquisition of these practices was the process of socialisation that shaped the relationships of workers to each other, to production and to politics. Workers who operate in environments shaped by these patterns of socialisation and circumscribed by these practices occupy an instituted and instituting 'proletarian standpoint'.

The other, latent register of worker experience is given its coherence in part by the degree of familiarity on the part of workers (or, more precisely, of worker writers) with the history of the workers' movement, which stands in for familiarity with the Marxist discourse that oriented this history as a political project.[29] This broader history stands in contrast to the instituted manifestations of a version of that history in the (bureaucratic) trade unions and main political organisations that use versions of that same discourse – the PCF and

---

28 This distinction between practices narrowly construed and that which unifies them, gives them a direction (a *sens*), the domain out of which they emerge and relative to which they acquire meaning has been elaborated in various ways. Merleau-Ponty does so in 'Cezanne's Doubt' in Merleau-Ponty 1964a or on Matisse in 1964b through his notion of 'l'oeuvre'. Lefort later took up the same issue in his work on Machiavelli (l'oeuvre of Machiavelli is the creation of the political). Developing in a separate direction, Castoriadis, following Freud, refers to this dimension of social practice as signification, that which brings into relation.

29 Lefort 1979a, pp. 91–2.

CGT in particular in the French context. Familiarity with this broader tradition provides space for alternate 'activations' of a heavily sedimented language that, by its sedimentation, provides a sense of legitimation. An example of this is the role played in the 1953 East Berlin June Days by the study circles devoted to reading Marx and Lenin directly rather than as mediated through official catechisms. In the analyses published in *Socialisme ou Barbarie*, these collective readings formed a horizon of instituted signifiers that enabled the articulation of political positions in revolutionary language outside the purview of the main bureaucratic organisations. Insofar as Socialisme ou Barbarie was concerned the reappropriation of this language was a condition of possibility for autonomous worker action, and an indication of the extent to which at this time the group understood it as a natural horizon against which these actions could take shape. Autonomous worker actions, then, instituted alternate interpretations of the language that structured the history of the workers' movement. In this, they were Socialisme ou Barbarie's proletarian doubles.

Socialisme ou Barbarie never explicitly said who these workers were: we will return to this point in the second part of this chapter. However, it is clear that when Socialisme ou Barbarie referred to the working class, they had in mind primarily semi-skilled workers like machinists and lathe operators.[30] In a context dominated by assembly-line production, these workers were under sustained attack. Semi-skilled workers worked in collectives, and not in the individuated image of Fordism. They retained some autonomy in the conception and execution of their work, though the extent of this autonomy varied considerably from factory to factory, and within the same factory as a function of the shop's place in the factory hierarchy. This autonomy enabled these shops to develop types of sociability that were for the most part tied to the transmission of skill. However, as French heavy industry, led by Renault, increasingly adopted American industrial organisation during the 1950s, the struggles of these workers to retain their autonomy and skill became more acute. The explosions engendered by this struggle were among the most intense and violent of the decade.[31]

These conflicts over the autonomy of semi-skilled workers within mass production were a continuation of what Benjamin Coriat called Fordism's war on

---

30 On the French salary scale, occupying the rankings of P1–P3.

31 The shipyard strikes in St. Nazaire and Nantes during the summer of 1955, for example, were triggered by Penhoët (and the state's) efforts to increase cadences by redesigning production in such a way as to tie together the wages and functions of workers involved with various stages of welding despite some operations being simpler and faster than others. See Oury 1973 and the accounts of the strikes published in *SB* no. 18 (Jan–Mar 1956).

skill, which he argues was the defining feature of its mode of industrial organisation. The genius of Henry Ford, from a capitalist viewpoint, was his reconceptualisation of skill as a block on accumulation. Ford's methods did not develop in isolation, but rather appear as a condensed expression of experiments in organisation that arose with monopoly capitalism. Previously, skill had been monopolised by workers. This monopoly lay at the heart of a contractual relation between them and employers: employers were beholden to worker as the actual source of wealth and workers were beholden to employers as providers of the means to exercise their skills.[32] The automobile industry, a product of monopoly capitalism, played a crucial role in developing the mechanisms by means of which the assault on skill was carried out. Henry Ford led the way in this domain with his aim of producing a low-cost automobile. Standardisation of product enabled standardisation of production process, which in turn made possible the assembly line. The assembly line initiated a massive transfer of initiative away from workers into management and wiped out previously sacrosanct limits to the rationalisation of production.[33] Most indicative of this pattern was the fact that Fordist industrial organisation encouraged the spatial separation of research and development from production, putting them into different buildings, and often in different towns, as a function of the more general trend of vertical integration.[34]

Technological developments closely tracked these organisational innovations in delimiting the situation of semi-skilled workers under Fordism. Machine tools were increasingly designed as variations on the lathe. Having learned to turn, a worker could with relative ease shift to another machine and pick up the necessary movements.[35] In hindsight, it is clear that the standardisation of tool design was a first step in both the standardisation and routinisation of tasks.[36] In French heavy industry of the mid-1950s,

---

32 Coriat 1979, pp. 16ff.
33 On the role of the automobile industry as leading edge of technological, organisational and demand changes in the twentieth century, see Bardou et al., 1982. For a litany of preconditions that allowed the American automobile industry to shape this revolution in industrial organisation, see Chapter 6.
34 On this process at Renault, see Freyssenet, 1979.
35 See Romano, p. 40. See also Touraine 1955 for a more detailed version of the same argument in the context of Renault's Billancourt factory.
36 This was often more true on paper than in actual factories. By the time covered in Touraine's book on work at Billancourt, it had become an awkward combination of advanced design and heavily modified older machinery that required an unusually large section of machinists simply to maintain – rather like the Boston MTA does today. A more thoroughgoing Fordisation of production could not be adapted to such conditions:

implementation of industrial Fordism rapidly changed overall production design; in the introduction of management; and in the imposition of a new division of labour that separated intellectual and manual work. Changes in tool design facilitated the atomisation of the factory itself into isolated units concerned with maximum rationalisation of what were initially component parts of the larger production process. The standardisation of tasks and increased specialisation of technology reopened the politics of wage rates and production speed. It also sparked, with more political variability, a move to integrate and depoliticise trade unions through the mechanism of collective bargaining. In these larger contexts, the fate of the machinists played a small, but symbolically important part.

Socialisme ou Barbarie collectively believed the relative professional autonomy of semi-skilled workers enabled them to develop the type of informal shop-floor culture presupposed by any revolutionary project that did not assume the intervention of a Vanguard Party. Therefore, when the group inquired into worker experience, they referred to semi-skilled workers in the context of Fordist mass production, the most advanced form of industrial organisation of the period. In this, they conformed to a general tendency of the French Left. *Les métallos* were, for the most part, French, and were highly politicised and volatile.[37] French heavy industry recruited and increasingly relied upon an immigrant workforce on the assembly-line. This policy set up political, cultural and professional fractures within the factory that Socialisme ou Barbarie member Daniel Mothé (Jacques Gautrat) wrote about candidly in 1956.[38] For Socialisme ou Barbarie, it was in general more significant that assembly-line work was unskilled. The lack of skill and collective life in the context of production as well as the nature of line work itself were more important than the plurality of ethnicities, nationalities and languages in preventing these workers from acting collectively. Like most French Left organisations, Socialisme ou Barbarie did not focus on the unskilled OS workers on the line.[39]

---

it was therefore cheaper and easier simply to build a new factory at Flins based on newer conceptions and employing more up-to-date equipment. When Flins opened in 1952, the writing was in a sense already on the wall for Billancourt. Demonstration that transitions take time: Billancourt, the closing of which was announced in 1980, closed in 1992, the same week EuroDisney opened.

37   For the French Left, the *métallo* was the quintessential revolutionary militant.
38   Mothé 1958, pp. 146ff.
39   These would only later be targeted by Maoist 'établis' after 1968. Les etablis were Maoist students who got jobs on factory assembly lines in order to be with the workers in the period following May 68. See Linhardt 1978. Dubost 1979 provides an interesting and

On Worker Narratives and Proletarian Experience

> Text means Tissue; but whereas hitherto we have always taken this tissue as a product, a ready-made veil, behind which lies, more or less hidden, meaning (truth), we are now emphasizing, in the tissue, the generative idea that the text is made, is worked out in a perpetual interweaving; lost in this tissue – this texture – the subject unmakes himself, like a spider dissolving in the constructive secretions of its web. Were we fond of neologisms, we might define the theory of the text as a hypology (hyphos is the tissue and the spider's web).[40]

The worker narratives that Socialisme ou Barbarie envisioned collecting would combine first person observation of shop-floor experience with an anthropological perspective on the processes that shaped that experience and a sociological view of industrial organisation. The worker/writer of such narratives had to be both involved with, and detached from, the experience described. The narratives were to be autobiographical and descriptive of worker experience generally. The descriptions provided by any one narrative would have obvious limitations with respect to completeness and universality.[41] Many narratives gathered together might overcome these limitations. A phenomenology of these texts would provide the general structure of worker comportments at the point of production as reproduced in these narratives and shaped by their genre. What Socialisme ou Barbarie wanted was a window onto factory experience that would enable them to see how workers processed structural conditions as horizons. Further, Socialisme ou Barbarie wanted access to the interaction of appropriation and resistance constitutive of the proletarian standpoint. The analysis would acquire its significance from the larger revolutionary project.

In 'Proletarian Experience', Lefort argues that a feature of the 'radical originality of the proletariat' is that it can only be known by itself. Consequently, others may understand the working class only on its terms and in its language. From this premise follows the necessity of interpreting worker writing. However, these texts were not without problems:

---

        oddly moving account of the conditions among immigrant workers on the line at Flins and of the disastrous mistakes the Maoists made while trying to organise them.

40   Barthes 1975.
41   Lefort 1979a, pp. 87–8.

> This does not mean that we will claim to define what the proletariat is in its reality from this angle, after having rejected all other representations that have been made of its condition, which view it either through the deforming prism of bourgeois society or that of the Parties that claim to represent it. A worker testimony, no matter how evocative, symbolic and spontaneous it might be, remains conditioned by the situation of its source. We are not alluding to the deformation that can come from an individual interpretation, but to that which narration necessarily imposes on its author. Telling is necessarily not acting, and even supposes a break with action that transforms its meaning. Making a narrative about a strike is entirely different from participating in a strike, if only because one then knows the outcome, and the simple distance of reflection enables one to evaluate what had not, in the moment, yet become fixed in its meaning. In fact, this is much more than a simple change of opinion: it is a change of attitude, that is to say a transformation in the manner of reacting to situations in which one finds oneself. To this must be added that narrative places the individual in an isolated position which is not natural to him either (...) Critique of a testimony must precisely enable one to see in the individual's attitudes that which implies the comportment of the group. However, in the last analysis, the former does not coincide exactly with the latter, and we have access only to incomplete knowledge.[42]

For Lefort, the basic issue is not defining what the proletariat is or substituting a new, better representation for existing ones, because the class cannot be an object of this type of knowledge. He argues that 'knowing' the working class is more 'being-with'. It is an imaginative transformation, carried out through reading and critique. Knowing the working class transforms the reader into a specular 'participant observer'.[43]

A vicarious 'acquisition' of the proletarian standpoint and its constituent practices is hindered by the necessary incompleteness of any given narrative. Such incompleteness is a result of perspectivalism and of the suspension of the 'natural attitude' implicit in the act of writing. To paraphrase from the quoted passage above: 'Writing about an action is not to act within it and

---

42   Lefort 1979a, p. 90.
43   The classic statement on participant observer sociology is Whyte 1993. More recent examples include David Simons and Edward Burns: *The Corner: A Year in the Life of an Inner City Neighborhood* (New York: Random House, 1998). Wacquant 2006 is a lovely demonstration of what can be done with this form.

presupposes a break with acting that transforms its meaning'. For a worker to adopt an anthropological relation to his own experience as worker places him inside and outside that experience at the same time. The writer retrospectively orders experience by writing it: experience is no longer an open-ended relation to a context on the part of an embedded subject who interprets and makes judgments about it based on incomplete information.[44] The consequence of this retrospective character is to render contingent aspects of human experience as necessary elements by giving experience a dramatic or narrative form. Doing so eliminates the space for creativity.[45] Not only is writing necessarily retrospective, but it re-orders and spatialises the environment in particular ways and re-temporalises experience according to criteria internal to the process of narration and the type of narrative being produced. While Lefort acknowledges these mediations, the real question for him does not concern the gap that might be thereby instituted between text and experience. Rather, the main problem facing the critic/reader is in recognising and bridging the divide that separates the 'unnaturally isolated' writing worker from the necessarily social character of that which is described. The role of phenomenological analysis is to search for traces of the collective comportments within individual, fragmentary accounts.

For Lefort, the worker writer is the phenomenologist's accomplice who sorts out, compares and reduces. He (almost always he) transforms experience into data from which a second order critique can derive fragments of 'authentic' experience. At the same time the worker writer remains a worker, writing like a worker, describing factory conditions in a recognizably 'prolo' manner. The worker writer is the critic's double: the critic watches the worker watching; the critic appropriates what the worker describes.[46] The writing worker is a vehicle for the militant/critic's identification with the workers, an identification given content through the discovery of their practices, the adoption of their standpoint and the theorisation of their self-production. Haunted by the fear of reverting to a form of Leninism, Lefort confines the revolutionary militant to the role of phenomenological observer. However, this same identification is encouraged and exacerbated by the formal characteristics of the narratives

---

44 This is the peril of the instituting. On this theme, see Castoriadis 1998 *passim*.
45 Consider the difference between a musical improvisation and a recording of an improvisation. See also Merleau-Ponty 'Indirect Language and the Voices of Silence' in Merleau-Ponty 1964b on the gap which separates Matisse painting from a film of Matisse painting and the wholesale transformations of meanings that accompany the passage from open-ended creative work to the representation of open-ended creative work.
46 I think the motif of doubling was inspired by Rancière 1981.

that Lefort treats as primary evidence. To show how this part of the circuit operates, we take up the two texts that Lefort considered exemplary: Paul Romano's 1947 'The American Worker' and Eric Albert's 1952 'Témoignage: la vie en usine'.

Socialisme ou Barbarie member Philippe Guillaume introduced his translation of Paul Romano's 'The American Worker' with: 'Nous présentons ici un document de grande valeur sur la vie des ouvriers américains'. The pamphlet's value, Guillaume argues, lay first of all in its demolition of the 'Hollywood and *Readers' Digest*' illusion that the American worker, rich and without class consciousness, is a living example of the benefits of class collaboration. More than this, Guillaume argues that Romano has produced the first example of a new 'proletarian documentary literature'. This documentary literature holds a mirror up to workers that reflects (politically) significant elements within their experience back to them in their own language. The pamphlet addresses the reader by soliciting recognition. Guillaume repeats this gesture, and it is repeated a number of times thereafter, before Romano's narrative actually begins. Guillaume writes:

> Every worker, regardless of 'his nationality' of exploitation, will find in it the image of his own existence as proletarian. There are, in fact, deep and consistent characteristics of proletarian alienation that know no frontiers ... The translator of this small brochure himself has worked several years in the factory. He was struck by the accuracy and the important implications of every line. It is impossible for a worker to remain indifferent to this reading. In our eyes, it is not by accident that such a sample of proletarian documentary literature comes to us from America, and it is also not by accident that it is, in some of its deepest aspects, the first of the genre.[47]

Near the end of this quote, Guillaume repeats the Marxist axiom that the most advanced industrial setting will produce the most advanced forms of worker resistance. These advanced forms of opposition, and their potentials for new modes of class consciousness, are reflected in the creation of a new form of written expression.[48] This new form of expression is itself reflective of the transition within the industrial working class away from more traditional types of political (revolutionary) action which amounts to postulating that a new revolutionary avant garde is developing out of worker experience of technol-

---

47   Guillaume 1949, p. 78.
48   Ibid.

ogy, conventional political parties, trade unions, and so on, at the point of production. All this is implicit in Guillaume's statement but it is made explicit in Ria Stone's 'The Reconstruction of Society', the extended theoretical essay that accompanied Romano's narrative in its original American edition.[49]

From the outset, Romano is presented as a part of a new 'revolutionary tide' rising within the American working class. The elision of the particular into the general is made all the more attractive by his use of a pseudonym or 'war name'. These names were normal amongst the anti-Stalinist left in both the U.S. and France. Within Socialisme ou Barbarie, adoption of an alias was simply a matter of tactical necessity. It should be kept in mind that revolutionary political activity amongst intellectuals occurred in a semi-clandestine zone. Groups were subject to surveillance by the political arm of the Parisian Police, the 'Renseignements Généraux'. Socialisme ou Barbarie included a number of foreigners who were actively engaged in a type of political activity that could get them deported, like Castoriadis and Alberto Maso (Véga).[50] These groups were also subject to surveillance and repression from the PCF. Anti-Stalinist politics in a PCF-dominated environment, like Renault's Billancourt factory, could pose real physical and career dangers to those who engaged in it.[51] These pressures affected different people in different ways, and Lefort is interesting in this regard. A philosophy professor during the day, he initially published in *Socialisme ou Barbarie* under the name C. Montal. He began to use his real name more frequently after leaving *Les Temps Modernes* in 1952, and exclusively after 1956.

The names take on another, quite independent function in the reading of these narratives. Scant information was provided about Paul Romano, the pamphlet's author. Even in 1972, in a preface to a new edition of the pamphlet, Martin Glaberman would only say that Romano was active in the Johnson-Forest Tendency, and worked at a General Motors factory in New Jersey that employed about 800 production workers.[52] The Introduction to the first edition, signed J.H., describes Romano as:

> Himself a factory worker, [who] has contributed greatly to such understanding [of 'what the workers are thinking and doing while actually at

---

49   Boggs 1972 was originally published along with Romano 1972. It was translated by Guillaume and published in *SB* nos. 7 and 8 (1950–1951). See the pamphlet's final flourishes.
50   Interviews with most members of *SB*, Véga in particular. This theme of the pseudonym recurs more extensively in Chapter 6 below.
51   Interview with Pierre Blachier. On this, see Chapters 5 and 6.
52   Martin Glaberman, Introduction to Romano 1972, p. v.

work on the bench or on the line'] by his description, based on years of study and observation of the lives of workers in modem mass production. The profundity of Romano's contribution lies not in making any new discovery but rather in seeing the obvious – the constant and daily raging of the workers against the degrading and oppressive conditions of their life in the factory; and at the same time, their creative and elemental drive to reconstruct society on a new and higher level.[53]

Romano's own opening paragraphs repeat this operation in a somewhat more complex manner:

> I am a young worker in my late 20s. The past several years have found me in the productive apparatus of the most highly industrialised country in the world. Most of my working years have been spent in mass production industries among hundreds and thousands of other workers. Their feelings, anxieties, exhilaration, boredom, exhaustion, anger, have all been mine to one extent or another. By 'their feelings' I mean those which are the direct reactions to modern high-speed production. The present finds me still in a factory – one of the giant corporations in the country.
>
> This pamphlet is addressed to the rank and file worker and its intention is to express those innermost thoughts which the worker rarely talks about even to his fellow workers. In keeping a diary, so to speak, of the day-to-day factory life I hoped to uncover the reasons for the worker's deep dissatisfaction which has reached its peak in recent years and has expressed itself in the latest strikes and spontaneous walkouts.
>
> The rough draft of this pamphlet was given to workers across the country. Their reactions were as one. They were surprised and gratified to see in print the experiences and thoughts which they have rarely put into words. Workers arrive home from the factory too exhausted to read more than the daily comics. Yet most of the workers who read the pamphlet stayed up well into the night to finish the reading once they had started.[54]

The first three sentences contain all the particular information we are given. From this point on, the individual is blurred into the collective, and vice-versa. For example, Romano claims to describe 'the innermost thoughts which the

---

53   J.H. Preface to Romano 1972, p. viii.
54   Romano 1972, p. 1. We return to this shortly.

worker rarely talks about even to his fellow workers'. The accuracy of such description is, in Husserlian language, intersubjectively verified, established quasi-scientifically, by means of a straw-poll of 'workers around the country' who stayed up late to read it because they (who? where?) recognised themselves in the writing. 'Paul Romano' itself is a nearly arbitrary name, a proper name that does not signify, that does not limit, that does not help establish some reference point around which to stabilise the shifting border between experience and writing about experience. The author, Paul Romano, is an empty function that generates propositions in the form 'the worker feels x...'; 'the workers see y...every day'. We are presented with a claim to a sort of 'lateral verification'. The workers stayed up late to read these propositions.

Romano delimits his intended audience in another way through the paragraphs on intellectuals.[55] The pamphlet is a conversation between workers: intellectuals 'so removed from the daily experience of the laboring masses' could not be sympathetic to its content. Romano argues that: 'They felt cheated' because there was 'too much dirt and noise'. This characterisation places the phenomenologist-cum-revolutionary militant, who in all probability has a romantic attachment to the idea of dirt and noise, in an ambiguous position. He seems to approximate an eavesdropper listening in on a telephone conversation between two others during which they begin to make disparaging remarks that could be about the silent third party. There is a certain voyeurism that attends looking at the 'elemental drive' of the working class in process through the act of reading. At the same time, the reader is encouraged to side with the workers, to embark on a voyage accompanied by a trusted native informant.

The pseudonym functions to turn the author into a contentless variable, an observing machine that generates a trail of propositions about factory life. I have argued above that there is a structural doubling of the militant/critic in the writing worker, and powerful political reasons for the former to project himself into the position made available within the narratives by the latter. The arbitrariness of the proper name in this context removes any brake that might otherwise have been set up on this identification by information on the empirical life of the author.[56] This identification, staged at the level of relation between militant/critic as phenomenologist and the worker writer, is furthered by the narrative's use of 'prolo' language. Philippe Guillaume touched on this issue again in his brief translator's preface, and on some of the problems he encountered while translating Romano's English:

---

55   Ibid.
56   Barthes 1968.

> It is impossible for a worker to remain indifferent to this reading. It is even more impossible to translate such a text in an indifferent, or even routine, manner. At several junctures, it was necessary to take a considerable distance from the letter of the English text to provide a really faithful translation. Some American popular expressions have an exact correspondent in French, but embedded in different imagery. Even in his descriptive style, Romano uses a proletarian optic.[57]

The translation problem in moving from popular American to a parallel French while not dissolving Romano's 'proletarian optic' was resolved in such a way as to make the version published in *Socialisme ou Barbarie* an interesting primer in 'prolo' French for an American reader. It also functions as a second order legitimation of Romano's status as worker, something which would go without saying were the pamphlet actually being transmitted worker to worker. For whom need a 'proletarian optic' be defined?

The various prefaces and introductions to Romano's pamphlet are important because they make explicit what is usually left unsaid in these narratives and is worked out at the level of style and through the manipulation of certain conventions. Once past these introductions, we encounter Romano's narrative proper. Here we shift to a more structural analysis, reading Romano along with Eric Albert's 'Témoignage: la vie en usine', published in the July 1952 issue of *Les Temps Modernes*, to isolate several common features that operate as genre markers informing/shaping 'proletarian documentary literature' as collected or generated by Socialisme ou Barbarie.[58]

In several ways, Albert's narrative is quite different from that of Romano. It was written for a different audience – the educated, progressive bourgeois readership of *Les Temps Modernes*. A journalistic exposé of conditions inside the newer types of factories, combined with elements of a travel narrative, it documents Albert's experience as an o.s. (an unskilled worker). Albert worked in two different factories owned by the same cable manufacturing company near Paris. The first, in which Albert learns his job, is older, roughly on the order of Billancourt; the second is a more recent building and an example of Fordist organisation on the order of Flins.

The point of Albert's narrative emerges through the contrast between his experiences in the two factories, which are staged as emblematic of the past and future of factory design. The former allowed a margin for worker auton-

---

57   Guillaume 1949.
58   Albert 1952, pp. 95–130.

omy, and thereby the creation of the types of informal shop and shift-specific collectivities that are the focus of Romano's writing. The latter offers no such margin. Its layout is entirely subordinated to what Albert calls the 'geometrical requirements of the machinery'.[59] Albert uses his experience to reveal the inhumanity, and the political danger for the left, of Fordist factory design from the vantage point of an unskilled worker. Romano's narrative, on the other hand, consists mostly of detailed descriptions of informal shop-floor communities from the viewpoint of a semi-skilled worker (who would be in the range of a P1–P3 according to the French professional hierarchy). Romano uses these descriptions to winnow out the political implications of their collective life.

There are thus significant divergences between the two narratives that Lefort takes as exemplary in 'Proletarian Experience'. There was an enormous gulf that separated the experience of an o.s. from that of a P1–P3 worker. The accounts were written for different assumed audiences. There is also a political difference between the two. It is difficult to pinpoint Albert's political viewpoint. He appears at times to be an old-style anarcho-syndicalist whose politics come from the pre-World War II period, and who is still attached to the traditions of the 'worker aristocracy'. At other times, he appears to have simply read a lot of material like Michel Collinet's 1950 *Esprit du syndicalisme*.[60] Romano's affiliation with 'Correspondence' would position him closer to Socialisme ou Barbarie.[61]

That said, the narratives nonetheless share a number of formal characteristics, though each deploys these features in a different order. This variation can serve as an index of the writer's political affiliation or aspirations. For example, consider the location of the initiation scene. Romano's narrative begins:

> The factory worker lives and breathes dirt and oil. As machines are speeded up, the noise becomes greater, the strain greater, the labor greater, even though the process is simplified. Most steel cutting and grinding machines of today require a lubricant to facilitate machining

---

59   Albert 1952, pp. 98–101. This section in Albert is an exact mirroring of a similar section in Georges Navels 1945 autobiography *Travaux*, which recounts his experiences in factories on either side of World War I. On Navel, see the section on proletarian literature in Chapter 6.

60   I know nothing about Eric Albert. The possibility of being an anarcho-syndicalist comes from pp. 125ff: Albert discusses what he considers to be the significant political tradition lost to younger workers in anarchist writers like Proudhon, Bakunin, Jules Vallès, Collinet and Friedmann. He also outlines on p. 117 an anarchist take on the Popular Front.

61   See Chapter 5 for an extended discussion of *Correspondence*.

the material. It is commonplace to put on a clean set of clothes in the morning and by noon to be soaked, literally, with oil. Most workers in my department have oil pimples, rashes and sores on their arms and legs. The shoes become soaked and the result is a steady case of athlete's foot. Blackheads fill the pores. It is an extremely aggravating set of effects. We speak often of sitting and soaking in a hot tub of water to loosen the dirt and ease the infectious blackheads.

In most factories the worker freezes in the winter, sweats in the summer and often does not have hot water to wash the day's grime from his body...[62]

This paragraph introduces two fundamental characteristics of Romano's narrative, and of these narratives in general. The universal and the particular are intertwined in a complex manner. The universal appears through the propositional form 'the worker lives...'; 'most workers in my department have oil pimples...'; 'we speak often....' The particular appears through Romano's evocation of pain. This usage of pain is a bit surprising, given its extreme particularity, its incommunicability, its tendency to 'unmake the world' available to the subject by forcing the body (roughly following Merleau-Ponty's notion of the body as social and spatial orientation for a subject) back onto itself. Another's pain is most distant from oneself.[63]

The collective first-person pronouns function in Romano's text to shift identification onto a very immediate level. The reader/militant/critic is encouraged to project himself into the empty space outlined by the author as generator of propositions, but left empty because of the arbitrariness of the proper name. The tone of the descriptions is on the order of: you and I know the extreme noise, the stress induced by machine speed-ups; the rashes and pimples caused by inadequate facilities and poor ventilation. The reader is squarely on the shop floor. Albert's narrative opens with a structurally similar 'reduction of the subject'. Because the piece is not designed as explicitly to draw the reader into the experience being described, though it is not without its vivid moments, the reader's initiation into the Textual Factory can be more abstract. Albert's experience is presented as universal in a rather different way: I ran out of money. I had to get a job. I got hired at this place. Here is what happened: 'When one no longer knows what to do to make a living, all that remains is finding a job as

---

62   Romano 1972, p. 3.
63   This discussion leans heavily on Scarry 1985.

an O.S. That is why I found myself one day on a street outside the large door of a cable-making plant, along with about twenty other men...'[64]

The intertwining of the universal and particular is repeated at the level of framing information. Romano's text features extremely detailed accounts of worker responses to concrete problems (using steel pipe to smash closed windows that should be open to provide ventilation) and resistance (the informally organised slow-downs accompanying the arrival of the time-study men [chronos in French] because everyone knows that working up to or over speed is self-defeating and results only in increased production quotas and cadences). In the section 'Why Such Inefficiency?' Romano provides descriptions of the shop-floor view of overall industrial organisation. These accounts are situated within a 'shop floor' that is itself decontextualised. The reader is provided with no information about where these acts occur, either within the geography of the factory (workers simply do this) or in the world (not a word).[65]

However, the shop floor is situated rather carefully with respect to the Abstract Factory that is produced within or by the text. The Abstract Factory is elaborated along one of two general lines. In the writings of Albert and Vivier, a sociologising gaze surveys the entirety of the Factory from top to bottom and generates a typology of worker strata and various personality types.[66] In the other pattern, the Abstract Factory is described from the standpoint of a particular shop. For Romano and Mothé, the Abstract Factory functions to legitimate and give content to the 'proletarian standpoint', which is a narrative position. The Factory environment locates the reader on the shop floor. The presentation of other workers from this narrative viewpoint is also presentation of types, but one that serves to fill out the reader's experience of the textual shop-floor. In his texts published in *Socialisme ou Barbarie* several years later, Mothé was able to take this much further than Romano, as will be seen in the next parts of my presentation, because the prominence of Billancourt for Parisian left politics enabled him to avoid having to stage the entirety of the Abstract Factory and because his writings appeared as a series of articles that frequently involved the same shop and characters. Mothé's readers become almost comfortable with them: they comprise something of a repertoire company.

---

64   Albert 1952, pp. 98–100.
65   Romano 1972, pp. 14–15.
66   Albert's typological chapters are entitled 'Les anciens', 'Les jeunes' etc. Vivier follows much the same model. That Viver's narrative is relatively ignored in subsequent development is indicative, I think, of SB's collective relation to this type of writing. See Albert 1952, pp. 118–26.

The point where the worker enters the effective life of the shop floor is also the moment the reader enters the 'interior'. The initiation scene in 'The American Worker' is retrospective, and is staged as an account of relations between a neophyte and the political culture of the shop:

> The Workers' Organization
>
> I arrived in the plant several weeks after the 'Big Strike' had ended. Things were tense for several weeks. Newcomers were eyed with suspicion by both workers and company so soon after the strike. My first day in the plant found me waiting in one of the departments for the foreman. A worker sauntered over to me. In a very brief discussion, he tried to determine my attitude toward unions. I shook him off and he walked away. His speech made it clear that he was anti-union. Union men made themselves conspicuous by their avoidance of newcomers.[67]

Romano only stays on this threshold for a paragraph: having passed an initial test, he is soon integrated into the political structure of the shop. This is a crucial passage in the pamphlet, as it marks more than Romano's passage into the interior of shop-floor life. The section of which this is the opening quickly turns to a detailed discussion of the gap that separates the union hierarchy from the shop floor; It is also a demonstration of, and argument for, the existence of a class perspective tied to this shop life and independent of union organisation and ideology. Only after establishing this perspective does Romano undertake his survey of the Abstract Factory: the function of this survey is the legitimation of the viewpoint from which it is carried out. The political implications of the position of the initiation scene can be seen by counterposing Romano to Albert. Albert's narrative conforms much more explicitly to the conventions of a travel narrative: the encounter, the threshold moment, the unanticipated test and passage into the interior all happen at the beginning. This passage into the interior is explicitly linked with the acquisition of skill, where this link remains a pervasive assumption only made explicit in Romano's final pages.[68]

At this point, a recapitulation. Lefort's essay is fundamental to understanding Socialisme ou Barbarie's efforts to gain access to and think about worker experience as the basis for a type of political work that did not subordinate this experience to the Higher Historical wisdom of the Party. Lefort's approach to worker narratives, and his phenomenology of worker experience that frames

---

67   Romano 1972, p. 21.
68   Romano 1972, pp. 34–41.

FRAME: ON CLAUDE LEFORT'S 'L'EXPÉRIENCE PROLÉTARIENNE' 133

it, would have combined the careful gathering and collating of texts with a sophisticated theory of reading. His theoretical framework was also shot through with problems of uncontrolled identification/projection. Efforts to control for this projection were impeded by the narrowness of the sample the group was able to collect. This small data set meant that, while the phenomenological apparatus was in place, the reductions themselves really could not be undertaken. The possibility remains that a more detailed phenomenological description of the 'proletarian standpoint', based on reductions performed with a larger data set, could have significantly reduced, or eliminated, the space for projection. Because Socialisme ou Barbarie's project belongs to the past, we cannot know.

Lefort's approach to the question of interpreting worker narratives as windows onto shop-floor experience took as central the problem of knowledge about social-historical phenomena, understood as spatially and temporally imbricated processes that entail or produce meaning structures or what Castoriadis would later call social-imaginary significations. Lefort's use of phenomenology to analyse these texts cut two ways. By focusing on them in terms shaped by the situation of their production, it allowed for the development of some interesting and fruitful conceptualisations, particularly in thinking about practice, which was the domain Socialisme ou Barbarie wanted to analyse as the everyday 'ground' of its revolutionary project. The situating of practice and how it unfolds within both the immanent and (potentially) revolutionary contexts at once clarifies the orientation of revolutionary theory with respect to the present. At the same time, Lefort's focus on the conditions of their production and indications of worker creativity, patterns of self-organisation and orientations toward the future entailed a curious neglect of these texts as texts, and of the experience of being a reader of them. At the same time as it enabled an isolation of potentials for revolutionary creativity, the phenomenology of worker narratives formalised a projective relation between analyst/critic/militant and worker. This projective relationship repeated within the texts, in the gaps that separated their extreme precision about concrete shop-floor experience and its presentation in a decontextualised, abstract manner, that is in precisely the way these narratives gave Socialisme ou Barbarie, as a community of readers (like ourselves), access to the shop floor, the proletarian standpoint, and the 'games' in the context of which that standpoint was instituted.

Lefort's phenomenology of worker narratives bracketed from the outset the possibility that this type of self-reflexive writing was as much a literary construction (a set of genre rules and expectations) as an account of actual experience. By treating these narratives as phenomenological data for a series of reductions that never get underway, Lefort's approach sets Socialisme ou

Barbarie up for a wholesale confusion of the signified of the narratives' discourse with the referent, taking for 'objective' history that which is highly mediated and processed through certain linguistic and generic conventions. The signified would be the internal world of the narrative, the Abstract Factory, the decontextualised shop floor, the Workers as types or as individual atoms, the upsurging revolutionary wave sweeping across the American working class, the formation of a class consciousness closely linked to the production of significations on the shop floor outside of and in direct opposition to the existing workers' movement. The referent would be the actual factory experience of Paul Romano or Eric Albert. The relation between the two would be difficult enough to establish even were Romano and Albert present in Socialisme ou Barbarie, as will be seen by way of Gautrat/Mothé. Here, the relation is undecidable. That Socialisme ou Barbarie took these narratives as direct accounts of experience, whose constructed character is simply a function of the temporal gap that separated the worker within a specific situation from that same worker writing about that situation, testifies to the power of what Roland Barthes called the 'realism effect' of these narratives.[69]

---

[69] See Barthes 1981.

CHAPTER 4

Working-Class Politics at Renault Billancourt

We Stop Briefly to Consult a Map

Socialisme ou Barbarie saw itself as operating in a new situation after the summer of 1953. The emergence of new forms of autonomous working-class action was the defining characteristic of this shift. The East Berlin June Days was the most politically advanced of these. The privileging of East Berlin followed from two assumptions, one explicit and the other tacit. The explicit assumption was that western, fragmented bureaucratic capitalism was tending toward consolidation. Bureaucratic capitalism in its Soviet and Eastern European forms was, in a sense, the future. The tacit assumption was that, while these autonomous actions resulted from conflicts set off by attempts to rationalise and deskill work, what made them potentially revolutionary was their re-appropriation of Marxist language.

Over the next years, the pages of *Socialisme ou Barbarie* reported on this new situation with a collage of reports and analytic essays on autonomous worker actions. While the actions themselves were spatially dispersed, their juxtaposition in the journal brought their commonalities to the fore. In the new situation, workers opposed not only conventional bureaucratic political parties and trade unions but also the types of politics they practiced. Workers expressed their opposition through their direct-democratic forms of self-organisation as well as in the demands they generated. The main events of the period – East Berlin 1953, St. Nazaire and Nantes 1955, destalinisation, Poznan and Hungary 1956 – organised these reports into a mounting wave of worker revolutionary action. The group took the Hungarian Revolution as its culmination.

Socialisme ou Barbarie saw in autonomous worker actions evidence of great revolutionary potential, the elucidation of which was the principal task confronting revolutionary theory. The group approached this elucidation with a theoretical framework organised around a central schema. Under bureaucratic capitalism, the main conflict set management against informal worker collectives. The everday experience of the latter at the point of production was a continuous struggle to both accommodate the workers' situation and limit alienation. The significations (patterns of sociability and/or meanings) that shaped this struggle contained potentials for a new revolutionary politics. As Lefort pointed out, in the context of everyday experience these potentials are latent. They become manifest in autonomous actions like wildcat strikes, as do the consequences of workers' experience of being dominated both by capitalist production and the main forms of political action. The job of revolutionary theory was to make explicit the links that connect everyday experience at the point of production to the characteristics of the new forms of autonomous collective actions, and to radicalise them by connecting them, in turn, to a vision of direct-democratic socialism.

As we saw in the last chapter, Socialisme ou Barbarie anchored their understanding of everyday experience at the point of production through first-person autobiographical narratives fashioned by working people. We outlined the rationale for according centrality to these narratives and looked at some of their formal characteristics. Lefort stages these narratives as part of a dialogue that would link Socialisme ou Barbarie with the worker avant garde. The dialogue would shape the production of texts that would enable worker-writers to theorise their own experience. The resulting texts would allow the group to deepen its revolutionary project. The teleological frame at the heart of the group's understanding of revolution would, in turn, have cognitive and political implications for the worker writers. The idea of this dialogue presupposed that workers would write, and only wanted a forum.

The rest of this book follows Socialisme ou Barbarie in their efforts to institute this dialogue, to gather worker writing and to mobilise politically a worker constituency in the process. These undertakings involved the group with the main Renault factory at Boulogne-Billancourt, just southwest of Paris. The contexts that shaped working-class politics there differed fundamentally from those which shaped Socialisme ou Barbarie as a group of Parisian intellectuals and political militants. They also differed from the ways in which workers and working-class politics were staged in the journal. The group encountered these differences through the worker-newspaper project, and resolved them with the writing done by Daniel Mothé, though in ways specific to the journal.

Socialisme ou Barbarie participated in launching *Tribune Ouvrière* in 1954. For the group, it was simultaneously a 'worker newspaper' and a platform through which a new type of revolutionary organisation might be developed. Understanding *Tribune Ouvrière*, and Mothé's autobiographical writings, presupposes an account of both the symbolic importance and the political sociology of Renault Billancourt. The political world in which *Tribune Ouvrière* operated was defined through the working of the political-union field structured by the confrontation between management and the PCF-CGT. Conflicts between the CGT and its trade-union opponents circumscribed the tactical parameters within which *Tribune Ouvrière* defined itself, its notion of the political and its project. While the crowded, stratified character of the field often made staking out clear positions difficult, *Tribune Ouvrière* tried nonetheless to do so by scanning the shop-level environment for political or professional conjunctures that raised problems that the national organisations would not or could not address. The paper sought to expose such problems, link workers together and mobilise them politically outside the control of the dominant organisations. Because of the political and symbolic importance of Billancourt in the landscape of French politics, the stakes were always very high.

This chapter is a general map of the political terrain at Billancourt. After surveying how the conflict between the PCF-CGT and worker opposition was inscribed in competing histories of the Popular Front, the analysis shifts to postwar Billancourt as a legal and institutional context. The bulk of this section is a structural account of the positions occupied by the PCF-CGT that focuses on the conflicting pressures to which they were consistently subjected. The structural account provides a way to critically situate Socialisme ou Barbarie's tendency to conflate the two organisations by discussing their strategies of aggregation-disaggregation developed to accommodate a complex sociopolitical position. It also explains some of the tactical choices made by *Tribune Ouvrière* by examining the institution of collective bargaining and its role in determining which issues were admitted into, and excluded from, political debate. The section concludes with a brief examination of politico-union conflict as one over the definition of the collective, its relation to the factory on the one hand and the party on the other, and the role of the militant.

Billancourt

> ... the space of tactics is the space of the other.[1]

> Concrete political aims must be set in concrete circumstances. All things are relative, all things flow and all things change. There is no such thing as abstract truth. Truth is always concrete.[2]

In schematic terms, the political terrain at Billancourt involved management, trade union organisations and workers. The overall framework that linked management to unions was collective bargaining, which was *de facto* before 1955 and *de jure* thereafter. The union context was pluralist, with multiple organisations competing for worker constituencies. Trade union pluralism had important consequences for the language of organisational contestation. The

---

1 de Certeau 1984, p. 101.
2 'Two Tactics of Social Democracy', Lenin 1977a, p. 482.

unions were bureaucratic organisations that attempted to navigate the tensions that arose because of the differences in interests that shaped negotiation with management in the bargaining context on the one hand, and those of the worker base on the other. At issue were various indices of power: influence over compensation and benefits, control over aspects of factory organisation.

Throughout the 1950s, the strategic game at Billancourt that set the Renault management and trade unions against each other was dominated by the CGT (*Confédération Générale du Travail*), which was ideologically tied to the French Communist Party, the PCF. For reasons that will be explained below, we treat these organisations as a system, and refer to that system as the PCF-CGT. The PCF-CGT was the *idée force* in the Billancourt factory's internal political and trade-union field. Even the most anti-communist of the minority trade unions[3] had to position themselves with respect to management and PCF-CGT before they could do so relative to each other. Struggles for symbolic capital – increased membership levels and organisational strength, and the ability to impose a dominant political discourse – were fought with reference to Stalinism. The resulting tendency to map union politics onto the conflict between East and West was a bit deceptive. All the main trade unions were national, bureaucratic organisations that accepted the legitimacy of state-owned capitalism, and the fixing of the terms of employer-labour relations through collective bargaining. However, these factors were not in question. Insofar as inter-organisational conflict was concerned, they disappeared into a war of position in which the players articulated their moves on East/West grounds.

In the margins of this context were a number of small, proletarian revolutionary groups. Operating in less complex tactical environments than the national trade unions, and in relatively close contact with the worker base, these groups generally tried to read issues and vocabulary off shop-level conflicts in order to split bureaucratic organisations away from the rank and file. Despite the overwhelming material and political dominance of the PCF-CGT system at Billancourt, at certain moments proletarian revolutionary groups could constitute a real danger. Proletarian groups could exploit the effects of the strategic complexities that often prevented national organisations from adequately responding to worker grievances based on local circumstances. They could also work to raise issues excluded from debate on other grounds. The tactics used by these small groups centred on autonomous strikes as a device for organisation building.

---

3 These unions were: the American-style Force Ouvrière (FO); the Confederation Française des Travailleurs Chrétiens (The Confederation of Christian Workers or CFTC); the company-sponsored Syndicat Indépendant Renault (SIR).

Proletarian revolutionary groups embodied the threat of a revolt from the left and a basic challenge to the PCF-CGT's claims to exclusively represent the French working class. The PCF-CGT developed managerial approaches to counter such local dissent. These ranged from mobilising base militants to publishing and distributing tracts, to direct coercion. The union also devised a pattern for containing local dissent as an organisation. The CGT would initially seem to acquiesce to local demands, but would quickly follow with moves to isolate, contain, redirect, and ultimately gain control over any unauthorised action. Because of the symbolic importance of Billancourt, at issue in these situations was the PCF-CGT system's claim to be the exclusive representative of the working class, which was central to the PCF's viability as a parliamentary party. Within the factory, at stake were the definitions of the workers' relationship with the collective or class, the function of the strike, the relationship between local and national issues, the role of Party discipline and the definition of militancy. This chapter examines the conflict between the PCF-CGT and proletarian opposition as a conflict over the definition of these fundamental terms.

Billancourt as a Social Signifier

The position of Renault's Billancourt factory as a signifier in the political landscape of the French left during the 1950s is indicated by the number and complexity of investments in it. Long a symbol of industrial modernisation (Fordism in the narrow sense) and the social and political conflicts specific to it, Renault was nationalised in January 1945, confiscated from its founder Louis Renault as part of the penalty for his excessive enthusiasm in filling German war-material orders during the Occupation.[4] In creating the *Régie Nationale des Usines Renault* (RNUR),[5] the state became involved with an enterprise of enormous economic, social and political importance. It was France's largest, most technologically sophisticated and internationally competitive automobile manufacturer.[6] Renault maintained its position in the automobile industry throughout the 1950s and 60s primarily through the strategies devised by

---

4   For a detailed account sympathetic to Louis Renault, see Hatry 1990, Chapters 18–23.
5   I use this abbreviation to refer to the Régie throughout this chapter.
6   See Tiano 1955, pp. 28–9 for overall production figures by vehicle-type, 1945–55 (p. 28) and market-share by percentage, 1938–54, and in comparison by production figures with Citroen, 1948–54 (p. 29). From 1946–54, Renault controlled between twenty-eight and thirty-seven percent of the automobile market in France; from 1951–4, market share levelled off at about thirty-three per cent.

the aggressive, technocratic management that succeeded Louis Renault.[7] The RNUR benefitted both from state financial support and relatively loose integration into the various plans.[8] The state only rarely intervened directly to set RNUR production goals. The immediate postwar period was an exception: the state directed that production be increased without an accompanying increase in rationalisation as an instrument of employment policy. It was also heavily involved in the development of the inexpensive, mass-produced 4CV.[9] Across the 1950s, however, this kind of direct state intervention did not happen. The RNUR operated like a privately owned corporation. Benefitting from a series of very successful automobiles, beginning with the 4CV, and from privileged access to state capital, the RNUR underwent rapid and intensive rationalisation along Fordist lines. It pioneered the automation and vertical integration of production in France. The goals of these processes, both industrial and political, were to maintain production levels and market position, and to create a deskilled and politically docile workforce where possible.[10]

Throughout the 1950s and into the early 1960s, the Billancourt factory remained the heart of the RNUR. Located on the *île Seguin* just west of Paris,[11] Billancourt had a largely urban, highly politicised and relatively skilled workforce. In 1947, Billancourt employed 83.8 percent of the Renault workforce (34,028 workers) and 70.2 percent (35,785 workers) in 1954.[12] The factory's importance as a Parisian employer, as a laboratory for the development and adaptation of American-style marketing and management, combined with the

---

7   See Depretto and Schweitzer 1984, pp. 43ff, for an account of splits amongst Louis Renault's protégés during the 1930s.

8   Renault was relatively difficult to integrate into the overall goals of the plan and operated, for the most part, like a privately-owned automobile manufacturer in its relations with the state. Its integration was relatively loose when compared to industries like the EDF that more closely embodied the plan's goals and logic. See Naville *et al.* 1971, Chapter 1.

9   Fridenson 1979, pp. 33–40. See also the invaluable overview-essay in Fridenson 1986, pp. 514–43.

10 Brachet, in Naville 1971, details the distinction between Renault's modernisation and the slower, less thoroughgoing reorganisation of Citroen, which was owned by Michelin and thought of largely as a subsidiary to the tire business, the family-owned Peugeot and the smaller, more vulnerable SIMCA (the principal victim of increasing American imports). On the double-edged nature of rationalisation, see also Dubost 1978. Dubost in particular discusses the differences between the urban, skilled and highly politicised Billancourt workforce and the rural, relatively unskilled and depoliticised workforce at Flins.

11 For an account of Billancourt's origins, see Hatry 1990, Chapter 11.

12 The difference in percentage is attributable to the opening of a new factory at Flins in January 1954. Tiano 1955, p. 33. On Flins and the reorganisation of Billancourt, see Freyssenet 1979, pp. 113ff.

fact of state ownership to make Billancourt a symbol for, and legitimation of, the French mixed planned economy. Billancourt also had a turbulent political past. The most prominent association linked the 1936 Popular Front and the PCF's emergence as a viable national-scale political force. This association was carefully maintained by the Party press. Billancourt's position at the centre of Renault's organisation, and Renault's within French heavy industry generally, its politicised workforce and history of explosive class conflict along with the extensive press coverage devoted to these conflicts made it a 'pilot factory' for technological development, industrial conflict and labour relations. It was the leading edge of French industrial Fordism.

The RNUR marketed the factory as a symbol of its own modernisation. The location of the first marketing department in France, Billancourt was the subject of an important photographic essay by a number of photographers, including René-Jacques, published by the RNUR in 1951 as *L'automobile française*.[13] The RNUR's book is an interesting index of the development of French consumer culture. Centring on the automobile as vehicle at a variety of actual and metaphorical levels, the essay anticipates the erasure of traces of production that made of the automobile the quintessential Fordist commodity. The process reflected in René-Jacques's photographs is that described in 1955 by Roland Barthes in his essay 'The New Citroen'.[14] Automobiles had become autonomous geometrical constructions, 'magical objects ... dropped from the sky ... explored with an intense, amorous studiousness' in showrooms and auto shows by potential buyers often constituted as such only through changes in the availability of consumer credit.[15] Barthes argued that effacing the automobile's commodity form, rendering it 'autonomous' and 'magical', construed traces of production as a new form of obscenity.[16] Indications of this process of autonomisation of the automobile from the conditions of its production can already be seen in the 1951 photo essay, particularly in René-Jacques's staging of Billancourt as a collection of complex geometrical forms.[17] The institution

---

13   Excerpts can be found in Borhan and Rogiers 1991. See also Ross 1995, Chapter 1. Contrary to Ross's argument, René-Jacques's fascination with industrial design is more symptomatic than critical of the replacement of a Marxian with a consumerist view of industry. Ross's argument here, as it so often does, recapitulates what it purports to criticise.
14   Barthes 1988.
15   These are the preconditions of Fordist consumerism. See Aglietta 1987 and Harvey 1989.
16   'I think that cars today are almost the exact equivalent of the great Gothic cathedrals: I mean the supreme creation of an era conceived with a passion by unknown artists and consumed in image if not in usage by a whole population which appropriates them as purely magical objects' (Barthes 1988, p. 88).
17   Borhan and Rogiers 1991, pp. 18, 120–2, 124.

of Fordist consumerism runs temporally parallel to the evolution of Socialisme ou Barbarie. The group's focus on the social consequences created for Marxism by the institution of Fordism and their rejection of the broader cultural logic that ran toward an autonomisation of the commodity makes *Socialisme ou Barbarie* fundamental to a counter-history of Fordism.

Billancourt was the 'transmission belt for social conflict', a PCF-CGT stronghold and an oft-consulted barometer of national working-class reactions and their magnitude.[18] Billancourt's position at the centre of French industrial, political and social conflict gave a certain advantage to the PCF-CGT in relations with the Renault management. When it suited the Party, Billancourt became the centre of national class struggle. Always protective of its autonomy, management sought to counter challenges by isolating Billancourt from larger problems as much as possible. For example, the Renault management actively tried to emphasise centre-periphery wage differentials during the summer of 1955 in order to prevent a general strike that was already spreading out from Nantes and St. Nazaire from affecting Renault. The PCF-CGT sought to dictate when and how links between Billancourt and national (or international) politics were to be made. Struggle over the relation between Billancourt and larger social conflicts acquired their importance in large measure through the associations between the Renault workers on strike and the escalating socio-political crisis.

Renault workers demonstrating *en masse* behind the banner of the Party and CGT allowed the Party press to suggest comparisons with the June 1936 Popular Front strikes. A moment of profound working-class solidarity and mobilisation around both political (anti-fascism) and syndical issues, the Popular Front prompted the reunification of the CGT and CGTU. It drove the abrupt transformation of the PCF from a small, 'ghettoised' militant organisation, working in competition with other radical groups to carve out a constituency at the expense of the Socialists, into a viable parliamentary Party.[19] For the Party press, to invoke the *'mythe de Billancourt'* was to recapitulate the origin myth of the modern PCF, to reaffirm the link between the working class and the Party, and to reposition the Party as the defender of worker interests *par excellence*. It also evoked the PCF as a parliamentary actor responsible for a series of important legislative initiatives of great material benefit to workers immediately after June 1936 and again, under the same publicity banner, during the 1946–7 Tripartite period.[20] Between 1954 and 1956, while the Party was jockeying to become a coalition partner in government, *L'Humanité* made the

---

18   Fallachon 1972, p. 111.
19   See Depretto and Schweitzer 1984.
20   For the official Party-interpretation of the Popular Front, see Thorez 1949.

period between the 1934 *Front Unique* and the *Front Populaire* into something of a liturgical calendar, serving to repeatedly affirm the connection between workers and Party. In 1936 the Party mobilised against fascism; in 1954 the Party mobilised against the 'monopoly of trusts'.

A 'Left Opposition' counter-history[21] of the Popular Front developed[22] alongside and against that of the PCF. Whereas the Party claimed that the working class rallied *en masse* behind it during May and June 1936, the largely Trotskyist Opposition claimed that PCF's 'opportunism' exploited, and ultimately betrayed, the 'revolutionary aspirations of the masses'. According to the counter-history, the new pattern of PCF relations with the working class was revealed clearly, for the first time, during June 1936. Not able to control the initiation of action, the PCF allowed events to unfold apart from it, while seeking to contain, limit, channel and eventually take control of the situation and turn it to the Party's own ends. The key moment in this story was the replacement by the PCF of the workers who had occupied the Billancourt factory with Party militants. This marked the beginning of a pattern of the subordination of worker actions to Party parliamentary ambitions. The counter-history was always articulated from the viewpoint of the aggrieved revolutionary masses, and turned on the prominent Trotskyist theme of betrayal. Because it is a recurrent construction of politically marginal groups, the precise links between the various organisational positions claiming to speak for the workers and the workers themselves have not been examined. For our purposes, the debate over the history and signification of the Popular Front establishes some of the terms taken up and transformed by opposition groups after World War II.

The PCF's transformation into a parliamentary 'working-class party' entailed a rapid and thoroughgoing organisational change. While in the process of elaborating its new organisational form, the PCF found itself pulled in competing, sometimes contradictory tactical directions. Many of the arguments articulated through the counter-history of the Popular Front were picked up and transformed by post-war opposition groups at Billancourt. The Party remained extremely sensitive to these challenges, despite the material and numerical weakness of their opponents. The opposition's arguments often recapitulated those made against the Bolsheviks by the Social Revolutionaries and the Workers' Opposition after 1917. Many of the same arguments were appropriated and raised again by Trotsky, designated 'Enemy Number One' in the *Short Course*

---

21   See Mothé 1980, p. 12.
22   A recurring construction, the main texts that comprise this counter-history include: Weil 1951 and Danos and Gibelin 1986, which was originally published by Maspéro in 1952 and Lefort 1956. The best overview of the history of this history is Broué and Dorey 1966.

of the History of the Soviet Communist: Party (Bolshevik).[23] The Party's furious attacks on its left-wing critics were often paranoiac responses to efforts to turn the Bolshevik model on the Party itself. Party doctrine labelled this threat the re-emergence of the 'Principle of Contradiction' in the shape of the Party's demonised negative image of itself, a never well-defined 'Trotskyism', which the Party would inevitably overcome by ferreting out and eliminating 'class enemies'. This response was predicated on the Party's tendency to present and legitimate positions in terms of its official history. More immediately, the symbolic importance of Billancourt made shop-level conflict between the PCF-CGT and opposition groups particularly explosive. The CGT's loss of control over Renault workers could entail disastrous consequences. The April 1947 wildcat strike that provided then-President Ramadier a pretext to expel the PCF from the government and end Tripartism gave ample proof of this ever-present danger.[24]

The PCF-CGT Press

The numerical and material dominance of the CGT at Billancourt extended the influence of a numerically relatively small PCF. The Party press dubbed the factory '*la Fortresse Ouvrière*'. Billancourt was both a Party stronghold and an exemplar of its successful 'Bolshevisation'. In France, Bolshevisation entailed the transformation of cell organisation from a regional to a factory basis. This transformation was framed as the material translation of Lenin's famous slogan: 'Every factory should be our fortress'.[25] Billancourt was the backdrop before which the Party's claims to be the Vanguard Party of the working class could be demonstrated, and the stage on which could be enacted the always-unanimous forward march of the workers behind the PCF-CGT.

To the extent that one views the Party press as the internal mirror reflecting the worldview of the apparatus, as does Annie Kriegel in *Les communistes français*, the endless repetition of the unity of workers and Party unfolding

---

23   Stalin 1939.
24   The best source on April 1947 is Fallachon 1972, which pays close attention to the material written both by the committee and by the political parties behind it, including *Internationaliste*, which is now exceedingly difficult to find. See also Pierre Bois, 'La greve des usines Renault', *Le revolution prolétarienne*, 304 (June 1947), pp. 9–73 through 12–76 and the testimonies reproduced in Tiano 1955 Annexe XXII, 'Récit de la grève d'avril-mai 1947 par deux jeunes ouvriers'.
25   This also was the title of Fremontier 1971, a book written under the auspices of the PCF. Among those less sympathetic to a preponderant weight of the PCF-CGT, Billancourt became known as the 'little Kremlin'. See 'Euro Disney ouvre, Billancourt ferme', *Courier International*, 75, pp. 25–6.

against the scrim of Billancourt can be read as an effort to conjure through iteration and to reassure.[26] For Bertrand Badie, in his *Strategie de la grève*, the interaction between the Party press and Renault workers was secondary to the fact of mobilisation around short-term obtainable material goals. The claims made in *L'Humanité* about these mobilisations fit into a larger pattern of Party management of worker grievances. The pattern emphasised the PCF's leading role as it worked to restrict or control relations with the external world. Mobilisations 'consolidated the identity and cohesion of the worker system' and demonstrated the 'working class character of the Party'. Party press coverage functioned as a gloss that emphasised the progressive nature of the Party's demands, regardless of what they were, and situated them in an overall narrative of progress.[27] The progressive narrative was grounded with reference to the Popular Front. Each repetition reinforced the centrality of Billancourt in the Party's internal Imaginary. The prominence in the press of Billancourt as the stage for continual assertions of Party unity with the workers explained the power behind Sartre's evocation of it, in a very different field of intellectual production, to limit critiques of the PCF from anti-Stalinist intellectuals: 'Il ne faut pas déséspérer Billancourt'.[28]

The general narrative of continual PCF achievement on behalf of the worker and the revolution was supplemented by extensive journalistic coverage of CGT actions in the factory. This coverage emphasised the achievement of limited tactical goals and the material benefits that accrued to the workers by supporting them. Taken together, Billancourt emerges as a junction that connected particular union actions with the more abstract ideological narratives outlined in Thorez's *Fils du peuple*[29] and the *Short Course*. Press accounts of particular events were processed in terms of heavily sedimented narratives which staged the Party claims to represent the working class, its past and its future. At the level of Party discourse, Billancourt was a fundamental signifier in the construction and maintenance of system identity. This identity was constructed around criteria internal to the Party apparatus.

---

26 Reading *L'Humanité* as a mirror of the internal world of the Party-apparatus is borrowed from Kriegel 1980. See also Gérôme and Tartakowsky 1988; Goulemot 1981 on the construction of the Stalin cult based on a reading of *L'Huma* during the 1930s; also his 'Du culte de Staline et quelques autres chez les communistes français' in the invaluable colloquium-proceedings, Dioujeva and George 1981.
27 See Badie 1976, pp. 167–75.
28 Roughly, 'Billancourt must not be made to despair'. I like 'Don't bum out Billancourt' better.
29 Thorez 1949.

The inward orientation of the Party press became clear at moments of crisis. During 1956–7, a series of conjunctural factors that culminated with the Soviet suppression of the Hungarian Revolution resulted in a breakdown in PCF-CGT's ability to manage relations with the rank and file. At the same time, the highly controlled and distorted nature of information published by the Party press became manifest. Serious damage resulted. At moments like this, the narratives that ordered system identity became detached from the range of social and political practices normally invested in and interpreted through them. The question of what else was revealed at the factory level by this folding back onto itself of the Party press will be central to my analysis in Chapter Six.

The Strategic Game at Billancourt

The ideological conflict over the signifier 'Billancourt' traced conflicts within the factory itself. For the state, Billancourt symbolised the success of a mixed planned economy. The Renault management was primarily concerned with asserting and maintaining its autonomy relative to both the state and the trade unions. The interests of management and the State coincided in the pursuit of an aggressive modernisation programme. Management translated its ambivalence over Billancourt as a pilot enterprise and its role within a nationalised enterprise into flexible bargaining tactics with respect to the unions. In the immediate post-war period, management sought to limit PCF-CGT influence by allowing the state latitude to directly intervene in the construction of an elaborate system of social benefits for Renault workers. Management consistently tried to turn Renault's 'pilot enterprise' status to its advantage in both formal and substantive labour relations. Management attempted to resist worker demands for wage increases on national interest grounds from 1944–7; in a different situation (1955) it used the relatively high wages paid to the Billancourt workers in comparison with their provincial counterparts to separate the RNUR from a national strike wave.

For the PCF-CGT, the central problems involved maintenance of position: relative to management as a partner in negotiating the shape of the enterprise; relative to other trade unions; and relative to the worker base. Tensions created by differences between national-scale and local political exigencies complicated the formulation of local strategies. Revolutionary opposition groups, whatever their spin on June 1936, worked at the level of particular shops to exploit gaps that emerged between the organisation and the base.[30] These gaps

---

30   For Socialisme ou Barbarie's view of the Popular Front, see Lefort 1956.

were the result of trade-offs necessary for the PCF-CGT to balance the pressures outlined above. Complexity increased with the progressive integration of the CGT into a collective bargaining system in the context of a nationalised enterprise. Collective bargaining was a defining feature of Fordist industrial relations: it assumed depoliticised trade unions and a terrain of management-union conflict limited for the most part to wage and benefit issues.

The PCF-CGT System

Bertrand Badie provides a useful 'dynamic functionalist' understanding of the interaction between the various pressures the PCF-CGT confronted and how they shaped the relations between the two organisations. Badie argues that the two organisations are best understood as constituent elements of a single system. The defining system characteristic is that the components aggregate or disaggregate depending on the situation created by relations with two 'reference systems': national politics and the working class.[31] Pressures brought to bear on the PCF-CGT by these reference systems determined the relation that obtained at a given time within an inter-organisational dynamic of autonomy and control. Between October 1947 and late 1952, the tactical and strategic priorities of the PCF – themselves largely dictated by its oppositional role in French politics and its unqualified support of the USSR in the Cold War – entirely dominated the tactics employed and demands formulated by the CGT. Subsequent relations between the organisations were more complex. During periods of autonomy, the CGT could be fairly ecumenical and was able to detect and respond relatively quickly to changes in the mood of the working class. Throughout, the CGT's role in this relation was to gather and correlate information from local militants and relay it to the Party. The PCF would, in turn, reprocess the grievances in terms of its own tactical priorities and relay those responses back to the CGT, which would then direct its militants to react accordingly.

In principle, this arrangement should have allowed for both considerable responsiveness and flexibility in the relationships between the PCF-CGT

---

[31] This schema is drawn from the dynamic functionalism of Alvin Gouldner, which takes the notion that in a shifting and complex historical context, systems confront situations within which equilibrium is not functional – that is, equilibrium would not allow the system to remain internally consistent, to retain its specificity or identity. The goal of functional analysis, then, is to isolate specific structural features by means of which the system retains its identity. See Badie 1976, p. 9 and Gouldner 1959.

system and the worker base and for relatively tight coordination between the two organisations.[32] However, from the shop-floor viewpoint as articulated by *Tribune Ouvrière* and Mothé, particular grievances reprocessed by the PCF never coincided with local realities. For groups like *Tribune Ouvrière*, whether this lack of fit resulted from unresolvable conflict between local demands relayed by the CGT and those placed on the PCF by virtue of its position in national and/or inter-bloc politics or from another cause was secondary to the continual emergence of a gap that separated workers from bureaucratic organisation.

Collective Bargaining and the Depoliticisation of Trade Unions

CGT participation in collective bargaining in the context of a nationalised enterprise added to the problems encountered by the PCF-CGT in formulating coherent positions on specific worker grievances.[33] In the early 1970s, Claus Offe thematised the problems that collective bargaining created as the result of unions being forced to adapt to the parameters of a game set up by capital in its own image:

> ... [A] vastly broader range of interests is involved in this case [the trade-union] than in that of the capitalists, who can satisfy a large part of their interests somewhat apart from their functioning as capitalists. In the case of the workers, those interests that have directly to do with, and are directly affected by, the exchange of labour-power that they are subject to include not only material rewards but such things as job-satisfaction, health, leisure-time, and the continuity of employment. Unions are, therefore, confronted with the task of organising the entire spectrum of needs that people have when employed as wage workers. The multitude of needs of 'living' labour is not only comparatively more difficult to organise for quantitative reasons, but it is also for qualitative reasons that there is no common denominator to which all these heterogenous and often conflicting needs can be reduced so as to 'optimise' demands and

---

32   Badie slides from using the functionalist approach to provide an abstract model for isolating the 'structural invariants' of the relationship between the PCF and the CGT to acting by the end of the book as if the model were descriptive.

33   For a more empirically detailed analysis of the history of collective bargaining and its implementation, see Jean-Pierre Bardou, 'Labor and Industrial Relations since 1945', in Bardou 1982.

tactics. How much in wages, for instance, can 'rationally' be given up in exchange for what increase in job satisfaction? The answer to this question cannot be found by any calculus that could be objectively applied; it can only be found as the result of the collective deliberation of the members of the organisation.[34]

For Offe, a trade union enters into sustained direct negotiation with capital as if each represented the same type of interest. This is already a move in the game, one that places the union at an immediate disadvantage. By conceding to capital the prerogative of defining the nature of the players and rules of the game, the union is forced either to ignore or misrecognise the very real differences in interests that distinguish it from capital. The problems this created were particularly acute for the CGT, which was not set up to develop positions on the basis of the 'collective deliberation of its members'.[35] While it tried to appear open, inclusive and responsive during periods of relative autonomy, the CGT remained in fact a hierarchical, democratic-centralist organisation that relied upon the discipline of militants to implement its decisions locally.

According to Offe's schema, it would be difficult to establish a strict *quid pro quo* according to which specific changes in the work situation could be compensated for by specific changes in wage levels. However, it was nonetheless a defining feature of collective bargaining that union demands were, for the most part, limited to wage and benefit issues. Problems of organisational awareness of this difficulty were compounded by the fact that, for the PCF-CGT, mobilising on the basis of wage issues dovetailed with traditional Marxist and Leninist positions on the political centrality of economic demands. From its inception, the PCF-CGT preferred economic strikes geared toward concrete, immediate goals. Wage issues were seen as class issues. They were crucial for marking off worker unanimity against capital. At the same time, wage issues demonstrated the homogeneity of the working class mobilised behind the PCF banner. Strike actions around wages also permitted the postwar PCF-CGT to refer, at yet another level, to the Popular Front.[36] The centrality of wage issues in the PCF-CGT tactical repertoire enabled the system to integrate itself smoothly into collective bargaining without forcing it to confront either the process of depoliticisation or its consequences.

PCF-CGT restriction of its activities primarily to questions of wages and benefits at Renault was reinforced by their position on nationalisation. Party

---

34   Offe 1986, pp. 178–9.
35   Compare this to the bottom-up structure of the CFDT.
36   Badie 1976, pp. 41–68; pp. 118–25.

ambivalence about technological modernisation extended to the Russian Revolution. During the 1920s, Party officials cited Lenin to argue that Taylorism implemented under existing socialism would not figure in the same way as it did under capitalism. Transformed ownership and redirected forces of production would necessarily transform the relations of production.[37] To say the least, this position reflects a deep optimism about the nature of Soviet socialism.[38] Ideologically, this argument was only possible in the context of Soviet-style Marxism, which ignored the relations of production in favour of a metaphysics of productive forces.[39] Socialist Taylorism was relevant at Renault because the RNUR had been nationalised. In 1946, nationalisation along with the PCF's participation in government under the Tripartite agreement confronted the PCF-CGT system with the possibility of its version of revolution. For the Party and CGT, socialism equalled nationalisation (the abolition of private property) and the integration of nationalised industry into a planned economy elaborated in the context of the dictatorship of the proletariat. The dictatorship of the proletariat could result from the assumption of power by the Party, which was characterised as a 'revolution by parliamentary means'. While not itself socialism, nationalisation was nonetheless a progressive step to be 'fought for, expanded, made a reality and protected from sabotage'.[40] 'Making nationalisation a reality' went beyond simply defending the change in ownership to include product initiatives like the 4CV and the active support of the modernisation of technology and production design. Protection from sabotage included not only opposing reprivatisation, but also preventing unauthorised strikes and resisting challenges from the Left.

The defence of nationalised French industry also brought to the fore the Party's patriotic motives. This combination was an important element of the PCF under the double sign of 1936 and the Resistance. Patriotic motives had prompted the Party to dub itself a 'mass parliamentary Party with a revolutionary core'[41] and to be fully participant in the project of reconstruction. It

---

37 Dorey 1976, especially pp. 146–53 and 204, n. 14. See also Linhart 1976 for a more detailed treatment of Soviet Taylorism, particularly on Lenin's views, and the works by Charles Bettleheim and E.H. Carr cited in Dorey, p. 204 n. 14.

38 Maurice Goedelier, Foreword to Dorey 1976, p. 7: 'Remarkably enough, French Communist newspapers from the period 1925–1935 perpetuated what is in effect a mythology about the virtues of introducing Taylorism in the Soviet Union. They *assumed* that the Soviet Union was the land of economic and political democracy, and the introduction of Taylorism would *immediately* lead to an improvement in the living conditions of the workers'.

39 See Castoriadis 1988b.

40 Jean Bruhat, 'Le guide de métallurgie', March 1947, quoted in Fallachon 1972, p. 113.

41 Characterisation taken from Kriegel 1980.

encouraged an increased state involvement in the economy while working to solidify its position amongst the working class positively, by advocating specific legislation designed to ameliorate their social situation, and negatively, by moving to block or isolate worker actions critical of Party positions. When the Party was forced into opposition after April–October 1947, the basic features of this earlier line persisted: the defence of nationalisation, modernisation and of legislative gains for workers. To this was added a general subordination of local tactical imperatives to the defence of the USSR.

The constraints given abstract formulation above were expressed concretely at Renault in the CGT's efforts to restrict contestation with management to wages, control over professional hierarchy, hiring and firing and '*politique sociale*'. Despite occasional protests from workers over the 'cadences infernales', the CGT was unable coherently to address the deterioration of working conditions that resulted from technological change. Lacking the collective, deliberative procedures that, as Offe argued, would have allowed the union to work out some type of acceptable '*quid pro quo*' – x degree of deterioration in working conditions for y gain in wages or benefits – the trade-off for collective bargaining was an intensification of the union's tendency to pull away from its worker base and the problems these workers confronted every day.

Collective bargaining reduces the arena of legitimate trade union action to questions of service delivery. It is a crucial instrument in the implementation of what Michel Aglietta called the American model of depoliticised trade unionism so basic to Fordism.[42] By depoliticisation, Aglietta refers to the abandonment of older types of trade-union activity rooted in any semblance of a vision of alternative socio-political organisation. The existing order becomes the inescapable horizon for all political action. Depoliticisation is synonymous with the transformation of syndicalism from political opposition to an interest group in a representative democratic context. It is an enabling condition in the deskilling and atomisation of the workforce characteristic of Fordism.

The General Structure of Collective Bargaining at Billancourt

The negotiations structured by collective bargaining opposed management and two representative trade-union bodies, the personnel delegates (stewards) and the *comités d'entreprise*. The '*délégués de personnel*' were to 'present to the employers all individual or collective requests relative to application of salary levels and professional classifications, the Labour Code and other laws and

---

42   See Aglietta 1987.

regulations concerning worker-protection, hygiene and social contingency funds'.[43] The *comité d'entreprise* managed social projects: 'it cooperates with management on the amelioration of collective conditions at work and in personal life'.[44] As a conduit for state involvement in the extension of its 'social politics' to the working class, the *comité* was a substantial bureaucracy. The industrial sociologist André Tiano referred to the Renault *comité d'entreprise* as a counter-enterprise that administered programmes ranging from retirement benefits to youth hostels and soccer leagues. Included among these social programmes were important benefits for working people that gave them access to services, facilities, organisations and retirement prospects they otherwise would not have been able to afford. By providing these services, the *comités* also provided the CGT with an important source of patronage and a powerful mechanism for disciplining dissident workers.[45]

Representatives to both bodies were proportionally elected each year before 1950, and biannually thereafter. For the CGT, which routinely won them, these elections affirmed its relation with the Billancourt workers, its claims to be a democratic union, and its relative position amongst competing unions. Given the stakes, each election occasioned an intensive PCF-CGT mobilisation of its constituency in the forms of a flood of posters and tracts, increases in militant activity and limited strike actions.[46] While the Party and CGT presses would report election results as reflecting the solidity and continuity in their relations with the base, as measures of actual strength the results were less than reliable. An electorate is not a membership. Accurate membership figures have never been forthcoming from either the PCF or CGT. Each routinely inflated its numbers by, for example, counting each stamp purchased as a different person, even though each member might purchase up to seven a year. Annie Kriegel

---

43 I use Tiano's definition (Tiano 1955) of the delegates to differentiate them from shop stewards. The CGT appointed its delegates and shop militants, while shop stewards (particularly in the UK) were directly elected by the workers. The British shop stewards movement was undergoing a revival during roughly the same period we are discussing here.

44 'The laws of 22 February 1945 and 16 April 1946 required that all businesses having more than fifty employees establish mechanisms for negotiating between the owners/management and trade unions' (quoted in Tiano 1955, p. 38). Others bodies at Billancourt included building and hygiene committees. The two entities discussed in the text are the most important for the structural argument we are making here, as well as for background information for assessing the various texts to follow.

45 This happened to Pierre Blachier in 1972; he claimed that it was not uncommon, and constituted one of the most important risks that militants ran in opposing the CGT.

46 For a survey of the CGT media that postdates the period I am analysing, but nonetheless provides a good idea of the extent of these resources, see Verdier 1981.

noted that, following the same logic that shaped the inflation of numbers, neither organisation was particularly interested in analysing its own social composition, particularly when compared with the German SPD. She offers the PCF's distinction between a worker party and a working-class party as a partial explanation.[47]

As is often the case in representative democracy, abstentions were not counted in reporting election results. In his analysis of voting patterns at Billancourt for trade-union elections during the early 1950s, André Tiano noted low levels of inter-union mobility: workers either voted for the same union each time or they abstained.[48] This low voter mobility was probably a function of the highly fragmented political context at Billancourt and, particularly, of the overlay of East-West politics and anti-communism introduced by CGT's ties to the PCF. A Party sympathiser would not vote for the explicitly anti-communist FO for example, even if his dissatisfaction with a CGT line prevented him from voting for it.[49] Inter-union contests therefore revealed little that could not be gathered from comparing the number of sections each union had at Billancourt.[50] Elections determined the relative position of the trade unions in each of the entities that confronted management. Shop militants were appointed by the organisation.

From the point where direct negotiations between management and unions over the shape of Renault were undertaken immediately after World War II, the unions were *de facto* engaged in collective bargaining. *De jure*, a series of steps separated earlier forms from the institution of collective bargaining proper with the Renault Accords of September 1955. Prior to 1955, the process was heavily weighted in management's favour, which was not legally bound to abide by negotiated agreements. Until 1950, the direct state control of wage levels minimised the stakes.[51]

---

47   See Kriegel 1980, Chapter 3; comparison with the SPD, p. 66. See also Buton 1985.
48   Tiano 1955, p. 47.
49   Mothé's articles on Renault during 1956–7 confirm Tiano's observations at the level of the Renault AOC. See Chapter 6, below.
50   Between 1944–55 at Renault, the relative strength of the various trade-unions was: CGT – sixty worker sections (15 of which were very active), one employee, three salaried workers. The Christian CFTC: twelve worker sections (four very active), one employee, one management, one technicians and foremen. *Force Ouvrière* (FO) split from the CGT in October 1947. It was created as an anti-communist, apolitical union modelled on the American AFL. FO controlled two worker sections, one management cadre and one of technicians and foremen. Source: Tiano 1955, p. 51.
51   Shorter and Tilly 1974, pp. 21–28, esp. p. 27.

On Strikes

Across the period during which *de facto* and *de jure* bargaining were being brought into alignment, the CGT implemented a number of changes in how it brought pressure to bear on management. Bargaining was predicated, if not on outright opposition to strikes (as with the FO and CFTC), then at least on their instrumentalisation (with the CGT). For the latter, strikes were displays of force, threats of production stoppage that were used to counterbalance management's right to walk away from any settlement. Such limited and specific use of strikes assumed tight control over their location and length, and a minimum understanding between the union and management as to the significance of each action.[52]

Socialisme ou Barbarie read such an instrumentalised use of strikes as delegitimating the CGT amongst the workers. The group argued that workers understood that they were being deprived of an important weapon by means of which they could intervene in the shaping of their social and economic situation. This recognition was not confined to Socialisme ou Barbarie. More traditionally Leninist opposition groups routinely called for unlimited general strikes, with each positing itself as the new Vanguard Party. Socialisme ou Barbarie supported a more autonomous, self-organising reappropriation of the strike consistent with their critique of Leninism.[53] Reclaiming the strike was crucial. Consistent with the revolutionary syndicalist tradition, Socialisme ou Barbarie argued that participation in such actions was fundamental to the formation of class consciousness.

The CGT position on the organisation and function of strikes was superficially similar. Participation in the '*grèves tournantes*' was considered important in providing individual workers with a tangible sense of their relationship to the class. The actual organisation of strike actions relied heavily on local militants and their ability to get people out. Once under way, the PCF-CGT press coverage framed officially sanctioned strikes using the same rhetoric as had been used before 1936. For Socialisme ou Barbarie's reading of the effects of CGT's instrumentalisation of the strike, this was important because the rhetoric of revolution, and an older conception of the strike as an instrument of radical social transformation, were constantly evoked even as the political content of the strike was being hollowed out by increasing legal

---

52   For a parallel development focused on control of the workers rather than on the institutional mechanisms of union-integration, see James 1956. Typescript on Walter Reuther.
53   See Chapter 2 on Socialisme ou Barbarie's reading of East Berlin and the 1953 PTT strike.

restrictions and the effects of informal understandings between management and the unions. Socialisme ou Barbarie argued that the gap which separated the CGT's focus on wage and benefit questions and the problems workers confronted every day replicated that which separated the revolutionary rhetoric used in the Party and union press to frame its positions and the depoliticised, interest group actions in which they were actually engaged. For Socialisme ou Barbarie, this gap explained worker passivity. But it also exposed them to the rhetoric of revolution. With the latter came the possibility that the French working class might break out of that passivity and move in a revolutionary direction.

Shop-floor Conflict

For Socialisme ou Barbarie, these larger tensions were recapitulated and played out on the shop floor. In this theatre of conflict the parties included: management, represented by the '*chronos*' (rationalisation) and foremen (surveillance); the trade unions, represented by the union delegates and militants; and workers, gathered in informally organised collectives who only represented themselves.[54] Management's efforts to extract higher production levels from the workers took the forms of technological change, the reorganisation and increasing compartmentalisation of tasks, and production speed-ups. From Socialisme ou Barbarie's viewpoint, all these were efforts to eliminate the margin within which workers creatively interacted with the machines to address and solve the problems continually posed in production. The efforts of management ran up against informal worker collectives, which devised strategies to resist or limit exploitation and to retain their margin for interaction with each other and their work.

Caught in the middle was the CGT.[55] In the complex positions occupied by CGT militants, the conflict given abstract formulation by Claus Offe became material. Unable to democratise, and thereby to become more responsive to the base, the CGT navigated almost constant conflict through the agency of its militants at the base, who tightened or relaxed the shop-level organisation. This could take a variety of forms, ranging from distributing tracts or postering to mobilising, or preventing the mobilisation of, union members and

---

54 Mothé 1957 and Castoriadis 1988.
55 The following concerns primarily semi-skilled workers at Billancourt. Non-CGT unions were marginal and intimidated in these shops.

sympathisers around protests or strikes. Local organisation mediated the tensions that arose between the union and its base as a result of the former's tendency to pull away from it.

The modalities of CGT action would vary in the same factory from sector to sector as a function of the strength of its political organisation relative to that of other unions, the professional level of the shop, etc. In highly organised sectors like the AOC, conflict between the union and its base could serve a range of purposes. It could function as an adaptive mechanism, informing the organisation of particular grievances and giving it a chance to formulate a response, be it management or damage control. Or a local conflict might present the union with a threat that it would move to isolate and co-opt. The selection from among the options was conditioned by the overall situation of the PCF-CGT system.

Of the range of practices that were available to PCF-CGT militants in the shops, the strike was the most powerful. In his *Strategie de la grève*,[56] Badie argues that the PCF-CGT strike tactics were predicated on providing members and sympathisers the experience of demonstrating as part of a mass of workers. This approach hinged on the ability of local militants to mobilise workers around union slogans. It did not require that the rank and file be informed of the considerations that shaped a particular position. The PCF-CGT relied upon the affect generated by the show of force, as interpreted and situated by the press, to create an immediate sense of connection between individual workers, the working class and the Party/USSR. The PCF-CGT system organisational models were well adapted to conditions at Billancourt to the extent that they evaded the division between the oral culture of the shop floor and the written political culture on which *Tribune Ouvrière* was to founder.

Defining the Militant

Daniel Mothé provides a schema for understanding the roles played by shop-floor militants in his writings from the 1970s and early 1980s. He produced three texts on the topic while transforming himself from a participant-observer of industrial conditions at Billancourt to an industrial sociologist. There are few alternative sources. Conventional historiography of the 1950s reduced politics to conflicts between consecrated intellectuals over various abstract correlates of political positions.[57] Political action proper is assumed but secondary, its

---

56   Badie 1976.
57   See Khilani 1993 for an example of this view of politics.

modalities unanalysed, the terrain across which the connection between politics and ideas were worked out largely occulted. Similarly, analyses of trade-union politics reduce their object to a series of official positions, relegating political initiative to the upper levels of Party-union hierarchy.[58] Between the disappearance of proletarian literature and the rise of the CFDT and, later, the Maoist établis, local conflicts at the intersection of syndicalism, political parties and Fordist industrial life were passed over in virtual silence.[59]

Mothé's accounts of his experience at Billancourt during the 1950s and 1960s, initially written for *Socialisme ou Barbarie* and later published in book form, provide unique glimpses of the shops and of everyday professional and political conflicts seen from that viewpoint. I discuss these writings separately in Chapter Six. Here we focus on his attempt to formalise an understanding of militant culture. The main text from the period is his 1973 *Métier du militant*.[60] The text is a sociological portrait of the militant based on Mothé's experience at Billancourt and the modes of thinking about that experience developed through his earlier autobiographical writings. Juxtaposed with this – at times awkwardly – are more formally sociological modes of analysis. The result is a curious amalgam of analysis, projection and polemic.

There is a sense in which Mothé's sociological description of the militant is compensation for its material disappearance, along with that of the political culture that produced both the social role and Mothé himself. Mothé's basic argument is that any understanding of how the union-base system functioned, and of the grounds on which proletarian opposition contested this system, requires a definition of the roles and/or positions occupied by the base militant. This definition was produced even as changing social, political and industrial conditions eroded the position itself. Mothé describes this erosion as a widening of the distance that separated political culture, within which militants operated, from worker/factory culture, from which the militants came and to which they invariably referred.[61] Militant action was predicated on a

---

58 See Ross 1982.
59 An exception was the nascent *sociologie du travail*.
60 Mothé 1973, p. 8. This section also refers to Mothé 1965 and Mothé 1976.
61 This splitting of militant and base is in part a function of the atomisation of worker collectivities. This process continues in various factories to varying degrees. For a more recent description of conditions in an automobile factory that parallels those described by Mothé, see Michel Pialoux 'Le vieil ouvrier et la nouvelle usine' in Bourdieu 1994, pp. 331–48. This text is a description of, and a transcribed interview with, a pair of workers from the Peugeot factory in Sochaux that deals with the past twenty years.

projective identification with the working class. As the bases for this projective identification broke down, the role of the militant was transformed from being affective and operational to an object of analysis susceptible only to description.

Mothé argues the social position of the 'militant' presupposes a specific political and organisational experience that should be considered a kind of trade. As with any trade, learning required the acquisition of certain competencies. The trade of the militant assumed both an abstract political framework that would make coherent and explicable the various conflicts in which the militant was engaged on the one hand, and a more diffuse, practical knowledge of the modalities of struggle and its management that could only be acquired through direct experience on the other. It follows from this definition of a unifying set of skills that Mothé considers the militant to be a single, internally differentiated social type or socially instituted construct. The instituted signifier 'militant' has a particular history, one that shapes, and is sedimented with, more contemporary variants. Mothé discusses this historicity by developing two analytical schemata. The first opposes the Leninist to older syndicalist types of militant. Each type is based on particular *a priori* assumptions about the nature of industrial politics that rest upon different priorities accorded to the relationship between theory and practice, between the organisation and the masses. Superimposed on this older opposition is a more 'modern' typology of militants as trade-union functionaries. This classification reflects Mothé's view of how the older, more revolutionary forms of worker politics were undercut. The bulk of the variables he adduces are derived from the Leninist position, which assumes a top-down relationship between the organisation and the workers. The syndicalist tradition, predicated on the inverse idea that the base should control the organisation, is staged as a fading element in the history of the militant as a social type.

The convergence of Mothé's experience and his analysis is evident in the derivation of his categories. The basic data comes almost entirely from his twenty-year experience with, and his observations of, the political-union field at Billancourt. The analysis departs from an overlay of the Weberian notion of ideal types on this experience. The same tension between political and academic approaches marks Mothé's subject matter, the sociology of the militant at the base, and his primary *problématique*, the development of an explanation for the abandonment of the base by trade unions as reflected in transformations of the role of the militant. At yet another level, Mothé uses this ambiguous position to build into his text a survey of post-68 political projects that operated in the tradition of Socialisme ou Barbarie, assessing their strengths and weakness from the viewpoint of elder statesman.

In *Métier*, Mothé generalises the position of the CGT within metallurgy to construct a vision of a national trade union politics dominated by it. This move enables him to treat the structure of the CGT as paradigmatic for all modern trade unions.[62] According to Mothé, the modern union tries to be, and imagines itself as being, a highly centralised bureaucratic organisation. But the image of the modern union as a well-ordered, coherent pyramidal structure is an illusion, circulated both in the press and historiography. The illusion is an expression of union ideology in its desire for a disciplined, party-like organisation. Mothé argues that this ideological emphasis on top-down organisation and discipline also reflects an institutional desire to operate in a political context in which membership would be compulsory and not a matter of voluntary association. Compulsory membership would minimise the latitude for dissent. From an organisational viewpoint, Mothé contends, the modern union would understand compulsion and the minimisation of the space available to dissent as adaptation in its way. This would normalise by eliminating the turmoil created amongst the base workers by the processes of depoliticisation.[63]

At this point, the strategic importance of the CGT for Mothé becomes clear. He argues that, from the viewpoint of politics at the base, modern trade union ideology converges with the managerial view of production. For both, organisation is the active principle.[64] Referring back to Socialisme ou Barbarie terminology, the reliance on organisation as a generative principle is symptomatic of bureaucratic capitalism in its transfer of all types of initiative away from the base. For Mothé, the main consequence of this transfer is increasing chaos, with all the paradoxes that this chaos generates for organisational ideology in train. To counter this cycle of bureaucratisation, chaos and increased bureaucratisation, Mothé argues for a return to more democratic modes of trade union action in terms that echo his political education in Socialisme ou Barbarie and his aspirations for the CFDT.[65] It is characteristic of Mothé's

---

62 The American AFL-CIO is the paradigmatic Fordist trade union in terms of organisation and politics for the Regulation School. To repeat what I noted earlier, the distinctive feature of trade-union politics in France is its pluralism, which prevented the formation of sectoral monopolies and put limits on depoliticisation.

63 Like the Regulation School did ten years later, Mothé describes modernisation as the progressive abandonment by the unions of their traditional role as defenders of worker interests against capital and their transformation into counter-enterprises that are primarily concerned with self-perpetuation, patronage, and providing alternative possibilities for social mobility.

64 The influence of Socialisme ou Barbarie's positions on Mothé cannot be overstated.

65 The CFDT is the Confederation Françias Démocratique des Travailleurs or the Democratic Union of French Workers. See the disclaimer appended to Mothé 1965 for Mothe's view

writing (and, to an extent, Socialisme ou Barbarie as well) to operate in two related modes. The normative mode brackets the complex problems involved in actually instituting such a unionism. The descriptive mode submerges the aspirations articulated in the normative mode in detailed accounts of prevailing conditions that offer no space for it.

Mothé's analysis provides images of the concrete implications of structural characteristics of the French trade-union movement in the post-World War II period as they affected the politics of the shop floor. A very different view of the situation, and an indication of the particularity of Mothé's and Socialisme ou Barbarie's analytical framework, is obtained if one pulls back momentarily from the tight focus on a CGT-dominated political context. In comparison with the UK and Germany, a relatively low percentage of the French workforce ever joined a union, even in the nationalised sectors. In their long-term, synthetic study of French labour unrest, *Strikes in France*,[66] Edward Shorter and Charles Tilly explain this relatively weak unionisation by referring to features that structure French industrialisation and politics. France industrialised late and intensively. For all its speed and intensity, however, this process involved a relatively narrow spectrum of the overall economy, which was, and remained, dominated by small to mid-sized production.[67] Efforts to form unions encountered fierce resistance from employers. Almost all, from Louis Renault to the smallest, saw unions as unnecessary, foreign imports that would ruin the (profitable) equilibrium they saw as characteristic of French paternalism.[68] I have noted in passing that the French metallurgy trade unions – the most visible and politically volatile sector of the French working

---

of the CFDT. His notion of the 'syndicalist militant' owes much to Descampes 1971. Descampes was an early, central figure in the break between the CFTC and CFDT in 1964. On the CFDT generally, see Georgi 1995. Mothé's post-*Socialisme ou Barbarie* texts, particularly *Métier de militant*, can be read both in the terms I develop and in terms shaped by politics internal to the CFDT.

66 Shorter and Tilly 1974.
67 This explains the recurrence of certain sectors in *Socialisme ou Barbarie*'s accounts of industrial conflict during the 1950s and early 60s. These sectors include: automobiles, shipbuilding, the PTT and transportation (particularly railroads), and coal. *Socialisme ou Barbarie* also published analyses of less conventional sites like insurance and school-administration.
68 Shorter and Tilly 1974, pp. 29–33. The relative weakness of the French working class is indicated by the low 'success-rate' of strikes – only one in five from 1830 to 1965. For another discussion of the conflicts between employers and trade unions across the nineteenth and early-twentieth centuries, as well as their impact on French salary structures, see Mottez 1966.

class after World War II – organised primarily amongst semi-skilled workers. In the 1950s, this sector was almost entirely French. The unions devoted little energy to organising amongst unskilled, often immigrant, assembly-line workers. Trade-union pluralism subdivided the world of French syndicalism even further. Competition amongst unions was restricted by East/West polarisation. This particular kind of pluralism both prevented any one union from gaining a monopoly in an enterprise or sector and placed at least superficial limits on the process of depoliticisation.

French trade unions can be seen as relatively small organisations operating in a highly fragmented context. Each union was internally divided between its apparatus and membership, and then divided again between apparatus, membership and a wider political constituency. Statistically, as Tiano argued, the polarised nature of syndical politics made the respective electorates unlikely to cross union-to-union in order to express dissatisfaction. Dissatisfaction was more often registered by casting blank ballots or abstaining altogether.

Militants were responsible for the effective institution of the union's particular definition of the collective or class, of relationships to the union as organisation and to the base and the local level. The unions, like any political machine, relied upon getting bodies out to vote. The linchpin of this system was the militant. Union militants agitated in a sort of permanent campaign to define, retain, and mobilise, or demobilise, the electorate. Militants were relays in a system of information gathering, transmission and delivery. They fine-tuned service delivery and solicited dues. They were key players in union struggles to maintain their relative position. Militants were also themselves embodiments of particular conceptions of the class. As Socialisme ou Barbarie repeatedly pointed out, trade-union definitions of the working class were not synonymous with those that flowed more directly from the experience of production, rooted in the informal worker collectives that formed by shop and shift on the factory floor. Nor were these definitions given once and for all: they were constantly reiterated and subject to contestation, directly at stake in each collective action.

By the early 1970s, following from the socioeconomic and political transformations instituted by Fordism, and only temporarily disrupted by May 1968, the militant and the culture that gave the role its coherence had become increasingly isolated and self-referential. This context enabled Mothé to think of patterns of militant action as belonging to a discrete social space. Conflict within this space, he argued, opposed two personality types, corresponding roughly to trade-union and (revolutionary) opposition militants.

Mothé divides trade-union militants into three types: the orator; the administrator; and the doctrinaire. Each type is conditioned or inflected by their particular organisational affiliation.[69] These trade-union types are encompassed and unified in the broader notion of the Leninist militant. The relation between specific types to Lenin was largely one of identification. CGT militants might have imagined themselves as operating in the tradition of Lenin as they set about their daily rounds of administrative tasks because Lenin's notions of what constituted a militant so thoroughly permeated PCF-CGT ideology, and this ideology shaped the way individual militants approached their activities.

However, Mothé points out, fine-tuning service delivery or agitating politically were not activities that could be undertaken simply on the basis of an identification with Lenin. Being a militant presupposed that one had both professional and personal credibility in the shop. It also presupposed that one had particular skills that were in relatively short supply in that context. These included facility with written and spoken language in general, and with the specialised language of politics in particular. This facility was, in turn, shaped by familiarity with the specific practices constitutive of the militant trade.[70]

These last characteristics were shared by both general types of militant, who opposed each other across a shared social space. For Mothé, the militant:

> [P]ossesses the characteristics of an intellectual: whether from a worker-origin or not, he adheres to an ideology by the intermediary of a certain type of knowledge; his actions are determined by the scientific knowledge of society. The workers themselves are led naturally to discover the scientific mechanisms of society by their confrontation with the reality of their exploitation. The two paths, of knowledge and experience, reconnect, but the role of knowledge is preponderant; it is that which allows him to take a position '*avant*', and why the revolutionary militant will be the '*avant-garde*'.[71]

The militant is an intellectual who traffics in a combination of experience in the shops and 'scientific' knowledge of society. For the Leninist type, the party

---

69   Mothé provides an organisation-by-organisation sketch of how militants function, and plots it onto a three part, ideal-typical schema. These three character types – the orator, the administrator, the doctrinaire – combine in various ways and to varying degrees in any given militant. The criteria that shape such combinations are noted in the main text, above. See Mothé 1973, Chapter 2: 'Le militant de base' and Chapter 5: 'Les trois types de militants'.
70   See Mothé 1956 pp. 73–100.
71   Mothé 1973, p. 22.

results from the accumulation of this knowledge and is the primary instrument for its preservation and dissemination. To access 'scientific knowledge' about society is to be linked to the party, to follow its directives and pursue its agenda. It follows that when party directives and local problems, 'knowledge and experience', came into conflict, the Leninist militant would subordinate the latter to the former.

Mothé opposes to this an older, syndicalist conception of the militant. Bearing the imprint of a history that begins before World War I with the revolutionary syndicalist forms of political organisation that were particularly powerful in France, this type of militant advocated precisely the opposite prioritisation of knowledge and experience (i.e. party and local conditions) from that advocated by the Leninist type. This is the conception of the militancy advocated by Socialisme ou Barbarie, to the extent that the worker-militant was theorised as such.[72] Mothé seems to have in mind the image of syndical militancy valorised by the CFDT after its 1964 split with the CFTC. A trade-union organisation interested in developing forms of organisation that afforded maximum control to the base without thereby getting involved with a revolutionary politics, the CFDT laid much more explicit claims to the syndicalist tradition than Socialisme ou Barbarie could have done. This type is:

> [S]omeone over 30, well integrated into the enterprise. Through a certain seniority, he had the confidence of his compatriots and through experience in various local struggles [*luttes revendicatives*] he has access to the 'trade' of a militant. The 'trade' no longer refers to the Leninist professional revolutionary whose knowledge is essentially theoretical, but to a trade which one learns like most others, as much by diverse knowledges (and not by 'Knowledge') as by practice and experience. This is the conception among the old syndicalist militants who, even if they officially are Leninists, remain very attached to this idea of the militant.[73]

The distinction between Leninist and syndicalist militants can be reduced to an opposition between militancy based on access to a single, codified, hierarchical type of knowledge, the condensed social and political expression of which is the party or organisation, and a militancy based on a more heterodox mode of knowing, assembled through a *bricolage* of scientific knowledge and

---

[72] Socialisme ou Barbarie would not make the distinction between the politically active worker and workers more generally, nor would they very easily recognise the existence of politics as a discrete social space/a discrete social activity.

[73] Mothé 1973, p. 23.

shop-floor experience. This opposition transposes very different notions of legitimate political activity. For example, a CGT militant would be appointed by the organisation, often on the basis of stamp sales. He was not elected by the workers he 'represented'. He therefore owed his position entirely to the union. Union activity would be a ticket off the factory floor, and the union hierarchy an alternate means of social mobility. The desire not to return to production work often substitutes for political aspirations. The pervasive use of revolutionary rhetoric in PCF-CGT ideology might well conceal this substitution. This pattern is one type of explanation for the process whereby the Leninist type of militant tended to invest in a notion of organisation as active principle and of politics, and the rhetoric of emancipation, as a separate, self-contained, self-legitimating theoretico-historical institution.

The syndicalist militant, the *bricoleur* whose political worldview would be consistently shaped by shop-floor experience and whose position would necessarily be established on (informal) democratic lines, is an echo of the type of politics imagined by Socialisme ou Barbarie. Mothé presents it both as an endorsement of the CFDT and as an idea made increasingly distant and normative by the progressive destruction of working-class political culture under the combined pressure of Fordism and the pulverisation of Marxist language under the weight of Stalinism.

In an interview with the author, Mothé outlined the following hypothetical situation to explain how he remembered himself as a militant. Workers in a particular shop have been complaining to the shop steward and foreman about speed-ups for some time, and nothing has changed. It becomes increasingly evident that the union will not respond to these grievances, any more than the corporation will. The workers in the shop express their displeasure by abstaining *en masse* from syndical elections, informally orchestrating slow-downs, perhaps even by sabotaging machines. A militant from a revolutionary group, with a command of language and a certain oratorical flair, gets up on a table and begins to talk. Emerging from amongst the workers, his politics are well known. Getting up on a table interrupts the sightline of the shop, gaining the workers' attention even though none of them can hear what he is saying. Gradually, the machines stop in the department, the workers begin to listen. Mothé described his having provoked a couple of small strikes in exactly this manner, referring to them as 'moments of *jouissance*'.[74]

---

74 Interview with Mothé, January 1992. I return to this scene and Mothé's quite striking language in Chapter 6.

CHAPTER 5

Looking for the Working Class

Introduction

This chapter examines Socialisme ou Barbarie's efforts to engage practically with the problems of organisation, politics and gaining wider access to worker experience through the medium of a 'worker newspaper'. The chapter is organised in three parts. The first is an overview of the *Correspondence* project, which Socialisme ou Barbarie took as the model. Based in Detroit, the *Correspondence* collective operated in a field of cultural production quite different from the one at whose margins Socialisme ou Barbarie found itself. Rather than provide an account of that context (a task that another is encouraged to undertake) I focus on the collective as an interlocutor to Socialisme ou Barbarie and the paper as a counterpart to *Tribune Ouvrière*. The main themes are the intertwining of organisation and worker writing.

The second part examines the relations between *Correspondence* and Socialisme ou Barbarie. While the former was of fundamental importance, what Socialisme ou Barbarie collectively valued was the kinds of writing that *Correspondence* was able to elicit. Insofar as the Correspondence collective itself was concerned, both theoretically and practically, there were basic disagreements. The second part of the chapter illustrates this through the analysis of C.L.R. James's presentation to the group in early 1956, and the range of responses to it. I then turn to Socialisme ou Barbarie's theoretical appropriation of the *Correspondence* model, focusing on two key texts: Castoriadis's 'Sur le contenu du socialisme (I)' and Daniel Mothé's 'Le problème d'un journal ouvrier'.[1] These texts together comprise a critical, but sympathetic, conversation with their Detroit counterparts.

The two groups employed the same basic approach to linking revolutionary organisation and theory to new forms of autonomous worker action. They shared similar views on a socialism rooted in direct democracy. The differences over organisation that separated *Correspondence* and Socialisme ou Barbarie originated with divergent understandings of the status of socialism as it related to working-class experience. *Correspondence* saw worker culture as already

---

1 Both articles were published in Socialisme ou Barbarie no. 17, along with translations from *Correspondence*, including extracts from the special supplement on organisation and *Tribune Ouvrière*.

containing elements of socialism. Socialisme ou Barbarie saw socialism as a future possibility, a telos, the nature of which was shaped by potentials generated in the course of everyday worker experience. This difference comes down to a matter of how each group construed the relationship between shop-floor worker collectives and the dominant culture. For *Correspondence*, workers rejected and took a distance from the dominant bourgeois culture. Socialisme ou Barbarie, by contrast, took the fact of domination more seriously. For them, workers were alienated from the dominant culture, but there was no outside. This characterisation is fleshed out in the second section.

The final section analyses *Tribune Ouvrière*, the problems it encountered and its failure to become a 'worker newspaper'. This section is based on reading and situating accounts of micro-political conflict in semi-skilled shops at Billancourt. The section moves from these readings to explore the cultural divisions that separated the realm of politics from the realm of everyday experience and the effects of the routinisation of political language. The sociological factors that shaped this routinisation of political language proved fatal for the idea of a worker newspaper, which asked workers to write about their own experience in a language close to the oral culture of the shop floor.

Correspondence

Like the Johnson-Forest Tendency before it, *Correspondence* was a fundamental interlocutor for Socialisme ou Barbarie. The header appended to the first *Correspondence* translations to appear in *Socialisme ou Barbarie* indicates the importance attached to the paper:

> [M]uch more than a new revolutionary publication, it represents a profoundly original effort to create a journal for the most part written by workers, to speak with workers from the workers' point of view. Whatever critiques or reservations that might be formulated regarding those issues which have already appeared – which are related to the fact that we are still taking our first steps – it must simply be acknowledged that *Correspondence* represents a new type of journal and that it opens a new period in revolutionary worker journalism.[2]

---

[2] Unsigned, 'Un journal ouvrier aux Etats-unis', *Socialisme ou Barbarie* no. 13 (January–March 1954), p. 82.

From the outset, Socialisme ou Barbarie was collectively interested in *Correspondence* as an experimental journal that tried to generate a new type of dialogue between militants and workers. The group was sceptical of the claims made in the paper about being a model of a new type of revolutionary political practice. The scepticism followed from the fundamental differences in the visions central to each group. This section focuses primarily on the area of agreement: the worker newspaper.

Becoming *Correspondence*

The collective that published *Correspondence* developed out of the Johnson-Forest Tendency after its 1950 split with Trotskyism.[3] Like Socialisme ou Barbarie, the Johnson-Forest Tendency argued for the fundamental importance of the relations of production in shaping how the workers practically elaborated the basis for class action in the course of everyday experience. The J-F Tendency saw this as a new culture that was unfolding at the point of production. The paramount task facing revolutionaries was to gain access to this culture and disseminate it in the form of written artifacts. The primary task of revolutionary theory, to the extent that there was space for it in the *Correspondence* project, was to facilitate this dissemination and provide contexts for it. This vision of worker culture was central to much of C.L.R. James's theoretical writings from the period, as well as to Grace Lee Bogg's essay 'The Reconstruction of Society'. These writings consistently returned to the idea that the revolutionary movement had to be reconstituted around this 'new culture' that was being socially elaborated by the modern proletariat.[4] Knowledge of the new culture was predicated on a direct analysis of the concrete relations of production. This knowledge could not be based on the work of 'outsiders'.[5] Instead, it had to be rooted in the understanding of the relations of production

---

3 See James 1950, p. 8. The Johnson-Forest Tendency 'became conscious of itself early in 1941'. Its best-known members were C.L.R. James, Raya Dunayevskaya and Grace Lee Boggs.
4 James often phrased his critique rather differently than Socialisme ou Barbarie members would, situating it as an effort to recuperate the 'spirit of Lenin' against Leninism. His approach to Marx was constructed along the same lines. This differing relation to the Marxist tradition is an effect of context and was the source of various misunderstandings between the groups.
5 'Outsiders' might come from academic-sociology or industrial backgrounds, for example. See Lee 1947 for a critical reading of Elton Mayo's *The Problems of Industrial Civilization*. Mayo, and Lee's reading of him, were important influences on Castoriadis 1988e.

expressed by the workers themselves, in writing their own experience.[6] The first, and in some ways the most important, result of these theoretical arguments was Paul Romano's 1947 essay, 'The American Worker'.[7]

The central role accorded to worker writing followed from the Tendency's critique of Lenin. Parallel to that worked out by Socialisme ou Barbarie, Johnson-Forest's critique of the Vanguard Party emphasised the political consequences of the division between intellectual and manual labour. The idea of a proletarian 'new culture' and its historical and social variability was based on readings of Marx's early writings, which the Tendency was the first to translate into English, and a critical, collective reading of Hegel undertaken by Johnson-Forest during the mid-1940s.[8] The worker newspaper as a means to access and disseminate aspects of this new culture had a number of sources in Marx and Lenin as well. One obvious model was the 'All Russia newspaper' programme Lenin outlined in *What is To Be Done?*[9] For Lenin in 1901, a newspaper could itself be a form of revolutionary practice. The newspaper would be the centre of a political education for an organisation through its assemblage, fabrication and distribution amongst a wider readership of a focus on everyday conflicts. Assuming ongoing interactions between the collective and the readership would make it a significant political tool and a formidable weapon in advancing the revolution. As Lenin put it:

> In a word, the 'plan for an All Russia political newspaper', far from representing the fruits of the labour of armchair workers, infected with dogmatism and bookishness (as it seemed to those who gave but little thought to it), is the most practical plan for immediate and all-round preparation of the uprising, with, at the same time, no loss of sight for a moment of the pressing day-to-day work.[10]

---

6   This is particularly evident in Boggs 1972.
7   Romano 1972. For a wider perspective on Johnson-Forest thought, see C.L.R. James, 'Dialectical Materialism and the Fate of Humanity', 'Class Struggle', and 'Popular Art and the Cultural Tradition' in Grimshaw (ed.) 1992, pp. 180ff in particular.
8   Johnson-Forest turned to Hegel and the early Marx in the mid-1940s as a 'return to the sources' that might enable them to develop a Marxist critical theory adequate to a rapidly-changing socioeconomic and political context. This turn enabled them to be innovative while still remaining firmly within the traditional Marxist lexicon.
9   See 'The Plan for an All-Russia Newspaper' in *What is To Be Done?* (Lenin 1977). In addition, one could connect the idea of *Correspondence* to the correspondence committees that made up the First International. On these committees, see Rubel 1975, Chapter 2, '1846–48'.
10 'The Plan for an All-Russia Newspaper' in *What is To Be Done?* (Lenin 1977).

In theory, *Correspondence* was a logical extension of the positions outlined by Johnson-Forest. In practice the paper signalled an abrupt change in their collective relation to Marxism: the abandonment of theory. The abandonment of theory entailed an abandonment of the form of militant action centred on the particular types of writing that were central to the mode of being-revolutionary particular to Trotskyism. Not all *Correspondence* militants were able to make this break. Their inconsistent responses indicated the political and psychological difficulties involved with a basic refashioning of militant comportment once it extended beyond cutting formal ties with a particular party. A lingering Trotskyism was often evoked internally to explain why the project of the self-theorising paper wholly written by its worker readership could not be fully realised.[11]

The *Correspondence* Collective

In 1954, the *Correspondence* group consisted of seventy-five workers and five self-described intellectuals divided into Detroit, Los Angeles, Pittsburgh and New York cells.[12] The centre of activity was Detroit, where the paper was produced and where the National Editorial Board was based.[13] Each cell had the autonomy to define itself, its membership and its main concerns.[14] But each cell had the same 'layered' structure: 'first layer' intellectuals were subordinated to 'second layer' worker-intellectuals (intellectuals by training working in factories), who were in turn subordinated to a 'third layer' of 'organic' workers.[15] The collective considered the subordination of upper-layer

---

[11] See C.L.R. James, 'On W', p. 25, point 1. This text is an unpublished, typescript-polemic against Dunayevskaya written during their 1955 split.

[12] Correspondence 1954, p. 1. Hereafter referred to as 'CBooklet'.

[13] Lyman Paine, an architect and the group's principal financial backer, lived in Los Angeles. C.L.R. James was thrown out of the US in 1953 for overstaying his 3-month visa by several years: he kept in contact with the group via a voluminous correspondence from the U.K.

[14] This was true more in principle them in fact. See 'On W' for information concerning Dunyevskaya's efforts to shift people from cell to cell, and James's response to them. Dunayevskaya is attacked repeatedly for indulging in tactics that were holdovers from the old Trotskyist days.

[15] These divisions rested on a theory of 'social types' made explicit in 'The Real Problem: We Solve This or Fail' in *Correspondence* no. 14, Special Supplement, 'Publishing Correspondence', p. S-l. An edited version was published in Correspondence 1954. The essay was translated as 'Intellectuels et ouvriers' in *Socialisme ou Barbarie* no. 17, pp. 83–4.

intellectuals to the third-layer workers crucial for *Correspondence* as a newspaper and the core of a practical solution to the 'organisation question'. One can read the *Correspondence* worldview off the metaphor of layers: one moves from surface to depth, superficiality to profundity, veneer to reality, by moving from intellectual to worker. At the same time, one moves through an inverted Leninism.

As the centrepiece of a political organisation that avoided the structure and problems of the vanguard, and as a vehicle for uncovering new social phenomena in a new language, *Correspondence* was conceived of as a continuing experiment in form and content. The first eighteen issues appeared biweekly in a fairly traditional opposition format for a political or trade-union journal: on cheap 8' × 11' paper, mimeographed from typed copy.[16] James later called these first issues an apprenticeship for the newspaper format that was adopted in October 1953, one that established its internal organisation and elements of its style.[17]

Just as the break from Trotskyism and the working out of relations between layers proved to be more complex and difficult than expected, so the shift from occasional writing to journalism created its own problems. The expenses of publishing a large-format newspaper without advertising and on a regular basis were considerably larger than those involved with producing occasional pamphlets and newsletters. This placed great financial pressure on the group. The newspaper format also entailed changes in the amount and type of writing collective members had to produce. Journalism required that writers develop a backlog of articles written in a straightforward, telegraphic style. For older militants, this required learning how to write in a genre quite different from the political essay and to work at a very different rhythm. For new worker writers, these same pressures shaped an accelerated education in journalism. Successfully navigating these problems was critical. For *Correspondence* to create and occupy a position in the field of working-class print media, and thereby have any chance of expanding its subscriber base or advancing its political project, it had to appear regularly, regardless of financial strain, and be internally consistent regardless of the stage of the writers' re-education.

---

16   The first is dated 15 November 1951.
17   See the letter from C.L.R. James to Johnny Zupan, 10 January, 1954: 'We sure are conducting a great experiment. We do not know. In anything really new the moves are in part guess work. They have to be'. James: untitled, unpublished typescript of extracts from letters on the *Correspondence* collective, Correspondence 1955, p. 7. Hereafter referred to as 'Letters'. Thanks to Scott Maclemee for providing me a copy.

In addition to these problems, the *Correspondence* collective was plagued with personal issues and conflicts that were connected to, but not synonymous with, political differences. Probably the most serious involved Dunayevskaya, whose difficulties with abandoning more traditional forms of political writing were a condensed expression of personal and political conflicts within the collective. One can imagine this having been manageable had C.L.R. James not been deported from the United States in 1953. The newspaper format had been his idea; he alone in the group had experience as a journalist. James also had the clearest vision of the links between publishing the paper and the organisation problem. More important for the fate of *Correspondence*, James was a central member of the core of the Johnson-Forest Tendency. He had tremendous influence within the group – even as he talked endlessly about the need to renounce it – and was the only member with enough personal and symbolic capital to manage relations between Dunyevskaya and the rest of the group.

While the collective grappled with personal and organisational problems, the paper evolved into an interesting, if eccentric, media outlet. Its most distinctive elements were the articles. Organised under the rubric 'Labor-Women-Negro-Youth-Organization-Culture-Editorial', articles reflected the composition and preoccupations of the various cells and the social *milieux* in which they were immersed. The New York cell produced articles that analysed working-class youth gangs as forms of revolutionary resistance.[18] The Detroit writers devoted much effort to articles on union, labour and race relations in the automobile industry.

Identifying Worker Writing

All *Correspondence* members had to write for the paper.[19] But it was not always clear what should be written about, how it should be written, and for whom. In this regard, the first issues of *Correspondence* are particularly interesting for their explicit statements showing how the editorial board tried to set the parameters for writing. The first issue opened with a journalistic account of

---

18   See Correspondence 1954.
19   During the 12 January 1955 meeting between Socialisme ou Barbarie and members of *Correspondence*, which included James and Lyman Paine, writing for the paper was presented as the sole criterion for membership in the collective. Socialisme ou Barbarie's questions indicated that they suspected the *Correspondence* collective of Menshevism.

a wildcat strike in the West Virginia coal fields.[20] The second article, 'Forging Steel and Men', was *Correspondence*'s first attempt at 'worker journalism'. Written in a clipped, declarative style by (an) uncredited member(s) of the Pittsburgh cell, 'Forging Steel and Men' describes the 'coffee gangs that gather in a greasy spoon outside the mill gate' each morning. It develops a loose taxonomy of worker characters by correlating the time each 'gang' assembled in this diner with types of comportment inside the mill. The article was written in response to a solicitation from the National Editorial Board in Detroit. It was not, however, quite what the board had in mind. Board discussions about the piece prompted one of the very few programmatic statements about worker writing and its content:

> Pittsburgh writes that they are in 'a real state of uncertainty about just what sort of article we should be submitting'. And they request 'critical comments, suggestions and advice'.
>
> The state of uncertainty is understandable and appreciated, and the request is an unusually large one; however, some comments and suggestions will be attempted.
>
> The article 'Forging Steel and Men' is suitable for publication; however this type of article should not dominate or characterize the type of material we want to publish.
>
> The article describes an aspect of workers' lives, and our paper should reflect every aspect of working-class life. The question is to what purpose.
>
> The primary function of the organ we are publishing is to reflect the attitude that workers have to their role in production, in society, to the other classes and all other capitalist institutions that exist either for the purpose of exploiting or alleviating the many evils that are visited upon him.
>
> Only in this way can be seen the revolutionary rejection of the way in which a worker works for a living and of the life he lives in general with his wife, children and fellow man.
>
> Production is the most vital function not only of society but also of the working class. Naturally the role of the worker in production and his attitude is our most important concern. It is here that the nature of the crisis

---

20 My analysis is directed more toward the development of explicit genre criteria for worker-journalism in the sense that was central for Socialisme ou Barbarie. It leaves aside the content of the reports on the coal industry. It should be noted that these reports gave the collective the first real sense that what they were writing could be used as 'a weapon in the class struggle'. See C.L.R. James, 'Letters'.

is revealed, and above all the nature of the new society that the workers are struggling to create. [...]

The articles can describe, analyze, generalize and interpret the experience of the working class in production, society, organizations of the workers (unions, political parties, fraternal organizations), the relationship between classes or any phenomena [sic] that illuminates the life, struggles and experiences of the workers.

The best way to learn how to write is to take our material to the workers, not with the idea of teaching them something, as is generally done by everybody, but rather to see their reactions, comments and criticism; and to encourage their involvement or to understand their failure to become involved.[21]

The opening paragraph not only states the pretext for such a direct intervention by the editorial board; it also frames *Correspondence* as the public manifestation of a continuing conversation. The print conversation begins with a frame that positions it as an aspect of broader conversations already under way both within the collective and between the collective and workers. Operating without a clear definition of borders (between the oral and written, inside and outside) this broader conversation had public and semi-private dimensions. It was an aspect of an already ongoing editorial exchange that implies a broader circulation of articles and letters. What was published in the paper did not include everything that the editorial board had received. Beyond the obvious function of suggesting editorial standards, *Correspondence* situated itself from the beginning as an aspect of a wider socio-political process.

The device of a continuing conversation moved the paper's experimental character to the fore. At the same time, the device positioned the paper as itself a reflection of worker culture's dynamism. At moments of crisis, however, this framing conversation could turn suddenly inward.[22] Internal disputes played out in both editorials and letters from readers that quickly reduced the conversation device to a mere conceit, making the paper seem sectarian, self-referential and self-congratulatory, caught in its own very proletarian little world. The conversational device, crucial for selling the paper's self-image in this earliest period, was symptomatic of a larger tendency to blur inside and outside and to efface the borders that separated the paper, produced by a collective organised in terms of a shared worldview, the working class generally, and the

---

21 'Suggestions for Articles' in *Correspondence*, vol. 1 no. 1 (15 November 1951), p. 6.
22 A similar phenomenon occurred in the PCF press during the period following the Hungarian Revolution of Autumn 1956.

revolutionary culture that *Correspondence* tried to articulate and empower. Given the claims *Correspondence* made about itself and its project, this blurring indicates a confusion of internal desires and external realities.

The editorial argues that 'Forging Steel' was both too particular and too vague. The daily gathering of workers in a diner outside a steel mill at a sequence of times was an element of the shared experience of the workers at this mill. The article's problem was therefore not empirical. Rather, it did not construct for its readers a particular worker subject-position. Anyone who spent enough time in the same diner could arrive at the same conclusions. The editorial board's conception of worker journalism was rooted in a Marxist variant of autobiography. Individuals were supposed to recount a particular experience in terms of its 'objective determinants'. This entails a highly self-reflexive mode of writing. Ideally, articles would strike a balance between the detailed information necessary to demonstrate a life's particularities and social conditions that shaped them. Writing that managed to intertwine the particular and general in this manner would resonate with an ideal readership of shop comrades and provide a sociological perspective on the experiences that were recounted that would position it as 'working class'. Successful worker writing would combine worker experience and working-class life. The pieces would use autobiography to stage a particular experience in ways that included description, analysis, and interpretation. While these general aesthetic criteria are evident enough, they do not answer the question of what to write about or how to write about it. One could look at the 'Suggestions for Articles' editorial as a call for writing on the order of Paul Romano's 'The American Worker' written about different industrial and social environments.[23] But Romano's pamphlet is not presented as a model. There is good reason for this: a call for experimental work that uses an accompanying example makes of that call a request for the example to be imitated.

Worker writing was to 'reflect the attitude that workers have to their role in production, in society and to other classes' as a means of revealing, and understanding, their 'revolutionary rejection of the way in which a worker works for a living and of the life he lives in general'. 'Suggestions for Articles' is predicated on a vision of *Correspondence* as producing a total description of working-class life from a collage of individual perspectives. This formulation of the project converges with that outlined in Lefort's 'L'experience prolétarienne'. In both, workers' writing should provide a narrative viewpoint that allows the reader to imaginatively occupy sightlines along which shop-floor experience of the

---

23 I analysed Romano's pamphlet in Chapter 3, particularly its blurring of individual and collective experience by its use of the propositional form 'The worker feels x…'; 'The worker knows y…'.

factory is organised. By occupying those sightlines, readers take over the author's subject position. What anchors this imperative is the capture of thoughts and sensations universal for those with experience of the shop floor in contemporary industrial settings. For a militant reader, encounter with this sort of text entails a rethinking of revolutionary politics from this perspective. For a worker reader, the encounter is the recognition of common experience and a clarification of the links between this experience and possibilities for collective action.

A degree of workerism is implicit in the conception of *Correspondence* both as a group and as a newspaper. If there was a pedagogical function for the newspaper, then it was primarily directed at intellectuals. If the paper was successful, workers would already in a sense know about what they read, and would recognise themselves and their experience in it. Workers were already implicated in the social 'molecular processes' constitutive of the 'new culture'. Theory in its traditional form was beside the point, as the new culture was already developing at a level and according to a logic that intellectuals could not apprehend because they were steeped in bourgeois forms of knowing by virtue of their social position.

> When I think of politics as we are talking about today, I see something entirely new. The essence of this newness is that the American working class has adopted a new form of the class struggle. Picket lines, wages and hours, union bureaucrats and even union meetings do not command the lively interest of the workers that they held in the past. Yet from the stories that we get every day from the shops, we can see a new form of struggle emerging. It never seems to be carried to its complete end, yet its existence is continuous... This struggle is not the old one. This is the struggle to establish here and now a new culture, a workers' culture.
>
> Culture for the American workers does not necessarily mean attending lectures, visiting museums, reading or writing books. For him [sic], it is a way of life, his relations with his fellow humans on the job, his relations with his neighbors, the kind of house he lives in, what he does in his spare time, the things he likes or dislikes, this is his culture.
>
> It is this we must be extremely sensitive to. We must watch with an eagle eye every change or indication of the things that these changes reflect. It is these things that must fill our consciousness and the pages of this paper.[24]

---

24   'Editorial: A New Culture' from *Correspondence* no. 6, 12 December 1953, reprinted in Correspondence 1954, p. 38.

Again, there is a mixture of agreement and divergence here between *Correspondence* and Socialisme ou Barbarie. Both were groups agreed on the necessity to reclaim, reinvent, and reinvest traditional forms of worker struggle with a revolutionary significance. The divergences arose over whether 'worker culture' could be construed as the domain through which this reinvestment might occur. For revolutionary politics, locating progressive elements in a dominated culture is a base-line problem. *Correspondence* tended to ignore domination and its effects by positing a radical separation of the workers from dominant culture. Worker rejection of the dominant culture opened space for the emergence of positive political and cultural forms. These forms were socialism.[25] Socialisme ou Barbarie did not assume such a separation. Rather, the group saw Fordism as destroying any autonomous worker culture. From this, it follows that Socialisme ou Barbarie would find the abandonment of theory to be impossible if political activity is to remain coherent. For Socialisme ou Barbarie, socialism would develop from the unfolding of implications or potentials being posited in everyday resistance to exploitation on the shop floors of heavy industry. Socialist culture was a project to be worked out in the future. The divergences are rooted in the sociological and political assessments of the situation of the working class in the specific environments in which each group operated.

Practice: *Correspondence* as Organisation

> *Correspondence* is a paper that is written and edited by its readers. This one fact, and it is no small one, is the program and the line of the paper. The editorials, the political articles and analyses of current affairs will flow from what our readers have to say. The attitudes to the unions, the needs, interests and problems of the workers, Negroes, women and youth, as they are expressed in the pages of this paper, issue after issue, will clearly establish the line, program and direction of the paper ...
>
> The simplest problem for the paper is to draw up a list of demands in the interest of workers, Negroes, women and youth. The hardest problem is to avoid doing that very thing.
>
> The only problem we have is to establish the paper, to make it a living reality. No amount of agitation in our paper will result in the six hour day. No amount of agitation in our paper will solve the questions of war,

---

25 See James, Lee and Chaulieu 1974, pp. 106ff, 110.

peace and depression. An important step in that direction would be the establishment of a paper that existed solely for the purpose, and made it unmistakably clear, that what is decisive in this moment of history is what workers have to say.[26]

Correspondence provided workers a forum in which to 'speak'. The problem was how to make the paper available as such a forum. Internally, this meant that the intellectuals had to relinquish the informal power they had by virtue of academic training, facility with language, techniques of argumentation and familiarity with Marxist discourse. *Correspondence* tried to refashion the intellectual worker relation through its 'layered' organisation, and through the structure of the National Editorial Board.[27] The *Correspondence* collective considered an editorial committee essential to the regular appearance of, and continuity within, a weekly newspaper, even if the paper was undergoing a (much desired) fusion with its readership. The organisation question was therefore addressed in the board's structure. This was the motivation behind electing Johnny Zupan to the editorship, a 'third-layer' worker with fifteen years at Chrysler. Zupan was to give *Correspondence* its 'worker' form and outlook.

In the letters he wrote to the collective from his UK exile, C.L.R. James was concerned with the internal dynamics of the editorial board and in particular with the process of defining a role for Zupan in relation to his comrades on the editorial board (which included former Johnson-Forest intellectuals Dunyevskaya and Grace Lee Boggs). James endlessly lectures Zupan on the importance of his role as editor, pushing and cajoling him to use his position to imprint the paper with his working-class vision. To Dunyevskaya and Boggs, James wrote with equal persistence to stay off Zupan's back, not to argue with or correct him. These letters show James trying, unsuccessfully, to persuade the intellectuals, Dunyevskaya in particular, to relinquish control over the political project that they had been instrumental in developing and their dominant positions within the group. From James's viewpoint, Zupan was the key to entering into the circular relation between field and audience. To get to its desired audience, *Correspondence* had to create and occupy a position in the field of cultural/political production directed at the working class. The paper

---

26 'Our Aim and Our Program', *Correspondence* no. 15, April 17, 1954, reprinted in Correspondence 1954, p. 30.
27 Space does not permit an intricate reconstruction of the problems within the Editorial Board and with Dunyevskaya in particular. Such a reconstruction would indicate how, at nearly every point, conflicts within the board were displaced versions of personal conflicts within the group.

could only gain such access by acting from the outset as if it already had access. If the audience failed to materialise, organisation was the obvious explanation. Paradoxically, this pushed *Correspondence* back onto the narcissistic terrain of small Trotskyist groups and their obsession with the 'correct' line and the 'correct' structure.[28]

Zupan's 'worker viewpoint' was to be reflected both in his writing and in the paper's content and layout. At the level of writing, Zupan encountered the central problems of adjusting to journalism mentioned earlier. Zupan had already been an important writer in setting the general tone for *Correspondence*.[29] His role as editor required that he rework his relation to writing, build up a backlog of finished articles, and abandon the topical, last-minute writing typical of oppositional journals published by small militant groups. James placed great emphasis on the backlog, arguing that it would enable him to stay closely involved in the production of articles, would remove him from the scramble to meet deadlines, and would allow him the space to visualise the paper as a whole. Amateurish copy would doom the paper from the start: layout had to be both thought-out and precise if its content was to get through to the readership.[30]

Zupan's editorship was also crucial for defining publication criteria. The collective hoped his influence as worker-editor would empower other workers associated with the collective to write and encourage their development. Editorials in *Correspondence* often noted with pride that the paper had provided a forum for experimentation to several workers who had never written before. Some of them developed into skilled, productive writers:

> One of the most remarkable things that has happened to us is the discovery of exceptional literary talents among our workers. One or two of them who cannot even spell, write at the drop of a hat like trained and experienced journalists. Two of our finest pamphlets have been written by such people. The trouble was not to get them to write. No, our difficulty was to prevent the educated, trained intellectuals from first 'recognizing' their faults, instructing them, educating them, in other words, ruining their

---

28 This paragraph draws heavily on James, 'Letters'.
29 See James 'Letters' on Zupan's CIO article from *Correspondence* no. 10 as a model for this type of writing. This article was reprinted in Correspondence 1954, p. 22.
30 James 'Letters', *passim*.

natural gift for style. A stern fight had to be waged to beat off the intellectuals from these natural writers.[31]

The premise in the above is that there is a 'natural' mode of worker writing that is linked closely to the oral culture of the factory floor. This mode of self-expression involved an active appropriation of written English that bent it to the cadences of an oral culture without regard for staid, 'proper' conventions. The worker writers who surfaced through *Correspondence* used their 'natural gift[s] for style' in ways that intellectuals not only failed to appreciate but frequently could not even recognise as indicative of anything other than incorrect usage. This incomprehension is evident in the 'politically sympathetic' intellectual's attempt to 'instruct' and 'educate' the worker writer – and thereby 'ruin' their writing. If intellectuals were incapable of recognising the outline of 'authentic' worker culture in these writings, how could one expect these same people to generate a coherent theoretical description of that culture? One could not. Intellectuals, by virtue of their training and regardless of their political sympathies, are products of the systems of education and socialisation rejected by the workers. Hence, passivity is the only attitude possible for intellectuals. They could support *Correspondence* by contributing to the creation of a forum for worker self-expression. But intellectuals could not theorise that expression in a coherent manner. Theory, as the mode of being-political that the *Correspondence* collective associated with intellectuals, was useless or worse.

The division that separated workers from intellectuals extended beyond questions of proper spelling and the interpretation of worker texts, to divergent notions of what constituted politics. In the 'Publishing *Correspondence*' supplement, an article entitled 'The Real Trouble: We Solve This or Fail' confronted the problem by recounting an internal debate about McCarthyism:

> There is an editorial meeting of three people to discuss an article, it consists of one working man as chairman, one woman who has worked in the plant for years and still works there but is an intellectual, and one intellectual of great knowledge and political experience. Nothing could be better. The question before them is an article on McCarthy, on some aspects of the McCarthy business.

---

31   'The Real Trouble: We Solve This or Fail' in 'Publishing *Correspondence* Special Supplement no. 1' to *Correspondence* no. 14, April 3, 1954, p. S-4. Abridged version published in Correspondence 1954, pp. 3–4.

The worker in the chair says that he does not think that the paper should concern itself too much about McCarthy. The workers, he says, are not much afraid of McCarthy. If McCarthy tried to touch the working class, he would get a mass of blows. And having expressed his opinion briefly, he stops. The politically experienced intellectual says 'But it is not a question of McCarthy as such. There is the question of the freedom of the press... [that] affects everybody'. The worker replies 'The workers are not particularly interested in freedom of the press'. The politically experienced intellectual says at once, 'But that is absolutely untrue and even if it were true it is the duty of the paper to point out to the workers that freedom of the press is a matter of life and death for the country as a whole and the workers more than anyone else'...[32]

As a result of this argument, *Correspondence* published an article on McCarthyism that was, in the view of the author of the above, indistinguishable from what had appeared in any number of mainstream newspapers. The author claims that the piece:

> ...meant nothing at all to a majority of the workers in the country. If *Correspondence* does not say what the workers think, not only does is not deserve to exist. It will certainly not continue to exist.[33]

With this pronouncement, the author derives a political moral from the story:

> The criminal thing is that the worker chairman did not say what he thought, that what he thought did not go into the paper. He knows workers, he has lived among them all his life. He spoke out of a tremendous depth of experience. I can say that after 25 years of studying the workers' movement in theory and practice, I have arrived at this conclusion. Whenever a worker of some political understanding says something that contradicts what I, as an intellectual, think, I do not correct him, I do not argue with him. *I ask him to tell me more.* I do not interrupt him. I listen. And when he has said all he has to say, and I have questioned him with the sole purpose of finding out what he was driving at, I ask him to write his views down. I spend days and weeks thinking it over.

---

32 'The Real Trouble: We Solve This or Fail', p. s-l.
33 Ibid.

> My experience, and it has taken me years to learn this, is that as a rule, what he is talking about is not what I am talking about at all, and that what he is talking about is what matters.[34]

The workers know what is going on. Intellectuals do not. The only attitude possible for intellectuals, relative to workers, is respectful, considered silence. By virtue of their training and dispositions, intellectuals are obstacles. The workers must be allowed to speak for themselves. Ironically, this injunction is presented as the fruit of twenty-five years of engagement with the workers' movement on the part of a highly trained intellectual. The exchange gives a good idea of what James saw at stake in the organisational issue.

Correspondence had to consistently demonstrate its close relationship to its working-class readership. These demonstrations would necessarily fail if the paper's definition of politics diverged from what workers were thinking. Such divergences were expressions of the group's failure to resolve the organisation issue. The failure obstructed the emergence of a new definition of politics consonant with what the worker-participants/readers said and/or wrote. The new politics would break with the traditional left rhetoric of political engagement. The questions of perspective and language were crucial if *Correspondence* was to create a distinctive space. The problem of distancing *Correspondence* from its Trotskyist origins arose again:

> The article 'A Revolutionist With Worn-Out Principles' was originally written for 'Two Worlds: Notes from a Diary'. Before publication it was sent around for comments. The comments from a working woman sum up so precisely the habits that an intellectual must overcome in writing for *Correspondence* that we publish the original article and comments side by side.[35]

'Two Worlds' was Dunyevskaya's regular column. This particular article, which had circulated amongst the collective, was almost a caricature of Trotskyist polemic. Working Woman's critique zeroed in on the immersion in the internal history of Trotskyism evident in Dunyevskaya's denunciation of James P. Cannon. Working Woman argued that this 'made workers feel dumb'. Her response then demonstrated, through a line-by-line critique of the article, that the language of the piece constructed for the reader a particular, non-worker subject position.

---

34 Ibid.
35 'Writing for Workers to Read' in 'Publishing *Correspondence*', p. S-2.

By the fourteenth issue of *Correspondence*, the residual Trotskyist rhetoric was increasingly at cross-purposes with the paper's development. The juxtaposition of this rhetoric with other forms of writing provided the paper with a distracting gloss that drew attention to small-group sectarian politics. Perhaps because it was more familiar to the intellectuals that produced much of *Correspondence*, this language took over at moments of internal crisis. The drift of this language outward to the readers' letters almost immediately undermined the framing conversation that was to connect the paper to a wider worker constituency.

Correspondence needed to develop sustained relations with 'ordinary' workers outside the collective and a language for communicating them. 'Working woman' emphasised the role that diary-columns could play in this, assuming that each was 'as intimate in its own way and as personal, and I mean this in the political sense, as the autobiography of the Negro auto worker in "Indignant Heart"'. Charles Denby, the author of 'Indignant Heart', was the most visible of the workers who emerged as a writer through the *Correspondence* project. An African-American worker who had never previously written, Denby's regular column, 'A Worker's Diary', was among *Correspondence*'s most vivid and successful experiments.[36] Denby's column constituted an autobiographical fulcrum around which the paper as a whole could turn, grounding in descriptions of concrete social relations the paper's assemblage of genres that ranged from journalism written from a worker's perspective to strike reports to detailed accounts of a particular social *milieux*.[37]

Behind questions of finances, organisation and position lay the vexing problem of extending the paper's reach into the working class and increasing worker participation in its production. An article entitled 'Attitudes behind Correspondence' tried to explain the paper's limited circulation and the collective's failure to expand as problems of 'worker confidence'. In fact, the

---

36   See his 'Workers' Journal' column in *Correspondence*. More accessible is his autobiography, Denby 1989. See also *Correspondence*, vol. II no. 1 (May 1, 1952), entirely taken up with the unattributed 'A Negro Soldier's Story of World War II', possibly by Denby. Extracts from his columns are reprinted in Correspondence 1954.

37   These letters pose at another level the problem of determining 'inside' and 'outside' in *Correspondence*. In the selections published under the title 'Intellectuals and Workers' in *Correspondence*, no. 16 (1 May, 1954) as responses to the 'Publishing *Correspondence* Supplement', two of the four clearly came from inside the group – 'A Woman's View' and 'An Intellectual Replies'; 'A housewife' is hard to determine. Of them, then, only 'A University Professor' clearly originated outside the group. The same problem shows up with the transcribed conversations: see, for example, 'Workers' Conversations' in *Correspondence*, vol. I no. 5, (January 10, 1952), p. 6.

collective's insular and divided internal life and a lack of clarity about what constituted participation prevented most workers who tried to join the collective from remaining active for long.[38] Cutting across all these problems were tensions created by conflict between organisational layers.[39] Regardless of the explanation, the fact was that very few workers actually participated in the production of this 'worker newspaper'. Given the centrality accorded the links between the paper's orientation and what workers wrote, and the marginalisation of theory undertaken on the assumption that workers would write and that the paper would, therefore, be self-theorising, worker indifference to 'their' paper threatened it with total collapse. One could argue that the blurring of the collective's edges through the device of the continuing conversation between it and a broader worker-audience is what enabled this small group to produce this newspaper for years under very adverse conditions. It may have reassured them to think that, with patience, reality might come to approximate this 'conversation', and *Correspondence* might begin to fuse with its readership and become a model for a new type of revolutionary organisation. There was a sense of fragility to the project. At times, the paper in general, and the framing conversation in particular, seem like little more than bizarre screens for the fantasies of a group of isolated militants.

The collective fragmented in 1955. The editorial board remained hopelessly divided. The collective's intellectuals, Dunayevskaya in particular, could not renounce their informal power. Most fundamentally, the paper was not able to resolve the political and logistical problems that the collective felt prevented it from becoming an outlet for worker writing, the 'new culture' and a revolutionary politics based on it. In 1955, Dunyevskaya and workers committed to her left to form 'News and Letters'. Charles Denby was among those who left. C.L.R. James could only watch from the UK. The remaining members did not have the material capacity to continue putting out the paper. *Correspondence* disappeared for four years.[40]

---

38   An ambiguity which the writer helpfully resolved by introducing a notion of 'total participation'.
39   'Attitudes behind *Correspondence*' in 'Publishing *Correspondence* Special Supplement', p. S-3.
40   The paper reappeared in the late 1950s. More work really should be done on *Correspondence*, particularly on its relations with the political-syndical field in Detroit.

Socialisme ou Barbarie and the Worker Newspaper

The dialogue between Socialisme ou Barbarie and *Correspondence* was in the main a most productive one. *Correspondence* was central to the way Socialisme ou Barbarie came to define worker writing in principle, and was a significant source for the clips from the 'worker press' that helped the group position the journal as approaching the working class in ways that Trotskyism could not. Socialisme ou Barbarie regularly received and discussed issues of *Correspondence*.[41] Individual members of the two groups corresponded more or less privately. Castoriadis was in regular contact with Grace Lee Boggs and, to a lesser extent, with C.L.R. James. Philippe Guillaume, who was in general more sentimental about his Trotskyist past, also stayed in contact with several members of the *Correspondence* collective.[42] However, neither influence nor personal contacts were shared evenly across Socialisme ou Barbarie. Jacques Signorelli (Garros) pointed out during a 1992 interview that *Correspondence* played a differential role in the group because not everyone in the group read or spoke English. Efforts to undo the informal hierarchies that separated intellectuals from workers in one context reinforced them in another.[43]

The differential roles played by *Correspondence* in Socialisme ou Barbarie did not prevent fruitful interactions. The groups' shared origins in the Left Opposition of the Fourth International prompted both to see the USSR as a primary reference point for thinking about the logic of contemporary capitalism. They were in general agreement about the direction in which the modern revolutionary movement should develop. Both groups tried to work out forms

---

41 Issues were noted as received at the beginning of nearly every meeting during 1954 and 1955. The paper would figure in conversations about *Tribune Ouvrière* frequently, as a point of comparison.

42 Castoriadis's suitcase, full of correspondence between himself, Grace Lee and C.L.R. James, was lost in 1958. Traces of the relationship with Guillaume can be found in the articles translated in later *Correspondence* issues. In a conversation with Grace Lee Boggs in April 1992 (Providence, R.I.), she indicated that both she and her (late) husband James were quite fond of Guillaume. Within Socialisme ou Barbarie, Guillaume was among the members who had fond memories of his Trotskyist past and stayed in contact with militant friends who stayed in the PCI after Socialisme ou Barbarie left – rather like the impression Grace Boggs gave of her own Trotskyist past, despite the great political distance separating her from it.

43 Interview, Jacques Signorelli, February 1992. To nuance this further, see Claude Lefort's *Anti-Mythes* interview (Lefort 1974, p. 2). Lefort notes Castoriadis's close relationship with Grace Lee (whom Lefort confused with Dunayevskaya) as a significant factor in explaining his disaffection with Socialisme ou Barbarie.

of organisation shaped by a critique of Lenin, and to fashion ways of thinking about politics and theory consistent with that critique. There were significant divergences as well. *Correspondence* framed the situation of the working class around an idea that alienation had prompted withdrawal from the dominant order. From this followed the idea that informal worker collectives were already developing a form of socialism. Socialisme ou Barbarie factored domination into their framework and saw no such distance. The emphasis in *Correspondence* on a 'natural' style that workers bring to writing for a worker newspaper was a consequence of their views on socialism in the present. As we will see, Socialisme ou Barbarie saw the situation quite differently.

C.L.R. James Meets Socialisme ou Barbarie

On 15 January 1956, after a clandestine journey from the coast that involved switching cars and covering tracks, the militants from Socialisme ou Barbarie were welcomed to a 'historic meeting' with C.L.R. James. While there had been extensive contact between the groups, face-to-face encounters were infrequent. Those that did take place were mostly informal. The meeting with C.L.R. James was exceptional. The typescript of this meeting is a map of the convergences and differences which linked and separated the groups. The centrepiece of the evening was James's presentation, 'The Problem of Proletarian Organisation and Current Tasks'. In the presentation, James argued that every stage of the history of the workers' movement had been characterised by particular forms of organisation that originated from deep within the movement and that served particular class interests in particular contexts.[44] Following much the same logic as Socialisme ou Barbarie had developed independently, James argued that, in 1956, 'the essence of proletarian struggle is the struggle against bureaucracy'. James's discussion of bureaucracy turned on the categories of 'elitism' and 'centralisation'. The elitism *motif* played out through the language he worked with and in references to the psychological consequences of investment in the notion of the Vanguard Party among revolutionary militants. The *motif* of centralisation oriented the critique of the Leninist party itself:

> So as Marxists, what kind of organisation do we propose? We don't propose anything.

---

44   Typescript Reunion Speciale du 15 Janvier 1956 (Johnson, du groupe Correspondence, groupe 'Raoul' et *Socialisme ou Barbarie*), pp. 1–2.

> But as Marxists we must have a general perspective, not in order to teach the proletariat or argue with our enemies, but in order to guide ourselves and know the paths of worker struggle.[45]

For James, the development of general perspectives on contemporary capitalism and revolutionary socialism remains necessary, but loses its status as an independent theoretical project. Not only can a revolutionary organisation produce no theory or engage in actions that resemble older forms of revolutionary politics, but the organisation itself should have no independent status. The only organisational objective is to locate autonomous worker movements. Theoretical perspectives should be limited to contextualising and helping to orient specific worker activities, elaborated in pamphlets and other documentation and distributed while the organisation merges with the worker movement.

> One mustn't think there is nothing to be done: we are Marxists and have to believe that we are the only ones who preserve the heritage of Marxism. This kind of task existed well before there were parties. The link must be broken between Marxism and the idea that, to be a Marxist, one must be for an avant-garde party.[46]

James extends this line of argument into a call to abandon traditional factional work:

> We are not looking to construct a 'left wing' within other organisations. Reform is a hopeless undertaking. In the US you can't throw Reuther out of his building: he built it; he's going to stay there.[47]

James goes on to explain what he has in mind by documentation and analyses. The initial projects he outlines are quite general; historical works on the *les Enragés* and *Hébertistes* in the context of the French Revolution and a historical work on the Russian Revolution. He announces a forthcoming publication on Athenian democracy.[48] The autonomous worker actions of the time that seemed to him particularly significant involved the UK shop-steward's movement and docker unions. After short overviews of recent actions by the shop

---

45   Typescript Reunion Speciale du 15 Janvier 1956, p. 2.
46   Typescript Reunion Speciale du 15 Janvier 1956, p. 3.
47   Typescript Reunion Speciale du 15 Janvier 1956, p. 4.
48   'Every Cook Can Govern', published in *Correspondence*, Vol. II, No. 12. June 1956.

stewards and dock workers, James provides a more specific indication of the direction in which his thinking was heading:

> The shop-stewards have no history. We are going to make one. The dockers have no journal. We are going to start one. We are also going to publish something called 'State Capitalism and World Revolution'. We will distribute it as well, but that is not the future. That is a way to liquidate the past. It is itself a relic from the past.[49]

Socialisme ou Barbarie's Responses

Correspondence and Socialisme ou Barbarie shared an overall approach to thinking about questions of revolutionary organisation and related matters. But differences in their respective assessments of the situation of the working class resulted in conflicting positions. From Socialisme ou Barbarie's side, these differences were not evident when the relation between the groups was limited to exchanges of letters and publications. The differences emerged clearly with the responses to James's presentation.

James's positions were those of *Correspondence* in general. Socialism was already in the making amongst informal collectives of workers on the factory floor who expressed their alienation from bourgeois culture by rejecting and withdrawing from it at once. If socialism is already in the making in the present, there would be no need for a political line formulated by a group of militants except as a way for those militants to orient themselves. Militants would have nothing to 'teach the workers' and the workers nothing to learn from them. In fact, the situation would be the opposite. To think intellectuals had something to teach workers was to perform the idea resulting from the psychological consequences of involvement with the ideology of the Vanguard Party. To break with the latter would require breaking with those consequences as well. The result was an erasure of revolutionary politics. Militant intellectuals simply did what their specific skill-sets enabled them to do: fashion, publish and disseminate information. The organisations they form amongst themselves would have no independent standing. To participate in revolutionary action was to integrate themselves with autonomous worker organisations.

James elicited a range of critical responses from the members of Socialisme ou Barbarie. The reactions bore on questions of organisation rooted in assessments of the situation of the working class in France that differed

---

49 Typescript Reunion Speciale du 15 Janvier 1956, p. 6.

fundamentally from the assessments James articulated in his talk. The explicit disagreements centred on the 'content of socialism'. For Socialisme ou Barbarie, the central positive task of revolutionary theory lay in the elaboration of a vision of direct-democratic socialism rooted in the forms of self-organisation adopted by autonomous worker movements. The group connected these forms back to everday experience at the point of production. Because Socialisme ou Barbarie understood the working class as dominated and socialism as a construct oriented toward the future, the group tended to focus in an analytic mode on forms of practice and self-organisation in production that shaped the nature of autonomous actions. The content of socialism was the vision of a post-revolutionary situation. Its articulation was the main task for revolutionary theory. In the context of an ongoing dialogue with the worker avant garde, theory would provide autonomous actions a teological framework basic to their political orientation. So theory, and the organisation that produced it, retained an independent status.

For Daniel Mothé, what James proposed jettisoned revolutionary politics itself: 'Being opposed to bureaucracy is only a first step. It does not solve anything'.[50] Worse, Mothé continued, James provided no direction, no indication of what, if anything, militants might conceivably do or even of what, if anything, they might bring to worker actions. As if explaining to James what Mothé had said, Castoriadis countered that James had outlined an approach to the integration between revolutionary militants and worker actions that could be agreed on as a long-term goal for the revolutionary movement. But such integration presupposed at the least a conception of socialism shared by the worker avant garde and revolutionary organisation. Castoriadis asserted that there was no such shared conception at present. That lay behind Mothé's response. Castoriadis then said that the presentation had not gone far enough. Neither opposition to bureaucracy nor the fact of direct democracy could solve anything on its own.

Barois (Benno Sternberg) was more sympathetic to James's ideas. He related an overview of the situation in East Germany after 1950 that was analysed in Chapter Two. Communist Party attempts to co-opt local level factory committees had opened up space not only for the East Berlin June Days, but for other autonomous actions with significant political resonances. The underlying claim seems to be that actions like the East Berlin June Days could be understood in the terms James presented. But the explanations Sternberg adduced in his more detailed analyses are not symmetrical with this. The intervention seems shaped by personal affinity. Vega rejected James's basic arguments. By

---

50   Typescript Reunion Speciale du 15 Janvier 1956, p. 7.

way of demonstration, he pointed to the history of committee-based council movements. He argued that the Soviets between 1918 and 1920, the Italian factory committees in 1920, the Belgian miners of 1933, and a significant strike in Amsterdam in 1955 had all exhibited similar patterns of drift in the absence of some kind of broader view of revolution and its relation to socialism. A revolutionary organisation was necessary for the elaboration and dissemination of this broader view. For Philippe Guillaume, the central question to emerge from James's presentation was one of collaboration amongst revolutionary groups, one centred on a shared conception of socialism.[51]

The responses from members of Socialisme ou Barbarie can be interpreted in two ways. The first demonstrated the uneven impact of *Correspondence* within the group that Jacques Signorelli described. Members who spoke English, Castoriadis, Sternberg and Guillaume, were motivated by a sense of personal affinity with James. Mothé and Vega were not. The second manner of parsing the responses shows them to be versions of the exchange between Mothé and Castoriadis. If one took James's talk as accurately describing the situation of the working class in January 1956, there would be nothing for militants to do. On the other hand, the group in the main agreed that the revolutionary organisation would seek to merge with autonomous worker movements once there was a shared view of socialism. But such agreement did not currently exist.

The exchange was generally cordial despite the disagreements. James took umbrage to Vega's remarks. Perhaps it was a matter of tone or something else that remains ineffable in the transcript of a meeting.

Socialisme ou Barbarie's 1955 Map of the Revolutionary Project

For Socialisme ou Barbarie, the working class was dominated not simply due to its position within the relations of production proper, but more generally as an expression of those relations of production. So while the differences that separated James from Socialisme ou Barbarie were partly attributable to a 'field effect',[52] they also followed from significant differences in the assessment of the situation of the working class in contemporary industrial contexts. A more fully elaborated counter-position can be found in two texts from *Socialisme ou Barbarie* no. 17. Castoriadis's 'Sur le contenu du socialisme (I)' can be read as

---

51 Typescript Reunion Speciale du 15 Janvier 1956, pp. 8–11.
52 The example Bourdieu points to of this mutual incomprehension characterised relations between the Partisan Review and *Les Temps Modernes*. See Bourdieu 1984, 'Preface to the American Edition'.

assimilating James's vision of the working class as a source for the 'thinking differently' required of revolutionary theory across a prism of domination. Were the state of affairs as James outlined it, theory would be redundant. If theory was still produced, it would be merely descriptive. Castoriadis's essay is a defence of revolutionary theory and a call for the transformation of its content. Daniel Mothé's 'Le problème d'un journal ouvrier' is a normative design for, and critical assessment of, the worker newspaper as a model for revolutionary organisation. This essay synthesises Mothé's understanding of *Correspondence* with an analysis of the tactical binds that faced *Tribune Ouvrière*, the monthly with which Mothé had been involved at Renault Billancourt since May 1954.

'Sur le contenu du socialisme (I)' is the first in a series of three synthetic articles published under the same title that Castoriadis wrote between 1955 and 1958. Each essay in the series summarised Socialisme ou Barbarie's project to that time and used this summary to raise basic questions about the project and the assumptions that shaped it.[53] The series is quite heterogenous. The second is an extended description of a socialism organised around a pyramid of direct-democratic councils inspired by the Hungarian Revolution and Socialisme ou Barbarie's new visibility during 1957. The third, which is discussed in Chapter Six, formalises and reframes the problem of worker experience as of early 1958. Each text responds both to internal developments and shifting strategic situations.

In 1955, Socialisme ou Barbarie still operated in near-total isolation. 'Sur le contenu du socialisme (I)' is written as if anticipating new readers for the journal amongst elements of the worker avant garde. The essay opens with a review of Socialisme ou Barbarie's political and theoretical development. It rehearses the steps whereby the group moved from the analysis of the USSR and the development of the theory of bureaucratic capitalism to its preoccupation with the new revolutionary possibilities that the group felt were beginning to emerge after Stalin's death. The opening of new possibilities leads to the need for revolutionary theory to rethink the 'content of socialism'. The second section moves in three steps: it states what socialism is in outline; it poses the problem of revolutionary theory being embedded in the rationality that socialism will negate; and it attempts to move to an account of 'the content of socialism' beyond that rationality. The general solution arrived at leans on assumptions within the Marxian tradition similar to those Lefort outlined in his essay on proletarian experience. In the context of its collective experience at the point of production, the proletariat is working out the basis for socialism

---

53   Castoriadis 1988d (1957a) and 1988e (1957b).

just as the bourgeois order had worked out the basis of its rationality from inside the aristocratic and absolutist orders which preceded it.

For Castoriadis, the transition to socialism can only be effected through a conception of what socialism would be:

> The proletarian revolution will only realize its historic program to the extent that it suppresses this distinction [between *dirigeant* and *exécutant*], reabsorbs all particular directing strata, and collectivizes – more exactly completely socializes – the functions of direction. The problem of the historic capacity of the proletariat to bring about a classless society is not whether it can physically overthrow its exploiters from power (which it undoubtedly can), but whether it can positively organize a collective, socialized management of production and of power.[54]

Socialism is not just the abolition of exploitation. Socialism is the institution of functional social relations that would permit maximum collective control over the nature of the society and its means of reproduction. With this end in mind, the salient features of worker experience conditioning their desire to overcome alienation lay in the workers' capacity to direct or control production. The direct control over production – the socialisation of determinations of outputs and distribution – would entail a basic alteration in the relation of the instituted and the instituting. This terminology, which is drawn from Castoriadis's later work and which I am adopting analytically, brings together older dichotomies on the order of the relationship between dead and living labour and the separation of the *dirigeant* from the *exécutant*:

> The proletariat can only bring about socialist revolution if it acts in an autonomous manner, that is, if it finds within itself the will and the awareness of the necessary transformation of society. Socialism can be neither the inevitable result of historical development, nor the theft of history by a party of supermen, nor the application of a program deriving from a theory that is true in itself. It can only result from unleashing the free creative activity of the oppressed masses, an unleashing that historical development makes possible and that the action of a party, based on this theory, can facilitate enormously.[55]

---

54 Castoriadis 1988c, p. 10.
55 Castoriadis 1988c, pp. 10–11.

Theory and autonomous proletarian political actions were separate but complementary aspects of an overarching revolutionary project. As was the case in Lefort's project for interpreting worker narratives, revolutionary theory can provide the 'worker avant garde' with an image of itself, its experience and actions that would be differently weighted for having fitted within this context by situating these social-imaginary significations in the context of a teleological view that posited direct-democratic socialism as its end. The production of this 'clarified' image was the task of revolutionary militants. Making it available to the workers was the primary task of revolutionary politics. But neither theory nor the organisation that produces it can bring about socialism:

> To be a revolutionary means to think at once that only the masses in struggle can resolve the problem of socialism and to think that the essential content of the revolution will be given by the original and unpredictable creative activity of the masses, and to act oneself on the basis of a rational analysis of the present and a perspective anticipating the future. In the end, to be a revolutionary means to postulate that the revolution will entail a disruption, and enormous enlargement, of our rationality and to use that same rationality to anticipate the content of the revolution.[56]

In this passage, Castoriadis raises the central problems confronted by revolutionary theory. The institution of socialism would 'entail an enlargement, and enormous disruption, of our rationality'. Theory had to 'use that same rationality to anticipate the content of that revolution'. This meant that revolutionary theory had to incorporate into itself aspects of the new rationality being practically worked out at the point of production. Theory cannot be limited to description. Rather, it is an active reordering and re-conceptualising of social relations and their consequences. Theory shuttles between the patterns of meaning being worked out in the course of production and the radical extension of these patterns in the revolutionary organisation's collective vision of socialism.

As was the case for Marx, this conception implied a break not only with bourgeois ideology but also with the larger system of bourgeois thought that conditioned it. This break raises the problem of the social-historical position of the theorist. Marx's response to this problem centred on bourgeois intellectuals' relation to the proletariat. Renegade bourgeois intellectuals could

---

56 Castoriadis 1988c, p. 11. This paragraph is, in significant measure, a condensed restatement of Castoriadis's paper on organisation, 'La direction prolétarienne', published in *Socialisme ou Barbarie*, 10.

refashion themselves politically and intellectually by identifying with the proletariat. This identification would, in principle, enable these intellectuals to develop a new subject-position beyond the purview of bourgeois ideology and thought. The break with the dominant ideology would not be absolute. Marx's characterisations of the proletariat always emphasised its contact with the most advanced forms of bourgeois rationality from a viewpoint conditioned by their radical exclusion from the social order. At the same time, the proletariat's position was different enough that it could afford bourgeois intellectuals the basis for the construction of an image of ideology as a system. Such an image was difficult to construct because the dominant ideology shaped the categories in terms of which the world was understood. The role of these renegade intellectuals was crucial for radical politics because they brought analytical and literary abilities that played a key role in clarifying and radicalising working-class political action.[57]

In terminology drawn from Castoriadis' later work, the problem can be formulated with more clarity. Inherited or bourgeois thought unreflectively incorporates alienation into its founding assumptions and modes of apprehension. To contain the social-historical – and avoid the possibility that intellectual systems are historical products, the validity of which are a function of particular, transient social and institutional conditions – bourgeois thought universalises its logic. The universalisation of logic renders the thinking subject transcendent, and naturalises its objects. This style of thinking, which is shared by both Kant and Hegel, is incapable of interrogating the social-historical in a radical way. The same relation to logic shaped Marx's conception of history as well, which was worked out through engagement with Hegel and largely remained trapped at the moment of reversal. But there are indications of more radical ways of thinking about the social-historical in Marx.[58] One such way appears in an 1848 letter to his Russian correspondent Annenkov:

> Thus M. Proudhon, mainly because he lacks the historical knowledge, has not perceived that as men develop their productive forces, that is, as they live, they develop certain relations with one another and that the nature of these relations is bound to change with the growth of these productive forces. He has not perceived that economic categories are only abstract expressions of actually extant relations and only remain true while these relations exist. He therefore falls into the error of bourgeois economists, who regard these categories as eternal categories and not as historical

---

57   This schema is implicit in Marx 1988, pp. 61, 65–70.
58   My paragraph derives from arguments presented in the first part of Castoriadis 1998.

laws which are valid only for a particular historical development, for a definite development of productive forces. Instead, therefore, of regarding the politico-economic categories as abstract expressions of the real, transitory historic social relations, M. Proudhon, owing to a mystic inversion, regards real relations merely as reifications of these abstractions. These abstractions are formulae which have been slumbering in the bosom of God the Father since the beginning of the world.[59]

Following a parallel intellectual trajectory, Castoriadis enumerates the main effects of inherited or bourgeois thought on revolutionary theory in 'Sur le contenu du socialisme (I)'. These effects included: the tendency to reduce the unknown to the known; the assumption that theoretical work can take the individual, or individual economic motivations, as the premise for building useful descriptions of social phenomena or processes; and the treatment of social phenomena or historical processes as particular manifestations of abstract universal rules. Revolutionary theory would not only have to work through these problems, but would also have to work through those aspects of Marx that incorporated them as well. Rejecting conceptual stasis – the reduction of the unknown to the known – had been used since the 'Socialisme ou Barbarie' editorial in *Socialisme ou Barbarie* no. 1 to justify the group's iconoclastic relation to Marx and to other political organisations. The autonomous working-class actions that the group analysed had developed in opposition to both Marxist and bourgeois politics and organisations; it made little sense to think of them in old language. More substantively, the kind of social organisation Castoriadis saw as central to socialism was new. The point was to work out a relationship to the present through the mediums of critique and theory that enabled one to imagine the future and to use that imagined future to shape relations to and within the present.

Treating history as if it were governed by abstract rules made of it a closed system. Creation was thereby reduced to the recombination of existing elements. The premise of revolutionary theory was that human beings had the capacity to create a new social organisation, just as they have created the existing organisation. Revolutionary theory had to shift the social to the centre of its analytical dimension. Castoriadis argued that Marx's political economy did not do this. While other arguments had been worked out in the *Capital* seminars, the problem in this context is that Marx assumed the individual,

---

59 Marx 1982, p. 34. See Castoriadis 1955, p. 12: 'Marx was well aware of this problem: his rejection of "scientific socialism" and his statement "one step forward in practice is worth more than a dozen programs" are exact translations of his contempt for "bookish" solutions which are left behind by the living development of history'.

defined in terms of its economic interests, was an adequate premise for social analysis. This implicated Marx in the inherited thought that he tried to oppose: the bourgeois notion of '*homo economicus*' lay at the heart of his critique of political economy.[60]

The tendencies shared by bourgeois and Marxian thought converged in the definition of revolution. For Socialisme ou Barbarie, revolution should result in the collective institution of non-alienated social relations between both individual actors and the collective and between the collective and its modes of material and cultural reproduction. If this was the *telos* of revolution, it made little sense to retain older definitions that emphasised the simple overthrow of the dominant classes (a *coup d'état*), or that viewed revolution as a discrete event. Reworking Trotsky's notion of permanent revolution, Castoriadis argued that revolution was the moment of reversal within a much longer process. Its core lay not in the reversal, but rather in the working out of forms of life and politics based on continuous, collective self-institution made possible by the reversal. The shapes of socialism and revolution were intimately linked to the types of self-organisation developed before the revolution.

The juxtaposition of terms in 'Le contenu du socialisme' opened other avenues as well. For example, if it is true that revolution necessarily entailed a transformation of all social relations, then why should revolutionary theory privilege the analysis of the working class to the exclusion of other types of struggle, like those involving gender and/or sexuality?[61] At this point, Castoriadis's response would have remained firmly within the Marxist framework. Basing himself largely on Wilhelm Reich, he argued that revolution would entail an abolition of the bourgeois nuclear family and a freeing of sexuality from arbitrary constraints. These changes would entail a redefinition of gender roles. It is clear that these social relations remained derivative and that their transformation depended on the action of the (mostly white, mostly male) industrial working class.

Daniel Mothé's 'Le problème d'un journal ouvrier'

Castoriadis's 'Sur le contenu du socialisme' is also part of a conversation staged in *Socialisme ou Barbarie* no. 17 with *Correspondence* over revolutionary politics, the worker newspaper and the problem of organisation. Daniel

---

60 A theme developed in the 1950–1 *Capital* lectures and, in greater detail and with a different outcome, in Castoriadis 1998.

61 See Castoriadis 1955, pp. 21–3, in particular p. 23. For a brief discussion of Reich see pp. 23–5.

Mothé's 'Le problème d'un journal ouvrier' is the second element in this conversation. Mothé's essay is a normative conception of the worker newspaper as a political project. In its detail, the text considers problems encountered by *Tribune Ouvrière* during its first year of publication at Renault Billancourt. Mothé's text was a position paper in the group's ongoing debate about organisation; it was also Socialisme ou Barbarie's first public comment on *Tribune Ouvrière*.

The group considered *Tribune Ouvrière* an important, but often exasperating, experiment. From the first transcribed Socialisme ou Barbarie meeting, there was a wide range of attitudes about the paper and its implications.[62] The following is one of the group's first discussions of the paper. The group is canvassed about its prospects:

> Mothé: On *Tribune Ouvrière* no. 3: No discussion amongst the workers (holidays) or critiques from the Stalinists. The workers seem to be aware that *Tribune Ouvrière* expresses a current outside the traditional forces. [...]
> Conception of the journal: Because of different degrees of consciousness amongst the workers, it is necessary to translate their concrete experiences and formulate their political viewpoints. At the beginning, the factory-journal must tend toward being political. To avoid straying politically, a core should be constituted at Renault to select the articles. On the other hand, the group could assure the largest liaison with workers in other factories, prepare documents on the worker-press, and elaborate projects for articles.
> Véga: Conception: It is not possible to make *Tribune Ouvrière* a spontaneous expression of the workers. They discuss politics in a general way, but with a certain confusion caused by party-propaganda. An editorial organisation is necessary, having a political conception corresponding to the national experience of the workers.

---

62   *Socialisme ou Barbarie* began to transcribe their meetings and circulate typescripts on a quasi-regular basis after 22 July 1954. The official *Bulletin Intérieur* appeared after 1958 in a mimeographed and numbered format. The *BI* was initiated to keep those members like Lyotard and Souyri, who were posted to teaching jobs in the provinces, and Chazé, who lived in southern France, up to speed with debates in Socialisme ou Barbarie. The transcripts were not complete: for example, they omit the ritual recitation of those behind in their dues that began every meeting. Between 1954 and 1958, the coordination of the *BI* was apparently informal. This has resulted in a number of gaps in the collection that I was able to assemble from the papers of Jacques Signorelli, Henri Simon and Cornelius Castoriadis. I refer to the earlier, informal meeting transcripts by date.

Chaulieu: At the beginning, *Tribune Ouvrière* cannot be given a precise character. The experience has been undertaken almost outside of Socialisme ou Barbarie. It appears that a tacit agreement has formed around the editorial in number 1. The assistance given to editing the last issue by workers with past political experience could lead to a change in this original line.

It comes to this. Either *Tribune Ouvrière* becomes a political journal for the use of workers – and past experience warns against this, particularly with the core that seems to be constituting itself – but even if it turns out this way, the group should participate directly in its production. Or *Tribune Ouvrière* remains a worker-journal without a dominant political orientation at the beginning; but will tend to become a political journal. In this case, the journal must have a new format and break with those elements that tend to block all personal support from the workers.

Guillaume: Conception: The experience should be continued following a certain empiricism as much in the content as in the control of its orientation. There is a synthesis to be made between the viewpoints of comrades from different tendencies. Those who ask to participate should not be excluded because of their past experience. The character [given] by the direct expression of the workers should be preserved [...]

Guy: A journal should be created where the workers express their class-reactions. Starting with the experience the workers have, the important issues will emerge by themselves. The workers are not interested in party-politics but in the expression of these politics across the relations of production in the factory... Wanting to produce the journal by selection, with an editorial committee, comes to making a political journal with a bureaucratic organisation. A discussion with a Renault worker revealed him to be preoccupied with the journal's orientation and the hope that it will not be too ephemeral.[63]

Tribune Ouvrière was started at Billancourt in May, 1954 as an experimental factory-monthly that was to be written entirely by workers. Within Socialisme ou Barbarie, members had quite divergent interpretations of the project and its prospects during its initial phase. The more pessimistic arguments called for an interventionist editorial committee that could 'translate' worker experience and extricate it from dominant ideologies (Mothé and Véga). At the opposite end of the scale was the anarchist contention that any such committee would fatally contaminate the paper with the germ of bureaucracy (Guy made

---

63 Again, see the next section for detailed information on this point.

this point by referring to another Renault worker). In short, there was little agreement in Socialisme ou Barbarie over *Tribune Ouvrière*, its structure and implications. Neither was there any consensus about how to deal with relations between Mothé and the the Trotskyist elements in the collective.[64]

Mothé's 'Problèmes d'un journal ouvrier' is divided between a general theory of the worker newspaper and a pessimistic account of the problems that such a project might face. For Mothé, a successful worker newspaper would redefine the relationship between journalism and audience. By so doing, ithe reunification of the ways of being political that had been split apart by the definitions circulated by existing political and trade-union positions would become possible. This reunification would reject extant definitions and the more general patterns of thinking that subtended them. From this follows the emphasis in 'Problèmes' on the worker newspaper as an experience.

Like the vision behind *Correspondence*, Mothé defined the worker newspaper as based on active worker participation in its writing, production, and distribution. A successful worker newspaper would become a new space for workers and revolutionary militants, a forum for dialogue, and a junction for revolutionary theory and practices:

> We remain faithful to a preoccupation with the link between revolutionary organisation and the working class, between theory and the practical experience of workers. These two elements must necessarily reconnect, and their juncture will not only be the assimilation of revolutionary ideology by the working class, but also an assimilation of the experience of the working class by revolutionary militants. In this article, we will confront our fundamental theoretical conception and the dynamic of the efforts of workers who participate in this newspaper. We will always be guided by these two elements [...][65]

The underlying assumptions about organisation and the role of revolutionary theory are quite close to those Castoriadis had articulated in 'Sur le contenu du socialisme (I)'. For both Castoriadis and Mothé, theory could develop only through dialogue with the 'unpredictable, creative action of the masses'. To this dialogue, theory brought the capacity to clarify. The workers brought dynamism. The worker newspaper would be a forum for such a junction between theory and practice and would itself be a form of practice. From the experience of producing the paper might follow a redefinition of politics and the

---

64 On the composition of the group, see pp. 203ff. below.
65 Mothé 1955, p. 28.

ways in which social actors engage in politics.⁶⁶ The redefinition of politics was itself quite radical. It was antithetical to what Mothé saw as characteristic of working-class politics in 1955. Politics had become a discrete arena shaped by specialists for specialists. Politics, as bureaucratic discourse, unhinged the concrete experience of workers from the vocabulary that had developed through the history of the workers' movement and Marxism to express that experience and politically mobilise on that basis.

Mothé argued that abstracting Marxist terminology from its material referents ran parallel to the integration of trade unions and political organisations into parliamentary democracy. This separation had far-reaching consequences. The most immediate of these were confusion and the alienation of workers from the discourse that had developed to express their desire for emancipation. Alienation from the discourse of politics had a marked effect on the training of militants, who entered political life assimilating this abstract, bureaucratic politics as normal. This alienation extended to the formation of revolutionary militants as well. More precisely, Mothé argued, the dominant form of politics enabled militants to incorporate a basic theoretical error into their worldview by conflating two distinct types of politicisation, 'one particular to militants, and one particular to the working class':

> If the training of a revolutionary militant is almost entirely an intellectual training, particularly in periods like that which we have experienced, during which the lack of revolutionary movements has uprooted the revolutionary minorities from the class, the political training of workers is, on the contrary, almost entirely practical. It is in the course of its various struggles that the working class assimilates, in a more or less durable way, a certain political experience, and creates its own methods of struggle.⁶⁷

Ideally, the experience of the worker newspaper would set up new interactions or 'osmosis' between militants engaged in intellectual work and workers, whose knowledge of their situation was largely practical.⁶⁸ Following Mothé's

---

66 For now I will put aside the practical problems involved in this project. In fact in different contexts and for different reasons, both *Correspondence* and *Tribune Ouvrière* foundered on them. I address the latter's problems in the next section.

67 Mothé 1955, p. 30. In a footnote, Mothé argues that these processes are abstractions only, neither existing in its pure state.

68 '... [S]i la classe ouvrière a besoin de l'organisation révolutionnaire pour théoriser son expérience, l'organisation révolutionnaire a besoin de la classe pour y puiser cette expérience. Ce processus d'osmose a une importance déterminante', Mothé 1955, p. 30.

organic imagery, the paper would heal the wounds inflicted on working-class politics by the bureaucratisation of working-class organisations. So far as the relation of politics to writing was concerned, Mothé saw the paper as reuniting three main elements that had been separated by the conventional trade-union and political press.[69] Mothé defines the political as the internal deliberations of the Party apparatus, substituted for the activities of the base. The syndical pertains to economic issues. The documentary distinguishes the worker newspaper from a type of tourist literature that allows people without shop-floor contact to acquire the atmosphere. This position translates directly the decision to make *Tribune Ouvrière* a self-consciously 'internal' newspaper for Billancourt. The type of writing Mothé hoped would result from the experience of the worker newspaper would be a reappropriation of the tradition of worker writing that extended back through proletarian literature to such early nineteenth-century efforts like *L'Atelier*.[70] For Socialisme ou Barbarie, the reappropriation of writing was an exact parallel to the practical reappropriation of the general strike by the new 'worker avant garde'.

Mothé's vision of the worker newspaper was parallel to, and in conflict with, that of *Correspondence*. Both placed maximum importance on the paper as a catalyst for dialogue between revolutionaries and workers. They differed on the role each party could play in it. Both imagined that the paper would tend to fuse with its audience in the long term. *Correspondence* maintained a more anarchist position. For it, the fusion of paper and audience would mirror that of intellectuals and workers in the context of a revolutionary organisation. This fusion would be impossible unless intellectuals abandoned their specific modes of activity, beginning with the production of theory. The *Correspondence* group argued that a worker newspaper could have no political orientation, or line, other than what the worker readership wrote. For Mothé, the dialogue initiated through the worker newspaper would always involve workers and militants. Each would benefit from the competencies the other brought to it. Their interaction would determine the paper's line. However, the contemporary political climate did not permit a free-floating paper:

> A newspaper without some directing editorial line would be automatically a contradictory newspaper which, sooner or later, would fall under

---

69 See Mothé 1955, pp. 32–3 on these points.

70 The study circle run at Renault by Socialisme ou Barbarie member Andre Charconnet suggested a reading of a reprinted *L'Atelier* during its 1954 cycle of courses. See 'Introduction & Programme du Cercle Ouvrier Renault (année 1954–5)', p. 2. Document from Henri Simon's collection.

> the influence of the most experienced political elements. The newspaper has a line. That line is the discussion and confrontation amongst workers. But it is only revolutionary militants who have understood the enormous significance of this discussion and this worker-participation in [the discussion of] social, economic and political problems that can prevent the suffocation of this discussion by the experienced politicians.[71]

Mothé's position was that the existing political context tended to assimilate new or deviant positions, and that more experienced militants tended to marginalise the less experienced. Therefore, a political line was necessary, as was a core of revolutionary militants willing to take control of the paper and retain it.

It is clear from this that Mothé and *Correspondence* differed in their assessment of the ideological situation within which the working class operated and the impact this had on literary production. Mothé was far more pessimistic than his Detroit counterparts. Mothé did not see a revolutionary proletarian culture forming as a function of the workers' rejection of the dominant order. Rather, his experience at Billancourt showed him that the workers were too much under the sway of the dominant ideologies, too internally divided and too passive and alienated from politics. Mothé rejected the *Correspondence* vision of worker culture, their theory of social types and their belief that workers possessed a 'natural style' when they wrote that would flourish if only the intellectuals would let it get into print. Mothé saw the situation that the worker newspaper faced quite differently:

> It must not be assumed that when the workers want to express themselves, they will do so in an article free from literary prejudices. It is customary to talk one way and write in another. Also, articles written by workers are the most often influenced by journalistic form, full of clichés and prefabricated, inexact formulations. The workers who are most likely to write are those who have most fully submitted to this journalistic influence, thinking that they cannot express themselves except in a tortured manner or with the aid of expressions that are most often incomprehensible to the majority of workers. The task of the newspaper is: to disabuse the workers of these literary prejudices and to encourage them to express themselves in a way as simple as their natural form of spoken expression.

---

71   Mothé 1955, p. 35.

Allusions, images, references, comparisons should only be marked by everyday proletarian life.[72]

Mothé argues that workers are subject to a variety of influences that tend to devalue their modes of oral self-expression and the culture of which it is a part. There is no 'natural' style of worker writing. A worker writer's style is a construct. Mothé argued that it should be a written approximation of speech. It should be minimalist and describe the everyday experience of work in simple, direct language. It is a literary form with very few masters.

The idea of the worker newspaper was a potential solution to the vexing problem of organisation. The prospects of launching such a paper in France were quite dismal for several reasons. Of these, the most important, and most devastating for the project, was that there was no natural style of writing. If a paper wanted to use writing as a vehicle for developing self-consciousness amongst the workers, the level of political work that had to be done was very basic indeed. A proletarian style had to be constructed and a way cultivated of treating the adoption of this style as a political act. We will see in the next section that these were not the only problems encountered by *Tribune Ouvrière* at Renault Billancourt.

Tribune Ouvrière

This section analyses how the *Tribune Ouvrière* collective tried to create a political space for the paper at Renault Billancourt from 1954 to 1956. Based loosely on the notion of the worker newspaper outlined by Daniel Mothé in his 'Le problème d'un journal ouvrier', the collective wanted to make the paper into a forum that would both echo and politicise factory-floor-level experience. For Mothé, this aim could only be achieved through sustained worker participation in writing and producing the paper. We will see, however, that this vision of the worker newspaper was not shared by other members of the *Tribune Ouvrière* collective. Most felt that everyday experience could be politicised using more traditional forms of political agitation and language. This internal division is characteristic of the *Tribune Ouvrière* project.

The collective did desire worker input, even if they did not agree on its implications. All agreed that the paper should try to isolate and politicise issues that arose in the gaps that recurrently separated the problems that arose in the

---

[72] Mothé 1955, pp. 46–7.

context of actual production from the trade unions' ability to respond. The early issues of *Tribune Ouvrière* used the problem of professional hierarchy as a 'wedge issue'. The paper tried to oppose a notion of informal hierarchy, rooted in the everyday operation of production at the shop level, to official notions of hierarchy, rooted in what the paper argued was a bureaucratic vision of production. *Tribune Ouvrière* tried to use this issue to stake out a distinct, recognisable position for itself relative to the rest of the trade-union and political press at Billancourt. The issue of hierarchy was linked to demands for substantive worker participation in setting production norms. These demands were linked, logically and politically, to a broader call for democratic worker control over the pace and organisation of work. Ultimately, *Tribune Ouvrière* tried to use this position on hierarchy to redefine the nature and goals of working-class politics. Their ambition was to shift a politics rooted in analysis of the informal shop-and-shift-level worker collectivities – ideally generated by workers themselves – to the centre of a revolutionary politics.

Worker participation in writing the paper was important to this process of redefinition. The paper was started as a forum for workers. They were solicited to write for it, to describe what happened to them in their shops. The collective hoped that an accumulation of worker writings would at least give credibility to the paper's claims to speak for shop-level politics. For Mothé – and Socialisme ou Barbarie – a steady stream of writing by workers would have given the paper the potential to become a 'worker newspaper' in the sense outlined in the last section. Failing in that, a supply of worker writing could at least provide the group with data against which it could check the image of working-class reality it had constructed.

One can see from internal discussion of *Tribune Ouvrière* that Socialisme ou Barbarie collectively hoped that the paper could function as a point of contact between its revolutionary project and the working class. However, despite these hopes and the efforts of the collective that produced *Tribune Ouvrière*, few workers not part of the collective itself ever wrote for the paper or worked on its production. The next section examines this failure from a number of angles: as a function of disagreements within the collective as to the paper's goals; as a function of conflicts within the paper over what language to use; as an index of the non-contact between the cultures of the shop floor and those of politicised militants. I will also develop the last point to discuss the cultural specificity of Socialisme ou Barbarie's vision of the factory and working-class reality.

The *Tribune Ouvrière* Collective

Mothé's article on the problems of the worker newspaper was published in 1955 on the basis of about a year's experience with *Tribune Ouvrière*. The article is an account of the paper's development, its limitations and potentials, conditioned by Socialisme ou Barbarie and its internal debates on this topic. Mothé's analytical frame of reference is shaped by the group's concerns: the worker newspaper as a solution to the question of revolutionary organisation; the advantages and disadvantages offered by the *Correspondence* model; the general nature of working-class political culture and how that culture might shape/delimit the possibilities of worker writing. *Tribune Ouvrière* figures in 'Problèmes' as an experiment undertaken by a group of workers that had some interesting implications for revolutionaries thinking about the worker newspaper. In his 1975 interview with *Anti-Mythes*, Mothé gave a rather different account of *Tribune Ouvrière*'s origins:

> At Renault, I fell into the Stalinist fief of machine-tool operators. They offered me a CGT card, and I told them: 'Yes, but on one condition – it [the CGT] is directed by the PCF, which is wholly in the service of Russia, so don't be surprised [that] I think that it is an organisation largely sold out to Moscow. That said, if there is a union-action, I'll participate in it. I am going to write down what I just told you and put it into my union-card, so that later you won't accuse me of being a dirty traitor'. The guys said: 'Sure, sure, that's fine'. But they never came up with the CGT card. I was quickly classified as a Trotskyist. One day, there was a CGT tract laying out a position on salary-hikes. It suggested hierarchical raises, which they had calculated. So the raises would give 10 centimes per hour (?) to the OS; 15 centimes (?) for the P1; 18 (?) centimes for the P2; 25 centimes (?) for the P3 ... Even though this was a machine-shop, there was an outcry of indignation, of which I very soon made myself the spokesman. So I found myself suddenly the leader of the contestation. A certain number of workers agreed with my arguments. There was strong agitation in the shop. The guys discussed and discussed and I thought they were waiting for me to make trade-union style propositions to them. So I told them: 'OK, listen: everything you're saying is interesting: I'm going to write it as a tract [*on va l'écrire sur un canard*]'. Thus began *Tribune Ouvrière*. At the beginning, the articles were written as 'arranged' transcripts of our discussions. It was not the guys writing; it was always me. At the start, the paper had a certain echo. The Stalinists were beside themselves! But the comrades were pleased. They saw their arguments in writing. The folks

from FO, all of whom were terrorised by the Stalinists, were also pleased, but for their own reasons. That's how *Tribune Ouvrière* got started.

The Trotskyists got in contact with me. They were Pierre Bois and Gaspard, who was an old friend of Socialisme ou Barbarie. Gaspard had a certain influence in the shop where he worked, and a small number of young people joined up with us to put out this monthly journal.[73] Their shop was much better organised than mine was. Then there was Bois, the leader of the group that later became *Lutte Ouvrière*, who was a very traditional Trotskyist militant and very efficient organisationally. In my shop, there were a number of comrades who supported me morally, who agreed to discussions, who bought the paper, but who refused to do anything else. I think some of them saw my activities as a way to break with the CGT.[74]

For Mothé, *Tribune Ouvrière* was the result of a conjuncture. At its origin was the discontent in his shop, the Atelier Outillage Central (AOC), over a CGT position tract on professional hierarchy that circulated during the spring of 1954.[75] The shop's response was shaped by the nature of French trade-union pluralism. Because the East-West divide had been so thoroughly superimposed on trade-union activity, the workers loyal to the CGT could not express their unhappiness with the union's position by changing affiliation or voting for another union in elections. Instead, they had to seek alternative ways to express themselves. In the AOC, Mothé/Gautrat[76] was considered political but his position was ambiguous. Combined with his facility with language, this made him the logical person to be the mouthpiece. While functioning in this capacity, Mothé suggested to his AOC comrades that they write down the substance of their discussions and circulate it as a tract. Mothé's account links *Tribune Ouvrière* to a spontaneous mobilisation of AOC workers as a natural outgrowth of the struggle to make themselves heard by the CGT.

Mothé's is not the only account of the origins of *Tribune Ouvrière*. In an interview with the author, Pierre Blachier argued that the paper was the direct descendant of the April 1947 wildcat strike. Blachier was probably more

---

73 Gaspard is another pseudonym used by Raymond Hirzel, whose writing appeared under the name of Raymond Bourt in *Socialisme ou Barbarie*.
74 Mothé 1976a, pp. 3–4.
75 The AOC was a limited-run machine shop that primarily made production prototypes and replacement parts for production machines. For a Billancourt shop, the AOC had an extraordinary degree of professional autonomy.
76 On this name distinction, see Chapter 6, below.

important to the paper than was Mothé. An anarchist OS at Billancourt, he wrote extensively for *Tribune Ouvrière* from its earliest period through 1961, when the paper finally ceased publication. For him, the paper was never a 'worker newspaper' in the way Mothé tried to define it. Rather, it was the mode of self-expression for a community of worker militants, whose origin lay in the strike committee that organised the 1947 strike: Bois, Hirzel and the workers loyal to them from Billancourt's Collas sector. The paper was a mechanism that enabled workers to establish contact across shop and shift boundaries. Blachier argued that *Tribune Ouvrière* was primarily a network of friends who would meet not only to produce the journal, but with their families outside the factory. They would take trips together and organise group holidays. The centre was Raymond Hirzel.[77] Blachier emphasised that *Tribune Ouvrière* was never an extension of Socialisme ou Barbarie, nor was it under Mothé's control.[78] Both Mothé and Blachier claim a kind of proprietary interest in *Tribune Ouvrière* and build that interest into their respective histories of the paper. Mothé's version makes the paper the expression of a mobilisation in his shop; Blachier tries to trump Mothé by linking it both to 1947 and to another shop altogether.

This kind of disagreement about the origin, nature and function of *Tribune Ouvrière* runs back to its earliest days. For example, in the transcript of a 1955 'readers' meeting', published in *Socialisme ou Barbarie* no. 17, it is immediately clear that, while Bois and Hirzel did not agree about the nature of *Tribune Ouvrière*, they were united against Mothé and the notion of the worker newspaper articulated in 'Le problème d'un journal ouvrier'. Bois and Hirzel both emphasised how they found Renault workers to be divided and passive. In this context, *Tribune Ouvrière* should undertake 're-education' work. For Hirzel,'re-education' had to be carried out by certain groups: 'elements with training must teach the others about the history of the workers' movement and link everything to the central fact of exploitation'. For the Trotskyist Bois, the problem was: 'the discouragement of the workers, the feeling that they are zeroes politically and professionally. It is this discouragement that we must overcome by taking up again, with patience and obstinacy, the work of education and organization that has been undertaken by revolutionary parties of the past'.[78]

---

77 According to Simon and Blachier, Hirzel had a singular knack for organisation that extended to getting corporations to sponsor their holidays. Interview with Pierre Blachier, 10 April 1991.

78 Hirzel 'Les éléments qui ont une formation doivent enseigner aux autres l'histoire du mouvement ouvrier et tout relier au fait central de l'exploitation'. Bois: '[...] Le découragement des ouvriers, le sentiment qu' ils sont des "zeros" politiques et

Hirzel and Bois both argued for a strong party-like organisation as a counter to worker passivity. However, they differed on which historical precedent should be kept in mind while this organisation did its work: Hirzel emphasised the history of the workers' movement and Bois the history of revolutionary parties. Neither agreed with Mothé's idea that the paper should, in the long term, seek a fusion with the workers, nor with the claim that this goal was consistent with a new, open-ended dialogue of revolutionary militants and proletariat. Mothé's position assumed that direct contact with the contemporary working class was desirable and that political education should be limited to helping the workers find ways to express themselves and describe their experience free from the influences of major ideologies and 'legitimate' models of journalism and literature.[79] Pierre Bois's position assumed that the division and passivity of the workers was so deep that political work could be carried out only by a Vanguard Party. It is, of course, difficult to judge retrospectively which position was the more accurate evaluation of conditions at Billancourt in 1955. What is clear is that *Tribune Ouvrière*, its form and its goals were hotly debated from the outset by the various factions comprising the collective. These internal divisions are reproduced today in the competing claims about the paper, its origins, the most important people in the collective, the role of Socialisme ou Barbarie and the evaluations of the paper's ultimate success or failure.

Tribune Ouvrière and the Question of Hierarchy

It is empirically true that *Tribune Ouvrière* came about as a result of the agitation in the AOC over the CGT's April 1954 proposal for salary-increases that followed and legitimated the existing professional hierarchy. The tract that Mothé describes as the actual origin of the paper, 'Ouvrons le débat sur la hiérarchie des salaires', was written as an 'arranged transcript' of the objections raised by his AOC comrades to the CGT proposal. The tract was intended as an intervention in a long-running dispute between management and unions over salaries and control over the professional hierarchy.[80] To elucidate the tract, I will provide an overview of management and trade-union positions on these issues,

---

professionels. C'est ce découragement qu'il faut vaincre en reprenant avec patience et obstination le travail d'éducation et d'organisation qu'ont mené dans le passé les partis révolutionnaires' (Socialisme ou Barbarie 1955, p. 79).

79 See the previous section of this chapter.
80 'Ouvrons le débat sur la hiérarchie des salaires', reprinted in *Socialisme ou Barbarie* no. 15/16, p. 72.

and then turn to how the April 1954 tract set up the arguments that *Tribune Ouvrière* would develop in opposition to this entire debate.

Wage rates and professional hierarchy were intertwined issues subject to almost continuous conflict in French industry. At Renault, given the environment circumscribed by collective bargaining, questions of salary and professional hierarchy were both discrete problems and screens for the ongoing struggle between management and the unions over the shape of the enterprise.[81] Wage issues, which Lenin defined as always political, were the PCF-CGT's preferred mobilising tools. The status quo on professional hierarchy and training was equally important to the internal balance of power at Billancourt. The CGT's domination of trade-union elections gave it control over the *comité d'entreprise*. This control made the union an essential conduit for professional advancement.

From the early 1950s, the Renault management had tried to transform the professional hierarchy by tying base wage rates more directly to the level of skill and production output for specific workstations. Their basic argument was that wages should function as incentives to maximise production. Since skill and production levels were functions of overall production design, it followed that all variables shaped by that design should be assigned value by management. The management's proposal would have tied professional hierarchy (skill level) and base wages to piece rates. It also would have eliminated trade-union influence on wages. The problem with management's proposal was that it assumed vastly more detailed knowledge of, and control over, the production process than they possessed, and would only have been feasible after a radical extension of rationalisation and automation. Their redefinition of wages and hierarchy would have, in the short term, increased the activities of the time-motion people and increased the standardisation of tasks. It would also have reduced workers' physical mobility both at and away from the workstations. It would have accelerated the break up of semi-skilled sectors by extending assembly line production into the machine shops.

For the CGT, the bottom line was that the status quo on hierarchy had to be defended because, through it, the CGT occupied a central place in the reproduction of the factory's labour force.[82] The proposal from management struck at the heart of the existing professional hierarchy. This hierarchy stratified workers by seniority and skill level through a system of professional categories that determined the base wage rate. At Renault in the 1950s, a worker's wages

---

81 Collective bargaining was *de facto* before, and *de jure* after, the ratification of the Renault Accords in September 1955.
82 Tiano, Rocard and Lesine-Ogrel 1955, pp. 63–5, 69–95 and 185.

were calculated by multiplying a base rate by a production coefficient. The base rate was determined by the worker's place in one of three categories, each of which was divided into two or three grades: *Main d'oeuvre* [labourer] 1, 2; *Ouvrier Specialise* (OS) 1,2,3; *Ouvrier Professionnel* (P) 1,2,3.[83] Movement within categories was, for the most part, seniority-based. Movement between categories, on the other hand, was contingent upon passing a written examination. These exams were based on knowledge that was only theoretically linked to the experience of running machines: it was in fact impossible to pass the exam without specialised technical training. Workers could get the requisite training either through technical schools or through CGT-administered in-house training programmes.

This system was not optimal. As with American civil-service examinations, the passing score was determined by the aggregate number of available slots as unilaterally determined by management. Therefore, at any given time, a considerable number of trained workers crowded the OS3 level, waiting for P1 slots to open up.[84] There were also OS workers who had all the practical skills of any P1 but who were unable to advance because of limitations like illiteracy or other education deficits. These workers were trapped at a much lower base rate than would have been the case had hierarchy reflected what workers actually did in production.[85] The unions' defence of the system was not based on an assessment of how it functioned in practice. CGT control over in-house training programmes gave the union an important counterweight to the Renault management that forced it to take the union seriously. It was also a powerful coercive weapon. The union could, at any time, add political considerations to the other screening criteria that determined access to any hope of professional advancement.

Professional hierarchy and base wage rates were separated from actual production processes. Wages as a whole were reconnected to it through a complicated bonus system. This arrangement was a compromise that resulted from the long-standing conflict in French industry between fundamentally different ideas of how wages should be defined. These definitions were rooted in

---

83   Subsequent negotiations resulted in the near *ad infinitum* subdivision of these categories.
84   One might expect that a new employee with a technical certificate could enter Billancourt as a P1 – Gautrat/Mothé came to Renault in 1950 after having accelerated training as a milling-machine operator. Due to gaps between this training and the specialised factory requirements (real or otherwise), combined with position availability, Mothé worked two years as an OS before taking the examination. See Mothé 1975a, pp. 2–3.
85   This obviously does not exclude the OS who were, like Pierre Blachier, just not very good at this kind of work.

conflicting views of the social function and responsibilities of employers. The roots of this conflict extended back to nineteenth-century capitalism.[86] In general terms, employers favoured piece rates. This position followed from their view that the ultimate end of business was the extraction of maximum surplus value. Trade unions traditionally argued for flat base-wage rates. For unions, employers had an overriding social responsibility to their employees. Profits should be extracted only after a decent living standard was established for the workers.[87]

The compromise that Renault arrived at during the 1950s was subject to continual renegotiation. The flat base-wage rates reflected the worker's place in the professional hierarchy. Management was able to loosely tie these base rates to production output through the mechanism of incentives. At regular intervals, for example, a 'production coefficient' (a multiplier determined by the previous year's production rate relative to a norm [100%]) was added to the base rate. Other incentives reflected union victories in negotiations over social issues – increases in the cost of living, transportation allowances, attendance bonuses. To these were added a series of 'exceptional' bonuses of relatively obscure origin and periodicity. The complexity of this system – which is a history of conflict – effectively negated any psychological benefit that might have accrued to management because pay stubs were utterly indecipherable. Even this was subject to contestation. The spring 1954 conflict over wages and hierarchy was triggered by CGT demands for a simplified pay stub that would enable workers to keep track of their pay and determine if they were being cheated.[88] In response, management advanced its scheme to revamp wages and hierarchy by tying them to workstation production. Prevented by its position on modernisation from objecting to management arguments that increased production was desirable, the CGT based its opposition to this proposal on: (a) a defence of a socially-necessary minimum wage and (b) a defence of the existing hier-

---

86   For an account of the various positions, and the conflicts between them through the nineteenth and early-twentieth century across French industry, see Mottez 1966.

87   As employers were necessarily interested in assuring the reproduction of the labour-force, and given that in Western capitalism workers retained a margin of mobility that placed a break on the extent of exploitation, the debate here operated with draconian rhetoric in a situation within which the problems were less a matter of life and death for the worker than they would be under Soviet industry under Stalin, where the wage levels were artificially low and worker mobility was eliminated after 1940. See Castoriadis 1988a.

88   On the pay-stub dispute, see Tiano, Rocard and Lesire-Ogrel 1955, p. 65. A chart showing how salaries were calculated is reproduced as Appendix 2 in Tiano 1955, p. 186. It should be noted that the *comité d'entreprise* played an active role in the accumulation of bonuses; Tiano, Rocard and Lesire-Ogrel 1995, p. 67.

archy against management's attempt to unilaterally determine the rates to be paid. In reality, CGT objections centred on the maintenance of its institutional role in fixing base rates against what was interpreted as management's efforts to marginalise the union. As noted earlier, management advanced its position without having worked out the details of how the new rates would be calculated. In negotiation it was soon abandoned. Management then began to call for a revamped base-wage hierarchy that would have introduced new subcategories tied to actual production levels. The CGT countered by asking for the pay rises along the existing scale. Because of the irrationalities this system produced in practice, this proposal prompted an outraged response amongst the AOC workers that motivated Mothé to write the April tract.

The CGT approached this conflict in a classic Leninist fashion. For Lenin, following the *Communist Manifesto*, salary disputes were necessarily political because in them the specific conflict of interest that separated workers and capital emerged with great clarity and could be easily mapped onto the more general division between classes. Victories on wage issues provided important sources of political legitimacy for the PCF-CGT. Every pay raise obtained by union through negotiation with management directly affected the workers' standard of living and reduced an important, tangible, index of exploitation.[89] As Bertrand Badie pointed out, wage issues were fundamental in cementing the relation between the PCF-CGT system and the worker base. They provided the organisations with specific, obtainable objectives around which to mobilise, and were fundamental in the PCF-CGT system's efforts to balance the pressures to which it was subjected by operating between two very different reference systems, each with its own tactical exigencies. The Party and union press invariably read each achievement into the central, progressive narrative of working-class struggle behind the banner of the PCF-CGT.[90] In this particular situation, demands for a raise were linked to other objections that centred on management's vagueness on how and by whom the calculation of workstation production would be carried out, and what it meant for the existing professional hierarchy and particularly for CGT control over mobility between categories.[91]

Mothé's April tract, like *Tribune Ouvrière* thereafter, tried to stake out a different position. The tract rejected as non-political the jockeying for position

---

[89] The disparity between wage levels and prices/the cost of living is referred to as an index of exploitation.

[90] See Chapter 3, above.

[91] This account of the dispute over wages and hierarchy comes from Tiano, Rocard and Lesire-Ogrel 1955.

between the CGT, competing unions, and management. Its central argument was that current wage and professional hierarchies were simply arbitrary and should be abolished. Mothé used the technique of arranged transcription to frame the tract's arguments as originating, not in the AOC *per se*, but on the factory floor more generally. This shift is important because it gives an indication of how Mothé tried to integrate his professional and political experiences, weaving the AOC together with Socialisme ou Barbarie's theoretical interrogation of 'worker experience'. Mothé argued that, in a highly skilled, integrated and relatively autonomous machine shop, everyone knows who does what and how well. This ongoing, informal collective self-regulation is fundamental in production, particularly in isolating and solving problems that arise in the course of machining prototypes, limited-run specialty parts, etc. There are, therefore, two parallel hierarchies in the shop. Of these, the informal modes of self-regulation are the more legitimate and the more proletarian. They arise out of collective practice, are fluid and highly functional. In contrast, the official hierarchy does not connect directly with production. Like Castoriadis, Mothé argued that this hierarchy conforms to management's vision of how production ought to be. This vision, built around the logical criteria particular to bureaucratic systems, is rigid and arbitrary from a perspective informed by production. Even in this account of the tract's argument, one can see that Mothé shifted almost immediately from the AOC workers to 'the workers' in general, and from the AOC as a particular machine shop to 'the shop floor'. This universalisation set up one of the tract's main political arguments: not only was bureaucratic hierarchy arbitrary from a viewpoint informed by actual production, but it divided workers amongst themselves and obscured their basic commonality of interest. Following Marx, this commonality of interest was defined as a function of the universality of the proletariat's position in the production process.

Coextensive with this shared experience of production was a shared need for the proletariat to defend itself against exploitation.[92] Using the arranged transcript to construct a common workers' voice and interest, Mothé characterised management and trade unions as having agreed in principle about the legitimacy of the existing hierarchy, even as they argued amongst themselves over who would control it. This enabled Mothé to position the bureaucratic organisations together on one side of a political divide, and his vision of the autonomous working class on the other.

The strategies Mothé would use throughout his career as a writer to shift from the particular to the universal are evident here. Because it is such an

---

92 'Ouvrons le débat sur la hiérarchie des salaires', in *Socialisme ou Barbarie*, no. 15/16, p. 72.

important element of Socialisme ou Barbarie's notion of worker experience, I would like to walk briefly through the layers of generalisation before moving onto *Tribune Ouvrière*. In Mothé's description of how *Tribune Ouvrière* came about, this tract is linked directly to a shift in Mothé's social position in the AOC. Again, given the nature of French trade-union pluralism and the rigidity of union constituencies, the AOC workers, officially CGT supporters who, however, objected to the CGT proposal on wages, had nowhere to go to express their objections except to each other – whence the discussions that Mothé described in the *Anti-Mythes* interview. Mothé was able to position himself as the *de facto* spokesman by a process that he would later formalise in his 1975 image as characteristic of the 'older type of syndicalist militant' who rises from amongst the workers to assume a political role while remaining a worker in patterns of thinking and acting. The tract can be read, curiously, as both a catalyst for mobilisation and a confirmation and preservation of Mothé's (temporarily) changed status.[93] The tract also enabled Mothé to position himself for his readers as the voice of workers mobilising autonomously, beyond the control of conventional political organisations.

Another parallel process is discernible in the construction of the hierarchy issue. For Socialisme ou Barbarie, the anti-hierarchical demands that were issued by the workers involved in the summer 1953 actions were one of the main indices of each action's revolutionary significance. The group linked these demands directly to the workers' everyday experience. Clarifying these links was both an analytical and a political problem. Mothé's tract, and *Tribune Ouvrière* thereafter, can be read as an effort to shift from Socialisme ou Barbarie's *ex post facto*, analytical-descriptive mode to a proactive, political mode. Mothé's framing of the issue moved from the specific dispute and the reaction of AOC workers, to conventional Marxist arguments about the nature and meaning of hierarchy, to this argument, which could have come from *Socialisme ou Barbarie*:

> We know that hierarchy is the basis of all capitalist society and that is why we think it would be utopian to think that hierarchy could be suppressed within the capitalist system, but we think it is possible to limit its effects, and it is in this sense that the demand must be posed. It is only in this case that unity can be realised.[94]

---

93 See Chapter 6, below, for a more extended treatment.
94 'Ouvrons le débat sur la hiérarchie des salaires', in *Socialisme ou Barbarie* no. 15/16, p. 73.

Tribune Ouvrière

Tribune Ouvrière was itself a product of the same debates that produced the April tract on salaries and the professional hierarchy. The collective – initially consisting of Mothé, Raymond Hirzel, Pierre Bois and a few workers loyal to Hirzel and Bois – hoped that the paper would prolong these debates, widen them to include more professional sectors in the factory and influence the range of issues being discussed. This was the spirit behind the declaration of intent that opened the first issue of *Tribune Ouvrière* in May, 1954:

> What do we want?
>
> A strong trade-union or political organisation can make suggestions and offer advice. A small group of workers cannot.
>
> What we want is an end to the tutelage that the so-called workers' organisations have exercised over us for many years. We want all problems concerning the working class to be debated by the workers themselves ...
>
> We think that contemporary trade-union and political organisations trick the workers, but the workers are not yet capable of creating other really autonomous organisations. As for us, it is not up to us to create from start to finish an organisation that only represents ourselves. A real worker organisation can be created only with the support and will of the workers themselves. We must prepare the basis for it.
>
> What we suggest is to make of this paper a tribune in which we ask you to participate. We would like this journal to reflect the lives and opinions of workers. It's up to you.[95]

This editorial, 'What Do We want?', announced what had inspired the collective to begin publishing *Tribune Ouvrière*. Socialisme ou Barbarie's analyses of 'real' working-class interests were derived from the descriptive analysis of strike actions, and Mothé's April tract from the concerns raised in the course of discussions in the Billancourt AOC. This *Tribune Ouvrière* editorial reframes the problem of 'real' working-class interests as a political question best addressed by the construction of a 'real worker organisation'. Ideally, the paper would be but one aspect of the debate it called for on the issues that shaped working-class life and a reflection of the community that would begin to coalesce through these discussions. The interaction of debate, community formation

---

95   Unsigned, 'Que voulons-nous?', in *Tribune Ouvrière*, no. 1 (May 1954), reprinted in *Socialisme ou Barbarie*, no. 15/16, p. 74.

and *Tribune Ouvrière* would constitute the framework for this 'real worker organisation'.

The *Tribune Ouvrière* project seems to have taken the debate about hierarchy and salaries as the latest in a long chain of such debates that together demonstrated that the workers at Billancourt were alienated from the trade unions and political parties that controlled the factory. However, the fragmentation of the working class prevented workers from bringing to this alienation any sense of how widespread it was. In this, *Tribune Ouvrière* seemed more pessimistic than Socialisme ou Barbarie, which saw in the wildcat strikes evidence of a legitimation crisis.[96] Collective action seemed to carry with it a particular image of working-class consciousness that enabled Socialisme ou Barbarie to imagine the working class as approaching politics like intellectuals did, with clear ideological commitments and a sense of community that preceded and shaped any organisational affiliation. Socialisme ou Barbarie's analyses worked from collective action backward to a vision of everyday experience, moving from the present of action to the past of experience. *Tribune Ouvrière* began as an attempt to politicise experience, hoping to contribute to autonomous actions at some time in the future. Hence, for *Tribune Ouvrière*, building a sense of collectivity was a political task of the highest importance.

The paper frequently argued that working-class life was already shaped by a *de facto* legitimation crisis. The second article in *Tribune Ouvrière*, no. 1, made this point by contrasting the cynicism that greeted a carefully staged, but largely ignored, 24-hour strike called by the CGT in April 1954 to the impressive action of the four million workers who participated in the August 1953 general strike. In general terms, the article followed the interpretation developed in the pages of *Socialisme ou Barbarie* by Hirzel, among others.[97] According to this reading, French workers had grown tired of the CGT's use of limited '*grèves tournantes*' to protest against industrial issues and larger, purely political strikes to support the PCF's objectives. Increasing numbers of PCF-CGT actions were ignored by the rank and file. Hirzel's article claimed that this trend was already apparent in 1950. One could see in this pattern of refusal a limited practical critique of particular kinds of tactics: the '*grèves tournantes*' were too limited, and the political strikes were only concerned with supporting the USSR. Socialisme ou

---

[96] The term 'legitimation crisis' is taken from Habermas, 1975. I use it throughout as a convenient designation for the withdrawal of worker consent from bureaucratic trade unions that Socialisme ou Barbarie saw as a basic pre-condition for revolutionary politics at this time. The group did not itself use this terminology, which is therefore somewhat anachronistic.

[97] See Bourt 1950.

Barbarie took a more totalising line, arguing that these rejections of the PCF-CGT's strike calls were symptomatic of a wider legitimation crisis. As we saw in Chapter 2, Socialisme ou Barbarie went a step further by tying the rejection of these particular strike tactics to the resurgence of wildcat strikes and explained the two together as part of an almost conscious strategy on the part of the worker avant garde to reclaim the strike. By 1957, Castoriadis had connected the various strands of Socialisme ou Barbarie's theoretical position and argued that the re-appropriation of the strike was an implicit critique of the purely formal, representative democracy characteristic of Western bureaucratic capitalism in general.[98] The *Tribune Ouvrière* article did not go this far, limiting itself to suggestion.

Already one can see some of the parallels and tensions characteristic of the relationship between Socialisme ou Barbarie and the collective that published *Tribune Ouvrière*. Socialisme ou Barbarie's vision of the working class was built into a theory of revolution and the social-historical process that took moments of collective action as its premise. The group's analysis of these actions tried to derive logical connections from highly wrought images of the actions and the everyday experience the group saw as conditioning them. This mode of *ex post facto* interpretation enabled Socialisme ou Barbarie to unify the phenomena and to see collective action, and the various phenomena linked to it by virtue of their theory, as manifestations of class consciousness. Worker writers provided an alternative access route to the development of this consciousness. The worker newspaper was therefore but a forum for the autonomous development of this collective will. The arguments generated by Socialisme ou Barbarie about working-class consciousness were legitimated by criteria applicable to intellectual groups. Working in a highly circumscribed factory context, during a period without any great political action, *Tribune Ouvrière*'s articles were often in general agreement with Socialisme ou Barbarie's positions. However, this agreement, when it was present, was shaped by the paper's immersion in a very different context. The differences between the contexts that shaped Socialisme ou Barbarie and those that shaped *Tribune Ouvrière* were often underestimated by the former, perhaps as a function of their fascination with the working class as an analytical and political object.

In the early issues of *Tribune Ouvrière*, this correspondence of arguments was a function of the role played by Mothé. The first part of this section indicated that there was considerable disagreement over what *Tribune Ouvrière* was and who controlled it. Mothé's was not the dominant view either within

---

[98] This argument is elaborated most fully in Castoriadis 1988e in language heavily influenced by Mills 1956.

the collective or in the paper. Socialisme ou Barbarie was a very interested observer of the *Tribune Ouvrière*. The group published excerpts in *Socialisme ou Barbarie* and included a subscription to *Tribune Ouvrière* along with a subscription to the main journal. Socialisme ou Barbarie was materially quite important in assuring that the paper was printed. *Tribune Ouvrière* was printed on cheap paper and in limited quantities. It is now almost inaccessible. The easiest place to see it is in the excerpts printed in *Socialisme ou Barbarie*. These excerpts were selected to make *Tribune Ouvrière* appear like a worker newspaper, constituting both a particular interpretation of the paper (one that emphasised Mothé's articles) and of *'la presse ouvrière'*.[99] What factors, apart from the ones presented in *Socialisme ou Barbarie*, prevented *Tribune Ouvrière* from becoming a worker newspaper? And what does this failure tell us about the relationship between revolutionary politics/militant culture and working-class culture? These questions are the central preoccupations of the rest of this section.

The worker-newspaper project assumed conditions obtaining amongst the working class that seemed reasonable from the viewpoint of revolutionary theory but which were in fact quite particular to that theory. Two fundamental assumptions were: that workers have something like an 'authentic' writing style that is essentially ready-made and awaiting the appearance of a forum, and that such a forum would be recognisable to the worker readership for what it was. A third, that I will discuss later, is that workers in some way shared the teleological view of their experience developed through theoretical investigation and would write in a mode that reflected this view. The first two issues were closely connected and can be discussed in terms of the tactical problems or binds that faced *Tribune Ouvrière*. It is here that the political divisions within the paper's collective take on particular significance. These differences were written directly into *Tribune Ouvrière*. Each political position utilised a particular rhetoric of engagement, shaped by broader assumptions about revolutionary politics. In thinking about the relationship between the party and the masses, between organisation and the workers, a militant also makes assumptions about the type of language that is most appropriate, based on the function this language should fulfil.

Regardless of which version of the history of *Tribune Ouvrière* one finds to be the most compelling, it is clear that the collective formed around Mothé in the weeks after he wrote and circulated the April 1954 tract. The other principal actors – Pierre Bois, a Trotskyist from the *Lutte de Classe* group, and Raymond

---

[99] Since the paper is now extremely difficult to find, the views of *TO* outlined in *Socialisme ou Barbarie* are dominant.

Hirzel, a Bordigist from *Internationaliste* with a long, conflicted relationship with Socialisme ou Barbarie – each brought with them more cultural capital and more bodies than Mothé was able to muster. The cultural capital derived from Bois and Hirzel's roles at the centre of the April 1947 wildcat strike which toppled the Tripartite government.[100] While they managed to squander most of this capital by trying to construct the '*Syndicat Democratique Renault*', a task quite beyond their means, both retained a sort of 'revolutionary aura' and were, therefore, important players in the micro-politics of the Billancourt Collas sector.[101] Despite the collapse of the SDR, both managed to salvage relatively strong organisations in their respective shops. These informal organisations enabled Bois and Hirzel to each join with Mothé, accompanied by small phalanxes of politically active workers. Mothé had no such network and soon found himself isolated and outvoted in the collective he had helped start. The following shorthand overview of what happened was delivered to Socialisme ou Barbarie at the meeting of 21 May 1955:

> 'Historique' on the development of *Tribune Ouvrière*
> 1st period: writing in both direct and indirect form: organisation which regulated itself in an automatic manner – later political support of workers diminishing as a function of the contemporary situation in the factory.
> 2nd period: the creation of an editorial committee – though elected democratically, the same comrades – not possible with Gaspard (Hirzel) and Bois. Most of the workers sent by Hirzel came to counterbalance the influence of our comrade in the group. No longer a worker journal. Errors by the Group.
> 3rd period: elimination of Mothé.[102]

Pierre Bois came to the *Tribune Ouvrière* collective with views about the relationship between the party and the workers shaped by his long involvement with the small 'proletarian' Trotskyist group *Lutte de Classe* [Class Struggle]. *Lutte de Classe* considered itself the legitimate heir to Trotsky. The group distinguished itself in the period just after the Liberation, during which the Fourth International was struggling to reconstitute itself, by refusing to accept the International on grounds that the movement had 'lost its worker base'.[103] This ultra-left position issued into a relation to the lexicon of Trotskyist-Leninism

---

[100] See Fallachon 1972.
[101] See Fallachon 1972, Tiano, Rocard and Elsire-Ogel 1955.
[102] *Socialisme ou Barbarie* meeting, 21 May 1955. Handwritten notes by Henri Simon.
[103] Pluet-Despatins 1980, pp. 226–8. See, more generally, Chapter 6, n. 15.

consistent with an organisation that was attempting to out-heretic the heretics – a rigid faith in the necessity of using traditional language and forms. Bois's influence on *Tribune Ouvrière* was evident from the first issue. His contribution to the first issue was a snide 'Necrologie' [Obituary] for the 'class-enemy', Jouhaux, the deceased Renault CEO and 'servant of the bourgeoisie'. It is a classic Trotskyist-style *ad hominem* denunciation. In the fashion evident in nearly all his writing, it is little more than a collection of slogans.[104] This article, and others like it that appeared in a steady stream in *Tribune Ouvrière* until 1956, made the paper's political situation quite difficult, particularly if viewed from the viewpoint of the worker newspaper project.[105] Bois's commitment to a 'classic' Leninism prompted him to write in the same language as that used by the PCF-CGT but with a recognisably Trotskyist twist. This adherence to the rhetoric developed in pre-1917 agitation within the Second International followed from the belief, despite all evidence to the contrary, that small militant groups and the massive PCF-CGT system competed for worker allegiance on a more or less even playing field. The workers would gravitate toward the more correct line at the moment of revolution. This rhetoric limited the possibilities for any basic rethinking of politics, and the categories that ordered it, by adopting a strategy relative to the dominant PCF-CGT that was geared toward an ideological *coup d'etat*. Revolution would be marked by the workers' rejection of the PCF-CGT, not because its language was outmoded or no longer signified, but because these organisations could not claim to have either political legitimacy or an 'authentic' link to the working class.

The effects of this rhetorical conservatism were interesting. In his 1975 article on reading in the factory, Mothé argued, on the basis of his experience as a militant, that the Billancourt workers were for the most part neither involved in politics nor interested in political discourse. He claimed that the general attitude of Billancourt workers was that politics – and particularly the 'speaking Bolshevik' characteristic of left-wing political language – was part of contemporary formal democracy. Political language was a type of code constructed for, manipulated by and referring to actors in a specialised social milieu. This specialized milieu, Mothé argued, did not directly concern most workers. Politics unfolded in a highly ritualised linguistic and social space. Across the postwar period, these ritual elements gradually changed from marking politics to being politics.[106] If an article or tract read a certain way, it was political. If it read differently, it was not. Mothé's 1975 article reflects a history not yet evident

---

104   Interview with Véga, April 1991.
105   Bois and his allies left *Tribune Ouvrière* in 1956 to form Lutte Ouvrière.
106   Mothé 1976b, pp. 122–5.

to the *Tribune Ouvrière* collective in 1954, and I will discuss his description of the pivotal period after the Hungarian Revolution in the next chapter. However, in this context the implication is clear. The side-by-side coexistence of traditional political language and another language that tried to break with it, and to encourage workers to do so, decisively shaped the reception of *Tribune Ouvrière*.

To explain how and why, a brief detour into Pierre Bourdieu's work is useful. In Bourdieu's terminology, the PCF-CGT system functioned as the '*idée force*' in Billancourt's internal political universe. A basic feature of the '*idée force*' is that it thoroughly dominates a given field of cultural reproduction, which means that 'logic' (the range of available options, both strategic and linguistic) structuring the field is made over in the image of that position. Its internal symbolic system and its priorities become the necessary reference points for any 'war of position'. Any new group that wants to contest the legitimacy of the dominant position immediately encounters the problem of how to relate to this 'logic'. Bourdieu gives an interesting account of how important these problems are for a new group. To be legitimate, opposition has to take into account, and position itself relative to, the '*idée force*'. The main effect of cultural domination is that the dominant position remakes in its own image the terrain of conflict between producers and the relationship between producers and consumers:

> A field of production, which clearly could not function if it could not count on already existing tastes, more or less strong propensities to consume more or less clearly defined goods, enables taste to be realized by offering it, at each moment, the universe of cultural goods as a system of stylistic possibilities from which it can select the system of stylistic features constituting a life style.[107]

The PCF-CGT's domination of the politico-syndical field tended to reduce politics to consumption and to transform fundamentally the signification of Marxian vocabulary in the process. This process occurred as a result of the nature of the PCF-CGT's cultural production and the adjustment of worker-comportments relative to politics as articulated in its image. The same process can be applied to objects circulating within any field of cultural production:

> A cultural product – an avant-garde picture, a political manifesto, a newspaper – is a constituted taste, a taste which has been raised from the vague semi-existence of half-formulated or unformulated experience, implicit or even unconscious desire, to the full reality of the finished product, by a

---

107   Bourdieu 1984, p. 230.

process that is almost always the work of professionals. It is consequently charged with the legitimizing, reinforcing capacity which objectification always possesses, especially, as is the case now, when the logic of structural homologies assigns it to a prestigious group so that it functions as an authority which authorizes and reinforces dispositions by giving them a collectively recognized expression.[108]

This passage from *Distinction* has both the advantage of describing the circular relation between field, subjective dispositions formed by and through it (*habitus*) and the products that circulate, and of recapitulating elements of the analysed system in the analysis itself. Bourdieu wants to find culture to be exclusively about the reinforcement of hegemony because it increases the prestige accruing to Pierre Bourdieu, the master-demystifier, whose relation to his own discourse is often quite curious.[109] While one might argue that Bourdieu's view of cultural reproduction is overly rigid or even tautological, it is useful in indicating what was at stake for *Tribune Ouvrière* in the issue of political rhetoric. In the hands of the PCF-CGT, Marxism-Leninism became the language of command control. The Party translated the Leninist notion of the vanguard into types of political and cultural production that relegated action to professionals/specialists.[110] Political involvement, from the viewpoint of the worker base, was transformed from an active engagement to a Communist variant of machine politics. Workers were to be available for mobilisation around particular objectives that were glossed in the Party press as affirming the link between workers, class and Party.

This was an important part of the problem faced by *Tribune Ouvrière*. Trotskyist groups that tried to reclaim Leninist tactics and Marxist rhetoric from the dominance of the PCF-CGT were incapable of seeing the extent to which that domination had transformed its implications. Bourdieu's schema helps explain how workers might take Trotskyism, with its obsessive attention to rhetorical precision, as a variant of the same old thing. If one reads

---

108 Bourdieu 1984, p. 231.
109 Claude Grignon has pointed out that Bourdieu recapitulates the logic of the dominant culture in his analysis. Grignon argues that Bourdieu's stratification analysis of contemporary capitalist culture comes down to an intricately written variant of neo-liberal market theory. Supply and demand dovetail together and those positions that lose out do so because they deserve to lose. This amounts to an odd recapitulation of the logic of domination in a project purporting to expose and demystify that logic.
110 This maps Lenin's professional revolutionaries onto the post-1936 Party-apparatus. See Kriegel 1980.

Tribune Ouvrière in light of this problem, one can see that the context within which it circulated would invert the relative weight accorded the Trotskyist articles and those written along lines closer to those advocated by Socialisme ou Barbarie. Articles in a recognisable and conventional 'political' style like the 'Necrologie' would be read like the political articles in *Tribune Ouvrière*. Mothé's articles, and their recoding of Socialisme ou Barbarie positions, would be reduced to noise. To be recognisable, a new group had to use the dominant rhetoric. The price of recognition was assimilation into spectrum of existing opposition groups – Trotskyist, anarcho-syndicalist and anarchist – that tried to mobilise workers from the margins of conventional politics. Their success, when it came, had everything to do with conjuncture and relatively little to do with the ideological positions they articulated.[111] This pattern tended to filter out any basic challenge to the definitions of political action that subtended the dominant rhetoric.

The weight of the immediate context in shaping reception was one level of trouble that *Tribune Ouvrière* encountered relative to the worker newspaper idea. There were other problems as well. The worker newspaper project was aimed at establishing both intimate contact with the shop floor and a rhetoric adequate to communicating that contact. Mothé's programmatic essay made clear that this rhetoric was envisioned as closely mirroring the oral culture of the factory floor. The essay also made clear that developing this rhetoric was a central element in a process of re-education and redefinition. The paper would have didactic and political functions. The didactic function would consist largely in encouraging a style of writing disabused of literary or political cliché. The political function would consist in persuading writers and readers that this process entailed a fundamental shift in the nature of politics. However, if Bourdieu's description of the relation of *habitus* to field can be taken as accurate, then *Tribune Ouvrière* would find itself caught in a bind. While from the viewpoint of a revolutionary militant, this new rhetoric would both confirm the relationship between the militant and the worker and provide new avenues for writing, for workers the situation was quite different. If it was true that, for many, to be political was to employ a particular and ritualised written language, then to write as they spoke would be self-disempowering.[112]

---

111   The tracts generated by the April 1947 strike committee, for example, are primarily concerned with advancing wage demands in the name of the unified working class ('Les ouvriers en grève de chez Renaults addressent à vous...') The critique of the CGT is limited to detailing the union's inconsistent position on the question of wages and their relationship to the cost of living.

112   Mothé 1976b.

For whom, at this time, was the project of aligning written and spoken French a going concern? The literary avant garde took an interest, particularly through Raymond Queneau.[113]

The divide that separated the workers and the oral culture of the factory floor from the written culture of politics maps onto deeper social divisions. In particular, it maps onto the problems of differential access to literacy and the different functions literacy serves within/for various social groups. In the rigidly hierarchical French school system of the 1950s, literacy was an important means of exclusion that functioned to virtually assure that working-class children were channelled into the technical training that fed industry. The ability to read and write was a criterion used at critical junctures to stream the student population. Students were expected to have basic skills by the age of six-and-a-half years, at the end of the first year's schooling. These skills could not be acquired at that age by formal education alone. The transmission of such abilities relied on class-specific early socialisation. Working class and bourgeois families would not, in general, share the same relationship to reading and writing. The former might not have the time to spend teaching their children because of the demands of economic survival, or because their experience in the school system alienated them from print culture by setting it up as a domain for others.[114] If a given student failed a test measuring these skills at the end of the first school year, s/he would have to repeat it. The consequences of repeating the year could be quite significant down the line. The school system divided the student population a second time at the end of primary school, channelling some students into the *lycée* as preparation for university, and others into technical school. Age played a statistically determinate role in this selection process. If a student had repeated one year, the chances of gaining access to the *lycée* were substantially diminished; two repeated years and there was no chance. Older students were channelled into either an amorphous middle stream that fed the managerial cadres,[115] or into technical schools. If this passage through the educational system,[116] with its coding

---

113 See Chapter 6 for a detailed analysis of the rhetoric of authentic worker experience in relation to the proletarian literature movement.
114 On this point generally, see Willis 1981. For a critical reading of Willis, see George Marcus, 'Contemporary Problems of Ethnography in the Modem World System', in Clifford and Marcus (eds.) 1986, pp. 165–93, esp. 173ff.
115 The social origins of the management-cadres are analysed in Boltanski 1982.
116 Information about the French education system can be found in more statistical detail in the following sources, from which these paragraphs were constructed: Marceau 1977, particularly chapters 4 and 5; Baudelot and Establet 1971; Grignon 1971.

of literacy as a mechanism of exclusion, was an important shared experience of semi-skilled workers generally – the primary constituency of the politico-syndical field – it would follow that the alienation from print culture would precede, and to a certain extent explain, the nature of PCF-CGT politics and the kind of alienation from politics it engendered. *Tribune Ouvrière*, particularly in its worker-newspaper guise, would be predicated on misrecognition of this aspect of the cultural relationship between the factory floor and politics. If workers were asked, why would they turn, in order to free themselves, to skills that had functioned explicitly to exclude them from non-working-class possibilities for the whole of their lives?[117] And if they did, why should it have surprised Mothé that their writing tended to reproduce the surface features of literature, journalism or politics?[118]

While the logical conclusions to be drawn from the above are quite bleak from the viewpoint of the worker-newspaper project, at Billancourt any opposition could be dangerous given the proper circumstances.[119] The PCF-CGT therefore took no chances and mobilised its forces to contain and, if possible, eliminate all challenges from the left. Their pre-emptive strike against very small groups of dissident workers followed from the paranoiac view of the Left Opposition written into the official ideological catechism of the PCF. It also reflected the high symbolic stakes of conflict at Billancourt. In the *Tribune*

---

117 See below, Chapter 6, Section 2, on autodidacts, whose intellectual formation could be set against this characterisation of working-class politics. Note that this argument is limited to the problem of writing and should not be taken as a miserablist vision of the working class that sees them as victims bereft of creativity because they did not easily express themselves in more properly bourgeois formats like autobiography.

118 For a critical analysis of the Marxist assumption underlying this interpretation of what workers 'should' write about, see Rancière 1981 and his analysis of Saint Simonian poets that asks why it should not be more logical for workers to write in terms that allow them to temporarily escape their lots as workers. For an extended anthropological analysis of the effects of writing on previously oral cultures and the relationship between writing, power and memory, see Goody 1991, particularly parts 3 ('Written and oral culture in West Africa') and 4 ('Writing and its Impact on Individuals in Society'). There is an extensive literature on this problem, notably including work by Richard Hoggart (Hoggart 1998 [1957]) and Walter Ong (Ong 2002). See also Stephen A. Tyler, 'On Being Without Words' in Marcus (ed.) 1992, pp. 1–7. For a work bridging anthropological and radical perspectives on contemporary capitalist culture in these terms, see Willis 1981. Examining the interaction between written and oral culture in terms of class politics may open an interesting direction for contextually and formally reinterpreting Derrida's late 1960s work on writing, 'Structure Sign and Play' (Derrida 1978) and 'The Writing Lesson' (Derrida 1976).

119 I developed this argument in Chapter 4.

Ouvrière article 'Où sommes-nous au sujet de la hiérarchie des salaires?', the writer complains about members of the collective being 'called traitors, saboteurs and agents of the Bosses' by CGT people in the wake of the April tract. Their invective was drawn from the standard *Short Course* repertoire.[120] The PCF-CGT used a wide range of mechanisms to stifle dissent, ranging from the informal – gossip – to the formal – cutting off access to training or retirement benefits.

An individual's vulnerability to informal pressure was a function of who one was and where one was located. Mothé pointed out in his *Anti-Mythes* interview that each member of the core *Tribune Ouvrière* collective essentially represented a shop. Hirzel and Bois's superior organisational skills and strong political reputations in their respective departments gave each a group of loyal workers with whom they could present a collective front against CGT pressure. Mothé's situation was different. His AOC shop mobilised sporadically around specific issues but did not manage to construct on that basis any semblance of permanent organisation. One result of this was that, in political matters, the shop was constantly starting over again. When the shop did mobilise around a given issue, Mothé frequently found himself acting as the mouthpiece, repeating the process described earlier in this section. This transformation in Mothé's social situation had mostly to do with his command of language, his reputation for outspokenness and his lack of an obvious political affiliation. Mothé told the author in a 1992 interview that such changes in his social position did not imply any support for his personal views amongst the shop comrades.[121] The space he occupied politically would disappear with the agitation over a specific grievance. The whole process would begin again over a later issue. Mothé was both visible as a dissident and vulnerable politically because he was isolated in the AOC, except during periods of agitation. He was a particular target of CGT pressures:

> Question: What was your relationsip with the unions?
> Mothé: *Oh la la*, the shit I had to put up with! [*qu'est-ce qu'on prend dans la gueulel!*] It depended on the shop, but when you had a comrade isolated off in a corner, who had an entire cell around him, he could not hold up for long under the blows. There was constant pressure. That is what weighed on me most for twenty years: never having a moment's respite. You go into the locker room, you start to undress and you hear someone

---

120 'Où sommes-nous au sujet de la hiérarchie des salaires?', in *Tribune Ouvrière*, no. 1 (May 1954), pp. 3–4; Stalin 1939.
121 Interview with Mothé, January 1992.

calling you a bastard without being able to explain yourself to him. You've really had it by the end of the day. Everything you do is watched. I was divorced: 'A divorcee! What's up with this guy? He's depraved!' The least word is reported, twisted, distorted. You are always accused of being a traitor to the proletariat. There were some guys who resisted for a while, who hesitated before mixing in. In the shops, there were comrades who would say to me: 'You're going to circulate my article? Don't tell anyone it's mine'.[122]

While Mothé was among the more isolated and vulnerable members of the *Tribune Ouvrière* collective, similar pressure was directed against all members. *Tribune Ouvrière* was, therefore, a clandestine publication. Clandestinity carried significant consequences. It greatly complicated the collective's finances, making it almost impossible to actually sell the paper or build a subscriber base. The limited number of copies that were actually sold were the primary source of income, which meant that the price was too high.[123] *Tribune Ouvrière* was only purchased by a few people, as a gesture of support. The paper was therefore primarily funded through individual contributions.[124] These financial problems placed strict limits on the paper's form. Despite the complicated relations between the collective and Socialisme ou Barbarie, the latter appears to have been the former's most important source of financial backing. I assume that Socialisme ou Barbarie purchased the copies of *Tribune Ouvrière* it provided to *Socialisme ou Barbarie* subscribers. More directly, Socialisme ou Barbarie provided the collective with a Roneotype machine to produce copies.

Tribune Ouvrière was printed on cheap paper, with an abstract profile of Billancourt stencilled across the top. Titles were hand lettered and copy hand typed. Piles were left in the cafeteria, the locker rooms and the latrines. It could not be distributed by militants who stationed themselves at the main factory entrances when shifts changed, as most political and union tracts were. This type of distribution would have provided the collective with at least some kind of contact with the larger factory population. Mothé worked out a sort of informal semiotics of the worker reception of the tracts: the length of time spent

---

122 Mothé 1976a, pp. 5–6.
123 *Tribune Ouvrière* no. 2 opens with a pledge to find a way to lower the price of each copy.
124 I have not found any information on the financial arrangements. Usually, there would be dues; Bois's group may have been another way of getting support. Logistical problems were occasionally discussed at Socialisme ou Barbarie meetings.

glancing at them before they were crumpled and thrown away became a measure of how much of the message he imagined could have been taken in.[125]

Tribune Ouvrière circulated much as *Socialisme ou Barbarie* did: messages stuffed in bottles and thrown into the ocean.[126] It was impossible to know if *Tribune Ouvrière* was being read, who was reading it or how far it circulated. So the collective was always searching for what they called 'echoes' of the factory floor. Had workers written, the collective might have had another way to delineate the shape of its unknowing. However, the workers did not write.

> Response to readers
>
> On reading *Tribune Ouvrière*, many comrades have said: 'What you are saying is very nice, but what should be done?'
>
> In the first issue it was said that a very small minority of workers cannot give directives and cannot call for the constitution of new mass organisations. But this idea itself should be debated. It is not enough to say 'What is to be done?', it is necessary also to propose something, and we will have something to say on this subject in the future... We must first of all look around us, take stock of our situation... and react, not in the mistaken manner that we have up till now, but by rethinking how in the past the working class has reacted against diverse forms of exploitation. The exploiters have learned much from workers' struggles: the workers must now learn to react to the situation that has been made for us.[127]

The tactical binds that *Tribune Ouvrière* confronted from its 1954 inception were particularly destructive for Mothé's vision of it as a worker newspaper. The nature of the political-syndical field at Billancourt and worker passivity created a gap separating workers from politics that could not be broached by repeated appeals to them for writing. Factional divisions within the *Tribune Ouvrière* collective translated as rhetorical inconsistencies in the paper. The problems created by these inconsistencies could be mapped onto a tension between innovation and legitimation. To be recognized as legitimate, innovation often has to adapt criteria established as dominant by the context. This necessary adaptation can obliterate what is innovative by rearranging the

---

125 Interviews with Mothé, Blachier, Véga and Martine during 1992. See Mothé 1976b for a semiotics of tract disposal.
126 A paraphrase of a remark by Castoriadis.
127 'Réponse aux lecteurs', in *Tribune Ouvrière*, no. 2 (June 1954), p. 4; reprinted in *Socialisme ou Barbarie*, no. 15/16, p. 78.

relationship between voices: the innovative becomes a variant of the extant or is reduced to noise.

Tribune Ouvrière and Production Cadences

Despite these obstacles, the collective continued to search for issues on the order of hierarchy that could be translated into arguments framing everyday experience in the shops as political. *Tribune Ouvrière* functioned as if an outpouring of worker written expression was only the right problem away. The collective developed the issue of production cadences to this end.

Tribune Ouvrière no. 2 opened with the above 'Response aux lecteurs'. After reiterating earlier critiques of hierarchy that linked them to calls for substantive industrial democracy, the article broached the subject of production cadences. Even more directly than the hierarchy, a successful politics of cadences – the pace of work – would have entailed a politicisation of many other aspects of shop-floor experience. The trade unions were reluctant to raise the issue in any deep way because a critique of the pace of work fed directly into the critique of Fordist technology and production design. These were central elements of the industrial modernisation endorsed by the entire French political and trade-union spectrum. This approval of Fordist modernisation limited thinking about pace to cost reduction and increased output to the exclusion of quality of work issues.

Tribune Ouvrière introduced its position on cadences as another spin-off from the 1954 dispute at its origin. It should be recalled that the Renault management introduced cadences as a political issue through their effort to link base wage rates directly to the output of particular work stations. The CGT saw in this an attempt to undo the longstanding compromise that had been reached between the *patronat* in general and the unions over the nature of salary by changing base wages into piece rates:

> Piecework, while being already an old method, has been spread far and wide since the end of the war by the CGT leadership. All their lamentations about 'infernal cadences' should not lead us to forget that the union pushed workers to production-levels of 150 percent and in some shops even 200 percent.
>
> Meanwhile, entire shops were unable to reach 100 percent and were paid at the minimum.
>
> To struggle against piece-rates is to explain to our work comrades that they should not exhaust themselves trying to keep times down, that they

should not ruin themselves and not say anything, which would make the times seem feasible...

The struggle against piecework should depart from the principle that we consider base x 150 percent to be minimum and that we will not be fooled by any fake calculations.[128]

Initially, *Tribune Ouvrière* framed the question of cadences as a salary issue. Given the terms of legitimate debate already in place at Billancourt, this linkage set up the article to be received by its readers as having origins in some 'deviationist' trade-union tendency.[129]

The collective reframed the issue in two later articles. The first, 'Deux grèves aux vilebriquins de la 4CV', reported on two isolated strikes in the 4CV assembly area sparked by the near-simultaneous imposition of new machinery, new organisation and faster cadences.[130] The second, 'Un exemple à mediter', used the issue of work speed in general as a point of departure for the only article to appear in *Tribune Ouvrière* that could be called worker journalism, a first-person account of the contradictions between high-speed production and demands for precision in the differential assembly area.[131]

The two strikes were spontaneous actions in relatively isolated and politically unorganised shops located in the 4CV area of Billancourt. The 4CV was a low-cost automobile introduced after World War II to allow France to fill the market position occupied in Germany by the *Volkswagen*. Production was geared to keeping costs down by using a compartmentalised assembly process that operated at the highest possible speed. The first of two strikes was provoked by the installation of new lathes and a new work configuration in department 76.40 during the spring of 1954. Both the conflict as well as the response of trade unions and management were portrayed as paradigmatic of the political situation that workers faced and indicative of the need for an alternative outlet like *Tribune Ouvrière*. Shop foremen expected the 76.40 machinists to adjust to the new machines while maintaining an output level of 16 crankshafts per hour. The workers were not given any training on the new machines, which made the adjustment 'particularly difficult' because of the

---

128 'Réponse aux lecteurs', p. 79. I write this on 27 December 1997. While editing this note I found out that Cornelius Castoriadis died last night.
129 Echoing Mothé 1976b.
130 'Deux greves aux vilebriquins de la 4CV', in *Tribune Ouvrière*, no. 8 (January 1955).
131 'Un exemple a mediter' in *Tribune Ouvrière*, no. 14 (September 1955).

workers' 'outdated mechanical knowledge'.[132] In July, management apparently decided that the transitional period was over, and increased the pace to 17.5/ hour. The *Tribune Ouvrière* article claimed that the reason given by management for the increase – that the workers had mastered the new machines – was a lie. The real reason for the speed-up, the article charged, was that management needed to accumulate a backlog of finished crankshafts to set up a planned speedup in the 4CV motor assembly line after the summer holidays. Whatever the motives, the machinists, who had already been pushed to their physical and mental limits by the 'adjustment' process, refused to accept the increase, and stopped working. When the machinists stopped, the assembly line stopped as well.

The first skirmish around 76.40 was won by the machinists. Management immediately isolated a single worker on the new machine and ordered him to either match the new rate of 17.5/hour or be fired on the spot.[133] Because this action took place within days of the summer shut down, management relented after a brief stand-off and work resumed for a couple of weeks at the old pace. The conflict began again after the factory re-opened at the end of August. Management and the unions greeted the returning workers with what the article's author described as a Stakhanovite display by a 'demonstration worker' able to produce 18 crankshafts per hour to the applause of a group of union delegates and managers. At this point, Department 76.40 went on strike. By the day's end, it had spread to two adjoining sectors.

The rest of the article details the CGT's efforts to contain, isolate and undermine the strike. On the second day, the CGT told the 76.40 workers that they had the union's full support, even as the strike was allowed to collapse in the adjacent sectors that had earlier stopped in sympathy. The CGT said nothing about the action beyond the confines of 76.40. Isolated and wavering, the workers soon realised the situation was hopeless and the strike collapsed.

The *Tribune Ouvrière* article only appeared in its January 1955 issue. It was the first information about the action to circulate throughout the factory.

---

132 'Deux greves aux vilebriquins de la 4CV' in *Tribune Ouvrière* no. 8, p. 1. The tension on the automobile assembly is enormous. I heard an NPR radio report that included a number of interviews with Detroit car workers about their work. One interviewee described a fellow worker who had spent twelve years putting a right-hand screw into the driver's side door. One day, management asked him move across the line to put a left-hand screw into a passenger door. He could not adapt to it, and within a couple hours had begun to have a sort of nervous breakdown.

133 The absurdity of this 'demonstration' should be evident: the worker would probably match the rate to avoid being fired. If he managed not to get fired, management would argue that the rate was not excessive. If he failed, he would be fired.

'Deux grèves' framed the story of the strike and its collapse as a cautionary tale. It contrasted the willingness of the shop's workers to act in concert with each other to make a political statement about technological change being forced upon them with the machinations of the unions that tried to isolate and undermine their action, in collusion with management. For the author of the *Tribune Ouvrière* account, the most telling moment was what greeted workers upon their return from vacation. The spectacle of management and union-functionaries applauding the demonstration worker showed clearly the identity of their interests. 'Deux grèves' argued that the analysis of this strike could only lead to the conclusion that there was a practical need for a new, 'properly proletarian organisation' which could coordinate actions, transmit information beyond isolated shops in a timely manner, and enable spatially circumscribed actions to be generalised. *Tribune Ouvrière* could function in this capacity, enabling workers to establish connections and, in the process, to begin to recognise the commonality of interests linking all workers, and to build a new worker community.[134]

'Deux grèves' was not a first-hand strike report, but was, rather, a detailed journalistic account. It raised two different problems. The first would emerge more sharply through Mothé's 1956–7 accounts of life at Billancourt. By 1954, the absurdity of acting in isolation had begun to erode workers' willingness for shops to act on their own or in concert with shop comrades. Trade-union resistance to actions that originated 'from below' reinforced this growing reluctance to act. The trade-union press became the sole conduit for transmitting information across the whole of the factory. For *Tribune Ouvrière* – and this position was consistent from 1954 to 1961 – this realignment of worker politics was temporary or superficial and could be overcome, perhaps with the paper as an important organising tool. In Mothé's later articles, *Tribune Ouvrière* itself was in the past, and the crisis affecting working-class politics was unfolding at a deeper level. From the perspective of *Tribune Ouvrière*, the 76.40 workers' resistance to increased production levels was also a struggle to retain some control over their tasks, their organisation and pace, to be able to define the content of a given unit of time and to assert a degree of political and professional autonomy. While these goals were not in themselves radical, what mattered was that they acted autonomously, organised themselves and formulated coherent, specific demands. Such action was an end in itself. From a viewpoint informed by Mothé's later writing, the instructive thing about the 76.40 action was not simply the action but its position in a continuum of such

---

134   This was the idea behind *Tribune Ouvrière* outlined for me by Henri Simon and Pierre Blachier.

actions, and their cumulative effect on the workers' ability to appropriate the Marxist Imaginary and act in an autonomous manner.

The overwhelming material advantages of the mechanisms of containment and enforcement available to the dominant political and union organisations and brought to bear on autonomous, local worker actions was, to an extent, compensated for in *Socialisme ou Barbarie* by concentrating on actions that managed to be generalised and by assembling accounts of these actions into a collage. This superimposition of local actions appeared to show that the proletariat was acting with growing intensity and increasing political radicalism. Tensions increasingly emerged within Socialisme ou Barbarie between the normative – the vision of autonomous proletarian action given meaning through the schema I have discussed throughout this book – and the descriptive. These tensions mirrored the distance that began to separate the revolutionary movement, whose politics were centred on the possibilities created by autonomous working-class action, and the situation facing actual workers. These tensions would surface within Socialisme ou Barbarie's revolutionary project beginning with Mothé's essays about life at Billancourt written during 1956 and 1957, which I will examine in the next chapter. The processes that Mothé detailed were already, to a certain degree, operative in *Tribune Ouvrière*. While Socialisme ou Barbarie tended to interpret its collapse as a worker journal in terms of factional fighting and tactical mistakes made by the group, I would argue for a more complex view. *Tribune Ouvrière* tried to break down the distinction between the militant and the worker by repoliticising everyday worker experience at the point of production. The collective located problems which conventional parties and trade unions were unable or unwilling to address that bore directly on the quality of life and work of thousands of Renault workers, and were symptomatic of the lot awaiting workers under Fordism more generally. As a worker newspaper, it foundered on the division between oral and written culture that could not be theorised within Socialisme ou Barbarie's highly productivist notion of class. The blurring of the distinction between oral and written culture paralleled Socialisme ou Barbarie's blurring of militants and workers as well as militant efforts to politically mobilise and the more complex, often passive, political comportments of workers in general.

Tribune Ouvrière was not simply a failure. For Pierre Blachier and Henri Simon, the paper served a concrete political function by providing workers with a mechanism they used strategically, on occasion, to redress specific power imbalances in specific shops by naming foremen and detailing abuses. From their anarchist viewpoints, this was justification enough for the project. For them, it was never a political paper. Rather, it was an expression of certain problems that arose in the course of production and an avenue for redressing them. Both considered Socialisme ou Barbarie's efforts to 'politicise' *Tribune Ouvrière* – to make of it an extension of themselves on the shopfloor and to encourage a particular type of writing that they considered interesting – to be an unnecessary and destructive act of hubris.[135]

It is therefore ironic that an article written by Blachier most closely approximated what Socialisme ou Barbarie hoped to obtain through *Tribune Ouvrière* as a worker-journal. 'Un exemple à mediter' – renamed 'Il faut se débrouiller' in *Socialisme ou Barbarie* – portrays the struggles of an unskilled worker in the context of high-speed production, who had to fight through contradictory work organisation to keep up with the cadences:

> The increase in the intensity of does not only happen by the intermediary of time; it also demands more and more precision from the worker.
>
> The more that precision is demanded by quality control, the longer the worker has to spend on it. This would appear to be self-evident to any normally constructed human being.
>
> Meanwhile, the factory is organised in such a way that the control services and the time-motion departments ignore each other... One demands precision, the other speed. If you add to this *tableau* a third person, the 'foreman' who wants the worker stuck to his machine like a fly to its excrement, the situation becomes infernal.
>
> Let's summarise:
>
> *To be precise, one has to*:
> 1. Not be pressured by delays or cadences.
> 2. Be able to move from your place from time to time.
> 3. Find the necessary tools.
>
> *To be fast, one has to*:
> 1. Not be precise
> 2. Sometimes be able to stop and change ideas, and by the same token, one's place.
> 3. Have the necessary tools.
>
> *To be assiduous at his machine, one must*: Have a very intense inner life that allows one to think entirely of things other than work, particularly when this work involves repeating three or four successive movements all day long. But in this case, one cannot be precise or necessarily fast.

---

135 Interview with Simon and Blachier.

To have the necessary tools, one must: More often than not be very lucky in order to stumble across them just at the moment that they are needed. It is particularly important to have patience when you don't find them.

The organisation of such separated services places the worker in an impossible position; he cannot make everyone happy. Therefore, it is no secret that everyone requires the worker to improvise [*se débrouiller*].[136]

The reaction to Blachier's article within Socialisme ou Barbarie provides a good ending tonality:

22/12/55. Discussion of *Tribune Ouvrière* no. 17:
Chaulieu found some very interesting things in the last issue, and in particular an article by comrade Gilles (Blachier). The article shows that the worker has to 'improvise' to make the time while struggling against the demands of service that bear on him in a contradictory manner, and to not take account of the realities of work, to find tools that are not there when he needs them. This definitive article shows in a few lines how the entire functioning of the factory rests on the capacity of the worker to improvise in order to do his work.

Marie-Rose complains that we talk too much about the factory, that we constantly find things that speak about the factory and asks herself how our talking to them constantly about things they are in contact with could interest the workers, and if they might not prefer to talk about something else.

---

136 'Il faut se débrouiller', reprinted in *Socialisme ou Barbarie* no. 18 (January–March 1956), pp. 123–4.

CHAPTER 6

Reading Daniel Mothé

This chapter analyses the 'autobiographical' narratives published in *Socialisme ou Barbarie* between 1956 and 1957 under the name Daniel Mothé.[1] It is divided into three parts. The first analyses Daniel Mothé as a signifier, a textual subject-position fabricated by both Jacques Gautrat and Socialisme ou Barbarie that reproduced significant tensions in Gautrat's relationship with Socialisme ou Barbarie and in Socialisme ou Barbarie's relationship with the working class more generally. I examine the signifier 'Mothé' as an expression of the relationship between Gautrat, his biography and the place of radical politics in it. Mothé was the Worker in and for Socialisme ou Barbarie, and a hybrid worker/intellectual/journalist and sociologist who used his position in the group to gain access to a broader public through publications in journals like *Arguments* and *L'Express*.

The second section focuses on Mothé as a narrative function in the *Socialisme ou Barbarie* articles. It positions Mothé relative to two synchronic frames that situated him as a worker writer. The internal (Socialisme ou Barbarie) frame was constituted by Romano's 'The American Worker', Lefort's 'L'expérience prolétarienne' and the worker newspaper project. The external frame, the traditional representations of the 'authentic' French working class formalised in the proletarian-literature movement, explains the inclusions and exclusions that shaped Mothé's portrait of worker experience.

The third section begins with a close reading of the first and paradigmatic text of the 1956–7 writings, 'Journal d'un ouvrier'. This essay, through a condensed first-person account, stages Socialisme ou Barbarie's conception of working-class political mobilisation and its fate in the contemporary environment. The analysis discusses mobilisation as the collective appropriation of language games instituted through the field of political/cultural production dominated at Billancourt by the PCF-CGT. The balance of this section tracks the dissolution of these language games. It analyses Mothé's account of the aftermath for the PCF-CGT of 1956, a politically disastrous year. Mothé's

---

1 'Journal d'un ouvrier', in *Socialisme ou Barbarie* no. 19 (July–September 1956), pp. 73–100; 'Chez Renault, on parle de la Hongrie' in *Socialisme ou Barbarie* no. 20 (December–February), pp. 124–33; *Socialisme ou Barbarie* no. 22 (July–September 1957), 'L'usine et la gestion ouvrière', pp. 74–111 and 'Agitation chez Renault', pp. 126–44; 'Les grèves chez Renault', in *Socialisme ou Barbarie* no. 23 (January–February 1958), pp. 48–71. These texts were reprinted in Mothé 1959.

writings then split into what I call dominant and subdominant narratives after his account of December 1956 at Billancourt and its effects on worker politics. The dominant narrative tracks the evaporation of the informal spaces that once connected organisation militants to their broader worker constituencies. The disappearance of this space appears to signal the collapse of the language games that structured worker political action as well. The subdominant narrative attempts to contextualise the dominant in terms of what I have been calling Socialisme ou Barbarie's notion of legitimation crisis.[2] According to this crisis model, the workers had split away from conventional politics and the organisations that controlled it. This split was loosely understood as a reappropriation of the emancipatory elements in Marx and was therefore also an opportunity for the emergence of a new, revolutionary working-class politics. This new politics, as I have shown, derived its coherence and power from Socialisme ou Barbarie's interpretation of everyday professional experience. The two narratives stage mutually exclusive readings of the problems that faced working-class politics under Fordism. These two readings also define the general situation that Socialisme ou Barbarie would struggle to interpret between 1957 and 1965. One had either an emergent new revolutionary politics or a fundamental crisis affecting the categories and images that ordered and made possible any such revolutionary politics. One had, then, either a situation of great hope and excitement for revolutionaries – reflected in Castoriadis's 1955–8 series 'Sur le contenu du socialisme', for example – or a crisis of the Marxist Imaginary itself.

Mothé as Signifier 1: Jacques Gautrat on Becoming Daniel Mothé[3]

In 1940, fifteen-year-old Jacques Gautrat quit school. Despite his 'fascination with culture', he hated school and had to get away from his family. His father was a literate agricultural worker who had refashioned himself into a shopkeeper in the social flux that followed World War I:

---

2 Again, the term 'legitimation crisis' does not appear in *Socialisme ou Barbarie*. It was formalised by Habermas in the 1970s. The overlay of the crisis model outlined in Habermas 1975 on the group's interpretation of worker relations to bureaucratic union and political organisations is a generative exercise.

3 The following is a patchwork of my interview with Jacques Gautrat from 30 January 1992, Gautrat's CNRS office and Mothé 1976b. Quotations that are not cited come from my 1992 interview.

> He had a photo of Pétain in his window in 1940. All the other shops in the neighborhood did as well, but for me it was too much... I hated the trade, hated school, and wanted to be independent.

While Jacques and his father were at opposite ends of the political spectrum, their paths shared some basic features: a broken social trajectory disrupted by war that provided each of them with the chance to fashion a new identity and adopt a new politics. Where the father became a *petit commerçant* aligned with Pétain, the petit-bourgeois hero of the nation and a symbol of social stability, the son would become a '*métallo*', a machinist, part of the industrial working class and a revolutionary Marxist militant.

Leaving home for Paris, Gautrat was introduced to radical politics through the *Auberges de jeunesse*[4] during the first months of the German occupation (1940–1). The Occupation had forced the *Auberges de jeunesse* to fragment into a network of discussion circles and had broken down the barriers that usually restricted contact between its various left political positions. This was an unusually ecumenical climate for a political education: Gautrat's took place through discussion and debate with young anarchists, Trotskyists, pacifists, and Communists. Even after the Nazis banned the *Auberges de jeunesse* in November 1941, these small discussion circles continued to meet in different configurations and places. They comprised a network of young people who met to discuss politics, philosophy, and revolutionary theory. The experience was crucial for Gautrat: it gave him 'access to culture without the bullshit of formal education'. The experience also enabled him to select his political affiliation from the widest possible range of options, which increased the likelihood of political heterodoxy.[5] 'Convinced by their story of the Russian Revolution', and building what he called a romantic identification with 'the greater historical narrative' of the history of the workers' movement, Gautrat became a Trotskyist.[6]

---

4 The *Auberges de jeunesse* were established in the wake of the Popular Front as a youth club. *Socialisme ou Barbarie* member Jacques Signorelli (Garros), who, along with René Caule and later Jean Amory, devoted much energy to the movement, referred to the *Auberges de Jeunesse* as a sort of 'hunting ground for the Left' in search of new members. Interviews with the author, Spring 1992.

5 See the characterisations of working-class political trajectories by region and profession in Molinari 1991.

6 Gautrat noted in my interview that the grist for the identification-mill appeared at a variety of levels. This extended to things like being told: 'You look like Bukharin. He was also short'.

By the end of 1942, Gautrat was married and living outside the Occupied Zone.[7] During the day he worked in a mine at Albi. At night, he was part of a loosely organised Trotskyist group based in Toulouse that published the obscure *Front Ouvrier*.[8] Gautrat participated in the Resistance,[9] sheltering Jewish refugees and making false identity papers.[10] Working a physically demanding job during the day and on clandestine political activity at night fitted into a conventional pattern of the Leninist 'worker revolutionary'.[11]

At the war's end, French Trotskyism faced a number of problems. One important conflict resulted from tension between the Party, which sought to enforce its doctrinal and organisational authority, and a base accustomed to considerable freedom to act on and formulate positions during the Occupation. Another, more fundamental conflict resulted from Trotskyism's failure to routinise Trotsky's charismatic leadership. Trotsky's assassination in 1940, therefore, created an ideological and organisational void, the effects of which only began to emerge after 1944. Without any clear mechanism to negotiate the problem of succession, the question of where theory was to originate without Trotsky was played out through internal factional conflict within the reconstituted PCI.[12] Minority efforts to adapt Trotskyism to a changed post-war situation and to treat theory as an ongoing project were marginalised in favour of the Majority claims that Trotsky's pre-war writings were definitive analyses of contemporary capitalism and the USSR and could therefore be transformed into doctrine. A central and recurring issue in this conflict was the 'Russian Question', how to think about Stalinism and the socio-political nature of the USSR. The Party's 'Majority Tendency' and its allies adopted Trotsky's 1938 position, elaborated in *The Revolution Betrayed*,[13] that the USSR was a deformed

---

7   His ex-wife, Martine Gautrat, was also active in Socialisme ou Barbarie and, via the 'Groupe Renault,' in *Tribune Ouvrière*. She was a full-time *institutrice* [school administrator] who was very active in the SNI (*Syndicat National des Instituteurs*, the militant, professional trade union prominent during the resistance to the Algerian War). She figures in this project in her own right.

8   See Pluet-Despatins 1978.

9   Not all Trotskyist groups did so. The CCI – the organisation to which Claude Lefort belonged during the war – as an organisation considered the war to be a bourgeois affair that did not concern them, even while individual militants carried on Resistance actions on their own. A detailed account of the various Trotskyist groups and their activities during World War II can be found in Pluet-Despatins 1980.

10 Mothé 1976b, p. 2.

11 See 'What Is To Be Done?' in Lenin 1977, vol. 1, p. 194.

12 'Parti Communiste Internationaliste' or the Internationalist Communist Party.

13 Trotsky 1945.

workers' state. This position responded better to the problem of the routinisation of charisma and institutional continuity than to the theoretical questions posed by the nature of the USSR and Western capitalism in the post-war context. It entailed a series of other positions on the status of theory and the organisation's openness to change, the notions of the party, socialism, capitalism and the prospects of revolution that were also suited to the problem of routinisation.[14] In the context of these debates, the 'Russian Question' was a fundamental index that many of the competing positions within the PCI used to differentiate themselves from each other. It was also a preoccupation for Gautrat, who used it as a basic criterion for making his political choices.

During the reorganisation of the Fourth International in Autumn 1944, Gautrat aligned with the dissident 'Communistes Révolutionnaires'. In contact with the German RKD,[15] this organisation argued that the USSR was 'state capitalist'.[16] For Gautrat, this position enabled an accommodation of a range of written and oral accounts critical of factory conditions in the USSR and of the Gulag.[17] When the Fourth International officially adopted *The Revolution Betrayed*'s line on the USSR in November 1944, the 'Communistes Révolutionnaires' broke with it and with Trotskyism. Never tightly organized, they soon dissolved into the political scenery.[18]

---

14   In the sense that it made easier the rise of a centralised bureaucratic party structure claiming a monopoly on the production of theory and direction of politics. A rough analogy would be the 325 A.D. Council of Nicea, to the extent that it declared divine inspiration to be over, and selected 'legitimate' gospels partly on the basis of their compatibility with a centralised, bureaucratic church.

15   Mothé 1976b, p. 1.

16   After the war, the term state capitalism was associated with the Johnson-Forest Tendency. Central JFT texts include Raya Dunyevskaya 1942–3; James, Dunyevskaya and Lee 1947; James 1950a.

17   Ciliga 1938 developed, from a worker-opposition perspective, the theme of the Gulag as the core of Stalinist society forty years before Solzynitsyn. There were a range of other worker-opposition texts available, not to mention texts by anarchists, Mensheviks, etc. Other left-wing critics of the USSR whose works were known in Trotskyist circles included, on the Russian Revolution, Victor Serge (a social revolutionary) and Voline on Stalin, Trotsky and Boris Souvarine. Later books by ex-Soviet officials including Alexander Barmine and, particularly (and problematically) Victor Kravchenko confirmed and/or inflected earlier criticisms.

18   Mothé 1976b, p. 1. On the 'revolutionary communists' and their role (along with that of the RKD) in these debates during November 1944, see Pluet 1980, pp. 226–8. The CRs resignation letter ('Lettre de demission de la fraction communiste revolutionnaire lue par elle au Ier congres du P.C.I., avant de sortir') is quoted on p. 226; see n. 2 for mention of the 'Declaration des comrades de T'. from Toulouse – which would include JG – both of which

After the war, Gautrat moved to Marseilles to work on the docks and became involved with the Bordigist 'Gauche Communiste' ('Internationalist Tendency') which had been strong in the area since the Italian immigration in the early 1920s:

> I left them [the C.R.S] when I met the Bordigists... I found myself in agreement with Bordiga's 1924 'Rome Theses', which were very orthodox Leninist theory. What was interesting was that the Bordigists broke with the Trotskyist analysis of Russia, but they did so on the basis of a bizarre conception, according to which the USSR was a capitalist country. After a while, I found that this analysis did not correspond to the real situation... But this seems a bit false to me, because my attachment to militant action was not just theoretical, but was also affective. My militancy rested upon a classic Trotskyist conception with a different analysis of the USSR, which I characterised at the time as state capitalist. What's more, I found the Italian Bordigist militants to be impressive: they were people full of history, workers who carried a very rich experience, heroic militants in a sense. And they also had a certain coherence, not to say rigour, which came in a straight line from the writings of Marx and Lenin. This coherence gave reassurance and security to the young militant that I was.[19]

Gautrat's professional training overlapped with his politics:

> I am by origin a worker. I began working at fifteen as an upholsterer-decorator; in reality, I was an O.S. who made springs all day long. [Gautrat describes working at Albi, and briefly as a docker at Marseilles]. I went up to Paris after the war. I became a clerk thanks to false credentials. I was fired for professional and political reasons. And then, as in the traditional Trotskyist-Leninist conception [according to which] the revolution would happen with the metal-workers, I became a '*métallo*'. I underwent accelerated professional training and came out a milling-machine operator. But I still had to work as an O.S. for a year and a half, before entering Renault as a professional.[20]

---

were printed in the *Bulletin Intérieur du PCI* no. 9 (nov. 1944). A more schematic picture of the same period can be found in Alexander 1991, pp. 371–2.

19   Mothé 1976b, p. 1.
20   Mothé 1976b, pp. 2–3. For the 'classical Trotskyist-Leninist conception' of the role of the '*métallos*' – see Trotsky 1961, vol. 1, pp. 420–1.

In Gautrat's biography, there was extensive cross-cutting of his political and professional lives. As politics was his most coherent and important trajectory, it is perhaps not surprising that his decision to become a '*métallo*' was driven by the political imagery of revolution. Ideological positions not only framed professional choices, but also served to both integrate him into, and differentiate him from, his professional environment.[21] This use of politics to frame his professional life can be read as the precondition for the simultaneous involvement with work and a contextualised understanding of that involvement characteristic of the writing that Gautrat would later develop through Mothé.

As with most workers who get involved with politics, for Gautrat politics reflected not only an ethical commitment structured by and structuring a larger worldview, and a means of professional integration and marker of distinction. It was also a means of social mobility. Mobility for Gautrat did not imply the usual pattern of involvement with a party or trade union, eventually rising in the hierarchy as a way of getting off the factory floor,[22] but centred on the much riskier proposition of becoming an intellectual. He used his involvement with small groups constituted around the production of theory to gain access to, and actively participate in, a 'culture' that would otherwise have been foreclosed because he lacked the requisite cultural capital (particularly a university education).

Once in Paris, Gautrat remained a Bordigist, joining the small group around 'Internationaliste' that included Alberto Maso, Raymond Hirzel, Jacques Signorelli and others. This group merged with Socialisme ou Barbarie in 1951. Gautrat did not immediately follow the rest of 'Internationaliste' into Socialisme ou Barbarie for non-political reasons.[23] During this year of hesitation, Gautrat worked politically with the 'Fédération Anarchiste' (FA) at Renault. While never officially joining, he was known enough to act as a delegate from Renault at the FA congress that year (1951). He also was active with writing and publishing the short-lived *Le Libértaire Renault*. Gautrat's 1952 arrival in Socialisme ou Barbarie coincided with an explosion of the recurrent dispute over the problem of Socialisme ou Barbarie's status as

---

21 See the Mothé 1976b quotes on his professional life at Renault in Chapter 4, Section C.
22 This was a typical scenario for PCF-CGT worker-militants. Fear of being sent back into the factory played a considerable role in assuring loyalty. See Kriegel 1980. For an analysis that emphasises this dimension almost exclusively to explain working-class adherence to the PCF-CGT, see Heldmann 1989.
23 He and his wife Martine had divorced and she was then beginning a long-term relationship with Véga (Alberto Maso).

an organisation.[24] Of this, he said: 'It was not my problem. The problem, for me, was the rupture with Bolshevism and how to analyse bureaucracy which neither the Trotskyists nor the Bordigists could do'. The group was still quite small and loosely structured at this time, more like the clandestine groups Gautrat had experienced during the war than a conventional left-wing party.[25] The position of Daniel Mothé began to be constructed as soon as Gautrat began writing under that name in 1953: 'In Socialisme ou Barbarie, I was accepted, valorised in an intellectual milieu. Mothé was not Gautrat at Renault: Mothé provided me with a space to live, to breathe'.[26]

Mothé as Signifier 2: Mothé as a Position within Socialisme ou Barbarie

Gautrat's relationship to his pseudonym is unique among the Socialisme ou Barbarie members I interviewed during 1991–2. For the most part, the names were simple necessities, covers for foreigners engaged in political activities for which they could have been deported (Véga, Castoriadis) or screens behind which politics could be hidden from professional lives (for example, teaching careers not yet developed to the point where publication in a radical journal could become a source of symbolic capital – Lefort, Lyotard, and Souyri). While the separate names were functional as markers of integration into a secret society, most Socialisme ou Barbarie members viewed them instrumentally, as tools that enabled them to be political during a repressive period structured first by their opposition to the PCF during its ascendancy and later by the state's response to the escalating Algerian War.[27] They were not particularly important in themselves, nor did they signify a discontinuity between the

---

24   The textual dimension of this debate was published in *Socialisme ou Barbarie* no. 10 as 'Discussion sur le parti révolutionnaire'; Chaulieu, P., 'La direction prolétarienne', pp. 10–18 and Montal, C., 'Le prolétariat et le problème de la direction révolutionnaire', pp. 18–27.

25   Véga in particular emphasised this aspect of Socialisme ou Barbarie's appeal during my interviews with him He contrasted it with Trotskyist groups, particularly around Pierre Lambert.

26   Interview with author.

27   In my Interview with Albert Maso (Véga), he claimed to have selected war names for a number of Socialisme ou Barbarie militants including Lyotard (Laborde) and Sebastien de Diesbach (Chatel). Others were chosen in a more casual manner. Daniel Blanchard, for example, decided to use Canjuers because it was a town near his childhood home.

actors' daytime lives and what they did at night.[28] Symptomatic of this instrumental relation, a number of the group's academic members (Lefort, Lyotard, Yvon Bourdet) began publishing articles in *Socialisme ou Barbarie* under their own names after 1956, once the journal emerged as a position in 'progressiste' debates and their professional positions were secure enough to benefit from publication in a radical journal.[29]

For Jacques Gautrat, Mothé was a separate identity, a social position constructed by and around him within Socialisme ou Barbarie that permitted him to function as an intellectual and opened up a different range of political and cultural possibilities than were available to him at Renault. This position – Mothé – was only possible, however, because of Gautrat at Billancourt. Socialisme ou Barbarie's revolutionary theory was constructed with constant reference to the industrial working class as the centre of their political hopes, theoretical analyses and affective investments. Because Gautrat was a worker who thought his professional position through a Marxist political and sociological framework, and because he could write, he possessed both a kind of experience significant in the group's imaginary and the capacity to rewrite that experience in terms shaped by it. Because there were almost no other workers in Socialisme ou Barbarie, Gautrat's integration into the group was not just as Mothé, but also as the Worker. A *'métallo'* at the symbolically important Billancourt factory and Socialisme ou Barbarie's representative of the working class, Mothé confirmed the relationship between Socialisme ou Barbarie's theoretical project and the working class at its centre, and was an actor in his own right shaping that project.

The peculiar position Mothé occupied was discussed in Claude Lefort's 1975 interview:

> There is no doubt about the workerist dimension. In this respect, we still situated ourselves in the Trotskyist tradition. Our principal concern was,

---

28 David Ames Curtis told me about asking Castoriadis if he stopped to change clothes between his day job at the OECD and the café where Socialisme ou Barbarie would meet. Castoriadis did not see the interest of the question. Like most of the other members I spoke with, he saw what he was doing in Socialisme ou Barbarie as part of a continuum of activities. Not so with Mothé.

29 Lamont 1987 analyses the risks and possibilities of creating an academic trajectory defined both by virtuoso-work and breaking or ignoring the conventional markers of professional distinction and institutional advancement amongst French academics and intellectuals. Lamont argues in part that this social gambit – the old virtuoso-model transposed into a professionalised academic system – played an important role in defining a mystique around Derrida that in turn shaped the initial French reception of his work in the early 1970s.

obviously, to build for ourselves a 'worker base'. Even though we did not have the means to create it, we discussed very early and interminably the worker-newspaper project. Besides, a new link to the working class was soon glorified. The words of Mothé – often very rich, but also at times confused and summary – had an excessive weight for many because it was felt that he 'represented' Renault. It seems to me, moreover, that while he was conscious of the role that he was expected to play and took advantage of it, it eventually began to exasperate him. The climate would have been different, undoubtedly, if we had among us more workers.[30]

Jacques Gautrat at the Renault AOC and Daniel Mothé, the proper name given the position created by and around Gautrat within Socialisme ou Barbarie, were mirror images of each other. Both Gautrat at Renault and Mothé in Socialisme ou Barbarie fashioned their social/political personae within relatively small collectives by defining themselves through valued but scarce competencies. Because Mothé was constructed with reference to Gautrat at Billancourt, we have a detailed image of how he operated as a channel for dissent in the AOC annex – catalysing debate, generating tracts, serving as an unofficial spokesman at union meetings. He acquired these functions because of his facility with spoken and written language, which enabled him to formulate the responses of his fellow workers, and a dissident political position, which gave him latitude to use these skills publicly.[31] A vaguer image can be assembled of Mothé functioning in a parallel manner in Socialisme ou Barbarie, as its link to Billancourt workers, articulating Mothé by passing Gautrat's experience through Socialisme ou Barbarie's theoretical grid.

Gautrat felt himself to be an anonymous worker in an immense factory, personally isolated in his shop because of his politics (due to PCF-CGT dominance) and his personal history (his divorce and his eccentricities).[32] This isolation would break down when the shop comrades disagreed with a PCF-CGT position enough to want to make a public stand without incurring the considerable personal risks that could follow from doing so. Mothé's accounts of Gautrat the militant indicate that he imagined his position and its possibili-

---

30   Lefort 1974, p. 8.
31   See quotes in the previous chapter from Mothé 1976b regarding his militant role at Billancourt, and below, on the accounts of that activity he produced for *Socialisme ou Barbarie*.
32   In my interview, Gautrat recalled a screaming match with Hirzel over the political consequences of his penchant for wearing used American Army fatigues when not in work overalls. On his divorce as a weapon, see Mothé 1976a, quoted above in Chapter 5, n. 44.

ties in terms of the revolutionary narratives that attracted Gautrat to Marxism. The gap separating these imagined contexts from his actual isolated situation conditioned Mothé's narratives by casting them as stories of failure. Gautrat was unable to effectively communicate the link between his actions and their revolutionary narrative framework to his fellow workers. He was never able to use his position in the AOC to build from conjunctural actions to some kind of organisation, nor did his political activities yield the kind of results his theoretical conceptions deemed most valuable – the worker newspaper, autonomous organisation, strikes, etc. Mothé provided Gautrat the luxury of textually reprocessing his failures in the AOC. He used them through Socialisme ou Barbarie to secure the social distinction, the 'validation in an intellectual milieu', that he desired.[33]

In this regard, Lefort's remark that Mothé's role as Worker was a direct function of Socialisme ou Barbarie's social composition and would have been probably quite different had there been more workers in the group is crucial. Throughout this project, I have argued that despite Socialisme ou Barbarie's talk about the working class and its desire to build a worker base, the distance that separated the group from its proletarian object of desire was reiterated in every effort to focus their project more completely on it. The gap can be explained by the highly theoretical core of Socialisme ou Barbarie's revolutionary project and its specialised, difficult language. This project constructed a view of the working class and workers' everyday experience that incorporated assumptions particular to an intellectual milieu – for example the assumptions about the nature of and relation to writing – that separated the group's vision from the workers even at the points where the contact appeared closest.

This gap was doubled by that which separated the field of cultural production within which Socialisme ou Barbarie operated from that in factories. For workers, Socialisme ou Barbarie not only presented problems of comprehension and a view of the political possibilities inherent in their professional lives that was quite distant from their experience, but the group could also not even offer any guaranteed short-term payoff in social mobility to justify the night meetings (after a long day) and other demands on time and energy. The workers that did become involved with Socialisme ou Barbarie usually only stuck around for a short time. They tended to be workers who, like Mothé,

---

33   Over the longer term, Mothé was refashioned again as a CFDT militant and later as a researcher in industrial sociology at the CNRS. He still publishes in *Esprit* under the name Daniel Mothé. On Mothé's texts, see Ragon 1974, pp. 252–7. For a more recent reference to Mothé's 1950s writing as an important documentary source of Billancourt life in the 1950s, see Fridenson 1986, p. 531 n. 52.

framed their understanding of their professional position in political terms.[34] Socialisme ou Barbarie's most sustained contact with workers besides Mothé/Gautrat was with the *Tribune Ouvrière* collective at Renault. Raymond Hirzel (the strongest personality in the collective, whose conflictual relation with Socialisme ou Barbarie was discussed in the previous chapter) could easily have been Mothé's rival for the role of 'Worker' in Socialisme ou Barbarie as he had been for influence in *Tribune Ouvrière*. Working in a highly politicised shop and benefitting from his association with the April 1947 strikes, Hirzel was a charismatic and dynamic person with a gift for organisation. He used his abilities not only in the factory but also socially by arranging commercially sponsored trips and holidays for workers and their families.[35] He was never consistently part of Socialisme ou Barbarie, perhaps because his influence amongst workers at Billancourt and his temperament made him unable to submit to the group's informal division between intellectual and militant. Mothé considered Hirzel both a 'classic paranoiac' and an example of a personality type drawn to Trotskyism by the belief that the next revolution will make of them 'the next Lenin'.[36] The Hirzel/Mothé rivalry was played out both in Socialisme ou Barbarie, where Mothé won, and in the *Tribune Ouvrière* factional fighting, where Mothé lost.

---

34   Among the longer term involvements by industrial workers: Hirzel; J. Dupont, who wrote as Georges Vivier 'La vie en usine', was a Citroen worker and part of Socialisme ou Barbarie from the beginning until around 1955; Marcel Kouroriez, a pressroom worker at *Le Monde* was active in Socialisme ou Barbarie from 1956 until 1958, but did not write. At the time, Socialisme ou Barbarie also included Henri Simon and a couple militants from the A.G. Vie (Guy in particular) were employees (white-collar workers whose positions were becoming more automated). Castoriadis and Guillaume were economists at the OECD. Lefort, Lyotard, Sternberg and Souyri were academics. Martine Gautrat was a school-administrator [*institutrice*] and active in the SNI union, with its own long tradition of radicalism. Véga was a full-time translator of Spanish, Catalan and French. Garros was a salesman for a dental-supply company and Michel (Georges Petit) a physical therapist. The 'generation' that entered the group after 1956 were for the most part university students (Daniel Blanchard, Sebastien de Diesbach) or recent graduates (Yvon Bourdet, Gérard Genette). The position workers were placed in was parallel to that faced by married women with children, who had to expend tremendous amounts of energy to participate in the group. Martine Gautrat, Andrée Lyotard and Louisette Signorelli all described how the mothers had to assume the role of 'super-mum': political activity was an additional demand, beyond working full time and taking care of a family. The group made no allowance for child care.
35   Interviews with Henri Simon and Pierre Blachier, April 1992.
36   Interview with J. Gautrat, February 1992.

Because the rivalry played out in *Tribune Ouvrière*, it later provided Henri Simon[37] (through his ICO/ILO groups)[38] a means to claim that he and his proletarian/anarchist group were the more legitimate successors to the 'real' Socialisme ou Barbarie legacy (defined by the centrality of the problem of relations with the working class between 1953 and 1958) than Socialisme ou Barbarie itself. Implicitly questioning Mothé's proletarian 'authenticity', Simon has argued that Mothé was central within Socialisme ou Barbarie not because he actually represented the workers, but because he mirrored Castoriadis's positions. By feeding the group what it wanted to hear, Mothé was able to conceal, or compensate for, his isolation in the factory. For Simon, the demonstration of this thesis was the crucial role played by Hirzel in *Tribune Ouvrière*, coupled with his troubled relationship with Socialisme ou Barbarie. From this, Simon concluded that Hirzel's conception of 'real' factory politics caused him to keep the overly intellectual Socialisme ou Barbarie at a distance. Consistently anarchist, Simon argued that Mothé's notion of the worker newspaper imposed a false, non-proletarian revolutionary frame on a paper that operated as a tactical weapon in local struggles at Billancourt, and that it continued to do so after Mothé had moved on. *Tribune Ouvrière* was used differently at different times by workers to intervene in particular situations and tip the balance of forces in their favour. For Simon, this was, and is, the essence of politics. In the context of this project, which has returned again and again to the notion of the worker as a central signifier in a Marxist Imaginary, Simon's counterposition of a 'real' and a 'false' proletariat, and a type of politics consonant with each, seems beside the point. That said, it is true that Mothé's position as 'worker' was fashioned by the group in its own image to the exclusion of other possibilities – including Simon – and that Mothé usually sided with Castoriadis in internal debates.

The crucial factor in fashioning Mothé was neither his '*prolo*' credentials nor his relationship with Castoriadis. It was rather his writing ability and the

---

37 Simon's arguments along these lines do not appear In Socialisme ou Barbarie transcripts prior to his departure from the group in September 1958. They are *ex post facto* efforts to ground his claims that ILO/ICO, and not Socialisme ou Barbarie, best continued the proletarian revolutionary tradition initiated during the period between 1953 and 1958 examined in this project. Another effort toward the same end is the *Socialisme ou Barbarie* anthology he edited for Arcatie covering the same period. For a more detailed résumé of the mid-1970s state of this tiresome dispute, see Simon and Mothé's respective *AntiMythes* interviews, particularly the exchange over Mothé supposedly being a 'trade-union careerist' for joining the CFDT, and Mothé's jabs at ILO/ICO in Mothé 1973.

38 Simon split with Socialisme ou Barbarie in 1958 to form 'Informations et Liasions Ouvrières' (ILO), later known as the 'Informations et Correspondances Ouvriers' (ICO).

confirmation it provided Socialisme ou Barbarie of its tendency to equate writing and self-consciousness. The ability to write also played an important role in defining Gautrat's position in the AOC. If one followed Simon's argument, Gautrat/Mothé's AOC role would have been more 'authentic' had he functioned like a corner letter writer who simply transcribed shop-level dissent. An enormous gap separates this transcribing/formulating function and the writing of tracts (specific interventions that try to alter a local strategic situation) from the production of autobiographical narratives that contain situated accounts of that transcribing function. But the gap is not that which separates the authentic from the inauthentic, but that which separates Gautrat from Mothé, and shop-floor experience from theoretical accounts of it. That Socialisme ou Barbarie would assimilate Mothé as if he and his writing were reflections of Gautrat at Renault indicates the distance that separated Socialisme ou Barbarie from the structuring cultural conditions of the factory life that so preoccupied them. This gap is in no way addressed or clarified by Simon's inversion of the traditional conception of militant practice, according to which the intellectual/militant had to be the same as the factory worker. Simon's defintion of the militant eliminated the space for self-consciousness. It translates into a writing that only describes. Presumably, these descriptions would be sent to a journal like ICO whose editorial role would consist of juxtaposing them with other such accounts as if the parts and the whole spoke for themselves. Interpretation, for Simon, only contaminated.

So How are We to Think about Daniel Mothé?

The first part of this chapter provided an overview of the various elements/social roles that constituted a sort of circuit around Daniel Mothé. The name Mothé is both the pseudonym under which Jacques Gautrat operated as a part of Socialisme ou Barbarie and a proper name given a social position jointly fabricated by Jacques Gautrat and Socialisme ou Barbarie in terms of their own interests, desires, etc. The writings signed Mothé are are rooted in Gautrat's factory experience, but are not simple reproductions of that experience: Mothé is rather a perspective on Gautrat's experience defined in terms of Socialisme ou Barbarie's theoretical grid, itself fashioned as a relation to working-class experience valued in, and intelligible to, an intellectual-militant social context. For a *Socialisme ou Barbarie* reader, Mothé excluded Gautrat – or better, encompassed, comprehended and stood in for Gautrat. For his Renault comrades in the AOC, Gautrat had no relation to Daniel Mothé. For Socialisme ou Barbarie, Mothé's position integrally assumed Gautrat's connection to Billancourt, while for Gautrat, Mothé and Socialisme ou Barbarie represented a separate position as an intellectual, a separate set of social and intellectual possibilities. It is not enough in this context to simply demonstrate the autonomy of the proper name: Mothé is rather the intersections of identities and the place within which the tensions between them are reproduced and covered over. These tensions lay at the heart of Socialisme ou Barbarie's construction of the worker: part empirical worker, part proletarian, part imagined double of the Marxist theorist.

The proper name Mothé is rather like an object, a 'determinable x' as Husserl would have it, and each constitutive social relation a predicate. The relation between each predicate and 'x' is discrete to the extent that each implies a certain directional relation that is (in some cases) exclusive of others (e.g. Gautrat's notion of Mothé as naming a separate social space and set of cultural possibilities as opposed to Socialisme ou Barbarie's tendency to treat Mothé/Gautrat as synonymous). Each version of Mothé is hyletic: a particular view from a particular position. Each position is shaped by a certain number of directional social relations. All of the various predicates that defined Mothé would not be operative at any given time. In fact, to show them all at once, as we are doing here, tends to dissolve Mothé into a fiction. The most important of the predicates, the one on which the others rely, that organises and enables them to exist, is the narrative function. If one analyses Mothé as narrative function, the designation of the various constitutive social relations as predicates is shown to be metaphorical: they cannot be extracted from Mothé's text, but rather shape the perspective from which these texts are written. There is no template with which one can distinguish clearly what is Gautrat and what is Mothé as a perspective on Gautrat. The textual descriptions of everyday professional and political experience at Billancourt only appear as already overlaid with the political/sociological perspectives shaped by Socialisme ou Barbarie and constitutive of Mothé as a social position. This, more than anything else, explains Mothé's centrality to *Socialisme ou Barbarie* for the textual staging and legitimation of the group's vision of the worker-militant.

Gautrat's rewriting of his experience as Mothé, by passing it through Socialisme ou Barbarie's theoretical grid and recoding that experience in a particular type of writing, reinforced Gautrat's internal position with Socialisme ou Barbarie and made possible for Mothé a public role somewhere between worker writer, journalist and sociologist who reported on the working class for the largely university-educated left that became *Socialisme ou Barbarie*'s primary audience/context after 1956.

Mothé's articles appeared not only in *Socialisme ou Barbarie* but also in *Arguments*, whose readership reached into the theoretical vanguard of the

Les Temps Modernes audience.[39] Occasionally, pieces appeared in the influential progressive weekly *L'Express*,[40] which had a much larger circulation than *Socialisme ou Barbarie* and a direct role in shaping debate on the left.[41] Marxism remained the central organising and legitimating political framework underpinning this *'Progressiste'* Left. Despite the problems encountered by the PCF during 1956, the field remained marked by its dominance. There was, for example, an intense interest in working-class responses to political events. This interest resulted in some remarkably superficial journalism. The combination of interest and superficiality can be read as parallel to the Party's lack of interest in a precise sociological understanding of its constituency so long as its theatrical politics of mass mobilisation continued to operate. This situation created a space for a writer with Mothé's expertise. In the weeks that followed the Soviet suppression of the Hungarian Revolution, Mothé published a version of his *Socialisme ou Barbarie* account of the impact of Budapest on politics at Billancourt that contrasted sharply with the straw poll based articles by Roger Stéphane.[42] Gautrat only had access to the publication as Mothé, who was in turn legitimated through the association with Socialisme ou Barbarie. The association with Socialisme ou Barbarie was able to function as legitimation partly because the group's visibility had increased quite suddenly as a result of their having available the only coherent interpretation of the Hungarian Revolution from a left-wing perspective in the months that followed the revolt.[43] Mothé's publications, in turn, gave *Socialisme ou*

---

39 The *Arguments* collective appears to have grown out of the *Comité des intellectuels révolutionnaires* that included Edgar Morin, Aimé Césaire, Dionys Mascolo, and Robert Antelme. The *Arguments* collective also included: Kostas Axelos, Frangois Fejto, and Roland Barthes. Poster 1975 contains a general account of the group's development. See also the two-volume reissue of *Arguments* edited by Olivier Corpet and Corpet 1987.

40 At the time, *L'Express* and *Le Nouvel Observateur* were competing weekly magazines aimed at the *'progressiste'* audience. Both worked in the shadow of *Les Temps Modernes*. *Le Nouvel Obs*, run by the *'trotskysant'* Gilles Martinet and Claude Bourdet, was close to *Les Temps Modernes*, while Jean–Jacques Servan-Schreiber's *L'Express* functioned as a 'forum for debates on the intellectual Left'. See Deli 1981.

41 Deli 1981 (pp. 78–9) cites the average press run for *L'Express* as one hundred and forty-eight thousand per week with average sales of around ninety thousand copies. *Arguments* had a larger subscriber base than *Socialisme ou Barbarie*, but nowhere near the base of the weekly. *Socialisme ou Barbarie* press runs, which were usually around one thousand per issue. They did not begin selling anywhere near that number until after 1957.

42 Stéphane 1956.

43 See the Socialisme ou Barbarie pamphlet, 'L'insurrection hongroise', published in November 1956 and later reprinted as part of *Socialisme ou Barbarie* no. 20: 'Questions aux militants du PCF', pp. 66–84, and Lefort, 'L'insurrection hongroise', pp. 85–116.

Barbarie much-needed publicity and at the same time reinforced the group's proletarian revolutionary credentials.

Mothé was an important element in Socialisme ou Barbarie's public self-presentation after 1956 as well. He was taken quite seriously in his hybrid worker-militant-sociologist role, particularly by the sociologists loosely working on what later became the sociology of work. An index of this was the reception of the 1959 publication of his *Socialisme ou Barbarie* writings, heavily edited and rearranged, as *Journal d'un ouvrier*.[44] Mothé's sociologising first-person reconstruction of '*la vie parallèle*' in the factory, his writing's generic position between autobiography, proletarian literature and sociology, also made its reception an index of how the '*sociologie du travail*', which was still constituting itself as a legitimate academic discipline, differentiated itself, its procedures and object of study from other analytical approaches.[45] Serge Mallet's *Le Nouvel Observateur* review[46] tried to position Mothé as a successor to Georges Navel and the proletarian literature tradition,[47] because both were autobiographical and provided thick descriptions of factory life, overlaid with a sense of despair.[48] Mallet's comparison of Mothé and Navel was as much a trivialisation as appreciation. Mallet used it to buttress the distinction that he drew between Mothé's 'authentic' testimony of life at Billancourt, and what he saw as the political framework 'imposed' by Socialisme ou Barbarie. The distinction enabled Mallet to attack Socialisme ou Barbarie in two ways. First, he dismissed the core of Socialisme ou Barbarie's critique of contemporary industry, centred on the role of bureaucracy, as the impractical creation of a bunch of 'coffee-shop revolutionaries'. Mothé's 'authentic' content was also distorted by his vision of a new type of trade-union organisation. For Mallet, Mothé's 'modern syndicalism' rested on politically and intellectually marginal views:

---

44   See note 1, above.

45   The most obvious rival to academic sociology's monopoly on knowledge of the working class was Marxism, both in political analysis and literature. The limitations of American social-science approaches to industrial sociology, particularly in the realm of understanding social practices, was explicitly posed as a problem in Barbichon 1956, esp. pp. 192–5. On the subsequent construction of *sociologie du travail* as an academic discipline, the professionalisation and scientisation of the field and the role played by the journal by the same name in deciding the conflict in favour of more conventional types of sociological analysis, see Rose 1979 and 1985. On the nineteenth-century conflict between sociology and literature, of which this was a general repetition, see Lepenies 1988.

46   Mallet 1959.

47   The main referent was Navel 1945.

48   Mothé's relationship to proletarian literature, codified in Poulaille 1986, was heavily mediated. See below for a discussion.

'But – and this is the bee in Mothé's bonnet – how to bring to trade-unionism "this really modern role?" The general theses of Socialisme ou Barbarie are known and shared by diverse schools of French Trotskyism'.[49]

Mallet tried to assimilate what was not naive or marginal in Mothé's argument into Alain Touraine's 'embourgeoisement' thesis, even though Touraine's arguments were fundamentally different. One explanation for Mallet's hostility is that Mothé's main point – that Fordist methods of organising both trade-union politics and industrial production were destroying the Marxist-based social-imaginary significations upon which mass action relied – contradicted Mallet's arguments, which he later presented in elaborate form as *La nouvelle class ouvrière*. In this text, Mallet very loosely adapted Alain Touraine's 1955 book on Renault to argue that a new quasi-artisinal class consciousness and new set of political possibilities were emerging within a highly skilled 'new working class' created by the rise of automated production processes.[50] Mallet's review was also a specific moment in the larger border dispute between the academic *sociologie du travail* and Marxist political groups over who could speak about the working class. This explains Mallet's attempt to assimilate Mothé's central sociological argument to Touraine and his dismissal of other arguments Mothé embedded in more autobiographical passages by linking them to the excessive influence of Socialisme ou Barbarie's (external and not authentically working class) 'bureaucratophobia'. Mallet's comparison of Mothé's writing to Navel operated in a parallel manner. It domesticated the innovative elements in Mothé's writing and rendered the whole '*folklorique*' even as Mallet claimed to be simply using Navel as a template that enabled him to isolate the 'authentic' content of Mothé's book. In the next section of this chapter, I shall return to the problem of positioning Mothé's writing in the tradition of proletarian literature from a rather different angle.

Socialisme ou Barbarie wrote and published a collective rebuttal to Mallet. It was a point-by-point critique of the latter's treatment of the group, and his 'distortion' of their project. It was also a statement about Daniel Mothé's relationship to the group. While the critique of Mallet is largely restricted to

---

49 'That would be naive – something that Mothé's friends in SB who have never set foot in a factory do not seem to recognize'. And: 'Mais-et c'est la le bât qui gene terriblement Mothé-comment rendre au syndicalisme "ce veritable role modern?" On connait la thèse générale que SB partage avec les diverses écoles du trotskyisme français'. (In English in the text above). Quotes from Mallet 1959, pp. 7–8.
50 Mallet 1963.

statements that can be summarised as 'what an idiot', the paragraph treating the relationship between Mothé and the group is quite interesting:

> What Mallet learns, therefore – since he apparently does not know it – is that Mothé's book is entirely made up of large extracts from articles published in our *revue* over the last ten issues and all discussed collectively by our group, which is not made up of workers on one side and 'theorists' on the other, but simply of political militants: that this 'theory', presented by Mallet as 'the bee in Mothé's bonnet' was elaborated in isolation by professional abstractors and then injected into Mothé, this theory was, in reality, the result of the confrontation and most rigorous possible systematisation of workers' experiences, including that – fundamentally – of Mothé, and of a reflection on the workers' movement and, in particular on the most recent developments by militants who, for the most part, have actively participated in them from the inside.[51]

Mallet's distinction between Mothé's 'real' account of factory life that one could isolate by juxtaposition with other, more explicitly autobiographical works and the 'injected' theoretical schemata of Socialisme ou Barbarie was irrelevant. For the Socialisme ou Barbarie collective, theory was a constitutive element of Mothé's writings because they were the production of the group as a whole. The crucial relationship was not, as Mallet had argued, between the real workers and the 'coffeehouse revolutionaries', but between political militants, some of whom worked in factories, some of whom did not, but all of whom had extensive experience at the forefront and inside of political struggle both in and out of the factory. This response gives a much different account of Mothé than did the header appended to his 'Journal d'un ouvrier' for the benefit of *Socialisme ou Barbarie* readers. The header claimed that the manuscript had been deposited with *Socialisme ou Barbarie* by an anonymous Renault worker.[52]

Mallet's response to Mothé's book in such a public forum is an index both of the problematic relationship between *sociologie du travail*, proletarian literature, and Marxist political organisations, as well as of Mothé's visibility on the intellectual left. Socialisme ou Barbarie often used his relatively high profile during the public meetings that were the group's only form of public

---

51 Socialisme ou Barbarie 1959, p. 85.
52 Given Gautrat's image of himself as a worker in the AOC, separate from Mothé, this is almost not a lie.

self-presentation and of meeting with its readership.[53] These meetings were held at important sites in the symbolic geography of 'Paris Rouge' like the *Société des Savants* or *Mutualité*.[54] The meetings were quite open-ended affairs, the quality of which varied with the composition and mood of the audience.[55] More important for the format, the same French laws that forced foreigners to employ pseudonyms also prevented them from publicly engaging in politics. For Socialisme ou Barbarie, this meant that neither Castoriadis nor Véga, two of the group's more dynamic speakers, could be at the podium. Each meeting therefore posed the question of who would be the group's 'public face', presenting a position-paper and moderating the transition from seminar format to floor discussion. The lot frequently fell to Mothé.[56] Once the floor debates began, however, the centre of gravity would abruptly shift and the meetings would take on their distinctive, decentred openness that many members cited as one of the group's most attractive features and what drew them into it.[57]

Mothé was also occasionally used during a meeting in a more specifically tactical way. During the spring of 1959, Socialisme ou Barbarie organised an open debate with group members and sociologists Michel Crozier and Alain Touraine over the questions raised in *Arguments* no. 12/13 about what it would mean for the French working class to oppose de Gaulle. Castoriadis is supposed to have listened to the sociologists for a while and then have stood up to announce: 'And now, Daniel Mothé, a worker, will respond to Michel Crozier, a sociologist' in a tone clearly intended to trump and reduce the offending

---

[53] There was talk during early 1957 of renting office space, but the cost was apparently too high. No doubt this contributed to Socialisme ou Barbarie's mystique as a shadowy, extremely radical and clandestine group, even though Socialisme ou Barbarie was never able to use it to their advantage with the public-relations skills of a Guy Debord.

[54] On the geography of the left in Paris during this period, see Bernard 1991.

[55] This openness became problematic at times when rival groups would show up *en bloc* solely to disrupt, or later, when a younger generation of Socialisme ou Barbarie members, influenced, to varying degrees, by 'L'Internationale Situationiste', began to treat disruption as a form of political action.

[56] Many of the Socialisme ou Barbarie members who described themselves as ordinary militants did not feel capable of managing a public meeting. Guillaume was too erratic, Lefort too professorial. Complicating the problem was the periodic change in teaching assignments that sent Socialisme ou Barbarie members who worked in schools or universities either out of the Paris region (Lyotard, Souyri) or the country (Lefort to Brazil; Sternberg to Morocco). The pool of options was always small and shifting.

[57] To write about the impression created by these meetings, I rely on interviews in December 1991 and Spring 1992 with Daniel Blanchard and Helen Arnold. Martine Gautrat was particularly helpful on the problems with speakers.

sociologist to silence.[58] But perhaps the high point of Mothé as 'the worker' was his appearance – as Jacques Mothé – in Jean Rouch and Edgar Morin's 1960 film 'Chronique d'un été' which used Rouch's highly improvisational ethnographic filming methods to portray the Parisian *metropole*. Its approach and the highly self-reflexive way in which the film was constructed, still raise questions for more conventional approaches to the documentary.[59]

Mothé as Narrative Function

The reader assumes a direct relationship between Mothé and Billancourt as the result of a textual 'realism effect'. This effect is not simply the piling up of seemingly gratuitous details that operate as 'proof' for the veracity of description, but results from this accumulation as performed by a particular kind of narrator. It relies on the successful construction of Daniel Mothé as a narrative function.[60] Mothé carrying out such a function required some of the central issues raised in his 'Problèmes d'un journal ouvrier' to have been effectively resolved. There had to be a functional definition of worker writing, its subject matter and mode of presentation. A set of literary cues had to be manipulated as well, linking the above to a 'legitimate' worker writer.[61] The worker writing that Socialisme ou Barbarie had hoped would develop out of the *Tribune Ouvrière* project would not have self-evidently been what it claimed to be: it would have had to develop and deploy legitimating genre rules and style markers. Synchronic frames would socially situate the textual 'I'; the narrative's diachronic frame would fit this 'I' to the experience and give it content. The synchronic frames that situated and legitimated Mothé as a working-class narrator had both internal and external components.

The internal frames – those developed by Socialisme ou Barbarie – directly shaped Mothé and delimited the possibilities for his texts. They would have functioned as such only for an ideal reader of *Socialisme ou Barbarie* who

---

58 This story was relayed by Sebatien de Diesbach, who was SB's representative on the dias for the meeting. He considered his presentation to be a disaster because he accepted SB's implicit view of the French left that it was divided into two groups – Socialisme ou Barbarie and idiots. Another version, different in some details, was told me by Daniel Blanchard.

59 An analysis of Jean Rouch's cinematic work that attends to the centrality of improvisation would be an interesting project.

60 The formulation of the notion of realism effect is taken from Grignon and Passeron 1989.

61 See Chapter 5 on Mothé 1955.

had followed them from the outset. The set of such readers may only have included members of the group. The ideal reader would recognise the interaction of *Socialisme ou Barbarie*'s theory of bureaucratic capitalism, the worker-narratives by Paul Romano and Georges Vivier, the phenomenological reading of these narratives developed in Claude Lefort's 'L'éxperience prolétarienne' and its relationship to the broader revolutionary theory Socialisme ou Barbarie had been developing in earnest since 1953. This reader might also have noted the relationship between the failure of the worker newspaper project and the emergence of Mothé as a prominent writer in *Socialisme ou Barbarie*. The externally constituted genre and style frames that enabled Mothé to position himself before a new *Socialisme ou Barbarie* audience included the extensive political coding of the narratives and manipulation of conventional representations of the working class. The coding enabled Mothé's autobiography to read as political allegory.

Representations of the working class are institutions linked to broader social-imaginary significations. While these representations have been, in the contemporary period, continually refigured through the conflict between the dominant political positions and their 'heretical' opponents, they also have a relatively autonomous history. Mothé's evocation and modification of conventionalised modes of representing the Worker can be clarified by positioning his writing against the French proletarian literature tradition formalised by Henry Poulaille. Poulaille's 1928 *Le nouvel âge littéraire* was the first attempt to fix the rules of this specifically French tradition of popular expression, the source of which lay, for Poulaille, in the work of Jules Michelet.[62] Poulaille's text was created in part as an intervention in the debate over how to represent the working class that occupied the PCF of the time as part of its larger efforts to occupy a new cultural and political space. After discussing Mothé's relation to this tradition, I will gauge the distance that separates Mothé from it by briefly examining Georges Navel's 1945 *Travaux*. The diachronic context involves the problems of autobiographical writing: the separation of the narrating 'I' and the textual staging of experience from the writing subject and its experience that involve specifically textual questions of emplotment, spatialisation, and coding.

This section works to suspend the naturalising of worker 'testimony' or 'witness' to their own exploitation that often accompanies the overlay of a Marxist epistemology and politics. Worker textual self-representation operates in a highly stylised literary domain within which the emphasis on artless-

---

62 I phrase this sentence in this way because other writers have linked proletarian literature to much broader and older currents of popular expression in France. See Ragon 1974.

ness and authenticity conceals a considerable degree of skill. Suspending the Marxist framework allows us to assume that Mothé was 'given' to readers as a function, a variable that operated with a particular range of possibilities, but without a specific initial value. Constructing Mothé as a Renault worker with authority to speak about life in the factory was the working-out of a value for him as narrator and for the narratives themselves.

Synchronic Frame 1: Socialisme ou Barbarie

I analysed the worker narratives by Paul Romano and Eric Albert that Claude Lefort used as the basis for a phenomenology of worker narratives and factory experience in Chapter Three. The assumption underlying Lefort's phenomenological project was that the writing of narratives necessarily implied a break with the action described in them and employed certain conventions in their expression. The combination of a large sample and phenomenological procedures could result in a type of reading that controlled for the effects of distanciation and literary conventions, just as transcendental phenomenology used the initial variation(s) to posit its object stripped of local socio-cultural determinations.[63] Assembling the sample and performing the reductions could, Lefort argued, provide militants/theorists with crucial information about the 'proletarian viewpoint'. The shop-floor perspective on production and its contradictions was the core of an imagined subject-position around which a modern revolutionary project should be articulated. This subject position, while not in itself providing a solution to the 'organisation question', was nonetheless an important imaginary interface that linked the separate, but complementary, tasks of theory and worker-resistance to exploitation in a common revolutionary project.

The narratives that Lefort used as exemplars were well suited to this analytical approach because they employed the conventions of the ethnographic travel narrative. The narrator, like the reader, was constituted as an outsider who journeyed to an alien, distant culture (spatial or social distances are, from this viewpoint, equivalent). After an initial period on the margins of this new place, the narrator underwent a kind of initiation into the inner workings of

---

[63] More precisely, the phenomenological analogy would be the proposition that the structuring effects of cognitive 'hardwiring' could be accounted for and bracketed in the positing of a transcendental object.

the previously opaque culture, usually assisted by a native informant.[64] The narratives thereafter often adopted the form of a *Bildungsroman* that traced the progression from innocence to experience through initiation and the construction of a new subject position for the narrator. For the reader, who remained physically separate from the experience being related, the narrator operated as a 'native informant' and reading was a 'deep tourism' that mapped its itinerary onto the narrator's *Bildung*. This doubling occurred through the piling up of increasingly detailed and intricate descriptions of the practical and spatio-temporal organisation of this social universe.

My analysis of Romano's and Albert's narratives demonstrated how each of them used this pattern and how it constituted the narrator as a sort of voice-over, whose relating of initiation and identity construction was always also the imposition of an 'outside' order. Lefort's phenomenological approach was aimed at working out ways to separate, with the greatest possible precision, this voice-over from the constitutive elements of the narrative's 'realism effect' (the textual 'I' from the experiences that give it content, in autobiographical terms).[65] The phenomenological reading of worker narratives and its ideal grid that would enable the reader/theorist to separate data from its ordering voice-over and from the purely autobiographical, necessarily particular context(s), was itself situated in Socialisme ou Barbarie's productivist framework. The reading of technology was geared to demonstrating the universality of politically significant aspects of experience at the point of production under bureaucratic capitalism. Because the role of the 'theorist' could not be assimilated to that of the 'Worker', the former was able to make the distinction between the universal and the particular only on the basis of epistemological assumptions and interpretive practices particular to his/her social position. Phenomenology was a type of theoretical practice that would permit theorists without direct contact with the factory to clarify the relation of the worker writer to factory experience. At the same time, it did not allow the theorist to forget that theory could only produce second-order descriptions.

---

64   Gayatri Spivak has pointed out that in the ethnographic travel narrative, the assumption that the native informant is telling the truth – when his/her self-interest would be better served by lying – is a legacy of imperialism. In these narratives, the situation is analogous. The wariness of politically active workers appears as an important aspect of the narrator's period on the periphery. Initiation into the factory culture proceeds through stages of learning the job and then, gradually, the job's social and political context. The process does not rely as much as most ethnographic narratives do on the agency of a particular native informant, without whom no integration could occur. The reliability of the native informant is not an issue in the same way.

65   Here used in the sense developed in Barthes, 1981, pp. 17–18.

Paul Romano's 'The American Worker' and its detailed descriptions of life at a New Jersey automobile-plant performed important political work for *Socialisme ou Barbarie*. It set up Socialisme ou Barbarie's reading of June 1953 as the signal of a new period of (potential) revolutionary action. The solutions Romano developed to balance the particulars of an individual life/trajectory/factory against the universal were important points of departure for thinking about how worker experience could and should be textually staged. Romano's solution was the propositional form 'the workers feel x ...' to map individual experience and social category onto each other.

Romano's pamphlet was the principal model for Mothé's writing.[66] Mothé's articles work against Romano in their rejection of the ethnographic narrative pattern. Mothé as a narrator is not initially posited outside the shop collective, and there is no initiation to double that of the reader. Instead, Mothé is positioned as part of the worker collective from the beginning. His viewpoint is always embedded and partial, while the experiences related are coded as universal. His narratives use movement through the political landscape of Billancourt as an allegory for working-class politics in general and as a naturalised emplotment of Socialisme ou Barbarie's assumptions about class formation and mobilisation. Mothé's abandonment of the ethnographic travel narrative form eliminated that form's tendency to dehistoricise the environment into which the narrator is initiated: for the ethnographer, the problem is to understand an existing social space, not the historicity of that space. It also freed Mothé from a *Bildungsroman* progression from innocence to experience. Mothé's general narrative begins at the end-state of the ethnographic narrative pattern and runs it in reverse. By the end, the narrator possesses the mechanisms for collective integration that no longer operate, as the collective falls apart around him.

Mothé's embedded narrator links his articles to the type of writing Socialisme ou Barbarie had hoped to acquire through the worker-newspaper project. Mothé's 'Problemes d'un journal ouvrier' outlined guidelines for articles that related to worker experience. They should be written in the first person, using concrete language, and should describe everyday experience in the factory, free of the dominant ideological frames and literary models. It will be recalled that Mothé, in contrast to the *Correspondence* Editorial Board, argued that there was no 'natural' mode of worker-written expression. One had to be cobbled together out of the debris created by the history of the workers' movement, turned against the dominant appropriations, and situated in terms of

---

66 Interview with Jacques Gautrat, January 1992.

suppressed counter-traditions.[67] The normative conception of worker writing outlined in Mothé's article assumed that, even if there was a problem of an 'authentic' worker voice, writing could nonetheless be considered coextensive with self-consciousness. This assumption led Socialisme ou Barbarie to look for a particular type of writing from Renault workers through *Tribune Ouvrière* that almost never came.[68] The exceptions, written by Mothé and Pierre Blachier, were fundamental data in Castoriadis's two major theoretical efforts to formalise Socialisme ou Barbarie's proletarian revolutionary project in the wake of Hungary.[69]

Synchronic Frame 2: Proletarian Literature

The set of *Socialisme ou Barbarie* readers who had read and retained the whole of the group's published output, and for whom these various internal frames could have situated Mothé's 1956–7 articles, was very small.[70] It may not have included anyone outside the group. *Socialisme ou Barbarie* published Mothé's articles during a period of great political turmoil for the whole French left. This turbulence was generated by the PCF as it stumbled through 1956. The degree of turbulence demonstrates the Party's centrality in the context of the left.[71] The crisis of the PCF opened up new possibilities for students and intellectuals: new political organisations began to occupy a cultural space

---

67 See my analysis of Mothé 1955 in the previous chapter.
68 Mothé's articles appeared at a time of great indecision within Socialisme ou Barbarie about how to respond to *Tribune Ouvrière*'s failure (on their terms) which reopened the problem of organisation. Part of the solution was to roll the *Tribune Ouvrière* project onto Socialisme ou Barbarie itself, a task made somewhat easier by the implosion of working-class politics after the winter of 1956, which was especially evident after May 1958. On this, see my analysis of Mothé's narratives below.
69 Castoriadis 1988e and Castoriadis 1988f (1960–1).
70 This section takes Grignon and Passeron 1989 as inspiration.
71 I will examine these elements in more detail later, but they are important to note. January 1956: anxious to get out of the parliamentary ghetto into which it had been forced since 1948, the PCF voted with Guy Mollet's Socialist government to intensify the Algerian War. March 1956 and thereafter: de-Stalinisation. The PCF aligned with conservative bureaucratic factions within the USSR that opposed both Nikita Khruschev's denunciation of Stalin and the personality cult, as well as the economic changes that made the attack necessary. July 1956: Poznan; October-November 1956: the Hungarian revolt and its violent suppression by the Soviet Army.

opened up by de-Stalinisation.[72] Most of these groups did not focus on the crisis of Marxism in general or the PCF in particular. Instead, they focused on the growing opposition to an Algerian War, which was officially supported by the PCF.[73] Socialisme ou Barbarie's relative position, as reflected in its audience and composition, changed as the PCF began to lose its dominance over the left.[74] Journal sales increased and the group became more important in political and theoretical debates. Socialisme ou Barbarie's new position assumed that they had sustained contact with a working class that was itself largely excluded from these debates and that was, in fact, evolving in a direction quite opposed to that imputed to it by the intellectuals who participated in these discussions. Mothé's major articles began to appear in the midst of this change in Socialisme ou Barbarie's position and audience. They could not have been written with exclusive reference to internal frames, but had to employ more broadly accessible generic and stylistic conventions so as to socially position them.

Representations of the working class are themselves institutions with an autonomous history that exceeds any particular appropriation of them. Without such a semi-autonomous history of representation, there would be no space for dissent, because the dominant appropriation could not be detached from and contextualised in terms of a larger frame of reference that exceeds it. In other words, there would be no way to demonstrate that the dominant

---

72   De-Stalinisation was presupposed in a way that nonetheless permitted the PCF to structure thinking about dissident politics: the *'progressiste'* left after 1956 increasingly focused on Poland to the exclusion of Hungary because in the former the Party 'reformed' from within, and continued to operate, while Hungary went much further, vaporising the Party within forty-eight hours. The preference for Poland can be explained by the inability of the intellectual left – the field of cultural production structured by *Les Temps Modernes* and including the *'trotskysant'* editorial staff around *Le Nouvel Observateur*, to imagine dissent without the party as a reference-point (see Sartre 1968 [1952–4]). In its insistence on the primacy of the Hungarian revolt, Socialisme ou Barbarie found itself marginalised in the field: the group was nonetheless a player in debates, which it had not been earlier. This shift implies a basic transformation in *Socialisme ou Barbarie*'s audience.

73   For a detailed account of the PCF difficulties in assimilating the students and intellectuals who joined as part of the 'Generation of '48', see Verdès-Leroux 1983 and Sirinelli (ed.) 1987.

74   Among the journals/groups that appeared in 1956–7 were the anarchist *Noir et Rouge*, 'L'Internationale Situationiste' and *Arguments*. Oppositional factions within the PCF were desperately sought by the major independent left-wing journals as a function of their effort to assimilate the PCF's problems to the Polish model. Some of these also began to publish journals (*L'Étincelle*, for example). For a comprehensive timetable, see Lourau 1980, Appendix 1.

appropriation is but one of many possibilities. Each representation of the working class is fashioned by specific, interrelated political parameters: the notions of class formation and consciousness; the historical role and function of the party; the conception of revolution and socialism. While Socialisme ou Barbarie claimed that their revolutionary theory was tailored to the specificity of post-1945 capitalism, the representations of the working class they employed were linked, not only to contemporary or internal referents, but also to a broader and older French tradition. This tradition, formalised in proletarian literature, portrayed the working class through internally nuanced, decontextualised descriptions that paid special attention to minutely described social practices. Transcribed speech, forms of skilled labour, types of domesticity and life in rural or small-town France were all conceptualised as aspects of a particular, lost 'fabric of being' rather than as sociological data. This tradition of representing the working class was associated with revolutionary syndicalism. Certain elements were later incorporated into the PCF's representations of the working class, often evoked to stage a 'fit' between the Party and the French working class and its history. This tradition was formalised as constitutive of a particular literary representation by the proletarian literature movement.

The 'movement's' chief ideologue, Henry Poulaille, located its origin in the work of Jules Michelet. In this section, I provide a limited account of the tradition concentrating on Poulaille's notion of authentic worker experience, its source in Michelet, its delimitation within proletarian literature, and the continuities and discontinuities that link it to Mothé. I do not undertake an exhaustive reading of either Michelet or Poulaille, nor do I offer a systematic account of the discontinuities, linked to profound socioeconomic and political reorganisation of France, that separate them from each other and together from Socialisme ou Barbarie.[75]

The PCF used its representations of the French working class to mediate conflicts between its national and international strategic constraints and the complexity of local conflicts in the manner discussed in Chapter 3 with reference to Renault. The repertoire of representations upon which the PCF drew was developed in the course of debates on the nature of working-class culture and its relation to the Party that preoccupied left-wing cultural critics during the 1920s. These debates were conditioned by several factors. The PCF came into being in the wake of the collapse of the left wing of the Socialist SFIO. Primarily occupied by revolutionary syndicalists, the Socialist left imploded

---

75 Accounts of these transformations include Noiriel 1986, Magri and Topalov 1989, Coriat 1979.

after the 1919 general strike debacle.[76] The PCF had to figure out how to occupy the political and cultural void left by this collapse. At the same time, the later 1920s and early 1930s were marked by Stalin's rise to power. This was reflected in increased central control over all aspects of party activity, and in the subordination to the Soviet model of national parties, histories and traditions. The Soviet Party's adoption of socialist realism, a process that began with the 1930 Kharkov conference, ended the debate about the nature of working-class culture in France, and how it should be represented.[77] Socialist Realism became the official mode of representing the working class in general.

At the same time as the PCF disseminated the Socialist Realist model, it relied on other types of representations to fit itself and its policies to conditions on the ground in France. These representations were developed before socialist realism, during the period when the Party and its press approached working-class culture, and the problem of constructing a relationship with it, in an explicitly syncretic manner, fashioning symbols from available debris and experimenting with literary forms.[78] This syncretism directly mirrored the Party's more general struggle to define itself as a distinct occupant of its political space.[79] Henry Poulaille's formalisation of 'proletarian literature' as a genre and canon came out of this fragmented political situation. Had the PCF adopted the conventions outlined by Poulaille, it would have linked itself to a

---

76 For a detailed account of the 1919 strikes as the last gasp of the pre-World War I left, see Kriegel 1964. The failure of the railroad strike not only shattered the extreme (revolutionary syndicalist) left of the SFIO as a political alternative, but also profoundly altered the political position occupied by the Socialists – 'La Vieille Maison' – in French politics more generally.

77 The end of proletarian literature as a viable option for the PCF's representation of the working class is aligned with the Kharkov conference by Arvidsson 1988; for a more detailed, Soviet-centred account of socialist realism, its development and characteristics, see Clark 1985.

78 See Poulaille 1986, pp. 47–8, on the early 1920s articles on working-class culture and literature appearing in *L'Humanité*.

79 The conflict within the Bolshevik Party before the Russian Revolution between syndicalism – in some ways of a piece with Bogdanov's 'god-builders', emphasising the importance of 'myth' and the 'epic frame of mind' and a tactical alternative with their emphasis on 'expropriation' in the form of factory-take-overs and direct action – and Lenin's more centralising conception of the party is detailed in Williams 1986, esp. 91ff. The point being made in these paragraphs could be expanded into an argument about syndicalism as the PCF's 'internal Other', particularly before 1936. For an account of the PCF's early militant practices at Billancourt, see Depretto and Schweitzer 1984. The relationship between Michelet, syndicalism and proletarian literature could also be developed in a different direction, emphasising the continuities between the two via the Sorelian notion of myth.

nationally specific, socially oriented vision of the relationship between workers, their work and politics. Proletarian literature's 'bottom-up' politics could also have been assimilated to the Party's account of its origins in the Russian Revolution.[80] However, by the time the International adopted Socialist Realism, the range of doctrinal resources the Party would adopt along with Stalinism was in place. Dialectical materialism, for example, used a reductive Marxism to 'prove' the absolute primacy of the Soviet model in all dimensions, including literature.[81]

Despite the marginalisation of proletarian literature by socialist realism, the PCF retained and used some of the former's stylistic markers because they connected to older forms of written 'popular expression'. They provided a set of conventions that could be deployed strategically to stage the relationship – or identity – of the working class and the PCF in press accounts and official histories. The relationship between the PCF's forms of representation and proletarian literature was staged in a second, somewhat more complex, way in Maurice Thorez's 'autobiography', *Fils du peuple*.[82] This text used Thorez's autobiography as a vehicle for a history of the Party expressed directly in its chairman's life. It was also a summary of the PCF's politics. *Fils du peuple* advanced some of the main claims made by the PCF made on French history and politics by, for example, equating the French and Russian revolutionary traditions, and the PCF with both the Jacobins and republicanism on the one hand, and Lenin on the other.

In the first chapters of *Fils du peuple*, proletarian literature and revolutionary syndicalism are mapped onto Thorez's childhood, and by extension onto that of the PCF. This mapping served several functions: it positioned Thorez as an 'authentic' worker, and explained his commitment to the French working class and its interests. It made this attachment sentimental. This sentimental overlay comes through strongly in the text's descriptions of the impression made on young Maurice by the spectacle of a syndicalist-led miners' strike, which was organised by local militants that prominently included his grandfather. The section was ghost written in the proletarian literature style, and its

---

80 For the fullest expression of the link between social movements and the party in this context, see Trotsky 1961.

81 See Clark 1985 for a survey of the history, conventions and function of Socialist Realism.

82 This text was one of several 'biographies' of PCF leaders to appear in the mid 1930s that tried to personalise the history of the Party in the figure of its chairman, and fit the dialectical materialist view of history to local conditions, using the biography as a frame for doing so. The value of *Fils* as biography is minimal, as argued by Robrieux 1975, esp. chapter 4, 'Fabrication et consecration d'un chef', pp. 169–228.

position in the text turns the conceits of that literature against it. This mode of expression, and the world of which it was a part, are textually positioned as elements of a vanished pre-World War I France and of Thorez's childhood. *Fils du peuple* incorporated proletarian literature's penchant for mapping social and individual histories onto each other. It diverges in its general narrative that relegates syndicalism and its traditions to the childhood of the Party, as an important but local and superseded stage in the dialectical unfolding of the international Party and its history.

The Party's adoption of socialist realism did not entirely preclude its assimilation of certain elements formalised by proletarian literature. It did, however, deal a huge blow to Poulaille as a cultural broker and to his aspirations for the stable of autodidact writers. The style soon began to fade away. Few writers still worked in it after World War II. Of these, the best known was Georges Navel, whose *Travaux* functioned somewhere between a template defining authentic worker writing and folklore.[83] A revival in interest in the sociological dimension of proletarian literature, particularly in its close descriptions of the workplace and worker sociability, was sparked by the rise of the *sociologie du travail*. It was a model for a sociology written with a novelist's sensibility capable of compensating for the descriptive limitations of American social science models. These limitations figured in a broad debate over what constituted the 'real' in the factory, whether it was to be understood through an analysis of production-design or technology, through statistical means or economic analysis, or by analysing social relations among workers.[84] At roughly the same time, following autonomous developments in literature, elements once associated with proletarian literature style – particularly the centrality of transcribed speech as evocative of an entire mode of being – began to figure in fragmented, displaced forms in avant-garde-writing, particularly in the work of Raymond Queneau.

Genre: Michelet

Proletarian literature claimed to be the most recent expression of an older tradition of workers writing about their own experience that had been ongoing in France since the mid-nineteenth century under the double influence of

---

83 Other problems with its mode of representation will be outlined below.
84 See Rose 1979 and 1985. Rose notes Serge Mallet, and, on technology, G. Friedman; production design and technology, A. Touraine; the growth of management and separation of tasks, M. Crozier; on changes in finance, P. Naville, etc.

Jules Michelet's 1846 book, *The People*,[85] and literary Realism.[86] From Michelet came the movement's quasi-mystical insistence on France, particularly rural or small-town provincial life: its generic delimitation of, and political justifications for, valorising 'the people' as bearers of an authentic, nationally specific poesis; the tendency to conflate a lost 'authenticity' or 'wholeness' in the lives of the people with the lost childhood of the writer; a folkloric concern with rural dialect and worker's speech; an emphasis on close descriptions of the workplace, its organisation and forms of sociability. This project, derived from Michelet, converged in certain ways with later developments in literary realism. In particular, Zola's ambition to paint a vast *tableau* of all French society in his fiction was adopted and reworked by proletarian writers in their own terms. Proletarian literature was therefore primarily the textual reconstruction of lost modes of popular existence. The centerpiece was the valorisation of rural life and meaningful artisanal work, often expressed through the decontextualised (sociologically speaking) restaging of a lost division of labour, a lost social life, and a lost relation to place. Reconstruction presupposed that the writer had a direct experience of this past and the reader an interest in vicariously acquiring it. Proletarian literature was a simultaneous interrogation of an individual and a collective past. Michelet's *The People* is the *ur*-text for this entire tradition:

> I have made this book out of myself, out of my life and out of my heart. It is the product of my experience rather than my studies. I have derived it from my observation and my conversation with friends and neighbors; I have picked it up along the highways ... I have found it above all in the recollections of my youth. To know the life of the people and their toils and suffering, I only had to question my memory.[87]

Written against both contemporary bourgeois fiction as well as to counter a tendency in popular writing to portray the people in urban/industrial – 'overly English' – settings, Michelet conceived of *The People* as a distinctive portrait of the popular classes and their specifically French ways of life. The normative centre of the book was country folk, for whom there was little discontinuity between working the soil and work in small artisanal shops. Their mode of living had already been destroyed. What Michelet saw as the connectedness

---

85   Michelet 1973. See also Barthes 1987 [1954] on Michelet's *'musée imaginaire'*.
86   In the Introduction, Ragon 1974 connects it directly to medieval forms of popular expression and is in general inclusive where Poulaille is exclusive.
87   Michelet 1973, 'Preface: To Edgar Quinet', pp. 3–4.

between spheres of existence had given way to the fragmentation brought with capitalism. This fragmentation of existence was the deepest of the various types of bondage to which the people now had to submit.[88] Michelet's text was an attempt to reconstruct a 'seamless' image of the people in their authentic being. This image was based largely on memories of his rural childhood. Memory was the cornerstone around which was built an extensive reconstruction of the popular mode-of-being. For Michelet, this reconstruction was not simply an act of nostalgia: the image of the people he constructed was also a template they could juxtapose to their contemporary, fallen lives. The political project would derive from the sense readers gained of how much had been lost to capitalism.[89]

Proletarian literature retained Michelet's nostalgia and emphasis on reconstruction. Later writers also exploited Michelet's technique of blurring individual memory into collective history. The people emerged as the locus of a destroyed wholeness that was closely associated with individual childhood. Proletarian literature also took from Michelet its politics of representation, echoing his concern with questions of who should control, construct and manipulate images of the People. This politics of representation was a class politics: Michelet reserved his harshest criticism for competing representations of the people that originated in other class positions.

For Michelet, the People's fall from grace, their 'natural' mode of existence, had been brought about by the French Empire and the class alliance that supported it. His notion of the people was directly associated with the French Revolution: the Empire and its 'alliance of wealthy classes' were obvious enemies, and the modes of representing the people developed by bourgeois writers were an element in a cultural war waged against the Revolution and all aspects of its legacy. Bourgeois writers, regardless of the exact form in which they worked, relied upon images of the People that shared certain assumptions. All were ironic, self-critical and distant in relation to their subject matter.[90] This distance, Michelet argued, reflected their (cosmopolitan) disregard for the 'real' France and their deductive relationship with the world. Characteristic of the latter was the bourgeois emphasis on law as opposed to duty as that which mediated individuals' relationship with the world. The

---

88   In Michelet 1973, Part 1, he delineates the various types of bondage to which the people must submit.
89   On the theme of seamlessness in Michelet, see Barthes 1987, pp. 77ff.
90   Balzac's portrayal of the peasantry particularly galled Michelet (p. 7). Stendahl and Georges Sand were also counted amongst the evil bourgeois writers.

wealthy classes could have no sense of place and could therefore have no idea of the connectedness to place that animated the 'real' lives of the People.

Michelet's class-specific opposition parallels Kierkegaard's distinction between the aesthetic and ethico-religious spheres. The wealthy classes live separated from the world. For Michelet, separation from the world is analogous to separation from faith in that both substitute for immediacy sets of abstract rules constructed according to the (aesthetic) criteria of interest.[91] Left to themselves, Michelet argued, the People lived in unmediated contact with place, with the nation, and with France. The nation is transformed into a god-term and the 'authentic' lifeworld of the people into a mode of being that Kierkegaard equated with the ethico-religious. Most of the other characteristics that Michelet considered central to defining the people are also in principle important to Christianity: simplicity; generosity of spirit, reflecting what Michelet called their direct contact with the 'profound realities of life'; innocence and a child-like purity of faith. Most important was a 'natural' relation to France, the 'living root'. Michelet saw this connectedness with place revealed in nearly every aspect of popular sociability. This is what gave popular sociability its interest and political valence.

For Michel Ragon, Michelet's construction of 'the People' was a performative category that enacted, rather than argued for, a relation to its object and the Revolution. Reading was also performative in the sense that it recombined elements in the reader's perceptual and affective fields in terms of a political project with a particular set of referents, each of which had a critical tradition and a wider history.[92] Ragon describes his experience of reading Michelet in these terms to show its power. For the text to work, however, the reader had to be predisposed to identify with Michelet's identification with his object, and thereby be available for Michelet's refiguring/reordering of the reader's world. This relationship between reader, text and author was set up by the 'rightness' of Michelet's descriptive set-pieces, like those that evoked the home or the workshop. The idea of 'rightness' itself presupposed a degree of shared experience. Michelet's text assumes complicity between Michelet and the reader at the levels of memory (real or acquired through immersion in the tradition of representations) and politics. The dyad behind the memory-

---

91 Many of Michelet's central concepts are only barely secularised religious concepts. See Barthes 1987 for an extended commentary on Michelet's commitment to a radical Christian renewal and his fascination with Christianities from the period before the Council of Nicea.

92 On Ragon, see n. 84. This is what Lefort later analysed as an effect of institution, 'le travail de l'oeuvre' in his Machiavelli book of that name.

politics association is nostalgia-revolution, a pairing extensively mined by the proletarian literary tradition inspired by Michelet. This later tradition crossed Michelet with elements drawn from Marx adequate to legitimate the form's shift away from an exclusive valorisation of rural life and artisinal work to a narrower focus on production itself. Michelet's lost wholeness was translated into Marx's problem of alienation.[93] This problem was framed by conventions derived from Michelet: the assumption that individual and collective histories were mutually intelligible, that reading was performative and that performativity was a route to politicisation. These assumptions informed the distinctive combination of precise description, decontextualised presentation and the emphasis on projection linking reader to scene described to workers that developed through proletarian literature. One can also see these same assumptions at work in Socialisme ou Barbarie's notion of 'proletarian documentary literature' and in Mothé's articles.

Genre: Poulaille

Henry Poulaille's 1928 book, *Le nouvel âge littéraire*, formalised the genre-rules and established the canon of proletarian literature. In significant measure, the book was a move made in the context of contemporary debates within and around the PCF over the status of working-class culture, how it should be represented and who should control these representations. I noted in the introductory paragraphs for this section that this debate can be read as an important index of how the PCF tried to define and occupy a distinct political and cultural space. This space was shaped by several factors that included the collapse of the radical wing of the SFIO, the prestige of the Russian Revolution and the USSR, and the PCF's articulation of itself by way of its symbolic relation to the French working class. As an active participant in the debate, Poulaille hoped to shape these representations, to have an impact on the relationship between the Party and the workers, and to reap the material and institutional benefits of winning a struggle for cultural power. Significantly figuring among these benefits was the prospect of gaining access to patronage and distribution for marginalised working-class autodidact writers like himself. His views of the nature, history and significance of proletarian literature were therefore shaped by multiple considerations, and a sustained analysis would have to demonstrate how they interacted with and conditioned one another. My interest in Poulaille, in this context, is limited to his view of what should link workers

---

93 Compare Michelet 1973 with Marx's 1993 [1844].

to organisation and the role that literature – and polemic about literature – should play in articulating that link.

Poulaille's politics were shaped by revolutionary syndicalism both in its insistence that the worker base should control any organisation and in its emphasis on the particularity of the French workers, their history and traditions. His proletarian literature, therefore, emphasised the work of writers influenced by Michelet, cross-voiced with Marx and the organisational and political views of revolutionary syndicalism. This balance reflected Poulaille's concern that the PCF address itself directly to the French working class and its traditions and history, rather than to a more abstract, international working class.

Poulaille defined proletarian literature as the result of a convergence of the tradition of popular writing influenced by Michelet and bourgeois literary Realism. Poulaille's was a realism recast and reworked by working-class writers in terms shaped by that class position. The emphasis on bourgeois literary Realism in *Le nouvel âge* was both a nod to Michelet and an attempt to insert his book directly into the conflict over legitimate types of literary production that occupied the PCF during the late 1920s. Bourgeois writers, like Gide, worked the literary tradition that began with Zola. Their panoramic sociological novels were the objects of extended critique in *Le nouvel âge*. Poulaille was particularly concerned that these writers should not be allowed to claim the position of the 'voice of the workers and peasantry'. His central arguments echoed Michelet: bourgeois art was conditioned by the class-origin of the artist, whose experience of the world was hopelessly mediated by characteristic categories and intentionalities. Poulaille considered bourgeois writers to be cosmopolitan and uprooted, incapable of making, much less communicating, the 'primordial connection' to the world that defined the authentically popular. The consequences of this non-relation to place were both aesthetic and political. Bourgeois portraits of the popular classes were full of 'artifice' and 'tricks' developed to simulate the authenticity that could only be known and communicated by worker writers like H. Poulaille. This 'artifice' was a defining element of bourgeois formalism, which he argued was the characteristic bourgeois mode of compensating for the loss of authenticity and was a direct reproduction of a more basic, class specific mode of apprehending the world.[94] This definition of bourgeois art enabled Poulaille to provide this succinct statement of the main forces fighting the cultural war in which he was engaged: 'Two cultures confront each other – two very dissimilar qualities – one that is

---

94 Arvidsson 1988, p. 77ff.

specifically formal, the other clearly instinctual. Aestheticism on the one side, authenticity on the other'.[95]

Zola's successors, who were Poulaille's specific targets, were symptomatic of bourgeois art in general. Their efforts to conceal what Poulaille saw as their non-relation to the world with formalist devices replicated the structure of bourgeois thought.

Poulaille's characterisation of bourgeois thought converges in some ways with Castoriadis's and Lefort's critiques of 'deductivism' and, in so doing, shows the debt both critiques owed to Marx. Bourgeois thought subordinated history and flux to ahistorical, atemporal concepts or forms, the contingency of institutional construction to a theory of history as governed by general laws. These characterisations of bourgeois thought dovetail neatly with Marxist ideology-critique. Many of the propositions central to Poulaille were logical extrapolations of Marx's characterisation of bourgeois ideology, its falsification of itself and the processes whereby it came into being and came to power. Particular and contingent institutions, dominated by the bourgeoisie, were ideologically cast as natural and eternal, for example. History, made through conflicts that issued onto manifold possible resolutions, was buried beneath a view of history as progress and the fetishisation of abstract principles and Law.

In *Le nouvel âge*, Poulaille read Zola as a complex writer whose work reproduced these dominant modes of apprehension and provided some ways to think critically through them. Zola's sociologising fiction, and its project of creating a vast portrait of French society capable of supplanting Balzac, had a salutary effect on many worker writers.[96] However, Poulaille argued, at least two important distinctions had to be made between Zola and his worker counterparts. Zola was 'typically bourgeois' in his quasi-Aristotlean psychological theory of hereditary social types and in his tendency to organise his fiction as a kind of demonstration of this theory. These problems were evident in his handling of working people.[97] Poulaille argued that Zola's assumptions excluded *a priori* any access to the popular 'fabric of being' that Poulaille saw as the core of authenticity. Zola's approach to popular language in *L'assomoir* was particularly telling. In it, popular speech floats as a kind of literary ornament, disconnected from its social context. The residents of Zola's working-class Barbès

---

95   Poulaille 1986, p. 519.
96   For the most part, Poulaille 1986 is a series of critical synopses of the writers that Poulaille considered part of the proletarian literary canon. Zola's influence is quite marked throughout.
97   Here, Poulaille's analysis and the later essay on Zola by Claude Grignon draw close together. My analysis intertwines both.

communicate in an already-outmoded pastiche of slang that was not drawn from Zola having lived amongst these people or intimate knowledge of the cultural milieu in which that speech had to be situated. Instead, Zola derived his worker speech from reading Denis Poulot's *Le sublime*. Not only was Poulot's text already twenty years old when Zola was composing *L'assomoir*, but it was also a moralising, diagnostic text, written by an employer for other employers. Poulot's motivation was to provide employers with a key for understanding and classifying worker speech and comportment so the employer reader could avoid hiring the more 'morally debased' of them. From Poulaille's viewpoint, then, beneath Zola's declared intent to use his fiction to create a comprehensive near-sociological portrait of French society lay a 'miserablist', condescending view of the people. This underlying condescension is what enabled Zola to assimilate an employer's adversarial portrait of the popular classes as a simple, unproblematic datum.[98]

Poulaille's critique comes down to the following: without having lived among the workers, without, therefore, having understood that popular speech is embedded in a particular mode of life, no writer, not even Zola, could portray them accurately. Accuracy, for Poulaille, entailed portraying the workers in their immediate context, with their relation to place and each other intact. Proletarian literature portrayed what bourgeois realism could not: the 'authentic' or 'real' mode of being specific to the working class, peasantry or the poor. This mode of being was not knowable in the abstract, in the way an object is knowable. It was only accessible through experience. Given the centrality of experience, it follows that Poulaille's *Nouvel âge* would valorise, as essential conduits for authenticity, 'l'écrivain ouvrier', who wrote without leaving his job and 'l'écrivain prolétarien', who was of working-class origin but who now tried to make a living by writing.[99] The implication for the sociological novel was clear. Social groups were not knowable from outside but only from within, through particular kinds of experience. This kind of experience gave access to a class-specific dimension of knowing about the world, to modes of

---

[98] For Poulaille's assessment of Zola, see Poulaille 1986, pp. 56–64. More generally see Grignon and Passerion 1989 and Lanoux 1978, pp. 143ff, esp. 145–147. On Poulot, see Poulot 1980 in particular, but also Alain Cottereau's 'Etude préable: Vie quotidienne et resistance ouvrière a Paris, 1870'.

[99] It was Poulaille's position on the autodidact that drew most contemporary fire from authorised intellectuals like Gide. The autodidact was figured as the eccentric double of the 'legitimate' intellectual, who was not equipped to filter information, often learning immense amounts about very narrow subjects and distorting the information for lack of context. See Sartre 1959 [1938] for a compendium of these attitudes. For a detailed reconstruction of Gide's attacks on Poulaille on these grounds, see Arvidsson 1988, 97ff.

interacting with it and with other workers conditioned by complex cultural preconditions[100] that were shaped or determined by histories, traditions, customs and profession. A writer had to acquire the entire 'fabric of being' in order to be able to convey working-class being-in-the-world with any degree of authenticity.

Poulaille's description of what proletarian literature ought to be maps onto larger political arguments. His description was an argument about who could write about the popular classes and why, which was also an argument about who should control the representations and what priority workers should enjoy in any political organisation. He also had strong views about how the worker writers ought to write. 'Authentic' proletarian literature, for Poulaille, should strive to 'banish aesthetic and literary concerns' from the form in favour of simplicity and directness.[101]

For Poulaille, authenticity was both a descriptive term that denoted a lost 'natural' attribute of the popular classes and also a criterion for reading and evaluating literary reconstructions. As a description, authenticity referred to many of the same attributes of the French People valorised by Michelet: childlike simplicity; an instinctive relation to the world; an unforced, natural sociability; generosity in the face of material hardship. The attitude of Poulaille's writers toward these attributes, and the people who lived with them, was like Michelet's as well: 'the family, the work, the humblest life of the people have themselves a sacred poetry'.[102]

The evolution of proletarian literature across the nineteenth century enabled Poulaille to juxtapose Michelet and Marx. The form had moved away from the sepia-toned rural world of Michelet. By the 1920s, reflecting the growing importance of Marx and his productivism, writers were focusing more narrowly on popular praxis as manifested in 'natural' modes of working on a 'human scale', in artisanal workshops or on small farms. In these spaces work was skilled. Skill gave workers a relatively high degree of personal autonomy, and made possible meaningful work. For Poulaille, as for the Marx of the '1844 Manuscripts', work was meaningful when it enabled producers to make useful objects and elaborate significations and to control both. In a shift away from Marx that indicates how pervasive Michelet's influence was, Poulaille linked the possibility of non-alienated labour to a specifically 'popular' temporality or 'rhythm of life'. Such a temporality would be established if the overall arrangement that conditioned, and was conditioned by, production, was organised in

---

100   These are what Gadamer would call predjudice structures.
101   See Ragon 1974, Chapter 2, pp. 73–81 and 112–114.
102   Michelet 1973, p. 9.

such a way as to eliminate any division between the rhythms of workshop and farm. Non-alienated production would, therefore, take place without disrupting the connections of worker-collectivities, their place/home and specific, local histories. This vision of rural, artisanally-based autonomy was a composite image of everything capitalism destroyed upon contact. For Poulaille, texts had to convey this kind of interconnectedness. Drawing readers into a vicarious experience of authenticity was central to Poulaille's vision of proletarian literature's political project, which hinged on a revolutionary project attached to a communism projected backward in time. Unlike Heidegger, for whom authenticity was a function of *Dasein*'s being-toward-death, Poulaille's notion of authenticity, while much looser, was embedded in a particular kind of social being. Like Heidegger, for whom authenticity was lost as a function of the forgetting of the question of Being, Poulaille's social authenticity was also lost, pulverised by capitalist mass production.

At the social level, Poulaille's authenticity had been forced into the past by an emergent (alien) socio-economic order. At the level of the individual, authenticity was linked to an irretrievable, lost childhood, as it had been for Michelet. From this followed proletarian literature's penchant for autobiography. As had Michelet, proletarian autobiography used the writer's memory to stage the text's central normative image(s) of 'authentic' life, usually conveyed in 'artless' but precise descriptions of workers interacting through the medium of work. The simplicity and 'artlessness' were understood as indicating 'fidelity' to the experience and to the writer's personal origins. Following this pattern, proletarian literature developed into a peculiar hybrid of autobiography and sentimental cultural anthropology. The central concern of this anthropology was the oral culture of the shop, and the central problem for writers was textually re-staging this oral culture. Detailed descriptions of the immediate context that shaped production were intertwined with transcriptions of popular speech. Popular speech was all the more authentic if it involved regional or class-specific dialects. Proletarian literature writers bent written French to approximate spoken French. Eventually, whole narratives were written in lyrical, but incorrect, or 'bad' French. The boundary that separated dialogue and context dissolved as did those separating the transcription from the transcriber, autobiography from history, integrated past from debased, shattered present.[103]

The power of this blurring of boundaries rested with the reader's empathetic understanding of the writer's identification with the reconstructed scene and a

---

103   It should go without saying, but does not in the context of a discussion of Poulaille, that accomplishing this feat required a high level of art.

performative notion of textuality that again reveals the influence of Michelet. The political power of these texts hinged on their ability to engage the reader. Engagement meant conveying in a direct, emotional manner a sense of this lost world and the authentic mode of existence destroyed along with it, in the hope that it would provoke at least a visceral reaction against the capitalist order responsible for its destruction. Poulaille's notion of the politics of proletarian literature, from the standpoint of the reader, went beyond this:

> For Poulaille, the experience of the proletarian reader almost never coincided with the image of existence offered by books. And it is precisely in the conflict that resulted from this that Poulaille hoped to find the very power of the proletariat, which discovered itself in discovering the vocation of writing.[104]

Poulaille's vision of proletarian literature shared several assumptions with the later, seemingly unrelated, *Correspondence* newspaper project. Both assumed that there was an authentic proletarian experience and written mode of communicating it. Only people who had lived experience could communicate that authenticity. The centres of experience were the workplace and its oral culture, whence the shared emphasis on combining close descriptions of immediate contexts – with a veneer of assumed familiarity – and transcribed speech. Both projects argued that the content of and control over representations of the working class were fundamental aesthetic and political issues, both in themselves and at the level of effect.[105]

There are also some important differences that separate Poulaille's project from *Correspondence*. Among these, the most obvious is context. Poulaille's vision of proletarian literature was articulated in the aftermath of revolutionary syndicalism's abrupt political collapse in 1919 by a critic deeply influenced by that movement's particular brand of working-class politics.[106] Poulaille's proletarian literature was therefore an avatar of pre-World War I revolutionary syndicalism, and it uncritically reproduced revolutionary syndicalism's highly sentimental, almost 'folklorique', view of a better society that turned on a version of blood and soil politics. This politics was faithful to Michelet,

---

104 Arvidsson 1988, p. 54.
105 The logic behind the internal struggles for control of the Editorial Board of *Correspondence* and to keep the politically sympathetic, university educated militants from correcting the writing of workers parallel that articulated by Poulaille, his valorisation of autodidact writers, and critique of bourgeois writers.
106 See Sorel 1981 [1918]. Sorel's relationship to Pouaille is discussed in Arvidsson 1988, p. 53.

his mystical notion of the French fatherland and a distinct French 'genius'. These general aspects of revolutionary syndicalist politics did not prevent the movement from developing highly efficient organisations, advocating positions that were quite radical, and developing militant forms of worker protest that made sophisticated use of the politics of spectacle and the taking over of public space. One might argue that its presence in '*la vieille maison*' gave this ideology a particular political configuration that it lost after 1919. The ideological ambiguities of the blood-and-soil politics built into this type of syndicalism were later expressed in the drift of prominent syndicalists such as Doriot into fascism during the 1930s.[107]

For both *Correspondence* and Mothé, Fordism precluded any attempt to ground revolutionary politics in a vision of lost authenticity. There could be no return to the past, to a lost wholeness; no nostalgia for a vanished more instinctual (rural/regional/traditional) mode of life. More Marxist than Poulaille had been, both considered Fordist socioeconomic organisation progressive and irreversible. Regressive, rural phantasms like Poulaille's were irrelevant.[108] Placing the vision of socialism in the past – a move that necessarily affected one's notion of revolution and its relationship to contemporary politics – foreclosed the main theoretical and political questions Socialisme ou Barbarie's revolutionary project was geared to keep open. A corporatist worldview traditionally assumed an 'organic' division of labour: the revolution Poulaille envisioned would restore this 'more natural' order. From a Marxist viewpoint, this 'revolution' would simply exchange submission to one repressive order for submission to another.

At this point, we can return to Serge Mallet's use of Georges Navel to interpret Daniel Mothé from an angle different to that which he developed. Georges Navel's 1945 *Travaux* is in the proletarian literature style. It is primarily a sentimental autobiography, written too late, that details Navel's childhood and adolescence primarily in terms of his various occupations. The book is broken up by World War I. The pre-war sections are accounts of a rural life dominated by agriculture, its temporality, and its relation to place, in which social relations were structured by a deeply held moral economy. These pastoral descriptions are interspersed with accounts of Navel's efforts to acquire a trade, first as a bricklayer and, later, as an apprentice in a small factory. He has two encounters with the factory in the text, separated by the war and the

---

107   See Rancière 1977.
108   The logic behind this can be found by looking at Marx's dismissal of Utopian and guild-socialism in Chapter 3 of Marx 1988. See also my analysis of Castoriadis 1955 in Chapter 5, Section B.

arrival of industrial Fordism. These encounters, and the differences between them, comprise the book's core. The first is a nineteenth-century-type factory, organised as a collection of discrete artisanal shops. Because each shop was highly skilled, production was largely self-regulating. The factory atmosphere was one of concentration and calm. After the war, Navel, now uprooted, gets another factory job. This was at a properly Fordist plant. He describes his first impressions of this new, modern factory with great precision, capturing the trauma of entering modern capitalism for a personality formed in an earlier, artisanally-based industrial culture. The factory had been rethought as a single productive unit and redesigned around a central assembly line. Tasks were recombined, broken up, and deskilled. Space was radically reconfigured, and a new, autonomous temporality imposed, organised around production considered as an abstract process and not around producers. Gone was the calm of the old factory, replaced by division, noise, speed, and monotony.[109] Navel's autobiographical 'I' stands in for the omniscient third-person realist narrator: each episode in *Travaux* is presented as a *tableau*. All action is firmly situated in the past, which enabled Navel to indulge his penchant for deliberately anachronistic pastoral lyricism *à la prolétarienne*.

Mothé's narratives read very differently. While necessarily retrospective, as a function of the distanciation that separates any textual staging of experience from the experience itself, the narratives are much more presentist than Navel's. They are written just behind the flow of the events described, occasionally dropping into the present tense. Fordist heavy industry, in its political and professional dimensions, constitutes the determining horizon of Mothé's articles. Within this industrial frame, the narratives are restricted to a single machine shop – the Billancourt AOC – and the adjacent spaces that comprise the shop's theatre of political action. The spatially and temporally narrow frame is legitimated on internal grounds by Socialisme ou Barbarie's productivist notion of class formation and the emphasis placed on the universality of worker experience in the autobiographical narratives published in earlier issues of the journal. Mothé never uses the word 'authenticity', as if Fordism had made the notion inoperative. He nonetheless retained, and manipulated, the conventions of representing worker practices, verbal and social, developed by proletarian literature as markers of authenticity and in the assumption that a factory as complex as Billancourt could be understood through close descriptions of a single shop.

Both Poulaille and Mothé tried to challenge the institutions and writers socially authorised to represent the workers at their respective times. For

---

109 See Coriat 1979 for an excellent analysis of these passages in Navel 1945.

Poulaille, who participated in debates within and around the PCF about the nature and mode of representing the working class in the relatively open period of the late 1920s, the primary target was bourgeois literary realism. For Mothé, writing in the mid-1950s, the central opponent was the PCF-CGT. Socialisme ou Barbarie was also engaged in a border dispute with the *sociologie du travail* – at the time still a semi-institutionalised, semi-legitimate academic field – over who should generate dissident images of the working class and what the function of these images should be. Mothé's writing was an integral part of Socialisme ou Barbarie's more general project that tried to challenge directly the legitimacy of the PCF's claims regarding the workers on political grounds, and, indirectly, the *sociologie du travail* by using a form of writing that was itself a critique of the latter's reliance on social science methodologies.

Reading Mothé

We have seen that the name Mothé designated a type of worker writer, a perspective on factory experience, shaped by Socialisme ou Barbarie's revolutionary project. Mothé's writings functioned to confirm contact with the working class for Socialisme ou Barbarie itself, and for the group as a whole in the context of the intellectual milieu of the anti-Stalinist Left that began to take shape during 1957. We discussed how Mothé was able to generate these effects by positioning him against the older tradition of 'proletarian literature'. This section turns to Mothé's narratives from the period 1956–7. It shows that his texts can be read as confirmation of Socialisme ou Barbarie's vision of the working class, and as a significant challenge to that vision. Mothé was the kind of writer that Socialisme ou Barbarie had been hoping to uncover since 1952. His texts provide the reader first-person, present tense descriptions of shop-floor life, built around a well developed sense of what was specific and what was universal in the experiences described.

Mothé's texts were written in the early moments of a profound crisis that seemed to transform the workers' relationship to the Marxist Imaginary. While the broader political implications of this crisis only emerged as it played out in French working-class politics over the next twenty years, it posed immediate and direct questions for Socialisme ou Barbarie's revolutionary project. Mothé's texts begin the slow erosion of the group's assumption that the working class was the necessary agent of revolutionary social transformation. His narratives describe the onset of a crisis of the Marxist Imaginary that manifested as a progressive unhinging of everyday factory experience from the discourse or significations rooted in Marx that gave that experience its political potential.

To show how the crisis of the Marxist Imaginary is staged in Mothé's texts, I analyse them in the order and form of their publication in *Socialisme ou Barbarie*. While this may seem an obvious sequence, it should be noted that it diverges from the *Socialisme ou Barbarie* context by treating these texts apart from the larger theoretical frames the journal placed around them. It also diverges from the order of publication in the 1958 collection, *Journal d'un ouvrier*. The first text, 'Journal d'un ouvrier', provides a narrative frame for the others. It describes the problems a group of AOC workers encountered when they tried to mobilise against the militarisation of the Algerian conflict during May, 1956. I focus particular attention on the essay's opening section, a first-person plural analysis of a symbolic strike initiated by the AOC in support of a fellow worker called up for Algerian duty. Mothé's staging of this action deviates from the Socialisme ou Barbarie pattern by not tying the strike, or its internal organisation, to the experience of production. What Mothé emphasises is a notion of mobilisation as the collective appropriation of Marxist discourse, or the collective enunciation of the language games that can be seen as the interface between worker collectivities and social-imaginary significations particular to the Marxist Imaginary. The balance of the essay describes how the bureaucratic organisations seem to work together to contain, or 'betray', this spontaneous effort to act politically.

The onset of crisis is described in 'Chez Renault, on parle de la Hongrie'. Using a spatial frame restricted to the Renault AOC, and a temporal frame limited to the first weeks of November 1956, the text describes the effects of the Soviet suppression of the Hungarian Revolution and the PCF's response to it. The AOC is a microcosm of working-class politics at Billancourt, and, thereby, of working-class politics in general. The crisis plays out as changes in the AOC workers' relationship to Marxist discourse. Mothé presents these changes as temporary, the results of a particularly intense period of political manoeuvring amongst the trade unions. With the next essays, Mothé's narrative divides in two. What I call his dominant narrative is elaborated in 'Agitation chez Renault' and 'Les grèves chez Renault'. The ideological crisis described in 'Chez Renault, on parle de la Hongrie' continued to evolve through 1957. Mothé's dominant narrative details the unfolding of this crisis as the draining of meaning from political discourse in general and Marxist political discourse in particular. This draining away of meaning left the workers to face their everyday experience as atomised individuals, caught in a motivation crisis afflicting an oppositional imaginary.[110] This narrative is the first indication to appear in *Socialisme ou Barbarie* of a fundamental problem that was at odds with the group's revolutionary theory in 1957. Castoriadis would begin to thematise it after 1959–60 as an effect of bureaucratic capitalism (Fordism) and its destruction of the significations that gave working-class informal self-organisation its political and theoretical meaning. Between 'Journal' and 'Les grèves', Mothé's narrative position shifts from a first-person plural – indicating his active participation in the action – to a first-person singular. Mothé becomes, with this shift, an isolated and bewildered militant who tries to understand the dissolution of the collective that had previously been his source of identity.

It is, perhaps, an index of the trauma associated with watching the dissolution of the imaginary, in terms of which he had previously articulated himself and his relation to the world, that Mothé did not see his texts developing in the direction for which I argue here. His subdominant narrative, 'L'usine et la gestion ouvrière', is a close, sociological description of modes of informal self-organisation and the contradictions that structured professional life in the AOC. It can be read as a fulfillment of the worker-journal project and a confirmation of Socialisme ou Barbarie's view that the source of a 'real' proletarian politics lay in the logic that structured the professional lives of workers at the point of production. This essay can also be seen in the context of 1957 as a reiteration of Socialisme ou Barbarie's vision of proletarian revolution originating in legitimation crisis. It limits the implications of the dominant narrative and assimilates the crisis described there to the optimistic reading from a revolutionary viewpoint of the contemporary political scene outlined in Castoriadis's main theoretical texts from 1957. It recontextualises the draining of content from Marxist discourse as preliminary to the reappropriation of that discourse by a new revolutionary movement. In this narrative, the imaginary is not itself in crisis.

Stylistically, Mothé's texts employ a range of forms. 'Journal d'un ouvrier' is a diary. 'Chez Renault on parle de la Hongrie' opens with a section of transcribed dialogue and shifts into a quasi-journalistic mode. 'Agitation chez Renault' and 'Les grèves de chez Renault' mix these stylistic options to trace a story of disintegration. 'L'usine et la gestion ouvrière' reasserts the first-person plural narrator in the context of elaborating a variation on the participant-observer

---

110 This allocution is included to differentiate motivation crisis in this context from motivation crisis as outlined in Habermas 1975, where it can be understood as the final stage of a theory of crisis as it would affect the dominant imaginary.

sociology.[111] Each essay deploys a variation on the socially embedded narrator whose viewpoint and status change as functions of the situation at Billancourt during this period.

Set-up: Daniel Mothé's 'Journal d'un ouvrier'

The first article Mothé wrote after his defeat on factional grounds appeared in *Tribune Ouvrière*. Because of Socialisme ou Barbarie's abandonment of it as a 'worker newspaper', the piece was not published under his name but anonymously in *Socialisme ou Barbarie* no. 19 with a header appended that claimed: 'A Renault worker sent us the manuscript we publish below'. The text was presented as a diary, not written for publication, that originated outside the limits of Socialisme ou Barbarie. Reading this text, one can see why Socialisme ou Barbarie would present it in this way. Important for its content, it was also an implicit demonstration of the correctness of the premise that writing was coextensive with self-consciousness, a premise that had informed the group's vision of the worker-newspaper project and their view of worker writing generally. The header was not exactly a lie: the imputation of anonymity to the author reflected Gautrat's sense of himself at Billancourt, apart from his Mothé *alter ego*. However, the text did not originate outside the group. And it is not a simple diary.

The conventional diary is an intimate textual space. A reader, who is not the author, eavesdrops on an imagined dialogue between writer and self and steals a look at a private, rough draft of subjectivity. The diary can be read – and often is read – as a document that reveals the nature and impact of socially and historically specific notions of interiority, of the prose of intimacy, and of the conventions that inform textual representations of the self in its staging of subjectivity. A diary written for publication is to a diary proper as modernism is to realist fiction. It adds a level of complexity, a space for conscious manipulation of self-representation as a particular type of fiction, governed by genre rules that produce certain literary effects. A reader of such a pseudo-diary does not trespass in a writer's private laboratory to watch experiments run on experience. Witold Gombrowicz, for example, used the difference between the two types of diary to turn the form inside out. His 'diary' mixed minutely observed accounts of daily experience with book reviews and fictional experiments to create an extended parody of the diary as a textual theatre of intimacy. In his

---

111   It is a variation because, unlike works in participant-observer sociology like Whyte 1993, Mothé does not start off outside the collective being he describes. His text is not directly a story of integration.

hands, the diary became a modernist form that he used to explore the interplay of form and formlessness, a theme that dominated his fiction.[112]

Gombrowicz's diaries are a highly aestheticised meditation on the relations of text, producer and experience that Socialisme ou Barbarie tried to build into its notion of worker writing. Charles Denby's regular *Correspondence* column, 'A Worker's Diary', was a more obvious, less complex, model for *Socialisme ou Barbarie*.[113] Denby's column often figured in *Correspondence* editorials as a demonstration of the potential in worker writing and of the paper's claims to be a worker newspaper.[114] Like Mothé, Denby is a fiction, a pseudonym used as the basis for constructing a perspective on factory experience, shaped by notions of worker self-representation that was developed by the intellectuals and militants of the 'Correspondence' group. His column used the play between the diary form and that of a diary written for publication to intertwine accounts of his experience with broader political arguments, conditioned by the specific interpretive assumptions. The results were deceptively complex, multi-layered texts.

Like Denby, Mothé gives the reader an account of a particular worker's experience filtered through militant conceptions of what that experience means. Mothé's 'Journal d'un ouvrier' opens with a description 'from the inside' of a spontaneous mobilization of AOC workers who wish to show their solidarity with a comrade called up for Algerian military duty in May 1956. The narrative follows these workers as they debate amongst themselves what to do and decide to organise a 'symbolic strike'. The opening can be read in different ways, changing with the context(s) brought to bear upon it. I use two contexts: Algeria and Socialisme ou Barbarie's internal frame as a window onto the crisis of the Marxist Imaginary.

Algeria

The AOC action was an isolated gesture of solidarity with a fellow worker (J.), who was being sent to Algeria. The action was typical of such throughout

---

112   Gombrowicz 1988. Gombrowicz's thematic obsessions lent themselves particularly well to this type of parodic treatment of the diary – assumption of a form of subjectivity, suppresses by definition the human conflict between form and non-form, maturity and the immature. This theme is at the center of *Ferdydurke* and operates at a variety of registers throughout his work.
113   Mothé's article uses the same title as Denby's column, perhaps to signal this relation.
114   Analysed in the previous chapter.

France during the spring of 1956. These actions were largely confined to 'les disponibles' and the populations closely linked to them and constitute a second wave of action against the escalation of the Algerian conflict.[115] Without networks that would have enabled them to publicise their case, and working in direct opposition to the PCF, which voted with Guy Mollet's government to militarise the war, the actions of the 'disponibles' had great difficulty making themselves known and almost no hope of coordination.[116]

An indication of the material scarcity and political isolation that confronted actions on behalf of the 'disponibles' can be seen in the handwritten tract from April 1956 that summarises the actions decided upon at a secret meeting of four hundred and twenty-eight 'disponibles' in Paris, along with three hundred and eight of their 'wives, mothers and sisters'. The inductees, backed by their female relatives, decided to reject the call-up and to refuse to report for duty. The tract argued that this was an extreme response to political gridlock. The announcement was coupled with a call for the adoption of 'other means of struggle'. Among these was a call for unified trade-union action and recourse to unlimited general strikes that would tap into what the tract's author(s) saw as working-class opposition to the war.[117] Given the primacy of a discourse built around ethical arguments to oppose the French use of torture after 1957, it is striking to note this tract's reliance on the rhetoric and tactical repertoire of the proletarian opposition. Even more so is the assumption that the working class would naturally oppose a war sold to it on patriotic grounds.[118]

---

115   'Les disponibles' were men who had already undergone compulsory military training. Mobilising these men was an important step in the escalation of the conflict. On the early efforts to mobilise against the war, see Stora 1992 Part I, 'France, 1954–1962: La noire violence des secrets familiaux', Section 1, pp. 13–20; Sec. 4, pp. 46–70, pp. 46–52 in particular; Sec. 5, pp. 74–8. For an interesting account of an early effort undertaken by intellectuals to mobilise, see Morin 1958, p. 187ff.

116   Compare this with the more broad-based 'resistance' to the Algerian War that emerged during the summer of 1957, mobilising diverse factions of the student and intellectual left around the issue of torture. See Vidal-Naquet 1989: 'Introduction', pp. 7–43, and 'Une fidelité têtue: la resistance française a la guerre d'Algérie', pp. 45–72. 'Resistance' is in single quotation marks in the text because it refers to a specific vision of the antiwar movement constructed by people like Vidal-Naquet. The 'fidelity' of the antiwar movement to the spirit of the Resistance was a powerful rhetorical tool for legitimating the positions adopted by this opposition.

117   'APPEL SOLOMNELLE AUX CENTRALES SYNDICALES CGT-CFTC-CGT FO ET AUTONOMES'. Tract in Castoriadis's papers, SB6A no. 7.

118   The combination of rhetoric and tactical suggestions may link the tract to Socialisme ou Barbarie. The call for trade-union unity and generalised actions in the belief that the

Other factors influenced the movement of 'les disponibles'. As a result of its parliamentary ambitions, the PCF had supported Prime Minister Guy Mollet's January 1956 decision to escalate the war in Algeria, even as Mollet argued for the 'recognition' of a distinct 'Algerian personality'.[119] In the spring of 1956, opposition to the war was unorganised and tied to the interests of a particular and politically ambiguous interest group. The spring of 1956 began the PCF's crisis period. The XXth Party Congress, and the PCF's attempts to initially conceal, and then minimise, the implications of the Congress in general and of Khrushchev's secret speech on Stalin's personality cult in particular, had not yet issued into the profound crisis that would follow the Soviet suppression of the Hungarian Revolution. In the spring of 1956, the PCF and its version of the Marxist Imaginary were still the frame of reference through which political dissent had to be articulated. What Vidal-Naquet called the 'Resistance' to the Algerian War presupposed fractures in the Stalinist Imaginary, the loss of a near-monopoly over legitimate dissent by the PCF, the mobilisation of new groups – particularly university students – into political action, and the creation of new possibilities for political organisation. Without these fractures of the PCF positions and the transformation of oppositional politics, there may have been no shift away from the traditional Marxist language of politics in the April 1956 tract to the language of ethics.

Socialisme ou Barbarie's Internal Frame

'Journal d'un ouvrier' can be understood as a description of the situation that faced the earliest movements in opposition to the Algerian War.[120] The article figures differently when read in the context of Socialisme ou Barbarie's revolutionary project. It describes a small-scale political mobilisation in the first-person plural, from an 'internal' viewpoint, and provides a wealth of detail about a level of working-class everyday experience Socialisme ou Barbarie had not previously been able to reach. Mothé does not, however, base his account on Socialisme ou Barbarie's productivist theory of class formation. The AOC action is not explicitly linked to contradictions in production and/or the professional lives of these workers. Mothé instead presents the action as taking

---

workers would, left to themselves, 'settle the issue' of the draft and Algeria, echo Mothé's positions on syndical unity and the possibilities of unified working-class action.
119 I will return to this in my analysis of Mothé's journey to the *comité d'entreprise*, below.
120 Very little work has been done on this period of opposition, and its modalities remain largely unknown.

place in an autonomous realm of politics. The AOC mobilises as the workers appropriate the language of class conflict. This appropriation constitutes the context within which the workers fashion themselves as a collective. Through this language, the workers refigure relations among themselves, and in their collective relation to their surroundings. These transformations set up and give significance to processes of collective deliberation.

The image of how workers appropriate the language of class conflict cannot be understood as the simple taking-over of categories. It is more an entry into, and activation of, a highly sedimented instituted and instituting social environment. The environment is instituted in that it gave workers access to the language of collective mobilisation associated with a history of such mobilisations by way of the central social-imaginary significations that ordered working-class politics. It is instituting in that the workers actively produce this environment as they enter into its language/significations.[121]

When 'Journal d'un ouvrier' opens, the AOC workers who knew J. had already been brought together as a group by the prospect of his call-up in the way that a family can be brought together by an impending death. Mothé emphasises the sense of solidarity by narrating the section in the first-person plural ('*nous savons tous...*'; '*nous étions etonnés...*'). The telephone rings, the inevitable happens, and the group shifts from anticipating to reacting: 'Everything that had been said about his departure became concrete, and we were surprised by the correspondence between writing, speech and reality'.[122] The telephone call causes expectation and actuality to converge. A second convergence is set off simultaneously: the group of workers shifts from waiting to thinking, acting and deliberating as a politicised collective. They decide to mount a symbolic strike.

Mothé appears to have wanted to set up this action as an ideal gesture of solidarity which was later betrayed by conventional political organisations. He also seems to have been interested in how this collective refigures itself by shifting its relation to Marxist language and, thereby, to politics. His account brackets what Elias Canetti called discharge by starting with the AOC workers already brought together. For Canetti, discharge is the spatial transformation of a group, the physical convergence that is the germinal point in the formation of a crowd. Thinking about the crowd as a second-order human organism that can be understood through the isolation of the quasi-natural rules governing its formation, Canetti defined discharge as spatial convergence and

---

[121] The language of institution and sedimentation are drawn from Husserl 1970. Sedimentation is Husserl's suggestive metaphor for the historicity of language.

[122] Mothé 1956, p. 77.

the shedding of normal social distinctions. Social distinctions are then rearticulated on an egalitarian basis in the temporary environment of the crowd. From this viewpoint, the shifters are movement through space and the physical convergence with others. A portrait of collective formation influenced by Canetti would start with the workers leaving their machines to converge and learn of J.'s fate.[123] For Mothé, the workers' appropriation of the instituted language of class politics triggers the abandonment of customary social and political identities[125] in favour of fluid, collectively defined, temporary identities.[124] This does the work of discharge.

Mothé's description of the AOC's response to J.'s call-up provides a glimpse of the workers' relationship to the Marxist Imaginary that is quite different from that found elsewhere in *Socialisme ou Barbarie*. The Marxist Imaginary is not treated as the natural horizon against which political action necessarily unfolds. The group constructed its image of Marx as a given in advance horizon in their analyses of proletarian politics that linked the patterns of worker appropriation directly to informal self-organisation that were articulated in the course of production. Mothé's description of the AOC workers shows them constituting themselves as political actors by appropriating the language of class politics.

Mothé's description of the AOC mobilisation can be mapped onto the model of 'enunciation' outlined in Michel de Certeau's *The Practice of Everyday Life*. This model has the advantage of providing an outline of the stages of activation/entry into a particular instituted social environment.[125] The point is to

---

123 'The most important occurrence within the crowd is the moment of "discharge" which creates it. This is the moment when all who belong to the crowd get rid of their differences and feel equal' (Canetti 1979, pp. 17ff). The term is taken in the sense of gunpowder. In Canetti's terminology, the type of crowd Mothé describes would be a 'crystal', a 'small rigid group of men, strictly delimited and of great consistency, which seem to precipitate crowds' (p. 73). This relation of the 'crystal' to the mobilised crowd would be a transposition of the logic of the general strike.

124 This network of relations is described in some detail in Mothé 1957a analysed below.

125 De Certeau divides his notion of enunciation into four elements: 1. a realisation of the linguistic system through a speech act that articulates some of its potential (language is real only through the act of speaking) 2. an appropriation of language by the speaker who uses it; 3. the postulation of an interlocutor (real or fictive) and thus the constitution of a relation of contract or allocation (one speaks to someone); 4. the establishment of a present through the act of the 'I' who speaks and, conjointly, since 'the present is the source of time', the organisation of a temporality (the present creates a before and an after) and the existence of a 'now' which is the presence to the world (de Certeau 1988, p. 33). See also Wieder 1974.

show that being-political is a function of the activation of particular social-imaginary significations, which can only be accessed through appropriating the language of class struggle. This appropriation process enables actors to refashion themselves and their relations to each other, their surroundings, as well as to past, present and future in predictable and recognisable ways. There are certain rules, then, and these rules operate (in part) through the medium of what Wittgenstein termed language games. De Certeau's enunciation model has advantages over earlier efforts to describe similar processes. In the early 1970s, D. Lawrence Wieder analysed the processes by means of which, in a California prison-system halfway house, inmates established and maintained themselves as a loose-knit social unit by interrogating the status and function of inmates 'telling the code'.[126] In *Language and Social Reality*, Wieder argued that the 'code' was an elaborate set of prescriptions and prohibitions that regulated social relations amongst inmates and between inmates and authority. While 'telling the code' was crucial to understanding the genesis of the inmate community, it remained conceptually problematic. The code performed a wide range of functions, but was not, Wieder argued, an objectively extant narrative that actors rehearsed in order to contextualise themselves and their action. What the code did was not separable from the act of telling it.

'Telling the code' was the active production of socially-instituted subject positions. The socially-instituted dimensions included not only subject position and relations to others: these relations established an alternative temporality only evident in contrast to the official temporal organisation of the house. 'Telling the code' introduced inmates to an alternative symbolic geography as well. While Wieder convincingly demonstrates that 'telling the code' had these effects, the ethnomethodological framework within which he tried to conceptualise it left him struggling with the problems of assigning it a logical status and of trying to break down the process of collective self-production into rules, much as Austin tried to do with Wittgenstein's notion of the language game.[127]

The collective appropriation of the language of class struggle by the workers in Mothé's AOC operated in a similar manner to Wieder's telling the code. Mothé describes both directly and indirectly the process of constituting themselves as a mobilised collective through debates over what kind of gesture would be best to show solidarity with J. and how to go about mounting it. De Certeau's enunciation model enables the reader to track the stages of this process. As the AOC workers debate through the medium of the language

---

126 Wieder 1974, Part III.
127 See Austin 1975.

of class conflict (point one) and articulate positions through that language, they begin to appropriate language games that enable them to abandon their everyday relations and to begin constructing new ones (points two and three). 'What is to be done to keep J. amongst us?...The "what is to be done" suddenly became the essential preoccupation of us all. All the answers we could give remained in the conditional. They all began with "it would be necessary...if all the guys...if the unions..."'[128]

Given Mothé's Socialisme ou Barbarie affiliation, it is not surprising that he would demonstrate how the AOC's deliberations positioned it in the more general rhetoric of class struggle. The collective almost unconsciously echoes the title of Lenin's best known pamphlet on the question of mobilisation in the course of their debates and does so from a perspective shaped by an experience of what Socialisme ou Barbarie would regard as 'real' working-class solidarity. These markers show that Mothé interpreted the AOC workers' actions in terms shaped by Socialisme ou Barbarie – 'real' worker interests were articulated autonomously through the active appropriation of Marxian language. This resulted almost immediately in a call for trade-union unity, which indicated that the collective was moving beyond conventional politics, albeit in a bleak strategic situation. Mothé writes melodramatically about these debates and the immense obstacles faced by the AOC action:

> As for us, what could we do, the 180 of the shop? 180 oppose a government decision, oppose a government supported by the ensemble of elected officials, 180 before a legal edifice, before a constitution, before a police, an army and a nation of more than 40 million inhabitants who remained, for us, a question mark. Were there other workers out there who were also upset? Other workers who felt themselves to be isolated and powerless but who would be ready to do something? Yes, these others had to exist, we were sure. But where were they? How to contact them?[129]

Almost immediately, Mothé and his AOC comrades recognised the particularity of their action, even as they suspected that it could resonate beyond the shop's confines. However, reaching across the nation was hardly their most pressing problem, when factory organisation prevented nearly all inter-shop communication. Thus the AOC ran directly into the basic problem of communication and organisation that *Tribune Ouvrière* had tried to and, from Mothé's revolutionary perspective, failed to address. Isolated within the shop, without

---

128 Mothé 1956, p. 73.
129 Mothé 1956, p. 132.

an organisational infrastructure controlled directly by the workers, the AOC action could only be a quixotic failure.[130] For the strike to succeed as a symbolic gesture, the AOC workers decided that some accommodation with the dominant CGT was inevitable. As an autonomous action, it was only redeemed in Mothé's text. And no one from Renault knew about Mothé.

While the action was unable to transcend the boundaries of the AOC, it was nonetheless public. Debates among AOC workers disrupted production, and the gathering of workers into small groups transformed the shop's spatial and temporal order.[131] Management almost immediately grew nervous over the stoppage and retreated to their glass offices to watch. Factory security moved around the shop perimeter, trying to figure out what was going on.[132] The arrival of security was a type of pressure that solidified the collective's sense of itself. The gathering was transgressive: security was the signal that the transgression had been noted. The collectivity now operated in public. Not long thereafter, the AOC workers also found themselves in a sort of dance with the CGT delegates. Here, the stakes were rather different. For the moment, the important point is that as the collective constituted itself internally, it was reinforced by the reactions it elicited from the outside. As the external responses reinforced the divide between inside and outside the collectivity, between the normal and transgressive, the process of the rearticulation of relations and identities intensified. Mothé portrays ordinary social relations, patterned by professional hierarchy and political affiliation, being reworked in terms explicitly shaped by the Marxist Imaginary. We have the example of M., a PCF militant turned advocate of direct action:

> M. explodes. And what other way is there? Petitions maybe? We won't change anything if we don't fight [*bagarre*]. M. is treated ironically by his former comrades as having an anarchist's spirit. M. is a union man, M. always followed the union and the Party. Today, his dynamism and his

---

130 Mothé 1956, p. 75.
131 'Nous discutons encore longtemps: le travail est pratiquement interrompu autour de la machine de J. depuis le coup de téléphone. Nous pensons qu'il faut faire quelque chose de symbolique' (Mothé 1956, p. 75).
132 'Des l'agitation a commence, des que des groupes se sont formes, la maitrise est sortie de son repaire vitré; les "blouses" passent, repassent, nous regardent a la derobee. Nos discussions les inquietent, ils se montrent, pour que nous cessions, pour que nous reprenions le travail. Mais leur passage n'a aucun effet' (Mothé 1956, p. 74).

initiatives ensure that he is condemned by those who quietly follow the organisation.[133]

While within the collective, this refashioning of identities continued, the confrontation with the CGT developed at its border. For the union, this confrontation was straightforward and the tactics standard. The isolated AOC action posed no direct threat to the CGT's position at Billancourt. However, because the union was as always on the alert to pressure 'from the left' and paranoiac about losing control of the rank and file, the AOC action had to be managed. The union's managerial techniques included the kind of 'repressive tolerance' Socialisme ou Barbarie had long analysed as emblematic of union cynicism about their worker constituencies.[134] The AOC workers seemed to view the CGT from a more instrumentalised perspective than Socialisme ou Barbarie was usually willing to concede. The only hope of success lay in cooperation with the CGT because the union possessed the communicative infrastructure the workers themselves lacked:

> At the same time, they can express themselves not only in thirty or fifty shops, but they can express the same idea in all the factories in France. But they say nothing, they get angry when we get angry. When one of us says, 'We have to do something', the union officials repeat, as if there was an echo, 'We have to do something'.[135]

For Mothé, a product of the type of politics geared toward the production and deployment of heretical arguments, it was crucial that the AOC workers expressed their opposition to the drafting of their comrade, and the militarisation of Algeria, by taking over the Marxist Imaginary directly. This imaginary was the unquestioned framework within which dissent had to be expressed. Mothé's emphasis on this ideological dimension implicitly positioned the AOC action within the framework of Socialisme ou Barbarie's theory of politics as structured by a legitimation crisis, which emphasised the significance of

---

133 Mothé 1956, p. 75. M.'s 'explosion' is an explicit critique of the PCF's tactics in organising opposition to the Algerian war through petition drives. Such a public outburst could be grounds for expulsion or at least internal discipline.

134 Other examples of union response to real or perceived threats 'from the left' analysed in this project include the pressure brought to bear on Gautrat in the AOC and the strike in Department 76.40. In this context, it appears that the CGT was primarily worried about controlling access to Marxist language.

135 Mothé 1956, p. 74.

workers using Marx against Marxist organisations. Mothé's description is not a point-for-point reproduction of this model, however. It did not retain Socialisme ou Barbarie's assumption that Marxism constitutes a natural horizon against which any political action must unfold and project onto the workers. Socialisme ou Barbarie also seemed to assume that workers were aware of this legitimation crisis as such. For the militants of Socialisme ou Barbarie, worker mobilisation resembled their own in that each expressed a clear, prior political commitment and registered a coherent protest. In contrast, Mothé shows his shop mobilising around very particular issues without any corresponding prior ideological positions. The workers' actions gained coherence and radicalism in and through the process of mobilisation itself. The central role is not occupied by judgement, but by affect – outrage at the drafting, frustration with the PCF-CGT, the sense of transformation, the knowledge of transgression.

While affect played a central role in generating a sense of cohesion, Mothé's description placed great emphasis on the process of deliberation. The AOC workers reacted to their situation in a more or less unified action as management sought to limit the action and the CGT sought to contain and channel it. They soon realised that they had taken this action as far as they could: the lack of a way to communicate with other workers and the spatial isolation of the AOC itself both placed strict limits on it. They decided to take up the CGT offer of 'collaboration' in an officially sponsored, half-hour strike. Mothé argued that the collective continued to operate within the CGT action:

> We retained our rage at them, we know that if they can sabotage the movement, they can also, by their support, make the hesitant decide to join in. Their support is fundamental. If we argue with them, there will be no strike. Those who don't know what to do will profit from our discord and will not protest.[136]

A meaningful symbolic strike could only occur with the cooperation of the CGT. For Mothé, the consequences of this cooperation were a loss of control, alienation, and bitterness:

> So we found ourselves, a good majority of strikers, in the central passageway: we stayed for a half-hour, at once victors and vanquished, at once happy to divest ourselves of our agitation and like the truly unhappy who cannot be satisfied with a half hour strike.[137]

---

136 Mothé 1956, p. 75.
137 Mothé 1956, p. 76.

The CGT strike was double-edged. Politically, there was no alternative to cooperation. However, this cooperation ceded control over the social dimensions of the action. Mothé describes the collective as continuing to function subjectively within the CGT action: the AOC workers feel, think and act and as a unit.

Socially, the formation of the collective was the result of an appropriation of the instituted language games that gave access to the Marxist Imaginary. Activating the Imaginary refigured social and political relations within the shop and transformed the area around the AOC from a space of production into a space of politics. Subjectively, this process was driven by a tremendous emotional charge. These emotions appear to have been the inverse of those that dominated production. Throughout his writings, Mothé claimed that factory work occurred in an environment of frustration and irritation. He emphasised these emotions, in part, because he read them as a nascent political response to the way work was organised. Collective action was characterized by intense exhilaration, communion, and 'jouissance'.[138] To mobilise was to merge with comrades through the larger narratives and images that organised the imagined present and the history of the workers' movement. It was a momentary transcendence of social and professional limitations and hierarchies, a little holiday away from the monotony of production, an ephemeral experience of freedom.

From Mothé's description, one could argue that this subjective dimension informed the AOC workers' understanding of what the CGT's involvement with the strike meant: it compromised the collective as a space of freedom from the constraints of everyday production and politics:[139]

> The guy who had just said that it would be necessary to fight added: it is necessary to be revolutionary. He who, in other times, would do nothing that would distinguish himself from his comrades, would he become blood-thirsty?
>
> I am surprised by smiles – 'he's made of good stuff'. Yes, but he freed himself with words. Others plotted every detail of their revenge: there, too, were words, excesses of imagination. But why these words,

---

138   This last term came up in my interview with Mothé in January, 1992, in the course of his attempts to describe what it was like to be at the origin of a strike.

139   A more thoroughgoing analysis of the relationship between the dominant imaginary significations and the subjective effect could be worked out using the model of subjectivity and the role of representations in Aulagnier 1975.

these bloody images? It's a way to staunch hatred, the easiest way, the most free.[140]

A second account of this action is found in the minutes of Socialisme ou Barbarie's 12 April 1956 meeting:

> Comrade Mothé asked to outline the situation at Renault. Mothé noted a strong reaction in his shop to the departure of the contingent [the men called up for Algerian duty]. Some young workers (a dozen Stalinists among them) came to find Mothé to do something generalised. In a neighbouring department, a half-hour strike was organised by the Stalinists, but three young workers wanted to do something outside of their control. In all, there are twelve or so very determined guys – what to do? Hand out fliers at the factory door? Intervene if Jacques Duclos takes the stand at the factory tomorrow? Call for a general strike? Publish an appeal? While the unhappiness is less clear in the other shops, I have to propose something to these workers.
> Mothé saw Henri and Gil Henri proposed a short, violent appeal demanding that [the workers] protest at the personnel-office, forcing a fifteen-minute stoppage for each man called up.[141]

If one scans Mothé's article for traces of this debate, it appears that he took Guillaume's response most seriously:

> The problem can be summarised simply enough. Can something be done to stop the mobilisation of the men? While there's nothing in the short term, one can and must do something. In this case, the classic fiction according to which, with good will and courage [something can be accomplished], must be avoided because what matters is making known what the workers feel. Succeeding in that would have great value. What is needed is a strike with a clear meaning. While this action would be very limited, it would have great repercussions.[142]

---

140 Mothé 1956, p. 77.
141 Typescript *compte-rendu* of *Socialisme ou Barbarie* meeting, 12 April 1956, pp. 1–2. Duclos was Thorez's assistant, no. 2 in the PCF. Henri and Gil were Pierre Bois and Pierre Blachier respectively, both members of the *Tribune Ouvrière* collective. Curiously, *Tribune Ouvrière* was not mentioned as an option in Mothé's article. This omission was probably the result of the ongoing factional fighting.
142 Typescript C.R. 12 April 1956, pp. 1–2.

Socialisme ou Barbarie had no more idea what the workers felt about the militarisation of the Algerian conflict than any other political organisation at the time. Guillaume's symbolic strike was a way to get some type of measure of that reaction in a context that presented little room for manoeuvre. Given Socialisme ou Barbarie's positions, one can imagine that the 'repercussions' which Guillaume hoped a symbolic strike might have would have included the emergence of cracks in working-class support for the PCF. While Lefort and Guillaume argued for the symbolic strike, others, including Castoriadis, argued for a more specifically political action, like a tract that directly attacked the PCF and the Algerian war. Socialisme ou Barbarie's consensus interpretation of the situation at Renault was that it was explosive and very dangerous for the PCF, which ran the risk of running into 'pressure from the base'.[143]

There are substantial differences between the two accounts. In light of this meeting, 'Journal d'un ouvrier' can be read as Mothé running through the various suggestions given to him in response to his request for advice. All options failed: the strike, the tract, his intervention at the *comité d'entreprise*. The AOC collective, the formation of which occupied the essay's opening section, did not remain intact through the week.[144] Mothé's text is an effort to derive some symbolic value from these failures by writing them up. From the gap separating the action as described for Socialisme ou Barbarie and that described in Mothé's text, one can deduce that 'Journal d'un ouvrier' opens with a composite account of collective mobilisation rather than with a detailed recreation of a particular mobilisation. Its conflation of the normative and the descriptive is of a piece with Socialisme ou Barbarie's tendency to substitute an internally produced 'working class' – an effect of the group's textually generated vision of worker experience – for the referent 'working class' – the actual experience of workers, including those who write narratives about it.[145] Mothé's interweaving of the composite and the particular, the descriptive and the normative, is obscured by the narrator's perspective, which presents the first section of 'Journal d'un ouvrier' as a first-person plural, 'real-time' account. This conflation of the signified and the referent, the composite and the particular, the normative and the descriptive, does not mean that the text is therefore false. Rather, it must be read alongside Socialisme ou Barbarie's revolutionary

---

143 The PCF 'se heurte a la pression de la base'. Lefort's comments. Typescript C.R. 12 April, 1956, p. 2.

144 The items listed here that are unfamiliar will be addressed briefly in the next section of this chapter.

145 This refers to the problem of the realism-effect that I discussed at the end of my analysis of Lefort 1952.

theory as a particular type of text that tries to describe and catalyse, to present a theory of history and to act upon that history by presenting an order and explanation at the same moment. These texts were written as political acts.

We have seen how Mothé's description also works against the dominant Socialisme ou Barbarie framework, particularly in its description of political action as the interaction of workers with the language of class struggle. This section has tried to show how a theory of the Marxist Imaginary as a social institution could be teased out of Mothé's description of the AOC workers: the subjective element; the almost unconscious repetition of the history of the workers' movement (and/or Socialisme ou Barbarie's vision of the strategic problems facing autonomous worker actions) as an effect of what Husserl called 'sedimented' language; the objective dimension of mobilisation evident in the responses of the various actors Mothé brings into play. One could imagine a more 'classical' *Socialisme ou Barbarie* reading of this same action that would emphasise the processes of collective deliberation, linking them to various types of sociability that shaped the informal organisation of production. This language – the language games that give access to the Marxist Imaginary and thereby shape workers' interaction with that language, with each other, and with their environment – becomes problematic in Mothé's other texts.

'Journal d'un ouvrier': On the Deskilling of Politics

The rest of 'Journal d'un ouvrier' unfolds in the realm of conventional politics. Narrating in the first-person singular,[146] Mothé journeys through the political landscape of Billancourt both as a transcriber of dissent and as a kind of modernist Odysseus, embarking on a long circular voyage only to find that returning home, to the mobilised worker collective, is impossible. The story is one of failure. These sections are closer to Socialisme ou Barbarie's line on conventional politics in their insistence that the bureaucratic organisation of political activity tends toward the political deskilling of the worker base. This deskilling is not complete, however, and this creates possibilities for resistance.[147]

Soon after the AOC's 'symbolic strike', the PCF, acting through one of the many '*comités fantoches*' ('phantom committees') it created to channel worker opposition to Algeria, circulated a tract that criticised the war and called for

---

[146] In Mothé 1956, the first-person narrator does not appear until p. 77.
[147] This is a translation of Socialisme ou Barbarie's 'central contradiction of bureaucratic capitalism' into the realm of politics.

petitions to be circulated in opposition to it.[148] Mothé's AOC reacted with 'outrage' to the tract, and Mothé was soon back in his usual role as unofficial spokesman for the CGT-dominated shop, delivering on its behalf messages otherwise too politically deviant for public exposure. He was delegated to speak (by whom exactly is not clear) first at a local meeting of the CGT and, later that week, before the Billancourt *comité d'entreprise*. Mothé circulated the text of what he planned to say in advance. The speech followed the outline of Castoriadis's suggestion in the April 12 meeting. It directly attacked the Socialists and the PCF, arguing that Algeria was already a colonial war. Designating it a colonial war was a central issue in the later mobilisations against it: in 1956, this position contradicted the line, shared by both left parties, that Algeria was a police-action aimed a quashing a particularly intense mutiny in a French department.[149] Mothé also attacked the PCF specifically, ridiculing its 'peace camp' posture and its reliance on petition drives as attempts to divert attention from its parliamentary position. Against these positions, Mothé argued for a broad-based resistance to the Algerian war that would manifest itself through coordinated general actions and would legitimate itself on anti-colonial grounds. The text was extensively debated in the AOC. Mothé saw the debate itself as healthy because it constituted a kind of rejection of trade-union efforts to confine such discussion to the official hierarchy.[150] The text, and the prospect of a speech, were vehemently opposed by the shop's PCF and CGT militants. This opposition was expressed

---

148   Mothé 1956, p. 81. I noted earlier that the PCF voted with Mollet to intensify the war, grateful to be part of a parliamentary coalition after 8 years of enforced isolation. Their line on the war, particularly early on, was extremely ambiguous. While space does not permit a detailed treatment of it, it can be summarised as follows: the Party officially supported the escalation under the logic of a police-action, driven by the exigencies of parliamentary politics. Consistent with its 'camp-of-peace' line, the Party also called for ceasefires and for the 'national fact' of Algeria to be recognised. Meanwhile, in an effort to maintain influence over the nascent anti-colonial movement, the Party multiplied petition-drives using the mechanisms noted here. This 'double game' continued, with some ideological variation, through 1962. See Hamon and Rotman 1987 for a detailed account of the Party's actions in the context of the student mobilisation against the war after 1959.
149   The problem here is that Algeria had been a French department since 1860 and was therefore not part of the empire. The independence movement was initially branded a 'mutiny' and the response a 'police action'. A police action could be militarised without ceasing to be a police action if one's primary criteria for defining the conflict derived from Algeria's administrative position as part of France proper.
150   'Les jugements étaient renversés, les anciennes valeurs bousculées, un vent nouveau soufflait dans l'atelier' (Mothé 1956, p. 80).

by what soon became a pattern of increasingly violent verbal confrontations between the workers, who generally favoured the position Mothé claimed to translate in his speech, and those militants who supported the PCF-CGT's positions.[151] In 'Journal d'un ouvrier', these verbal confrontations comprise the most evident signs that pressure was being increased on dissident opinions in the AOC. This pressure coincided with the arrival of the weekend. By the following Monday, the AOC workers had dissolved as an autonomous collective capable of acting politically. The dissolution of the collective makes unanswerable questions about the 'fit' between Mothé's polemic and the sentiments expressed by the workers, between the strike in solidarity with J. and the more ideologically-based opposition to the Algeria war.

Mothé's speech before the *comité d'entreprise* is set up to present his central argument about 'real' versus 'administered' politics. Communist, Socialist and Christian positions on Algeria are described as identical. All speakers behave in the same way, and the segments of the audience attached to each organisation do so as well. All the parties opposed colonialism. All supported education and urged the circulation of petitions. The audience applauded at the appropriate moments. The speakers and the audience seemed bored. There was no discussion or dissent. Mothé opposed to this type of politics that which emerged through debate in the shop:

> None of them, except the Christian, expressed his ideas with the least conviction. Each only recited, without any faith. Not a laugh, not a murmur, not a single flash of eloquence. Speeches without enthusiasm. Speeches by professionals. What a difference in our shop, where everything is said with such passion. How many pieces I have messed up while preoccupied with discussions? Yesterday, again, E. shattered his grinding wheel because he forgot the machine in the heat of discussion (...) we have to yell to be heard over the noise of the machines, but the discussions stay human, mixed with laughter and insults.[152]

The argument here is obvious. 'Real' and 'human' political discussions run parallel to production in the shop. These discussions are the basis for the social networks Socialisme ou Barbarie tended to downplay in their major analyses of shop-floor experience. For Mothé, political discussion is an opportunity to think independently and an escape from the monotony of work. The impassioned

---

151   This phrasing reproduces Mothé's view of the conflict in its opposition between 'workers' and 'militants supporting PCF-CGT positions'.
152   Mothé 1956, pp. 82–3.

nature of these discussions – their seeming violence – begins with having to yell over the noise of the machines. Mothé sets the trade unions and their shared managerial ideology against this. Were this managerial ideology fully implemented – were the political decision making process confined to the apparatus of each union or political party – then the effect would be a radical deskilling of politics. Paradoxically, this organisational ideology imputes great significance to ordinary political discussion by making it an act of resistance.

This view of politics is basic to the curious optimism that pervades this essay, despite its endless list of failures. For Mothé, the fact of dissent expressed in these shop-floor debates indicated that the bureaucratic organisations and their worker bases were split by a legitimation crisis. To exploit this toward revolutionary ends was a matter of finding the right occasion and language. A new organisation needed to be constructed in anticipation of that occasion.

'Journal d'un ouvrier' presents a vivid picture of factory life at Billancourt without much physical description. The embedded narrator rarely refers to the physical space, and when he does, it is simply to note certain details. Mothé mentions the circular rows of benches in the *comité* room, the banks of microphones arrayed across the front of the podium, and the incessant popping of flashbulbs that stopped the moment he took the stage. The technique is reminiscent of Robbe-Grillet in its assumption of familiarity, which forces the reader into a deciphering process that tends to collapse the distance between him or her, the narrator and the scene being narrated. Billancourt is presented as a space primarily by way of social interaction amongst workers. The few descriptions of individual workers' comportment provided by Mothé are made abstract by replacing their names with a single capital letter. The primary data, then, is speech either transcribed or embedded in tracts, which Mothé claims are indirect renderings of that same worker speech. The space within which the article unfolds is almost entirely social and political. 'Journal d'un ouvrier' includes only the briefest staging of the intersection of politics and production in the passage quoted earlier noting Mothé's 'missed pieces' and E's exploded grinding wheel. Instead, the article juxtaposes the 'humanity' of debates outside of organisational control to the mechanical 'horror of controversy', and dislike of *'les histoires'* typical of PCF-CGT militants, as a way to critique the deskilling of politics.

Pivot: 'Chez Renault, on parle de la Hongrie'

This article describes the earliest effects of the crisis into which the PCF slid after the violent suppression of the Hungarian Revolution by the Soviets. Like most Mothé articles, it employs narrow spatial and temporal frames: it details the crisis from the 'AOC viewpoint' as it unfolded during the first two weeks of November 1956. This narrowness makes the text difficult to decipher on its own terms. It provides a window into the still-nascent crisis of the Marxist Imaginary, which began as a sudden deepening of the effects of trade-union pluralism. At Billancourt, the most obvious short-term effects of Soviet actions were the PCF's isolation and paralysis. This paralysis presented the PCF-CGT's rivals with an opportunity to advance their relative positions. This scramble for position occurred at the level of discourse, with the CFTC and FO trying to appropriate significant elements of the Party's rhetoric and to use them for their own ends. Because of the general patterns that shaped trade-union politics at Billancourt, the scramble did not result in a shift of constituency away from the PCF-CGT, but in a withdrawal of the worker base from politics. Mothé argues that the workers not only withdrew from the politics dominated by the PCF, but from politics in general. While not presented as a theoretical argument, Mothé's article makes it clear that, in his view, the workers withdrew from politics because the rhetoric of working-class struggle had (temporarily) been drained of meaning, had ceased to signify. The discourse did not change: workers stopped investing it with particular meanings, stopped adapting a static language to a constantly changing environment.

For Socialisme ou Barbarie, had Mothé's reading of the effects of the Hungarian Revolution and the isolation of the PCF not been written so close to the events described, and had their effects not been framed as temporary, his text would have created theoretical problems. If his narrative was accurate, and the problem created by Hungary was the collapse of the language/language games that enabled the working class to access the Marxist Imaginary, then Socialisme ou Barbarie's entire revolutionary project was in peril. In early 1957, however, the group regarded Hungary as the crest of a wave of proletarian revolutionary action. In France, they alone were riding it. The legitimation crisis that Socialisme ou Barbarie argued had split the working class from its bureaucratic organisations had been intensified by the crisis of Stalinism that began with Stalin's death: it ran through the XXth Party Congres and seemed to culminate in Poland and Hungary. A massive reappropriation of the Marxist Imaginary by the working class in the name of proletarian revolution seemed more, not less, likely. Castoriadis, for example, argued that Hungary had to be understood as a new type of revolutionary response to total social crisis. The Hungarian people had acted almost as a unit against bureaucracy. Councils had been established all over the country, and had issued truly radical demands for the abolition of hierarchy and the delivery of substantive control over the economy to the people. Hungary was, therefore, a 'massive confirmation' of Socialisme ou Barbarie's work that marked the emergence of a new phase in proletarian-revolutionary action. The significance of this new phase was, Castoriadis argued, 'absolutely universal'.[153] From this, the dominant Socialisme ou Barbarie viewpoint, what Mothé described in his writing about Billancourt seemed local and transitory.

The background for Mothé's article was as follows. The PCF crisis flowed directly from the *L'Humanité*'s coverage of the Hungarian Revolution as a fascist putsch. While this line followed that advanced by *Pravda*, it was in sharp, and increasingly isolated, contrast to the extensive coverage in *Le Monde* and in weekly '*progressiste*' press outlets like *L'Express* and *France Observateur*.[154] Admittedly, the revolution was difficult to interpret *in vivo*: the lack of a single, coordinating source of information, the complexity and speed of events, the involvement of the whole of Hungarian society and the novel organisational forms developed by the revolution frequently had the reporters from *Le Monde* at a loss.[155] All observers agreed – each for his or her own reasons, of course – that during the last weeks of October 1956, Hungary was in a revolutionary situation, and that the Red Army tanks had violently suppressed a revolution in the name of revolution. It was obvious that *L'Humanité* was lying by portraying it as the work of a band of 'fascist counterrevolutionaries'.[156]

---

[153] The main *Socialisme ou Barbarie* articles on Hungary and its consequences for revolutionary theory include Lefort's 'L'insurrection hongroise' in *Socialisme ou Barbarie* no. 20 (December 1956–February February 1957), pp. 85–116. Originally published as a pamphlet around 20 November, it was the first comprehensive reading of Hungary to be published in France; Philippe Guillaume, 'Comment ils se sont battus' in *Socialisme ou Barbarie* 20, pp. 117–23; P. Chaulieu, 'La revolution prolétarienne contre la bureaucratie' in *Socialisme ou Barbarie* no. 20, pp. 134–171 (the quote above is from p. 134); Chaulieu, P 'Sur le contenu du socialisme' (II) in *Socialisme ou Barbarie* no. 22, (July–September 1957), pp. 1–73 and 'Sur le contenu du socialisme (III)' in *Socialisme ou Barbarie* no. 23, (January–February 1958), pp. 81–125. English translations of the Castoriadis pieces appear in Castoriadis 1988.

[154] See Deli 1981.

[155] See *Le Monde*'s coverage in particular, 25 October–10 November 1956. There is a considerable gap between the information reproduced without commentary in 'Le film des evénéments' and the main articles written from Vienna. The former are an important basis for Lefort's 'L'insurrection hongroise' cited above.

[156] In the context of this chapter I have bracketed the extensive theoretical disputes over the nature of the revolution and the relative merits of Hungary versus Poland that occupied Socialisme ou Barbarie as it shifted from being an isolated and marginal group to an underground influence on anti-Stalinist left-wing debates occurring on the edges of the *progressiste* public. Here, what matters is that *L'Humanité* was isolated and that a crisis of its readership translated almost directly into a crisis for the Party itself at Billancourt.

From this brief description of the situation can be seen the two general problems that shaped the situation at Billancourt: the obvious falsity of *L'Humanité*'s coverage and the contradictions generated by the Soviet suppression of a workers' revolution. Mothé's version of the crisis that followed centred on the theme of fragmentation. The essay opens with a series of 'transcribed dialogues' from the first week of November, 1956 that track, and comment on, the *L'Humanité*'s narrative on Hungary and the loss of faith it engendered amongst its (largely PCF) readership. These dialogues incidentally reveal the increased role of 'bourgeois' papers like *France Soir* and *Libération* as sources of information amongst Billancourt workers, and the extensive use in these publications of the rhetoric of popular revolt against a repressive state to describe the situation in Hungary. For the PCF readership, the fact that *L'Humanité* was ceasing to be the linchpin of ideological dissemination was symptomatic of a broader cultural crisis. This crisis cut to the core of the PCF's 'separate world' and the kind of commitment to it that would prompt Party members to cut themselves off from the bourgeois press and substitute for it a wide range of Party-controlled media.[157]

While this may have signalled a fracturing of the PCF as a 'world apart', Mothé describes the crisis at Billancourt as one of faith for *L'Humanité*'s readers, accompanied by the Party's collapse back onto its membership and paralysis amongst Party militants (for whom the questions raised by Hungary could have been traumatic). The problem faced by the PCF press was repeated in the context of Billancourt trade-union politics. Like the bourgeois press, Mothé argued that the FO, CFTC and SIR moved to colonise PCF-CGT discourse. An increasingly defensive PCF tried to ward off any further erosion of its position by playing up the themes of the conflict between East and West.[158] This context was particular, however, and the move revealed the depth of the Party's crisis: its 'antifascist' *mot d'ordre* failed to mobilise any support, even after a crowd of students attacked the offices of *L'Humanité* on 7 November 1956 in protest at Soviet actions.[159] At Billancourt, Party militants were increasingly isolated: some tried to stem the flood of criticism of the Party and the USSR,

---

157   On the PCF's mediascape as a 'world apart' see Kriegel 1980, Gérôme and Tartakowsky 1988, Verdès-Leroux, 1983.

158   This argument was not new. See Mothé 1954, pp. 27–38, and the other version of the same argument in the chapter on *Tribune Ouvrière*, above.

159   This slogan was created to equate the situation of the PCF in France with that of the Hungarian Party in Budapest. Both were 'under siege' by 'fascist bands' and 'counterrevolutionary elements' sponsored by 'international reaction'. To understand the extent of this, see *L'Humanité* from the days around 7 November 1956.

which seemed to be coming from all quarters, through intimidation and violence. Mothé saw this defensiveness as reactive and confused. Militants were acting out of the frustration created by what he saw as the Party's tortured, inflexible and contradictory positions.[160]

Problems for the PCF meant problems for the CGT. In the earliest moments of crisis, the union tried to portray the PCF as the victim of a 'campaign of lies'. This soon became untenable. The CGT, which relied on the PCF for ideological direction, was reduced to a parallel immobility. What appeared to be emerging through this crisis was a deep disruption of the patterns that shaped syndical politics – and politics more generally – at Billancourt. The informal links that had connected the PCF and CGT to their wider constituencies through the agency of their militants began to evaporate. These links were fundamental to the normal operation of the factory's political order.[161] Because this unfolded in a context divided on East-West grounds, there was little shifting of affiliation. The conventional mode of protest was, instead, abstaining from electoral participation. What Mothé described in the context of the AOC was a reflection of this pattern.

The effects of this particular crisis, however, seemed to run deeper as well. Mothé argued that the AOC workers did not react to the crisis by saying that the PCF had lied and that therefore we should begin building a new worker organisation, as he would (undoubtedly) have preferred to see and as his sense of politics, as conditioned by Socialisme ou Barbarie, could have led him to expect. Instead, Mothé claimed the workers argued amongst themselves that the PCF lied like all political organisations lie: there was, therefore, no point in continuing to be involved in politics.[162]

Mothé's reading of the situation tried to fit it into the Socialisme ou Barbarie legitimation crisis framework. The apparent collapse of the PCF-CGT's ideological legitimacy did not surprise him. Following Socialisme ou Barbarie, Mothé argued that the collapse of the political was temporary, and was a necessary precondition for possibilities to emerge which might transform working-class politics, perhaps moving it in a more revolutionary direction. This interpretive position explains the pervasive theme of 'trade-union betrayal'. After the initial sequence of transcribed dialogues, Mothé's text becomes a list of examples that converge on the argument that, in this situation, trade-union pluralism played into the cynicism of the workers and confirmed their withdrawal from

---

160   This is clear from Mothé's article and does not require his anti-Stalinist explanation.
161   See Chapter 4, above.
162   Mothé 1956–7, pp. 124–7.

politics. At one point, the FO and company SIR jointly called for a strike 'in support of the Hungarian workers'. Their call was directed primarily at workers who had previously refused to strike.[163] The novel thing was not that the anti-communist unions were trying to manoeuvre against the PCF-CGT but that unions predicated on the rejection of the idea of class conflict were now trying to champion the cause of the Hungarian working class by organising strikes. For Mothé, actions like this reduced the rhetoric of working-class politics to nothing more than the language of trade-union manoeuvre.[164]

One can see here indications of the deeper problem. PCF-CGT ideology – the Marxist Imaginary as figured in terms of its organisational history and interests – was the dominant reference point for the entire political and trade-union left at Billancourt. The political project of opposition groups like Socialisme ou Barbarie presupposed that these central signifiers retained an autonomous power despite the dominant appropriations of them. This assumption enabled the construction of the notion of proletarian revolution: in this situation, the workers would appropriate the significations that ordered class struggle and revolution to themselves, rejecting the dominant order's usage of them in the name of a new revolution. But Hungary introduced a new level of contradiction into the dominant position. Consider the range of terms directly at stake here: the USSR as a socialist workers' state; the knowledge of the historical process achieved by the Communist Party as a result of its role in the revolution; the status of the Russian Revolution as both end of history and culmination of the revolutionary tradition; the unity of the working class and its political project. Consider, further, the extreme nature of this contradiction as brought to the surface by Soviet actions in Hungary in the context of the broader crisis of Stalinism. Compounding all of this was the (temporary) shift to the left in the rhetoric used by the bourgeois press, which was doubled by the shift in trade-union politics. For Mothé, whose perspective was shaped by the project of proletarian revolution, this presented a dismaying *tableau*, in

---

163 Mothé 1956–7, p. 127. On workers who refused to strike in the AOC, see, for example, Mothé 1956, p. 80. There were many reasons why workers might not strike, ranging from disagreement over the particular issue and the particular organisation claiming to control it to a more principled rejection of class conflict.

164 Coming from Mothé, this is an ambiguous characterisation. The rhetoric of class conflict had always been the language through which conflicts over positions were fought out between competing organisations/positions at Billancourt. The difference in this situation here is that the Imaginary within which this vocabulary had been situated was in crisis as well. The language was being reduced to nothing more than the rhetoric of syndical manoeuvre. This pattern will become clearer in Mothé's subsequent texts.

which the words associated with the Marxist Imaginary were being reduced to mere words.

For Mothé, some consolation was available in the claim that some of this was clear to the AOC workers. The draining of content from phrases like 'solidarity with the Hungarian workers' did not go unnoticed: each action staged to exploit the PCF-CGT's problems was hotly debated in the shop. Mothé presents these debates as involving workers firmly on the left but equally disgusted with the PCF, the USSR and the anticommunist unions. The problem that crops up in Mothé's descriptions of these debates was the lack of a distinct language with which to articulate positions. This same problem made any organisational initiatives impossible. However, as in 'Journal d'un ouvrier', Mothé saw in the fact of debate reason for revolutionary optimism:

> Already we had begun to take up our human contacts a little. We began joking amongst ourselves even about politics and to discuss the problems of the factory and shop. The Hungarian affair began to raise the 'Russian Problem', and that is one thing, among many others, that the Hungarian workers have given us.[165]

Mothé argued that the Hungarian workers 'gave' the AOC a basis to renew 'human relationships' between themselves. He contrasted them with the 'robotic' comportment of Party militants who were, he claimed, reduced to repeating official phrases. More fundamentally, from a perspective informed by Socialisme ou Barbarie, Hungary offered a premise for a real discussion about radical politics by raising the problem of the status of the USSR. In these facts, Mothé found reason for a guarded optimism at the end of November 1956. However, the dominant images that emerge from this article are of fragmentation and paralysis. More profound a problem for the possibility of an oppositional politics was the crisis of language that would enable a new organisation to develop positions logically and politically distinct from those already circulating in the confused, temporarily radicalised context of Billancourt. Because of this, all opposition actions remained ephemeral.[166]

---

165 Mothé 1956–7, p. 133.
166 Mothé 1956–7, p. 132, describes a Trotskyist demonstration on the *Place Nationale* in these terms. The limited number of supporters appears to have prevented the demonstration from gaining any further support. This is understandable in terms of the theatrical nature of French working-class politics and its emphasis on the workers turning out *en masse*. See Chapter 4 for a more detailed analysis.

Dominant Narrative: The Fracturing of the Political at Billancourt

'Agitation chez Renault' and 'Les grèves chez Renault', written in April and October 1957 respectively, describe the medium-term consequences of the crisis outlined above on worker politics at Billancourt. As in 'Chez Renault on parle de la Hongrie', Mothé's main interpretive project is to scan the highly fragmented situation for signs that possibilities might be opening up for a new politics. At every turn, Mothé sees such possibilities and watches as they are blocked – betrayed – by either the PCF-CGT or by the effects of trade-union pluralism more generally. Beneath this narrative of betrayal runs another version of the fragmentation narrative. This affects the language of class struggle itself. Mothé does not always distinguish between these levels: some of the most direct remarks about fragmentation are presented as critiques of the PCF and trade-union pluralism, the key themes in the betrayal story. These two threads intertwine in descriptions of the repeated failures of attempts to mobilise and organise in the AOC. As these stories unfold, Mothé's narrative-position is transformed. His self-doubt indicates that he is increasingly prey to the effects of isolation. He becomes an actor who possesses the language of political integration in a context that no longer values that language – the ethnographer/traveller marooned in an inverted run of the standard travel narrative.

Mothé's arguments about the fragmentation of the political at Billancourt go as far as they do because he viewed it through the Socialisme ou Barbarie frame of reference. Fragmentation was symptomatic of a deepening legitimation crisis. Workers' rejection of the doctrinal ossification of the PCF and the depoliticising effects of trade-union pluralism were the necessary preconditions for the emergence of a new politics. This general position enabled Mothé to assume that the new revolutionary movement was developing autonomously within the working class and to explain the failure of all organisational efforts by recourse to the line of trade-union betrayal that Socialisme ou Barbarie inherited from its Trotskyist past.

'Agitation' opens with two exemplary tales. Each of the main unions called its own strike on 18 April 1957. At Billancourt it had been customary that workers were allowed to leave their workstations a few minutes before the official start of the lunch break. They needed the extra time to wash up and get to the cafeteria with enough time left to eat. Management proposed that this custom be eliminated. The unions responded to worker objections with calls for strikes. According to Mothé, however, the AOC workers were just as irritated by the competing strikes as by the threat to custom:

> We felt all of a sudden that our discontent was being used to feed the rivalry and competition between the CGT and FO. Thus, the discussion unfolded on this level… and the real problem found itself already half obscured.[167]

Mothé read the worker response in terms of Socialisme ou Barbarie's critique of bureaucratic trade-union practices:

> The total absence of preliminary discussion of trade-union directives under the pretext of efficiency, far from preventing controversies, only accentuates them. The workers are not allowed to determine their demands and forms of struggle. Therefore, they discuss the directives once they have been issued by the union-headquarters. Many refuse to participate in such actions because they do not agree.[168]

Following Socialisme ou Barbarie's logic, Mothé interprets abstention as a gesture of univocal protest over how trade unions made decisions. The unions prevented workers from having any input in the formulation of demands and development of strategy on the grounds of efficiency. Mothé argues that this exclusion is irrational and made ordinary grievances the main topic of conversation between workers at the political expense of the organisations.

The naturally political workers were therefore excluded from meaningful participation in the formulation of union positions. Because union visions of production closely mirrored those of management, the perspective in terms of which demands were formulated did not mesh with that of the base. Workers did not recognise their grievances in the versions promulgated by the unions. So they tended to withdraw. Given the East-West overlay on factory politics, this left them no recourse but abstention. Abstention was therefore a political act that registered protest over the lack of substantive democracy in the factory.

For Mothé, as for Socialisme ou Barbarie in general, the demand for substantive democracy was at the heart of a revolutionary politics. The October 1957 pamphlet, 'Comment lutter?', that Socialisme ou Barbarie generated to publicise its positions and take advantage of its new-found visibility reiterated Mothé's reading of abstention as a political statement. This understanding enabled Socialisme ou Barbarie to argue that a new type of politics and

---

167 Mothé 1957b, p. 127.
168 Ibid.

organisation might be possible if the underlying problem of substantive democracy was addressed.[169]

A similar position informed Mothé's assessments of the failure of the April strikes over the lunch issue[170] and of a similar story that unfolded soon thereafter over the question of whether Billancourt workers should stage actions in support of a CGT-run transit strike.[171] The premise behind this position came from Socialisme ou Barbarie: confirmation came from Mothé's involvement in shop-level conversations. Echoing the notion of militant-worker dialogue formalised in 'Le probleme d'un journal ouvrier', Mothé combined these conversations with his understanding of their political significance in his idea for a new 'bulletin d'atelier'. This shop bulletin would operate like an anarchist *Tribune Ouvrière*: it would be a basis for new personal and political connections between AOC workers and, possibly, between the AOC and other Billancourt shops. Almost as soon as he floated the idea of the shop bulletin, Mothé began to wonder if there might not be something more profound than unhappiness with the unions behind the workers' withdrawal from politics. The question arose in the context of his efforts to organise an action in support of the April transit strike. When Mothé discussed the action with his fellow workers, he was struck by the fact that 'many had concrete suggestions about how to organise a strike'. On this basis, he began to convene a series of informal meetings to discuss not only the sympathy action, but the creation of a shop bulletin as an organising tool. One such meeting involved militants from the AOC cell of the PCF:

---

169 This line was repeated in the fall 1957 pamphlet 'Comment lutter?', which marked *Socialisme ou Barbarie*'s turn away from the tendency that developed amongst the group's theorists to treat French and Eastern European Stalinism as if they were somehow the same. This tendency was itself the result of the register of analysis in which Castoriadis worked after the Hungarian revolt. See, for example, 'Sur le contenu du socialisme' II and III. It is not as if Socialisme ou Barbarie were wrong about this: the group seems to have overestimated the relation of this alienation to a revolutionary politics. The CFDT would later occupy this same issue, framing it as a more limited problem of industrial democracy.

170 See my analysis of the meaning of abstentions at Billancourt, cribbed from Chapter 3 of Tiano 1955.

171 See Sigfried 1958, pp. 181–2, and the Socialisme ou Barbarie meeting of 18 April 1957 for accounts of brawls between the CRS and strikers on Boulevard St. Germain. Mothé notes a 'certain admiration for the strikers' discipline' at the AOC.

I lay out the idea to the cell, along with two Stalinist militants. They listen with heads bowed, and seem annoyed. They suspect a manoeuvre, of that there is no doubt.

'In your tract, you asked that unity be realised in each shop. The publication of the bulletin is a solution'.

'Yes, maybe'.

That is the only response. They have no opinions, and can have none before they speak with their boss.

They too made a distinction between the propaganda of tracts, the Party line and reality. They are the points of an imaginary triangle, but these points have no real link between them and that is why there is, in fact, no triangle.[172]

Here, the problem seems limited to PCF militants, for whom the 'imaginary triangle' that linked Party rhetoric and particular situations had been broken apart by Hungary and its fallout. The Party had adopted a purely defensive posture, afraid that any action would do it further damage. As a function of its top-down structure, ideological paralysis left PCF militants adrift, without guidance, unable to comment. However, these PCF militants were still workers – and their relation to Marxian discourse was not that which Socialisme ou Barbarie assumed was the underpinning of the working-class relation to politics. Adding to the problems created by the breakdown in the capacity of Marxist rhetoric to signify was the emergence of Algeria as a political issue that galvanised students and intellectuals, two of the social sectors most directly affected by the Hungarian Revolution as an ideological crisis.[173] This combination of factors signalled the beginning of a transfer of political energy away from traditional working-class politics in France. This transfer paved the way for the Fordist redefinition of the relation of the working class to the dominant socio-economic order through the instrument of mass consumption.

For Mothé, the problem he outlined with reference to the PCF was not limited to Party members. The draining of meaning from traditional political language also affected the opportunities created by the paralysis of the PCF-CGT.

---

172   Mothé 1957b, pp. 132–3.
173   The PCF's problems with the antiwar movement were echoed at Billancourt. In the 18 April 1957 meeting, Mothé reported to *Socialisme ou Barbarie*: 'Il semble que beaucoup d'ouvriers pensent que seules les minorités de gauche sont capable de faire quelque chose au sujet de l'Algérie'. Mothé goes on to stipulate: 'Ces "minorities": opposition de la CGT, trotskyistes, MLP, Nouvelle Gauche'. There was no question about the workers mobilising 'as workers' (*Socialisme ou Barbarie* meeting, 18 April 1957, p. 1).

As Mothé put it: 'Words themselves have lost their meaning'. Mothé blamed this on the PCF. Attacking the Party for its continual use of the term 'fascism' to characterise its enemies, Mothé directly addressed the reader: 'You who rest on your memories of the Occupation or who have crammed in a little history, do not be upset by these examples. Propaganda, better than academicians, has changed the vocabulary's meaning'.[174]

From Mothé's viewpoint, the lexical and conceptual stasis of dominant Marxism, its mythologised history glossed by a Marx and Lenin reduced to a series of (endlessly repeated) clichés, meant that its only dynamism came from workers through their investments in it. This same view underlay Socialisme ou Barbarie's revolutionary project.

The problem that emerged in the wake of the Hungarian Revolution was that the dominant usage of Marxist rhetoric suddenly acquired an enormous weight. The institution began to crack. It was as if, in a different context, philosophy suddenly became illegitimate. The patterns of appropriation and reappropriation of metaphors central to philosophising that Jacques Derrida discusses in his essay 'White Mythology', for example, presuppose that philosophy continues to function as a social institution.[175] Within a viable social institution, it is possible to engage with the tradition of philosophical argumentation, to interrogate its history and to reinvest its words as a function of the kind of conversation with tradition that Husserl described as fundamental to the experience of being within a socially instituted space.[176]

In Mothé's text, in contrast, the framework was coming apart that had enabled working people to engage with the Marxist Imaginary more broadly. The Imaginary no longer provided workers ways to comprehend their situation, reinvent themselves and imagine possible alternatives. Its language was no longer an 'inhabitable site': the language games that the working class had developed in the course of their history of interacting with the Imaginary were breaking down. This did not mean that the language disappeared, of course: it remained intact and continued to be generated. The draining of meaning, from the viewpoint of worker politics, transformed Marxian discourse into an exclusionary, formal language. It collapsed back onto the dominant version.

---

174 'Vous, qui êtes restés sur vos souvenirs d'occupation ou qui avez un peu potassé l'histoire, ne soyez pas emus par ces exemples. La propagande, mieux que les académiciens, a modifié la signification du vocabulaire' (Mothé 1957b, p. 133).

175 See Jacques Derrida, 'White Mythology: Metaphor in the Text of Philosophy' in Derrida 1982, pp. 207–71.

176 The description of a mode-of-being proper to socially instituted space is central to Husserl 1970.

During 1957, militants became more separated from their wider constituencies and began to emerge as a discrete social group. Their way of speaking and writing became the professional discourse of bureaucratised trade-union politics.[177]

Mothé's position as narrator registered the transformation of the political landscape at another level. In his 1957 articles, Mothé presented himself as isolated and plagued with self-doubt. The breakdown of efficacy of the language of Marxist politics that appeared to be underway in the factory left him divided between his ideas about mobilisation and the processes that shaped it on the one hand, and his doubts about whether these ideas could be translated into action at any level on the other. A good indication of the distance that separates this context from that of the spring of 1956 is the difference between the opening of the 'Journal d'un ouvrier', with its evocation of the 'surprising correspondence of writing, speech and reality', and this description of the AOC's reception of Mothé's idea for a shop bulletin:

> I had come with my proposal [for the bulletin d'atelier] a little like a merchant offering his wares at market. What had to be done was what the unions do not do: inform ourselves, express ourselves, try to create connections amongst ourselves. All this was very worthy, and I was approved of, but was I not, myself, a merchant like the others? Perhaps more clever than the others?[178]

This self-doubt and sense of isolation is new. Rather than portraying himself as fully integrated into shop-level politics or as its roving expression, Mothé now presents himself as hawking ideas about self-expression. Where previously Mothé had not questioned the political value of organisational tools like the shop bulletin, here he wonders if his merchandise might not be the same as or, in a sense, worse than what it may replace. The change is a reflection of the pervasive worker-alienation from politics. In such a climate, the shop journal could not be a tool that enabled workers to establish connections among themselves and perhaps build a new organisation. Instead, the journal would steal their speech by committing it to writing and, eventually, alienate them from it. Just as the relation of militant to the working-class constituency had quickly dissolved in the wake of the Hungarian Revolution, so the breakdown of the Marxist Imaginary at Billancourt tracked the boundary that separated the written culture of politics from the oral culture of the shop floor. This explains why the workers' suspicion of the political did not, apparently, extend

---

177   See Chapter 4 on Mothé 1965. See also Castoriadis 1988e [1958b].
178   Mothé 1957b, pp. 133–4.

to discussions between workers themselves about political and syndical questions. Mothé noted that his fellow workers continued to evaluate trade-union action with great lucidity. While he saw in this lucidity important implications for a future worker politics, the current situation was such that even a project as small as a shop bulletin was impossible.[179] Mothé could not, as he put it, 'substitute himself for the will of his comrades'.[180]

Mothé's hesitations reproduce the tension between Mothé, the Socialisme ou Barbarie militant, and Gautrat, the worker. Where Mothé, a proper name that designated a perspective on factory experience conditioned by *Socialisme ou Barbarie*, might argue for the broader political implications of shop-floor discussions, Gautrat, the name of the frequently isolated, slightly eccentric person actually involved in these discussions, might be far more pessimistic and more aware of the limitations this split of political and shop floor cultures placed on action. The crisis of the Marxist Imaginary that manifested itself in general through the problem of Marxist language and the dissolution of language games, manifested itself in these texts through the convergence of Mothé and Gautrat. Gautrat gave his experiences at Renault meaning by reworking them through the lens he named Mothé. Mothé, in turn, secured him access to culture and validation as an intellectual. One can read the pessimism and self-doubt in these Mothé texts not just as a reflection of anxiety about the viability of Socialisme ou Barbarie's revolutionary project in these conditions but as traces of Gautrat's anxiety about the longer-term viability of his intellectual *alter ego*. A lasting crisis of the Marxist Imaginary could mean that, just as the working class found itself atomised and increasingly turned to consumption as a palliative, so Gautrat would be left only with Gautrat.

Like Socialisme ou Barbarie in general, Gautrat/Mothé was committed, for personal and political reasons, to maintaining the integrity of the revolutionary project. The narrative I have traced in this section was not that emphasised in the journal, nor was it front and centre in Mothé's texts. Socialisme ou Barbarie emphasised Mothé's subdominant narrative that detailed forms of collective self-organisation in the professional lives of the AOC workers. In the

---

179 'C'est la probleme de la démocratie ouvrière et celui de toute la society qui est mise en cause. Le simple fait de vouloir s'exprimer implique aussitot une serie de consequences qui poussent automatiquement dans l'engrenage de la politique. Vouloir s'exprimer. c'est nier que les forces syndicales représentent cette expression' (Mothé 1957b, p. 134).

180 'Les idées de J., R., ou M., ou de 80% des ouvriers, sont de bon sens même. Mais les faire déborder le bon sense les limites de nos rapports personnels représente pour le moment un effort souvent trop grand. Impossible de me substituer à la volonté de mes camarades' (Mothé 1957b, p. 134).

context of Socialisme ou Barbarie's more abstract framework, the deterioration of the language games that enabled workers to conceive of political action could be explained as an intensification of a legitimation crisis. Like all other types of bourgeois social arrangements, this crisis would be swept away by revolution. Yet for Mothé/Gautrat, there were creeping doubts. By saying that he could not substitute himself for the will of his comrades, he indicated that, in the climate of 1957, it was impossible to imagine a revolutionary workers' movement that would obliterate the distinction between militant and worker. The status of the working class as the agent of revolutionary social change seemed to be in flux: Mothé's notion of himself as a revolutionary militant was in flux along with it.[181]

Subdominant Narrative: 'L'usine et la gestion ouvrière'

As if to make explicit the tensions in his position, Mothé's 'L'usine et la gestion ouvrière' was juxtaposed with 'Agitation chez Renault' in *Socialisme ou Barbarie* no. 22. 'L'usine et la gestion Ouvrière' is a close, sociologically informed description of the professional lives of AOC workers and their modalities of informal self organisation. While Mothé considers these modalities from several angles, the primary focus is on the collective distribution of skill and its role in shaping resistance to Fordist rationalisation. It is also, even more than Romano's 'The American Worker', the paradigmatic example of 'worker writing' of the type that Socialisme ou Barbarie had hoped to elicit. Mothé's use of an embedded first-person narrator, and his descriptions of social networks at the point of production, made 'L'usine et la gestion ouvrière' a model of the kind of text Lefort had theorised in his 1952 essay, 'L'expérience proletarienne', as central for a definition of revolutionary theory around 'the proletarian standpoint'.[182] It is a fundamental *Socialisme ou Barbarie* text. It is situated at the intersection of the worker narratives, the newspaper project and the theoretical work Castoriadis began to develop after the Hungarian Revolution. It can be read against Mothé's dominant narrative as an attempt to get around the anxiety produced by the crisis of the Marxist Imaginary by emphasising Socialisme ou Barbarie's productivist notion of revolutionary politics. This section will provide an overview of Mothé's essay, which was fundamental to the

---

[181] Eventually, Mothé/Gautrat worked out a way to retain his commitment to industrial democracy outside a revolutionary framework by advocating more limited forms of self-management [*autogestion*] in the context of the CFDT.
[182] See Chapter 3, above.

most fully developed version of Socialisme ou Barbarie's revolutionary project in its Marxist phase. This overview will tie together many of the themes I have developed in this project.

The text does not innovate so much in what it describes as in how it does so. It avoids the 'workers feel x' propositional form Romano used to intertwine the specificity of his experience and the universal character of class experience.[183] Mothé substituted for Romano's propositional form a collective first-person narrator that associates the reader, Mothé and the AOC workers. Rather than trying to address the problem of generalisability at the level of sentence structure and repetition, Mothé thematises it in his opening lines:

> It is difficult to have an overview of the ensemble of things in our society: it is even more difficult for a worker, for whom the organisation of the world remains hidden like a mysterious thing obeying magical laws unknown to him. The worker perceives things in his very narrow purview: he has to fight to see further. Our horizon finds itself limited to the parcel of work that is demanded of and imposed upon us. Beyond that, we no longer know what there is. We no longer know what becomes of our work. It is launched out into the organisational machinery: we made it, but we do not see it again, unless chance causes us to run across it. More often than not, it would surprise, astonish or disappoint us to find that what we made goes into something completely useless. We must know nothing: the organisation of the world seems to be the organisation of our ignorance.[184]

Mothé's status as a worker, by definition, excludes him from access to general knowledge: he only has access to a fragment of the world shaped by the alienation specific to Fordism. Management claims general knowledge. For example, management sees the factory as a whole through the lens of its production design. Fordist production design embodies a series of necessarily political assumptions about the nature of work: that technology defines the essence of production; that work is an abstraction; that workers can be thought of as individuated bearers of quanta of energy. Fordist production design is the expression of bourgeois thought in general: its logical extension is automated production. Recapitulating Socialisme ou Barbarie's notion of the fundamental contradiction of bureaucratic capitalism, Mothé argued that this vision of

---

[183] Pierre Blachier's article on *le débrouillage*, *Tribune Ouvrière*'s closest approximation to this article, also employed this propositional form throughout.

[184] Mothé 1957a, p. 75.

the factory obscured the elements central to actual production. In particular, Fordism could not acknowledge the role played by worker collectives in everyday production. For Socialisme ou Barbarie, this meant that Fordism could not apprehend the 'reality' of production. This reality was knowable only by and through the working-class 'cogs in the wheel'.[185]

These worker collectives were under constant pressure: the perspectives available to any given worker were necessarily shaped by this pressure; workers' knowledge was, therefore, partial, local and particular. The partial becomes a marker of the writer's worker status:

> This article was simply made by a worker. That is why it only gives a partial view and it is for this reason that it does not pretend to respond to all the problems of factory organisation, but only to those that affect the sector of certain skilled workers: the machinists.[186]

This is false modesty. Skilled metalworkers were the traditional signified for discussions of the working class on the French left. Reference was routinely made to the working class as a whole by way of machinists. Further, the article is situated by the coordinates of Socialisme ou Barbarie's theoretical project. The idea of the proletarian viewpoint was to serve as the centrepiece for a counter-imaginary, opposed to the Fordist regimes of capital accumulation and social regulation that clarified and empowered the collective activity of workers at the point of production. This project presupposed, like all Marxist projects, that particular experiences at the point of production could be universalised because the capitalist system that structured that experience was itself universal. These assumptions were axiomatic for Socialisme ou Barbarie at that time. The publication of this account in the journal relieved Mothé of having to demonstrate all his assumptions.

---

[185] This argument about production design is a transposition of Socialisme ou Babrarie's critiques of the plan and of bureaucracy generally. It is not a coincidence that Mothé uses this formulation at the same moment when Castoriadis was using it as well to explain how the relations of production could become generalised to an entire society. This generalisation of industrial relations had been a central element in Lefort's definition of totalitarian regimes in his 'Le totalitarisme sans Staline – L'URSS dans une nouvelle phase' in *Socialisme ou Barbarie* no. 19, pp. 1–72, and was used extensively in Castoriadis's essays on Hungary and Poland. See in particular his 'La voie polonaise de la bureaucratisation' in *Socialisme ou Barbarie* no. 21, pp. 59–76, using the critique of the plan against Sartre and other '*progressistes*' who argued that Poland, not Hungary, was the 'real' revolutionary response to the Twentieth Party-Congress.

[186] Mothé 1957a, p. 78.

One important point of analysing professional comportment was to find modes of everyday self-organisation that could be logically connected to the forms of political self-organisation that Socialisme ou Barbarie saw as autonomous. As Castoriadis argued in 'Sur le contenu du socialisme (I)', if revolution necessarily entailed a 'radical expansion of bourgeois rationality', then imagining it posed a fundamental challenge to thought conditioned by that same bourgeois rationality. Revolutionary theory needed to focus on the source of political acts with revolutionary potential – the working class – to get an idea of what this 'radically expanded' rationality might look like. This new rationality would be expressed in and through modes of self-organisation that originated, Castoriadis argued, in everyday patterns of informal self-organisation by workers at the point of production.

In this text, Mothé emphasises the centrality of skill in the self-organisation of the AOC workers. Each group of workers is made up of individuals who possess different knowledges or abilities. Professional integration is as much about the shop getting to know a new worker's particular configuration of knowledge, abilities and limitations as it is about the new worker getting to know the shop. Implicit in this integration process is a broader and continuous worker self-surveillance. By means of this self-monitoring, workers in a shop develop a sense of the overall distribution of skill. This changes skill from an individual into a collective attribute.

The social mechanisms that shaped the use of skill – that enabled a collective to figure and refigure itself in order to cope with problems as they arose in production – were the centre of the broader social hierarchies that informally regulated professional life. Mothé argues that these same processes were fundamental in the socialisation and training of workers. These patterns of socialisation, organisation and regulation also shaped relations between workers more broadly, and amongst workers and management.[187]

To illustrate this point, Mothé reworked the notion of *débrouillage* developed in Blachier's piece in *Tribune Ouvrière* to make improvisation collective:

> This improvising [the collective type] has nothing to do with individual improvisation [like that described in Blachier's *Tribune Ouvrière* article]. The worker can only learn his trade or exercise his trade because he lives in a collectivity, because his comrades teach him and communicate to

---

187 This same mechanism of skill-deployment is also at the core of the regulation of relations both amongst workers and between the worker-collective and management. See, for example, the description of how 'un fayot, un ouvrier qui respecte trop la discipline de l'usine' soon finds himself isolated and facing hostility (Mothé 1957a, p. 81).

him their experience and their technique. Without this support of other workers, the irrationality of [management's] utilisation of manual labour would engender catastrophes in production. In a word, if the workers did not manage to assume, in addition to their jobs, the roles of monitors in an apprenticeship school for which they are not paid, it would be impossible for management to get such mobility and adaptability from the workers.[188]

The refiguring of skill as a social attribute is accomplished by the networks that order a given shop. These networks enable production to happen and workers to limit the impact of Fordist-style alienation. They were also the centre of Socialisme ou Barbarie's vision of the revolutionary proletariat, as they structured worker resistance and their capacity to control production.

Mothé's description of the AOC refers back to Romano in its aims and focus, and to Socialisme ou Barbarie's notion of the central contradiction of bureaucratic capitalism for its political content. In this vision of class conflict, the factory is divided in two. On the one side, there is Fordist technology and production design, built around the Taylorist assumption that each task can and should be executed in 'one best way'. Assembly-line production and the radical division of intellectual labour expressed in it operated in a shifting reality according to rigidly conceived, endlessly repeated schemata. The assumption of the 'one best way' – and the transfer of creativity in production from workers to managers and engineers – eliminates feedback loops and thereby renders production design increasingly vulnerable to entropy. Opposed to this organisation of production, Socialisme ou Barbarie argued, were workers and their ways of viewing, thinking about and organising production.

Socialisme ou Barbarie's theoretical descriptions of the place of these worker collectives in the factory and their implications are fastened to the factory floor and made tangible in Mothé's descriptions of the conflicts that pit semi-skilled workers and their desire to retain a collective mode of working against the Fordist rationalisation, individuation and deskilling of work.[189]

Mothé's AOC is an allegory for the larger conflicts characteristic of Fordist (or bureaucratic-capitalist) industry. He provides detailed descriptions of the processes of confrontation and negotiation that opposed the AOC workers to various representatives of factory administration – managers, foremen, '*chronos*' and security agents. A parallel register of contestation and negotiation pit the workers against trade-union representatives. Taken together, these particular

---

188 Ibid.
189 These broader theoretical conclusions are drawn in Castoriadis 1988e.

forms of conflict are elevated to the status of conflicts between workers and Fordism in general. Mothé's text moves the reader from a close description of specific issues, through a sequence of overlays informed by Socialisme ou Barbarie's notion of the proletarian standpoint, to the domain of industrial conflict in general.

This last level is presented indirectly in Mothé's texts: to make general theoretical statements directly would have contradicted the opening paragraphs and their characterisation of the workers' apprehension of the world as partial. The theoretical arguments are made in Castoriadis's seminal 1957 essay, 'Sur le contenu du socialisme III', which followed Mothé's text in *Socialisme ou Barbarie* no. 22. Castoriadis fits Mothé's arguments into a broader framework as integral to a summation of Socialisme ou Barbarie's vision of the factory. Reworking Socialisme ou Barbarie's notion of the fundamental contradiction of bureaucratic capitalism, Castoriadis argues that the conflicts Mothé describes are local expressions of the ontological divide that defines bureaucratic-capitalist production. This divide is conditioned by the coexistence of two fundamentally opposed modes of being-in-the-world. Management views production in terms of production design and the assumptions that shape it. Management literally cannot see worker collectives, or recognise what they do. Following Marx, and virtually the entire counter-tradition in Western philosophy as well, Castoriadis argues that the assumptions that shape Fordist production design are direct expressions of the broadest bourgeois assumptions about the relation of reason to the temporal flux. Worker collectives oppose this rationality. Shaped by confrontation with this bourgeois rationality and excluded from it, worker collectives are organised around process rather than around concepts, the collective rather than the individual. For Castoriadis and Mothé, the gap is unbridgeable that separates the managerial view of production, rooted in the politics of Fordism, and that of the workers. Production is therefore the site of continual conflict between incommensurate social imaginaries. This conflict explains why Fordist industry produces irrationality as it produces commodities. It responds to the former with continual, gradually escalating repression. Worker collectives respond by fashioning ways to both accommodate and resist this repression. Bureaucratic capitalism is civil war, stabilised by violence.[190]

For Castoriadis, as for Socialisme ou Barbarie in general, revolutionary potentials were created in the course of these shop-floor level conflicts through

---

190 This paragraph is drawn almost entirely from Mothé 1957a, pp. 81–97 reworked in Castoriadis, 'Sur le contenu du socialisme III'. Civil war and/or dual power was central to Trotsky's definition of the revolutionary situation.

strategies of resistance and self-organisation. The patterns of resistance shaped the political possibilities that surfaced in autonomous worker actions; the patterns of accommodation shaped the capacities of workers to assume direct control over production. The implications of the former emerged through strikes. The implications of the latter would only fully emerge in the context of direct-democratic socialism. Socialisme ou Barbarie's vision of socialism was, in these senses, the generalisation of the group's understanding of relations between workers at the point of production as they are elaborated in the informal social spaces that Mothé described.

This project has argued that Socialisme ou Barbarie's schema for proletarian revolution was rooted in a descriptive theory that took already-mobilised workers in situations like Berlin 1953, or Hungary 1956, as the starting point for thinking. Revolutionary theory tried to analyse, explain and radicalise the modes of self-organisation and patterns of demands developed by these worker actions. Analysis consisted largely in linking these aspects of autonomous worker action back to shop-floor conflicts. Both the choice of important questions from the actions and the search for the processes that gave rise to them in production were shaped by Socialisme ou Barbarie's vision of revolution and of socialism, which they imagined by extending these processes forward in time.

'L'usine et la gestion ouvrière' fits perfectly into this productivist notion of revolutionary class struggle. The group's emphasis on actual material production as the site wherein connections between various types of conflict and revolutionary possibilities are articulated, relegated the political proper – the Marxist Imaginary and the ways collectives gained access to and appropriated it – to the status of natural horizon. This imaginary was the assumed medium across which developed Socialisme ou Barbarie's 'dialogue' with the 'worker avant-garde'. Mothé's 'dominant narrative' raises problems for this productivism in its description of emergent cracks in the AOC workers' relation to the Marxist Imaginary. These cracks comprised the leading edge of a crisis of the Imaginary that manifested itself through the evaporation of language games and the reduction of the Marxist rhetoric of class struggle to the bureaucratic discourse of professional activists.

Socialisme ou Barbarie encountered a parallel problem in the failure of its worker-newspaper project. This project showed that, because of its timing, the failure of the worker newspaper did not so much pose a threat to the integrity of Socialisme ou Barbarie's notion of proletarian revolution as it raised questions about the nature of Socialisme ou Barbarie's descriptive theory of class conflict. The group's revolutionary theory was curiously directional: the links between its object – the working class, expanded into the bearer of revolutionary potential – and the horizon of political action appeared to be seamless from a vantage point shaped by that theory. The worker-newspaper project revealed the non-reversibility of the object-horizon relation. When Socialisme ou Barbarie tried to act in a proactive manner to politicise everyday conflicts in the factory, its descriptive theory became irrelevant and its efforts were drowned out by a political context very different from that in which the group operated.

Both *Tribune Ouvrière* and its American prototype, *Correspondence*, encountered this same basic problem. The advantage Socialisme ou Barbarie had over *Correspondence* was that the former never controlled *Tribune Ouvrière* and could not substitute its own desires for contact with the workers for the reality of such contact. However, because nothing about it raised questions about the nature of the Marxist Imaginary and the relation of workers to it, the failure of *Tribune Ouvrière* to develop into a worker newspaper could be explained in terms already available to Socialisme ou Barbarie's revolutionary theory. The group most often referred to factional fighting to explain it.

Mothé's dominant narrative introduced problems of a different order into the heart of Socialisme ou Barbarie's revolutionary project by raising questions about the social function played by the Marxist Imaginary itself in the period following the Hungarian Revolution. It is ironic that Mothé, the writer who embodied the contradictions of Socialisme ou Barbarie's relationship with the working class, would provide the group with both its closest description of how informal worker collectives operated at the point of production and an outline of a crisis of the Marxist Imaginary that threatened to undermine the revolutionary significance of these same collectives, not to mention Socialisme ou Barbarie's entire revolutionary project.

In 1959–60, Castoriadis wrote 'Modern Capitalism and Revolution', a text that signalled Socialisme ou Barbarie's first major break with the proletarian element of its revolutionary project. It was written in the wake of the failure of the working class to oppose the Fifth Republic in 1958 and after de Gaulle instituted reforms that integrated France into the transnational Fordist political order. In it, Castoriadis begins to address the implications of what emerged in an unthematised way through Mothé's dominant narrative. Castoriadis argues that Gaullist reforms eliminated the structural contradictions that had previously given local working-class actions their explosive potential.[191]

191　The reforms included the integration of France into the European Community through currency-convertablity and changed trade laws. This integrated France into the American-sponsored system that assured national stability at the economic and military levels. De Gaulle also began the administrative separation of France from its empire and shifted Algeria from a French department to a colonial holding.

Both politically and at the level of production, Fordism had triumphed. Castoriadis thematised this triumph as the result of a 'destruction of significations' visited upon the working class. By 'significations', Castoriadis referred to the forms of sociability and self-organisation that had been central to the group's understanding of informal worker collectives, as well as how they operated. Castoriadis argued that these networks had suddenly collapsed. With the collapse of these networks, the ability of workers to appropriate the language of class struggle, to act autonomously, and to carry the 'germ' of revolution went as well. This position is a productivist spin on the problem Mothé raises in his dominant narrative. It enabled Socialisme ou Barbarie to rethink its revolutionary project, while allowing the group to continue as if it was still Marxist in a substantive way. The key move here was Castoriadis's contention that the contradictions that had structured working-class experience at the point of production had been generalised to all of society. Where previously Socialisme ou Barbarie had been trying to analyse and work to empower a proletarian revolution, it now faced a version of total social crisis. The notion of total social crisis served two main functions: it enabled the group to argue that politically meaningful conflicts could originate from any number of social sectors. It also enabled the group to retain a Marxist frame of reference for thinking about these conflicts.

It was not until Castoriadis's 1964–6 essay, 'Marxism and Revolutionary Theory', that Socialisme ou Barbarie began to address the problem of Marxist language directly and to thematise the crisis of the Marxist Imaginary that Mothé could only describe in 1957. This move provoked a split within Socialisme ou Barbarie amongst those militants who had previously agreed with the arguments advanced in 'Modern Capitalism and Revolution'. The difference in reaction can be attributed to the later essay's assault on the Marxist Imaginary, which continued to operate for intellectuals and students as the legitimating framework of imagining dissent, the relation of politics to dissent, social roles for dissidents and a rhetoric for articulating dissent. A direct challenge to the Imaginary was profoundly disorienting for revolutionary militants, who had constructed their identities and notions of what it meant to be political through these categories/ significations. The issues at stake in 1964–5 are already implicitly raised in Mothé's dominant narrative. What is Marxism? How should one think about it in relation to the dominant social order? How does one think about a crisis of the Imaginary that enables one to imagine social critique itself? How do these questions bear upon the idea of dissent today?

Postface

> One thinks that one is tracing the outline of a thing's nature over and over again, and one is merely tracing the frame through which we look at it.[1]

These days I live next to a salt marsh. The months I spent reworking this book was time spent with a ghost of myself.

I made this project in the early 1990s. The underlying idea was to use Castoriadis's notion of the social imaginary to understand something about Socialisme ou Barbarie. It was less about continuities between the phases of his work than testing out the framework with an object of analysis that seemed uniquely suited to it. I was confused by the generality with which Castoriadis often used the category of social-imaginary significations in the seminars I attended at *L'Ecole des Hautes Etudes en Sciences Sociales*. I wondered if they could be used in more analytically specific ways. For this project, that raised a pragmatic problem: how to introduce both a body of material and a conceptual framework that remained at the time largely unknown to an English-speaking audience, and have space to do either well. The solution I arrived at was to use sparingly the categories I borrowed from Castoriadis's later work to illuminate the material.

I conceived of this book as an aspect of a larger project. There were two subsequent moves. One would continue the history of the group through its dissolution. It was to begin with the group's responses to de-Stalinisation, Poland and Hungary. The beginning of the second would overlap with the end of the first. The second project would explore the notion of the Marxist Imaginary and the long-term processes whereby it imploded. I thought accounting for them would be a collaborative undertaking that would produce a collection of fragments or partial views of the ways in which ideologies die.

I held these projects together in my mind like the impossible book in Borges's *Garden of Forking Paths*, an ideal assemblage that could be read in various orders. Each sequence would be a different logical extension of this book. Most would refer Socialisme ou Barbarie to contexts beyond itself. All but one would avoid containing the group's development in a self-referential narrative that reduces its interaction with the world to elements in a puzzle arranged in different ways over time. I juxtaposed with the philosophical elements entailed by the notion of the social imaginary the work I have since done in experimental music and fiction. Thinking this way made of much of

---

1 Wittgenstein 1997 [1953], p. 48e.

what I have been doing aspects of a single overarching project. But with this book, the situation changes.

> ... and she tried to imagine what the flame of a candle looks like after the candle is blown out, for she could not remember ever having seen such a thing.

This book ends with the demise of the canary in a mineshaft. The understanding of this demise seemed a way to begin the exploration of the broader question of how social-imaginary formations work in the world and not simply as philosophical constructions. The project also seemed to me a way to situate the Marxist Imaginary in the past. The idea was to shift the relations to the Marxian framework to something on the order of closure, a process of sounding out categories with the idea of moving beyond them. For the moment, I restrict myself to some observations based on what is in the actually existing last chapter.

The crisis of the Marxist Imaginary was driven by the collective withdrawal of affective investments in the significations that comprised it. Mothé's texts capture something of this in the breakdown of workers' capacity to reappropriate Marxian discourse. Framed by these texts, the breakdown refers in two directions: to the specific feedback loop instituted at Billancourt and to the general narrative Socialisme ou Barbarie brought to it. The last chapter described what happened at Billancourt as a collapse of language games in order to designate the disappearance of the relation to the discourse of revolution and the capacity of autonomous mobilisations to transform the space of production into that of politics predicated on its appropriation. This seems more an effect than a cause. The cause itself is absent.

It is not difficult to assemble a chain of preconditions: the weight of Stalinism in a context dominated by the PCF and the destabilising consequences of the Twentieth Party-Congress in the USSR; the effects of trade-union pluralism in reducing the language of revolutionary Marxism to the professional discourse of the PCF-CGT system, which acted like social-democratic organisations that talked about themselves in revolutionary terms; the comportments of CGT militants and their opposition to any actions not controlled by the union. The Hungarian Revolution presented images of a worker revolution being crushed in the name of worker revolution. But it was the sudden collapse of the political and media spaces occupied by the PCF and descent of the PCF-CGT into paralysis that appear to have disrupted the routines that framed the dissonances indicated above in a socially acceptable manner. That disruption brought the dissonance to a critical point.

To venture a general statement: ideological crisis follows from internal dissonances, ideological and/or material, in response to a disruption of the patterns of practical engagement that enframe them. They do not originate from the outside; they do not come about as a function of critique. Ideologies destroy themselves from the inside. In this case, the disruption of patterns revealed the extent to which the language of revolution appropriated by autonomous mobilisations leaned on that of the PCF-CGT system. From a viewpoint informed by Socialisme ou Barbarie, this would appear contradictory – in part because of the way the group framed Stalinism. But from a wider viewpoint, this language was operative because of myriad investments across the whole of the social machinery at Billancourt. Most of the forms of interaction bore no resemblance to those of Socialisme ou Barbarie (among ordinary PCF or CGT members, for example). It follows from this that while particular social-imaginary formations are not entirely separable from broader patterns of usage and/or language, they are local phenomena.

In the last chapter, I presented the crisis as if it followed from the images of the Hungarian Revolution. But that presupposed an understanding of the Hungarian Revolution close to Socialisme ou Barbarie's, which was alone on the French left in offering a revolutionary interpretation of these events. There is no evidence that this interpretation circulated at Billancourt. I also reproduced the position of Mothé's narratives in the context of the group's project through the positing of a unitary crisis of the Marxist Imaginary. But it is more likely that these narratives show an early moment in a diffuse series of particular breakdowns unfolding in a non-linear manner that, cumulatively, undermined the Marxist Imaginary itself.

In 1957, not even Socialisme ou Barbarie was looking at what was captured in Mothé's texts. The internal life of the group across 1957–8 was occupied with the same kind of concerns and activities as had occupied them previously. The group spent many meetings during 1957 trying to reorganise itself in order to respond to its increased visibility. According to a report delivered on 16 January 1958, the journal was sold in four Parisian bookstores. The sales had slowly increased: no. 18 sold 337 copies; no. 19 338. No. 20, which centered on Hungary, sold 453 copies; no. 21 644. The group sold around 75 copies per issue. Exact subscription numbers were not given. Each issue was printed in runs of 3000 at a Rouen shop. Increased visibility required quicker and more consistent fabrication of each issue and an expansion of the network of sellers. This strained both financial resources and organisation. The group considered brochures as an interim step. But they too had to be written and edited. The debates about reorganisation raised underlying tensions within the group that began to fray relations amongst the members.

At the same time, the group continued to track developments in Eastern Europe and to watch for echoes of these events in the West. They worried about their collective lack of contact with the working class. Castoriadis characterised this as an ongoing problem that was 'in no way mitigated by the fact that every so often Mothé writes an article for the journal'. Discussions resurfaced about launching a worker newspaper. It came to nothing: the group already felt its resources stretched. There was a sense of new opportunities with *Tribune Ouvrière* because of turnover in the collective that created it. But the understanding of the project had changed: it was now seen as a form of activity for the collective that produced it. Any sense of connection to the broader population at Billancourt had been broken. Mothé reported again and again that the workers there felt crushed and unable to mobilise. Bourgeois ideology was leaking in through the gaps created by the crisis of the PCF-CGT system.

The PCF continued to drift. At the same time, the political environment within which the group operated was being reconfigured by the mobilisation against the Algerian War. The group's relationship to the *tiers-mondiste* displacement of the working class onto the colonised was too complex to summarise here. There was a debate about an article by C.L.R. James on Nkrumah and Ghana that would have been published in the journal that entailed consideration of contacting the group that produced *Presence Africaine*. But the consensus was that they would not be interested. As the opposition to the Algerian War intensified, Lyotard became the central figure to articulate a position critical of the FLN and the French colonial order at the same time. By early 1958, members of Socialisme ou Barbarie were noting a mounting crisis triggered by events in Algeria that was unfolding before an entirely indifferent general population. The crisis of May 1958 issued onto de Gaulle's constitutional referendum in September. This received significant working-class support. With the modifications to the structure of the French system de Gaulle instituted soon thereafter, Castoriadis began to argue that something basic had changed – something that affected the basis of the group's revolutionary project.

Perhaps in the shorter run, nobody was looking because nothing appeared to change. The language and imagery associated with revolution and Marxism continued to be produced by the same media environments in the same ways as before. Quite apart from the obvious ideological motivations that might explain this, it is difficult for a top-down, representation-based media environment to register changes in relations to the representations it circulates. The frame of the apparatus, the position as auditor/spectator/reader being told about events in crisis by a voice that is not in crisis is one that, rather like the unnamed narrator particular to academic writing, knits anything and everything back into a version of the same.

Or perhaps it followed from a more general problem. We orient ourselves with respect to the world using various frames of reference (or, in a different vocabulary, particular social-imaginary significations and the associations they enable). In the instituting of everyday experience, these frames are, for the most part, transparent. They operate as an aspect of the process of reducing complexity. At the cognitive level, we manage complexity by creating forms. As is the case with any type of focus, the creation of form is a limitation of information. To the extent that the reduction of complexity is a mode of ongoing adaptation, we are information-limiting machines. In this lies our capacity to adapt continuously to shifting environments. If this sketch of the process of subjective orientation is at all accurate, then it follows that it would be difficult for anyone to know whether there was a fundamental problem with one or more of these socially instituted frameworks on which they rely.

Piera Aulagnier characterised investment in forms of radical opposition to the existing order as the rationalisation of alienation. It enables a sense of distance from a present in which one has an ambiguous sense of place. This ambiguity is attributed to a social order that is framed as irrational on any number of grounds. One transfers one's hopes for oneself, which find no coherent outlet in the present, to an alternate order that may be instituted in the future in which, presumably, one would find a less ambiguous sense of place. A break in one's investments in such a viewpoint, or the undermining of what enabled its elaboration, would result in a collapse of that sense of distance from the present. By 1960, one can find a reflection of this in Touraine's embourgeoisement thesis, or in attempts at displacement such as Mallet's new working class, or the transposing of the revolutionary proletariat onto the colonised.

The withdrawal of collective investment in a social-imaginary formation does not make any sound. It need not produce independent events. It is something that is recognised after the fact, through a sense of the consequences. Among members of Socialisme ou Barbarie, the recurrent story involved a retrospective moment of recognition that something had happened. These stories often unfolded years later. They differ from the narrative of loss of faith. Daniel Blanchard moved into poetry as a way of trying to write his way through a sense of being traumatised. Véga told of a realisation that accompanied the 1982 strikes in support of the early Solidarity-movement in Poland. Castoriadis was remarkable in the directness with which he worked his way along personal and philosophical trajectories in the moves into philosophy and psychoanalysis. Each maintained in their way a sense of connection to the possibility of political work. But at some point, each realised that the world they inhabited had already disappeared.

Bibliography

Alexander, Robert 1991, *International Trotskyism 1929–1985: A Documentary History* Durham: Duke UP.

Aglietta, Michel 1987, *A Theory of Capitalist Regulation*, London: Verso.

Albert, Eric 1952, 'La vie dans une usine', *Les Temps Modernes*, 81: 95–130.

Arvidsson, Karl-Anders 1988, *Henry Poulaille et la littérature prolétarienne française des années 1930*, Gothenburg: Actas Univeristatis Gothenburgennis.

Aulagnier, Piera, 1975, *La violence de l'interprétation*, Paris: PUF.

Austen, John Langshaw 1975, *How to Do Things with Words*, Cambridge, MA: Harvard University Press.

Badie, Bertrand 1976, *Strategie de la grève: pour une approche functionaliste du Parti Communiste Français*, Paris: Presse de la Fondation Rationale des Sciences Politiques.

Barbichon, Jacques 1956, 'La vie parallèle dans l'entreprise', *Esprit*, 235: 192–206.

Bardou, Jean-Pierre, Jean-Jacques Chanaron, Patrick Fridenson, James M. Laux, 1982, *The Automobile Revolution*, Chapel Hill: UNC Press.

Barthes, Roland 1968, 'L'effet du réel', *Communications*, 11:11.

―― 1975, *Pleasure of the Text*, edited and translated by Richard Howard, New York: Hill and Wang.

―― 1981, 'The Discourse of History', translated by Stephen Bann, *Comparative Criticism*, 3: 7–20.

―― 1987, *Michelet*, edited and translated by Richard Howard, New York: Hill and Wang.

―― 1988, *Mythologies* edited and translated by Richard Howard, New York: Noonday.

Baudelot, Christian and Roger Establet 1971, *L'école capitaliste en France*, Paris: Maspero.

Bauman, Zygmunt 2000, *Modernity and the Holocaust*, Ithaca, NY: Cornell.

Bell, Hugo 1950, 'Le Stalinisme en Allemagne Orientale', *Socialisme ou Barbarie*, 7: 1–45.

―― 1951, 'Le Stalinisme en Allemagne Orientale (2)', *Socialisme ou Barbarie*, 8: 31–49.

―― 1953 'Review of I. Deutscher *Les Syndicats Soviétiques*', *Socialisme ou Barbarie*, 12: 60–2.

―― 1954, 'Le prolétariat d'Allemagne orientale après la révolte de juin 1953', *Socialisme ou Barbarie*, 13: 10–12.

Bernard, Jean-Pierre A. 1991, *Paris Rouge; les communistes français dans la capitale: 1944–1964*, Paris: Champ Vallon.

Bettelheim, Charles 1945, *La planification soviétique*, Paris: Rivière.

Boggs, Grace 1972 [1947], 'The Reconstruction of Society', published along with Paul Romano's 'The American Worker', Detroit: Bewick.

Boltanski, Luc 1982, *Les cadres: formation d'un groupe social*, Paris: Minuit.

Borges, Jorge Luis 1999, 'The Garden of Forking Paths' in *Collected Fictions* New York: Penguin.

Borhan, Pierre and Patrick Rogiers 1991, *René-Jacques*, Paris: Editions Manufacture.

Boschetti, Anna 1988, *The Intellectual Enterprise: Sartre and 'Les Temps Modernes'*, translated by Richard C. McCleary, Evanston: Northwestern.

Bourdet, Yvon 1963, *Communisme et marxisme*, Paris: Editions Michel Briant.

Bourdieu, Pierre 1977, *Outline of a Theory of Practice*, translated by Richard Nice Cambridge: Cambridge University Press.

——— 1980a, 'The Production of Belief: A Contribution to an Economy of Symbolic Goods', *Media Culture and Society*, 2, 3: 261–93.

——— 1980b, 'Le mort saisit le vif: Les relations entre l'histoire incorporée et l'histoire reifiée', *Actes de la recherche en sciences sociales*, 32–3: 3–14.

——— 1980c, 'L'identité et la représentation: éléments pour une reflexion critique sur l'idée de region', *Actes de la recherche en sciences sociales*, 35: 63–72.

——— 1981, 'La représentation politique: éléments pour une théorie du champs politique', *Actes de la recherche en sciences sociales*, 37: 3–24.

——— 1984, *Distinction*, translated by Richard Nice, Cambridge: Harvard.

——— 1989, 'Flaubert's Point of View' in Dean, Ferguson and Griswold (eds.) 1989.

——— 1991 [1982], *Language and Symbolic Power* [*Ce que parler veut dire: l'économie des échanges linguistiques*], edited by John B. Thompson, translated by Gino Raymond and Matthew Adamson, Cambridge MA: Harvard University Press.

——— (ed.) 1994, *La misère du monde*, Paris: Seuil.

Bourt, Raymond 1950, 'Luttes revendicatives en France', *Socialisme ou Barbarie*, 5/6: 148–50.

Brandt, Stefan 1955, *The East German Rising*, London: Thames and Hudson.

Broué, Pierre and Nicole Dorey 1966, 'Critiques de gauche du Front Populaire', *Le movement sociale*, 54: 91–133.

Busino, Giovanni (ed.) 1989, *Autonomic et l'autotransformation de la societe: La philosophie militante de Cornelius Castoriadis*, Paris/Geneva: Droz.

Buton, Philippe 1985, 'Les effectifs du Parti Communiste Français (1920–1984)', *Communisme*, 7: 5–30.

Carrol, Lewis 2003, *Alice's Adventures in Wonderland*, Adelaide: University of Adelaide.

Canetti, Elias 1979, *Crowds and Power*, New York: Seabury.

Castillo, Greg 2001, 'Building Culture in a Divided Berlin: Globalization and the Cold War', in Nezar el Sayyad (ed.) 2001.

——— 2005, 'Blueprint for a Cultural Revolution: Hermann Henselmann and the Architecture of German Socialist Realism', *Slavonica*, 11, 1: 31–51.

Castoriadis, Cornelius 1949, 'La consolidation temporaire du capitalisme mondial', *Socialisme ou Barbarie*, 3: 22–67.

——— 1953, 'Sur la dynamique du capitalisme (I)', *Socialisme ou Barbarie*, 12: 1–22.

―― 1953a, 'Sartre, le stalinisme et les ouvriers', *Socialisme ou Barbarie*, 12: 63–88.

―― 1954, 'Sur la dynamique du capitalisme (II)', *Socialisme ou Barbarie*, 13: 60–81.

―― 1954a, 'Situation de l'impérialisme et perspectives du prolétariat', *Socialisme ou Barbarie*, 14: 1–26.

―― 1955, 'Sur le contenu du socialisme (I)', *Socialisme ou Barbarie* 17: 1–25.

―― 1973, 'Postface aux Relations de production en Russie', *La Societe Bureaucratique*, Paris: 10/18.

―― 1974, *L'experience du mouvement ouvrier 1: Comment lutter*, Paris: 10/18.

―― 1988a [1949a], 'Socialisme ou Barbarie', in *Political and Social Writings*, Vol 1, edited and translated by David Ames Curtis, Minneapolis: Minnesota.

―― 1988b [1949b], 'On the Relations of Production in Russia', in *Political and Social Writings*, Vol 1, edited and translated by David Ames Curtis. Minneapolis: Minnesota.

―― 1988c [1955], 'On the Content of Socialism I', in *Political and Social Writings*, Vol 1, edited and translated by David Ames Curtis. Minneapolis: Minnesota.

―― 1988d [1957a], 'On the Content of Socialism II' in *Political and Social Writings*, Vol 1, edited and translated by David Ames Curtis. Minneapolis: Minnesota.

―― 1988e [1957b], 'On the Content of Socialism III: Worker's Struggles against the Organization of Capitalist Enterprise', in Castoriadis 1992.

―― 1988f [1960–1], 'Modern Capitalism and Revolution', in *Political and Social Writings*, Vol 2, edited and translated by David Ames Curtis, Minneapolis: Minnesota.

―― 1988g [1973], 10/18 Postface to 'On the Relations of Production in Russia', in *Political and Social Writings*, Vol 1, edited and translated by David Ames Curtis, Minneapolis: Minnesota.

―― 1992, *Political and Social Writings*, volume 3, edited and translated by David Ames Curtis, Minneapolis: University of Minnesota Press.

―― 1997, 'The Only Way to Find Out if You Can Swim Is To Get In the Water' in Curtis (ed.) 1997.

―― 1998, [1964] 'Marxism and Revolutionary Theory', reprinted in *The Imaginary Institution of Society*, translated by Kathleen Blamey, Cambridge: MIT.

―― 2008, *Histoire et création: textes philosophiques inédits, 1945–1967*, edited by Nicolas Poirier, Paris: Seuil.

Chebel d'Appollonia, Ariane 1991, *Histoire des intellectuels en France, 1944–1954* Paris: Ed. Complexe.

Chollet Antoine 2012, 'Le désordre contre l'organisation: sur les divergences théoriques entre Lefort et Castoriadis à l'époque du *Socialisme ou Barbarie*', in Klimis, Caumières and van Eyde (eds.) 2012.

Ciliga, Ante 1938, *Au pays du grand mensonge*, Paris: Plon.

Clark, Katerina 1985, *The Soviet Novel*, Chicago: University of Chicago Press.

Clifford, James and George Marcus (eds.) 1986, *Writing Culture*, Berkeley: University of California.

Cohn-Bendit, Daniel 1968, *Obsolete Communism: The Left Wing Alternative*, New York: Harper and Row.

Coriat, Benjamin 1979, *L'atelier et le chronomètre*, Paris: Christian Bourgois.

Corpet, Olivier 1987, 'Arguments, 30 ans apres', *Revue des revues*, 4: 12–19.

Correspondence 1954, 'The Correspondence Booklet', Detroit: Correspondence.

Curtis, David Ames 1989, 'Socialism or Barbarism: The Alternative Presented in the Work of Cornelius Castoriadis', in Busino (ed.) 1989, pp. 290–332.

—— (ed.) 1997, *A Castoriadis Reader*, edited and translated by David Ames Curtis, Oxford: Blackwell.

de Certeau, Michel 1984, *The Practice of Everyday Life*, Berkeley: University of California Press.

Daniels, Robert V. 1993, *A Documentary History of Communism in Russia*, Hanover NH: University Press of New England.

Danos and Gibelin 1986, *June 36: Class struggle and the Popular Front in France*, translated by Peter Fysh and Christine Bourry, London: Bookmarks.

Dean, Phillipe, Priscilla Parkhurst Ferguson and Wendy Griswold (eds.) 1989, *Literature and Practice*, Chicago: University of Chicago Press.

Deli, Peter 1981, *De Budapest a Prague; sursauts de la gauche française*, Paris: Anthropos.

Delillo, Don 1997, *Underworld*, New York: Scribner's.

Denby, 1989, *Indignant Heart; A Black Worker's Journal*, Detroit: Wayne State.

Depretto, Jean-Paul and Sylvie Schweitzer, 1984, *Le communisme a l'usine; vie ouvrière et mouvement ouvrier chez Renault, 1920–1939* Paris: Edires.

Derrida, Jacques 1976, 'The Writing Lesson', in *On Grammatoloqy*, Baltimore: Johns Hopkins.

—— 1978, 'Structure Sign and Play', *Writing and Difference*, Chicago: Chicago Press.

—— 1982, *Margins of Philosophy*, translated by A. Bass, Chicago: O. Chicago Press.

Descampes, Eugene 1971, *Militer*, Paris: Fayard.

Descombes, Vincent 1979, *Le même et l'autre*, Paris: Minuit.

Dioujeva, Natacha and François George 1981, *Staline à Paris*, Paris: Ramsay.

Dorey, Bernard 1976 [1988], *From Taylorism to Fordism: A Rational Madness*, translated by David Macey, London: Free Association.

Dosse, François 1991, *L'Histoire du structuralisme t. 1: le champs du signe*, Paris: Le Découverte.

Dubost, Nicolas 1979, *Flins sans fin*, Paris: Maspero.

Duhnke, Horst 1959, 'Review of Sarel La classe ouvrière en Allemagne Orientale', *Journal of Central European Affairs*, 19, 3: 323.

Dunyevskaya, Raya 1942–3, 'An Analysis of the Russian Economy', in *The New International* December, 1942, January and February 1943.

Dussart, Robert 1954, 'Les greves d'Août 1953', *Socialisme ou Barbarie*, 13: 13–19.

Elgey, Georgette 1968, *Histoire de la IVe République: La République des contradictions, 1951–1954*, Paris: Fayard.

Engels, Frederich 2008 [1844], *On the Condition of the Working Class in*

England Cambridge: Harvard University Press.
Escobar, Enrique 2012, 'Sur l'influence de S ou B et, inévitablement, sur Castoriadis', in Klimis, Caumières and van Eyde (eds.) 2012.
Faber, Daniel 1954, 'La grève des postiers', *Socialisme ou Barbarie*, 13: 22–30.
Fallachon, Philippe 1972, 'Les grèves de la Régie Renault en 1947', *Le mouvement social*, 81: 111–42.
Fremontier, Jacques 1971, *La fortresse ouvrière*, Paris: Fayard.
Fridenson, Patrick 1979, 'La bataille de 4CV', *Histoire*, 9: 33–40.
———— 1986, 'Automobile Workers in France and Their Work, 1914–1945', in Kaplan and Koepp (eds.) 1986.
Freyssenet, Michel 1979, *Division du travail et mobilisation quotidienne de la main d'oeuvre: Le cas Renault et Fiat*, Paris: Centre de sociologie urbaine.
Gabler, Andrea 2001, 'Die Despotie der Fabrik und der Vor-Schein der Freiheit. Von "Socialisme ou Barbarie" gesammelte Zeugnisse aus dem fordistischen Arbeitsalltag', *Archiv für die Geschichte des Widerstandes und der Arbeit*, 16: 349–378, text available here: <http://www.magmaweb.fr/spip/spip.php?article543>.
Gérôme, Noëlle and Danielle Tartakowsky 1988, *La Fête de l' Humanité: culture communiste. culture populaire*, Paris: Messidor/Ed. Sociales.
Goody, Jack 1991, *The Interface Between the Written and the Oral*, Cambridge: Cambridge University Press.

Gombrowicz, Witold 1988–93, *Diaries*, 3 Vols, translated by S. McCleary Chicago: Northwestern.
Grignon, Claude 1971, *L'ordre des choses: les fonctions sociales de l'enseignement technique*, Paris: Minuit.
Grignon, Claude and Jean-Claude Passeron 1989, *Le savant et populaire*, Paris: Gallimard/Le Seuil.
Grimshaw, Anna (ed.) 1992, *The C.L.R. James Reader*, Cambridge: Blackwell.
Gottraux, Philippe 1997, *Socialisme ou Barbarie: Un engagement politique et intellectual dans la France de l'après-guerre*, Lausanne: Ed. Payot Lausanne.
Gouldner, Alvin 1959, 'Reciprocity and Autonomy in Functional Theory', in Gross (ed.) 1959.
Gross, Llewellyn (ed.) 1959, *Symposium on Social Theory*, Evanston: Northwestern.
Goulemot, Jean-Maire, 1981, *Le clarion de Staline*, Paris: Sycomore.
Guillaume, Philippe 1949, 'L'ouvrier américain', *Socialisme ou Barbarie*, 1: 83–94.
Habermas, Jurgen 1975, *Legitimation Crisis*, translated by Thomas McCarthy, New York: Beacon.
Hamon, Hervé and Patrick Rotman 1987, *Génération*, Paris: Seuil.
Harvey, David 1989, *The Condition of Postmodernity*, Oxford: Blackwell.
Hastings-King, Stephen 1997, 'On the Marxist Imaginary and the Problem of Practice: Socialisme ou Barbarie, 1952–6, in *Thesis Eleven* 49: 69–84.
———— 1999, 'L'Internationale Situationniste, Socialisme ou Barbarie, and the

Crisis of the Marxist Imaginary', *SubStance*, 90: 28:3.
Hatry, Gilbert 1990, *Louis Renault; patron absolu*, Paris: Editions JCM.
Heldmann, Henri 1989, *Les fils du peuple de Staline à Gorbatchev: aristocracie ouvrière, communisme et industrialisation en France et en URSS*, Paris: Henri Heldmann.
Hildebrandt, Ranier 1983, *Der 17. Juni*, Berlin: Haus am Checkpoint Charlie.
Hoggart, Richard 1998 [1957], *The Uses of Literacy*, New Brunswick: Transaction.
Howard, Dick 1988, *The Marxian Legacy*, Minneapolis: Minnesota.
Husserl, Edmund 1962, *Ideas*, New York: Collier.
——— 1970 'The Origin of Geometry', in *The Crisis of European Sciences and Transcendental Phenomenology* translated by David Carr, Evanston: Northwestern.
James, Cyril Lionel Robert *et al.* 1947, *Trotskyism in the United States, 1940–47, Balance Sheet: the Workers' Party and the Johnson-Forest Tendency*, Johnson-Forest Tendency.
——— Raya Dunyevskaya and Grace Lee, 1947 *The Invading Socialist Society* Detroit: Johnson-Forest Tendency.
——— 1950a *State Capitalism and World Revolution*, Detroit: Johnson-Forest Tendency.
——— 1950b, 'Balance Sheet of U.S. Trotskyism', typescript.
——— Anna Grimshaw and Keith Hart 1993 [1956], *American Civilization*, Oxford: Blackwell.
——— Grace Lee and Pierre Chaulieu 1974, *Facing Reality*, Detroit: Bewick.

Kaplan, Steven L. and Cynthia J. Koepp (eds.) 1986, *Work in France*, Ithaca: Cornell University Press.
Khilani, Sunil 1993, *Arguing Revolution; The Intellectual Left in Postwar France*, New Haven: Yale.
Klimis, Sophie, Philippe Caumières and Laurent van Eyde (eds.) 2012, *Socialisme ou Barbarie aujourd'hui: Analyses et Témoignages*, Cahiers Castoriadis no. 7, Brussels: Saint Louis.
Kravchenko, Victor 1947, *I Chose Freedom*, New York: Scribners.
Kriegel, Annie 1964, *Aux origines du Parti Communiste Français*, Paris: Mouton.
——— 1980, *Les communistes français*, Paris: PUF.
Lamont, Michèle 1987, 'How to Become a Dominant French Philosopher: The Case of Jacques Derrida', *American Journal of Sociology*, 93, 7: 584–621.
Lanoux, Armand 1978, *Bonjour Monsieur Zola*, Paris: Bernard Grasset.
Lee, Grace 1947, 'The Reconstruction of Society', in Romano 1972.
Lefort, Claude 1948–9, 'Les contradictions de Trotsky', *Les Temps Modernes*, 39.
——— 1952, 'L'experience prolétarienne', *Socialisme ou Barbarie*, 11: 1–19.
——— 1956, 'Review of Danos and Gibelin *Juin 36*', *Socialisme ou Barbarie*, 18: 112–15.
——— 1957, 'Reponse à Morin', *Arguments*, 4: 18–20.
——— 1978 [1952], 'Capitalisme et religion au XVIe siecle: le problème de Weber', in *Les formes de l'histoire: essais d'anthropologie politique*, Paris: Gallimard.

——— 1979a [1952], 'L'experience prolétarienne', in *Eléments d'une critique de la bureaucratie*, Paris: Gallimard.

——— 1979b [1956], 'Le totalitarisme sans Staline', in *Eléments d'une critique de la bureaucratie* Paris: Gallimard.

——— 1979c [1960], 'Qu'est-ce que c'est la bureaucratie?', in *Eléments d'une critique de la bureaucratie*, Paris: Gallimard.

——— 1974, 'Interview with Lefort', *Anti-Mythes*, 14.

Lenin, Vladmir Ilich 1970 [1903] 'The Position of the Bund in the Party', in *Lenin, Collected Works*, Vol 7, Moscow: Progress.

——— 1970 [1905] 'Two Tactics of Social Democracy' in *Lenin, Collected Works*, Vol 9, Moscow: Progress.

——— 1977 [1902] 'What Is To Be Done?' in *Lenin, Selected Works*, Vol 1, Moscow: Progress.

——— 1977 [1917] 'Imperialism, the Highest Stage of Capitalist Development', in *Lenin, Selected Works*, Vol 1, Moscow: Progress.

Lepenies, Wolf 1988, *Between Literature and Science: The Rise of Sociology*, Cambridge: Cambridge University Press.

Linhart, Robert 1976, *Lénine, les payans, Taylor* Paris: Minuit.

——— 1978, *L'établi* Paris: Minuit.

London, Kurt 1966, *Eastern Europe in Transition*, Baltimore: Johns Hopkins.

Lourau, René 1980, *L'autodissolution des avant-gardes*, Paris: Galilée.

Lyotard, Jean-François 1988 [1982], 'Pierre Souyri, le marxisme qui n'a pas fini', introduction to *Souyri, Revolution et contre-revolution en Chine*, Paris: C. Bourgois, reprinted in *Peregrinations: Law, Form, Event*, New York: Columbia.

——— 1989, 'L'Algerie, un differend', in *La guerre des Algeriens*, Paris: Galilée.

——— 1993, *Political Writings*, translated by Bill Readings, Minneapolis: Minnesota.

Magri, Suzanne and Christian Topalov 1989, *Les villes ouvrières 1900–1950*, Paris: L'Harmattan.

Mallet, Serge 1959, 'Review: *Journal d'un ouvrier de chez Renault*', *Le Nouvel Observateur*, 474: 7–8.

——— 1963, *La nouvelle classe ouvrière*, Paris: Seuil.

Marceau, Jane C. 1977, *Class Mobility and Status in France: Economic Change and Social Immobility 1945–1975*, Oxford: Oxford University Press.

Marcus, George (ed.) 1992, *Rereading Cultural Anthropology*, Durham NC: Duke University Press.

Marx, Karl 1959, *Capital: A Critique of Political Economy*, Vol 3 Moscow: International Publishers.

——— 1982, 'Letter to Annenkov on Proudhon', in *Marx-Engels Selected Correspondence*, Moscow: Progress Publishers.

1987 *Capital: A Critique of Political Economy*, New York: Penguin.

——— 1988, *The Communist Manifesto*, New York: Norton.

——— 1992 [1844], 'Economic and Philosophical Manuscripts', in *Marx: Early Writings*, edited by Lucio Colletti, New York: Hammondworth.

——— 2000 [1859], 'Preface to A Critique of Political Economy', in D. McLellan,

BIBLIOGRAPHY

ed. *Karl Marx: Selected Writings*, Oxford: Oxford UP.

Melville, Herman 2011, *Bartelby the Scrivener*, New York: Melville House.

Merleau-Ponty, Maurice 1964a, *Sense and Non-sense*, translated by Hubert Dreyfus and Patricia Allen Dreyfus, Evanston: Northwestern.

——— 1964b [1955], 'The Future of the Revolution', in *Signs*, Chicago: Northwestern.

——— 1965, *The Phenomenology of Perception*, translated by Colin Smith, London: Routledge.

——— 1970, 'Institution in Personal and Public History', in *Themes from the Lectures at the Collège de France*, Evanston: Northwestern.

——— 1973, 'Sartre and Ultrabolshevism', in *Adventures of the Dialectic*, Evanston: Northwestern.

——— 1998, *Notes de cours sur L'origine de la géometrie de Husserl*, edited by Renaud Barabas, Paris: PUF.

——— 2002, *L'Institution, la passivité: Notes de cours au Collège de France (1954–1955)*, edited by Claude Lefort, Paris: Belin.

Mills, C. Wright 1956, *The Power Elite*, New York: Oxford University Press.

Ministère fédéral pour l'unité de l'Allemagne 1954, *Soulèvement de juin – Documents et rapports sur le soulèvement à Berlin-est et dans la zone soviétique*, Berlin: Grunewald Verlag.

Michelet, Jules 1973, *The People*, translated by John McKay, Urbana: University of Illinois Press.

Molinari, J.P. 1991, *Les ouvriers communistes*, Thonon-les-bains: L'Albaron.

Morin, Edgar 1958, *Autocritique*, Paris: Minuit.

Mothé, Daniel 1954, 'La grève chez Renault', *Socialisme ou Barbarie*, 13: 34–46.

——— 1955, 'Le problème d'un journal ouvrier', *Socialisme ou Barbarie*, 17: 26–48.

——— 1956, 'Journal d'un ouvrier; Mai 1956 chez Renault', *Socialisme ou Barbarie*, 19: 73–100.

——— 1956–7, 'Chez Renault, on parle de la Hongrie', *Socialisme ou Barbarie*, 20: 124–33.

——— 1957a, 'L'usine et la gestion ouvrière', *Socialisme ou Barbarie*, 22: 74–111.

——— 1957b, 'Agitation chez Renault', *Socialisme ou Barbarie*, 22: 126–44.

——— 1958a, 'Les grèves chez Renault', *Socialisme ou Barbarie*, 23: 48–71.

——— 1958b, 'Les ouvriers français et les nord africains', *Socialisme ou Barbarie*, 21: 146–57.

——— 1959, *Journal d'un ouvrier*, Paris: Minuit.

——— 1965, *Militant chez Renault*, Paris: Seuil.

——— 1973, *Métier de militant*, Paris: Seuil.

——— 1976a, 'Entretien avec Daniel Mothe', *AntiMythes*, 18.

——— 1976b, 'Lecture en usine: pratique et subversion du tract politique', *Esprit*, 453: 117–33.

——— 1990, 'Le mythe de Billancourt', *Esprit*, 159: 11–16.

Mottez, Bertrand 1966, *Systèmes de salaire et politiques patronales*, Paris: CNRS.

Navel, Georges 1945, *Travaux*, Paris: Ed. Stock.

Naville, Pierre, Jean-Pierre Bardou, Philippe Brachet and Catherine Levy 1971, *L'Etat Entrepreneur: Le cas de la Régie Renault*, Paris: Anthropos.

Nezar el Sayyad, (ed.) 2001, *Hybrid Urbanism: On Identity Discourse and the Built Environment*, Westport CT: Praeger.

Noël, Jean-Francois 1977, *Les postiers, la grève et le service publique*, Grenoble: Presses Universitaires de Grenoble.

Noiriel, Gerard 1986, *Les ouvriers dans la société française*, Paris: Seuil.

Nove, Alec 1992, *An Economic History of the USSR, 1917–1922*, rev. ed. London: Penguin.

Offe, Claus 1980, 'Two Logics of Collective Action: Theoretical Notes on Social Class and Organizational Form', *Political Power and Social Theory*, 1: 67–115.

—— 1985, *Contradictions of the Welfare State*, edited by John Keane, Cambridge, MA: MIT Press.

—— 1986, 'Two Logics of Collective Action', in *Disorganized Capitalism*, edited and translated by John Keane, Cambridge, MA: MIT Press.

Ong, Walter 2002, *Orality and Literacy: The Technologizing of the Word*, New York: Routledge.

Oury, Louis 1973, *Les Prolos*, Paris: DeNoël.

Pluet-Despatins, Jacqueline 1978, *La presse trotskyiste en France de 1926 à 1968: Essai bibliographique*, Paris: Editions de la Maison des Sciences de l'Homme/ PUG.

—— 1980, *Les trotskvistes et la guerre*, Paris: Anthropos.

Poirier, Nicolas 2011, 'Retour sur la notion de l'expérience prolétarienne', *Première publication sur www.theoriecritique. com, 'La Haine'*. The text is available here: <http://variations.revues.org/105>.

—— 2011, *L'ontologie politique de Castoriadis: Création et Institution*, Paris: Payot.

Poster, Mark 1975, *Existential Marxism in Postwar France*, Princeton: Princeton University Press.

Poulaille, Henry 1986 [1928], *La nouvelle âge littéraire*, Bassac: Plein Chant.

Poulot, Denis 1980, *Le sublime*, edited by Alain Cottereau, Paris: Maspero, 1980.

Ragon, Michel 1974, *Histoire de la literature prolétarienne de langue français en France: littérature ouvrière, littérature paysanne, literature d'expression populaire*, Paris: Albin Michel.

Rancière, Jacques 1977, 'De Pelloutier a Hitler: syndicalisme et collaboration', *Les Révoltes Logiques*, 4: 23–61.

—— 1981, *La nuit des prolétaires: Archives du rêve ouvrier*, Paris: Fayard.

Rioux, Jean-Pierre 1987, *The Fourth Republic*, Cambridge: Cambrige University Press.

Robrieux, Philippe 1975, *Maurice Thorez: vie secrete et vie publique*, Paris: Fayard.

Romano, Paul 1972 [1947], 'The American Worker', Detroit: Bewick.

Rose, Michael 1979, *Servants of Post-Industrial Power? Sociologie du travail in Modern France*, White Plains: M.E. Sharpe.

—— 1985, *Industrial sociology: Work in the French Tradition*, London: Sage.

Ross, George 1982, *Workers and Communists: From Popular Front to Eurocommunism*, Berkeley: University of California Press.

Ross, Kristen 1995, *Fast Cars, Clean Bodies*, Cambridge, MA: MIT Press.

Rubel. Maximilien 1975, *Marx Without Myth*, New York: Harper and Row.

Sarel, Benno 1953, 'Combats ouvriers sur l'avenue Staline', *Les Temps Modernes*, 95: 672–94.

—— 1958, *La classe ouvrière en Allemagne Orientale*, Paris: Editions Sociales.

Sartre, Jean-Paul 1959 [1938], *Nausea* New York: New Directions.

—— 1964, *Situations VI*, Paris: Gallimard.

—— 1965, *Situations VII*, Paris: Gallimard.

—— 1968 [1952–4], *The Communists and Peace*, New York: George Braziller.

Scarry, Elaine 1985, *The Body in Pain: Making and Unmaking the World*, Oxford: Oxford University Press.

Shorter, Edward and Charles Tilly 1974, *Strikes in France. 1830–1968*, Cambridge, MA: Harvard University Press.

Siegelbaum, Lewis 1988, *Stakhanovism and the Politics of Productivity in the USSR, 1935–1941*, Cambridge: Cambridge University Press.

Sigfried, André, ed. 1958, *L'année politique 1957*, Paris: Editions du Grand Siècle.

Simon, Henri 1956, 'Une expérience d'organisation ouvrière: Le conseil du Personnel des Assurances Générales-Vie', *Socialisme ou Barbarie*, 20: 1–64.

—— (ed.) 2007, *Socialisme ou Barbarie, une anthologie*, La Bussière, France: Editions Acratie.

Simons, David and Edward Burns 1988, *The Corner: A Year in the Life of an Inner City Neighborhood*, New York: Random House, 1998.

Singer, Brian 1979, 'The Early Castoriadis: Socialisme ou Barbarie and the Bureaucratic Thread', *The Canadian Journal of Political and Social Theory*, 3, 3: 35–56.

Sirinelli, Jean-François (ed.) 1987, 'Generations intellectuelles – effets d'age et phenomenes de génération dans le milieu intellectuel français', *Les cahiers de l'Institut de l'Histoire du Temps Present*, 6.

Socialisme ou Barbarie 1949a, 'Presentation', *Socialisme ou Barbarie*, 1: 1–6.

—— 1949b, 'Lettre Ouverte aux militants du PCI et de la IVe Internationale', *Socialisme ou Barbarie*, 1: 90–101.

—— 1950, 'La vie de notre groupe: Bilan d'une année', *Socialisme ou Barbarie*, 5/6: 136–47.

—— 1950a, 'La situation internationale', *Socialisme ou Barbarie*, 7: 95–103.

—— 1952, 'La guerre et la perspective révolutionnaire', *Socialisme ou Barbarie*, 9: 1–14.

—— 1953, 'La situation internationale', *Socialisme ou Barbarie*, 12: 48–59.

—— 1955, 'Le réunion des lecteurs de *Socialisme ou Barbarie*', *Socialisme ou Barbarie*, 17: 79.

—— 1959, 'Comment Mallet juge Mothé', *Socialisme ou Barbarie*, 28: 83–5.

Sorel, Georges 1981 [1918], *Matériaux pour une théorie da proletariat*, Paris: Statkine.

Souvarine, Boris 1940, *Stalin: A Critical Survey of Bolshevism*, translated by C.L.R. James, London: Secker & Warburg.

Stalin, J.V. 1939, *Short Course of the History of the Communist Party of the Soviet*

Union (*Bolshevik*), New York: International Publishing.

Stéphane, Roger 1956, 'Les ouvriers de Renault et la Hongrie', *L'Express*, 284: 6.

Stora, Benjamin 1992, *La gangrene et l'oubli: La mémoire de la guerre d'Algérie*, Paris: Découverte.

Swain, Geoffrey and Nigel Swain 1993, *Eastern Europe Since 1945*, London: St. Martin's.

Swain, Nigel 1992, *Hungary: The Rise and Fall of Feasible Socialism*, London: Verso.

Thompson, Edward Palmer 1966, *The Making of the English Working Class*, New York: Vantage.

Thorez, Maurice, 1949, *Fils du peuple*, Paris: Editions Sociales.

Tiano, André, Michel Rocard, and Hubert Lesire-Ogrel 1955, *Expériences francaises d'action svndicale ouvrière*, Paris: Editions Ouvrières.

Touraine, Alain 1955, *L'Evolution du travail ouvrier aux usines Renault*, Paris: CNRS.

Trotsky, Leon 1941, *Stalin*, New York: Harpers.

―― 1942, *In Defense of Marxism*, New York: Pioneer Publishers.

―― 1945, *The Revolution Betrayed*, New York: Pioneer Publishers.

―― 1961, *History of the Russian Revolution*, translated by Max Eastman, Ann Arbor: University of Michigan Press.

van der Linden, Marcel 1997, 'Socialisme ou Barbarie: A French Revolutionary Group (1949–1965)', *Left History*, 5:1 pp. 7–37. The article is available online here: <http://libcom.org/library/socialisme-ou-barbarie-linden>.

Véga, A 1954, 'Signification de la révolte de juin 1953 en Allemagne Orientale', *Socialisme ou Barbarie*, 13: 3–10.

Verdier, Brie 1981, *La presse syndicale ouvrière: Analyse statistique du contenu*, Sceaux: Centre de Recherches en Sciences Sociales du Travail.

Verdès-Leroux, Janine 1983, *Au Service du Parti: Le PCF, les intellectuels et la culture*, Paris: Fayard/Minuit.

Vidal-Naquet, Pierre 1989, *Face à la raison d'état: Un historien dans la guerre d'Algérie*, Paris: Découverte.

Wacquant, Loïc 2006, *Body and Soul: Notes of an Apprentice Boxer*, Oxford: Oxford University Press.

Wark, Mackenzie 2011, *The Beach Beneath the Streets: The Everyday Life and Glorious Times of the Situationist International*, London: Verso.

Wieder, Donald Lawrence, 1974, *Language and Social Reality*, Paris: Mouton.

Weil, Simone 1951, *La condition ouvrière*, Paris: Gallimard.

Whyte, William Foote 1993, *Street Corner Society*, Chicago: University of Chicago Press.

Williams, Robert 1986, *The Other Bolsheviks: Lenin and his Critics 1904–1914*, Bloomington: Indiana University Press.

Willis, Paul 1981, *Learning to Labor: How Working Class Kids Get Working Class Jobs*, New York: Columbia.

Wittgenstein, Ludwig, 1997 [1953] *Philosophical Investigations* Oxford: Blackwell.

Index

Albert, Eric   106, 108, 124, 128–132, 134, 257–258
　See also: Lefort, Claude *L'expérience prolétarienne*
Algerian War   91, 246n7, 250, 268–269, 279, 281–298, 324
alienation
　Fragmentation of work   11, 19, 50, 108, 115, 124, 143, 191, 193, 269, 316, 321
　　(*see also*: deskilling; rationality, bureaucratic/managerial)
　of workers from dominant politics   185, 195, 199, 215, 315n169, 318
　　(*see also*: legimation crisis)
　psychological   63, 299
　radical politics as rationalization of   3, 325
"The American Worker" (*see* Romano, Paul)
anarchism   137, 205, 208, 214, 230, 240, 269
　Fédération Anarchiste   43, 249, 255
AOC (Atelier Outillage Central at Billancourt)   27, 107–108, 110, 244, 252–253, 256, 280, 282, 285, 287–288, 290–292, 295–300, 302–305, 307, 310, 312–321
　See also: Mothé, Daniel; Renault Billancourt; semi-skilled workers; Tribune Ouvrière
Arguments (journal)   1, 41, 108n3, 235, 249, 250n35, 254, 261n74
artisanal workers *see* skilled workers
Aulagnier, Piera   3, 325
autonomous worker actions   14–15, 18, 34, 59, 68, 75–75, 105, 113, 116, 120, 135, 194, 295, 318
　see also: East Berlin June Days; general strike; wildcat strike
autonomy
　inter-organisational   147, 149
　　see also: PCF-CGT system
　Political   1, 9, 14, 45n65, 105, 116n22
　　see also: direct democracy; socialism, content of; worker councils
　professional   18, 43, 104, 118, 120, 142, 205n75, 231, 273–274
　　see also: deskilling; Fordism

Badie, Bertrand   145, 147
　See also: PCF-CGT system
Bailhache, Georges   69
barbarism, modern   64
Barois (*see* Sternberg, Benno)
Barthes, Roland   121, 128, 134, 141, 258n65
Bell, Hugo (*see* Sternberg, Benno)
Blachier, Pierre   126n51, 152n45, 205–206, 209n85, 227n125, 231n134, 242n35, 260, 295n141, 315
　Il faut se débrouiller   233–234
Billancourt *see* Renault Billancourt
Blanchard, Daniel   242n27, 246n34, 254n57, 256n58, 324
Bois, Pierre   144n24, 204, 206–207, 214, 217–219, 295
Boggs, Grace Lee   17, 167, 177, 184
Bologne-Billancourt   5, 30n30
　see also: Renault Billancourt
Bordigism   53, 71, 218, 240, 242
Bourdieu, Pierre   5, 22, 28–29, 52, 157n61, 189n52, 220–222
bourgeois
　political economy   39, 65–67
　rationality   9, 45, 107, 175, 192–195, 314–315, 317, 324
　society   9, 26, 55, 111–112
　writers (versus proletarian literature)   267, 270–272, 274–275, 278
bureaucracy
　and Leninism   53–59
　see also: dirigeant/executant; Organization Question; Vanguard Party, critique of
　in Trotsky   46–47
　situation with a social totality   53–59
bureaucratic capitalism, theory of   12n15, 13–16, 26–29, 33, 37, 38–46, 65–68, 105, 108–109, 113, 117, 134, 159, 191–191, 216, 256, 280, 295n147, 314, 316–317
　fundamental contradiction of   14–16, 41–42, 52, 68, 88n44, 107–108, 295n147, 313, 316–317
　See also: dirigeant/executant
bureaucratization   28, 33, 42–46, 100, 200

Castoriadis, Cornelius   1–2, 19–20, 43, 61–65, 68–71, 76, 102, 111n12, 125, 184, 187–189, 197, 212, 216, 227, 229n128, 234, 236, 242, 247, 254, 294, 324–325
   Chaulieu-Montal Tendency   13, 30–37, 39, 54, 69–71
   Modern Capitalism and Revolution   280, 319–20, 324
   On the Content of Socialism I   75, 165, 189–195, 198–199, 315
   On the Content of Socialism II   280, 299–300, 307n169
   On the Content of Socialism III   107n14, 167n5, 212, 260, 312, 315n185, 316–317
   Organisation Question   33–36, 53–60, 71, 76, 109–110
   post-*Socialisme ou Barbarie* work   4–9, 45n64, 45n65, 112n15, 114, 117n28, 123n44, 133, 193, 321
   Relations of Production in Russia   46–53
   Socialisme ou Barbarie editorial   26–28, 81n27, 88n44
   Socialisme ou Barbarie study circle on Lenin (1949)   63–60, 76
   Seminars on *Capital* (1950–1951)   39n49, 65–68
   See also: Chaulieu-Montal Tendency, *Socialisme ou Barbarie*
CFDT (Confédération Français Démocratique du Travail)   1, 149n35, 157, 159–160, 163–164, 245n33, 247n37, 307n169, 312n181
CGT (Confédération Générale du Travail)   219, 241n22
   at Billancourt   136–139, 142–147
      and collective bargaining   146–153, 154, 225
      strikes, uses of   154–155, 215–216
      militants, types of   156n43, 159–160, 162, 164
      relations with worker base   155–158
      PCF-CGT system   94, 137–139, 147–148, 220–225
      Production speed   228–231
      Wage disputes   149, 151, 208–213
      Micropolitics in the AOC   282–298, 299, 301–303, 305–309, 322
   PTT strike (1953)   90, 94–102, 118
   See also: PCF-CGT System; PCF

Chaulieu-Montal Tendency   1, 13, 17, 30–37, 39, 54, 69–71
   and Johnson-Forest Tendency   32, 34–35, 125, 166–167, 239n16
   See also: Fourth International; Johnson-Forest Tendency; PCI (Parti Communiste Internationale)
Chaulieu, Pierre (*see* Castoriadis, Cornelius)
chronos (time-motion men)   78n18, 87, 117, 131, 155, 316
Cold War   34, 37, 40–41, 59–65, 68, 80
   PCF-CGT and   146–153, 161, 205, 302, 306
collective bargaining (*see also* Renault Accords)   6, 15, 18, 120, 137–139, 147, 148–153, 208
concentration, tendency toward   59–65
   See also: Castoriadis, Cornelius Seminars on *Capital*; imperialism
construction trades, East German   79, 83, 84, 104
   See also: East Berlin June Days 1953
Correspondence   6–7, 16–18, 28, 129, 165–167, 276
   antecedents   167–9
   See also: Johnson-Forest Tendency
   Critique of Leninism   167n4, 168, 170, 185
   Organization   169–71, 176–9
   Worker Writing   171–7, 179–83
   relations with *Socialisme ou Barbarie*   184–190, 195–202, 259, 276, 282, 319
   See also: Boggs, Grace Lee; Denby, Charles; Dunayevskaya, Raya; James, C.L.R.; Paine, Lyman; Romano, Paul; worker newspaper; worker writing
Cottereau, Alain   272n98
class
   conflict   73, 141, 285, 288, 303, 316, 318
   See also: dirigeant/exécutant
   Composition, Chaulieu-Montal Tendency   35–36
   consciousness   12, 16, 33, 58, 64, 106, 124, 134, 154, 215–216, 252
      in-itself/for-itself   10, 112–115
   formation   112, 114, 259, 262, 277
      Soviet bureaucracy as a new class formation   46–52
   See also: bourgeoisie; working class

INDEX 339

de Certeau, Michel 137, 286–288
de Diesbach, Sebastien 44n62, 242n27, 246n34, 256n58
Denby, Charles 182–183, 282
de-stalinization 260–261, 321
dialectical materialism 11, 32, 264
direct democracy 188
   socialism as 14–15, 45n65, 113n18, 115n22, 136, 165, 188, 192
   worker councils and 74–76, 103–105, 135
dirigeant/exécutant 12–14, 24, 27, 33, 41–44, 50, 109, 191
   See also: bureaucratic capitalism; management; skill as collective attribute; worker self-management
Dunayevskaya, Raya 17, 167, 169, 171, 183, 186n43

East Berlin June Days (1953) 5, 77–90, 118, 135, 188
les établis 120n39, 140n10, 157

Faber, Daniel 91, 94–95
field of ideological production, delimited
   Renault Billancourt 135–164, 220–225
   Socialisme ou Barbarie 28–32, 36, 52–53, 68–70
   See also: Bourdieu, Pierre
F.O. (Force Ouvrière) 90, 95, 138n3, 153n50
Ford, Henry 119
Fordism, industrial 40, 78n18, 118, 139, 141–142, 157, 161, 164, 176, 232, 236, 276–277, 280, 313–314, 317, 320
   as war on skill 118–120
Fourth International 30–32, 37–39, 68, 184, 218, 239
fragmentation of work (*see* Alienation, fragmentation of work)
Friedman, Georges 107, 265n84
Front Populaire (1936) 27, 94, 129n60, 137, 141–143, 145, 146n30, 237n4
Front Unique (1934) 143

Gabler, Andrea 23
Gaspard (*see* Hirzel, Raymond)
Gautrat, Jacques (*see* Mothé, Daniel)
Gautrat, Martine 71, 238n7, 246n34, 254n57

general strike, unlimited 24, 74, 76–77, 90–91, 95, 98n72, 108–109, 142, 154, 206, 215, 263, 283, 286n123, 293
Gombrowicz, Witold 281–282
Gottraux, Philippe 22, 29n17
Guillaume, Philippe (Cyrille Rousseau de Beauplan) 23, 92, 124–125, 127–128, 189, 197, 246n34, 254n56, 293–294

Hayek, Frederich 67
Hennecke Movement (*see* Stakhanovism)
heretical argumentation/subversion 29, 30, 36, 52, 70, 219, 256, 290
Hirzel, Raymond (Raymond Bourt, Gaspard) 63, 71, 99, 205–207, 214–215, 218, 225, 241, 244n32, 246–247
hierarchy
   bureaucratic/managerial conceptions of 15, 18, 45, 76, 118
   informal, within worker collectives 42, 104, 203
   (*see also* Skill as collective attribute)
   politics of 43, 103, 151–153, 205, 207–213, 214–215, 228, 299
   (*see also* direct democracy)
   trade union 132, 157, 164, 241
   Tribune Ouvrière and the politics of 207–215
   See also: direct democracy, socialism, content of
L'Humanité (PCF newspaper) 93n58, 94, 99, 101, 142, 145, 263, 300–301
   See also: PCF, PCF-CGT system
Hungarian Revolution (1956) 19, 76, 103, 135, 146, 173n22, 190, 220, 250, 279, 284, 298–300, 308–310, 312, 319, 322–323
Husserl, Edmund 114, 116, 127, 249, 285n121, 295, 309
   See also: institution; phenomenology

idée force 220–225
   See also: Bourdieu, Pierre
industrial sociology 16, 107, 245n33, 251n45
informal worker collectives, shop-floor 15, 42, 81, 104, 104, 135, 155, 161, 185, 319–320
   See also: bureaucratic capitalism; management; proletarian standpoint; skill as collective attribute

imperialism   26, 54n86, 55, 59–65, 68, 70
  See also: concentration, tendency toward
institution (instituted/instituting)   27, 116, 142, 164, 191–192, 195, 256, 261, 268n92, 285n121, 295, 309
  See also: Husserl, Edmund; Merleau-Ponty, Maurice
irrationality   67, 110, 316–317
  See also: bureaucratic capitalism; Castoriadis, Cornelius seminars on Capital; rationality

James, C.L.R.   19, 46n66, 154n52, 165, 167–172, 177–178, 181, 183, 184–189, 190, 239, 324
  See also: Correspondence; Johnson-Forest Tendency
Johnson-Forest Tendency   17, 20n17, 32, 34–35, 125, 166–167, 171, 239n16
  See also: Correspondence

Korean War   63–65
  See also: World War III

language games   8, 116n27, 235–236, 279, 287–288, 292, 295, 299, 309, 311–312, 318, 322
  See also: de Certeau, Michel; Wittgenstein, Ludwig
Laniel, Joseph   90, 93–96
Laplanche, Jean   69–70
Lefort, Claude   2n4, 32, 46n66, 53, 64, 135–136, 238n9, 242–243, 268n92, 271
  on bureaucracy   38–42
  Chaulieu-Montal Tendency   13, 30–37, 39, 54, 69–71
  L'expérience prolétarienne   16–17, 105–124, 129, 132–134, 174, 190, 192, 235, 256–258, 312
  on the Hungarian Revolution   250n43, 300n153
  and Socialisme ou Barbarie   69, 184n43, 244–245, 254n56, 294
  Socialisme ou Barbarie's "Organisation Question"   33–36, 53–60, 71, 76, 109–110
  and Les Temps Modernes   77–78, 125
  Le totalitarisme sans Staline   314n185
  See also: bureaucratic capitalism, fundamental contradiction of; bureaucratization

legitimation crisis   215–216, 236, 280, 290–291, 298–299, 302, 305, 312
Lenin, V. I.   13, 20, 26–27, 30–31, 33–35, 47, 52, 53–62, 68, 75–76, 85, 268
  "All Russia Newspaper"   68
  See also: Correspondence; Tribune Ouvrière; worker newspaper
Leninism   79, 109, 137, 154, 158, 162–164, 208, 211, 218–219, 221, 263, 309
  factory cell organization   94, 144–145
  and wage disputes   94, 149–151
  See also: Vanguard Party
Leninism, critique of (see Socialisme ou Barbarie, Organisation Question)
limited strikes (grèves tournantes) (see CGT, Strikes, uses of)
literacy, French working-class   223–224
Lutte Ouvrière   16, 205, 219
Lyotard, Andrée   71, 246n34
Lyotard, Jean-François   1, 3, 71, 196n62, 242–243, 246n34, 254n56, 324

machinists   6, 19, 86, 118–120, 229–230, 237, 314
  See also: metalworkers; semi-skilled workers
"Malenkov Interregnum"   72–74, 77–90 passim
Mallet, Serge   107, 251–3, 265, 276, 325
management (industrial)
  As synonym for dirigeant   13–16, 26, 38, 40, 42–4, 50, 81, 86–7, 117, 119–120, 135, 313–317
  See also: bureaucratic capitalism; dirigeant/exécutant
  Renault management   136–138, 140, 142, 146–147, 151–155
  Micro-politics at Renault
    Tribune Ouvrière and   207–212, 228–232
    Mothé and   289, 291, 305–306
  See also: worker management
Marie-Rose   35, 234
Marshall Plan   62–63
Marx, Karl
  1844 Manuscripts   18, 273
  See also: alienation, fragmentation of work
  A Contribution to the Critique of Political Economy   47–69

Capital   11, 19–20, 39n49, 51, 60, 65–68, 107–108, 194
Communist Manifesto   9–10, 26, 110–111, 276
German Ideology   111
Letter to Annenkov   193–4
Marxism
   Construction of the worker   11–14, 106–123, 212, 224n118, 256–257, 261–262, 269
   See also: proletarian literature; Poulaille, Henry
   Marxist language
      As horizon for militant activity   167–169, 177, 185–186 236–242, 244
      As horizon of autonomous worker actions   76, 85–86, 89, 98, 102–103, 117–118, 135, 199, 236, 250, 279, 285, 289–291
      Worker disinvestment from   7, 160, 252, 278–279, 280–282
   Orthodox   11–12, 38, 46–53
   PCF-CGT   149–150, 220–221, 264
   See also: CGT; PCF; trade-union pluralism)
   Socialisme ou Barbarie relations to   25–37, 39, 49, 55, 60, 65–68, 111, 142
Marxist Imaginary   3–5, 8–9, 19, 21–2, 53–4, 69, 76, 232, 236, 247, 278–279, 284, 286
   Crisis of   278–282, 298–320, 321–325
   See also: Castoriadis, Cornelius, post-Socialisme ou Barbarie work
Maso, Alberto (*see* Véga)
Merleau-Ponty, Maurice   77, 111n12, 112–113, 116–117, 123n45, 130
   See also: institution; phenomenology
metalworkers (les métallos)   96, 98–99, 120, 237, 240–1, 243
Michelet, Jules   256, 262–263, 265–269, 270, 273–275
militant, typology   156–64
Mollet, Guy   260n71, 283–284, 296
Morin, Edgar   4, 41n41, 250, 255, 283n115
   See also: Arguments (journal)
Mothé, Daniel (Jacques Gautrat)   2, 4, 7–8, 17–19, 21–23, 71, 86, 91, 99–102, 120, 131, 134, 136, 146, 188–189
   Agitation chez Renault   305–22
   biography   163–204–205, 209n84, 225–226, 236–242

   Chez Renault on parle de la Hongrie   298–304
   Les grèves chez Renault   305–22
   in Socialisme ou Barbarie   243–248, 254–255
   Journal d'un ouvrier (book)   000
   Journal d'un ouvrier (essay)   281–98
   Lecture en usine   219–220, 227
   Métier du militant   156–64
   Le problème d'un journal ouvrier   190, 195–202
   pseudonym, relations with   220, 242–253, 255–257
   and *Tribune Ouvrière*   202–207, 211–214, 216–219, 222, 224–227, 231–232
   L'Usine et la gestion ouvrière   312–18
   writing   159–260, 276–278, 281, 322–324
   See also: Marxist Imaginary, crisis of; worker newspaper; worker writing

Nantes (*see* Shipyard Strikes, 1955)
Neues Deutschland (newspaper)   79, 84–87
Le Nouvel Observateur   250–251, 261

Offe, Claus   43–4, 148–151, 155

Paine, Lyman   169, 171
PCF-CGT system   94, 137–139, 147–148, 220–225
PCF (Parti Communiste Français)   4, 29, 135–164
   as idée force for Left political field   29–31, 34
   as idée force at Billancourt   136–139, 142, 219–224
   and CGT (*See* CGT, PCF-CGT System)
   and crisis of the Marxist Imaginary   284, 298–305, 322–325
   and Front Populaire   27, 94, 129n60, 137, 141–143, 145, 146n30, 237n4
   and Hungarian Revolution   235, 250, 260n71, 279, 298–305
   and Left Opposition   125, 139, 143–4, 224–225, 241–244
   and revolutionary discourse   68–69, 215–219
   See also: legitimation crisis; trade-union pluralism
   L'Humanité See *L'Humanité*

PCF (Parti Communiste Français) (cont.)
  micro-politics AOC, Algeria   242, 261, 283–284, 290–291, 294–296
  PTT strike 1953 93–95, 98–99
  representations of working class   134–164, 256, 260–265, 269–270, 278
    See also: Poulaille, Henry; Thorez, Maurice
    See also: CGT, de-Stalinisation; PCF-CGT System
PCI (Parti Communiste Internationale)   13, 23, 31–37, 53, 69, 77n10, 184n42, 238–239
    See also: Chaulieu-Montal Tendency
PCI Majority Tendency   36
Petit, Georges (Georges Petro)   71, 91n51, 246n34
phenomenology   17, 110–111, 114, 116, 121, 123, 127, 132–133, 173n22, 256–258
    See also: Husserl, Edmund; Merleau-Ponty, Maurice
point of production   5–6, 13–16, 42, 44, 46, 74, 89, 105–108, 110, 113, 117, 121, 125, 135–136, 167, 188, 190, 192, 232, 258, 280, 312, 314–315, 318–320
    See also: bureaucratic capitalism, fundamental contradiction of; dirigeant/executant
Poland   15, 261n72, 299–300, 3134n185, 321
Popular Front (1936) (see Front Populaire 1936)
Poulaille, Henry   256, 260–278
Poulot, Denis   272
production cadence, production speed   6, 18, 82–84, 93, 103, 110, 120, 131, 151, 155, 228–234
productivism   16, 49, 232, 258, 273, 277, 284, 312, 318, 320
proletarian literature   129, 157, 200, 223, 235, 251–253, 256, 260–278
    See also: Michelet, Jules; Mothé, Daniel; Poulaille, Henry
proletarian standpoint   16, 108, 111, 114, 117, 121–122, 131, 133, 312, 317
    See also: bureaucratic capitalism; informal worker collectives, shop-floor; rationality, bureaucratic managerial; skill as collective attribute
PTT   91–94
  PTT strike (August 1953)   86, 89, 90–104, 160n67

Queneau, Raymond   223, 265

Raoul (PCI militant)   69–71, 185n44
rationality
  Bourgeois, dominant   9, 10, 13, 191
  bureaucratic, managerial   43–45, 107, 110, 112, 193, 315, 317
  problem of revolutionary theorist   13, 55, 190–192, 315
  proletarian   107–110
  socialist   14, 16, 17, 192, 315
Régie Renault (RNUR)   139–144
Renault Accords (1955)   153, 208n81
    See also: collective bargaining
Renault Billancourt (factory)   5–7, 16–18, 21, 23, 30n19, 98–101
  collective bargaining   148–153
  PCF-CGT domination of   125–144–146, 208–213
  political situation   137–139, 146–147
  professional and wage hierarchies   208–213
  role of small proletarian revolutionary organisations   142–143
    (see also Front Populaire)
  roles played by militants   156–164
  semi-skilled workers   118–120
    See also: deskilling; Industrial Fordism
  Symbolic importance of   131–136–137, 139–144
    See also: AOC; CGT; Mothé, Daniel; PCF; PCF-CGT System; Tribune Ouvrière
Renault, Louis   139–140, 160
revolutionary organization (see Leninism, Socialisme ou Barbarie: organization question)
revolutionary syndicalism   90, 97, 129, 262, 264, 270, 275
revolutionary theory   1, 12, 15–16, 25, 56, 75, 165, 189–195, 198–199, 311–321
  and autonomous worker movements   74–76, 102–104, 300
    See also: East Berlin June Days 1953; PTT strike; shipyard strikes 1955; Hungarian Revolution
  and Correspondence   167, 188, 190
    See also Correspondence; James C.L.R.
  Mothé and   243, 256, 262, 280, 311–318
    See also: Mothé, Daniel

proletarian experience and   107–109, 115, 133, 135–137
  See also: Castoriadis: *Socialisme ou Barbarie* editorial; Leninism, critique of, Socialisme ou Barbarie: organisation question
Romano, Paul   125
  "The American Worker"   16–17, 75, 106, 108, 124–133, 168, 174, 125, 256–259, 312–313, 316
  See also: Lefort, Claude *L'expérience prolétarienne*; proletarian standpoint; worker writing
"Russian Question"   13, 31, 38–39, 54n87, 184, 238–239
  See also: Castoriadis, Cornelius, *Socialisme ou Barbarie* editorial; *The Relations of Production in Russia*; Chaulieu-Montal Tendency; Johnson-Forest Tendency; Leninism, critique of; Stalinism; Trotsky, Leon
Russian Revolution   14, 26, 27, 30, 32, 186, 237,
  and PCF   150
  See also: Castoriadis, Cornelius, Study Circle on Lenin; *The Relations of Production in Russia*; Leninism critique of; Stalin, Joseph; Stalinism; Trotsky, Leon

Sartre, Jean-Paul   77n15, 111n12, 145, 261n72, 314n185
semi-skilled workers   14, 18, 100, 104, 118–120, 155n55, 161, 166, 208–210, 224, 316
  and French industrial wage hierarchy   208–210
  See also: AOC; deskilling; Fordism as war on skill; metal-workers; Mothé, Daniel
SFIO (Section Française de l'Internationale Ouvrière)   95n69, 262–263, 269, 273
shipyard strikes, Nantes and St. Nazaire 1955   15, 90, 99, 118n31, 135, 142
Signorelli, Jacques (Garros)   71, 184, 189, 196n62, 237n4, 241, 246n34
Signorelli, Louisette   246n34
Simon, Henri   23, 71, 196n62, 206, 231–232, 235, 245–248
skilled workers   10, 50, 266, 273–274, 277

skill as collective attribute   17, 42, 45, 117, 315–318
  See also: bureaucratic capitalism; informal worker collectives, shop-floor; rationality, bureaucratic managerial; proletarian standpoint
social-imaginary significations   7n11, 12, 45n69, 106, 113–115, 152, 252, 279, 285, 321, 325
  See also: Castoriadis, Cornelius, post-Socialisme ou Barbarie work; Marxist Imaginary
socialism, content of   51, 75, 169, 188–195, 198–199
  See also: autonomous worker actions; Castoriadis, Cornelius; direct democracy; revolutionary theory
Socialisme ou Barbarie
  and Correspondence   184–189
  composition of group   19–20, 68–71, 242–243, 196n34, 254–255
  journal production and circulation   15–20, 24, 216–217, 226–227, 323
  Organisation Question   33–36, 53–60, 71, 76, 109–110
  pseudonyms   125, 242–243
    See also: Mothé, Daniel, pseudonym, relations to
  transcripts of group meetings   32–36, 53–59, 196n62, 185–189, 197, 234, 293–4
Socialist Realism   263–265
sociology of work (sociologie du travail)   1, 117n59, 251–253, 265, 278
  See also: Freidman, Georges; Mallet, Serge; Touraine, Alain
Soviet Union   2–3, 24, 26, 46–53, 59–65, 72–74, 77–90, 109, 190, 215, 238–240, 260, 302–304, 322
  PCF and   138–139, 143–147, 151, 155–156, 161, 269, 302–306
Stalin, Joseph   4, 13, 30–31, 39, 46, 68, 72–76, 79, 83, 85, 89, 145, 263, 284
Stalinallee (East Berlin)   78, 83–87, 93
  See also: East Berlin June Days   1953
Stalinism
  as epithet for PCF or CGT members   196, 204–205, 293, 308
  See also: AOC, micro-politics; Renault Billancourt

Stalinism (cont.)
  as synonym for Soviet system   13, 24,
    30–33, 36, 39, 46–53, 55, 64n105, 69,
    72–76, 78, 80, 82, 91, 238–239, 264, 294,
    299, 303, 322–323
    See also: Castoriadis, Cornelius, The
      Relations of Production in Russia;
      Russian Question
  in France   138, 164
    See also: CGT; PCF-CGT system, PCF
Stakhanovism   78–79, 81–82, 230
  See also: Fordism; Taylorism
Sternberg, Benno (Hugo Bell, Barrois, Benno
  Sarel)   77–90, 188–189, 254n56

"Telling the code"   285–287
Taylorism   150
  See also: assembly line; Fordism
Les Temps Modernes   46n66, 77, 83, 111n13,
  125, 128, 189n52, 250, 261n72
  See also: Lefort, Claude; Merleau-Ponty,
    Maurice; Sartre, Jean-Paul; Sternberg,
    Benno
Third International   12, 27, 48, 56
Thorez, Maurice   142–145, 264–265, 293
Tiano, André (sociologist)   139n6, 140,
  143–144, 152–154, 161, 208, 210–211, 307
Touraine, Alain   107, 119, 252, 254, 267n84,
  325
trade-union pluralism   95, 137, 159, 161, 205,
  213, 299, 302, 305, 322
Tribune Ouvrière   1, 17–18, 20–21, 109, 134,
  165–166, 184n41, 202–233, 255, 260, 281,
  288, 307, 324
  circulation and production   217, 226–227
  collective   196, 202, 204–207, 214, 216–218,
    232, 246–248, 319
  context at Billancourt   137, 148, 156,
    220–227
  on production speed   228–236
  on professional hierarchy   203, 207–216
  on wage levels   208–211, 213
  and the worker newspaper project   190,
    196–198, 200, 202, 227
  and worker writing   233–234, 315–317
Tripartite Government 1947   93, 142, 150,
  218
Trotsky, Leon   4, 13, 30–35, 46–47, 60, 195,
  289n80, 319n190
  See also: Lenin, V.I.; Russian Question;
    Russian Revolution; Stalin, Joseph
Trotskyism   5, 13, 16–17, 24, 28–39, 52–53, 55,
  59, 69–70, 74–75, 78, 89, 115n23, 143–144,
  167, 169–170, 178–182, 184, 198, 204–206,
  217–219, 221–222, 237–240, 242–244, 246,
  252, 305, 308n173
  See also: Chaulieu-Montal Tendency;
    Fourth International; Johnson-Forest
    Tendency; Lutte Ouvrière; PCI; PCI
    Majority Tendency

USSR see Soviet Union

van der Linden, Marcel   22
Véga (Alberto Maso)   2, 28, 70n116, 71, 78,
  125, 188–189, 196–197, 227n125, 242, 246n34,
  254, 325
Vivier, Georges   23, 131, 246n34, 256

wage disputes   10, 120
  PCF-CGT position on   149–151, 155,
    207–212
  See also: collective bargaining
  Tribune Ouvrière and micro-politics
    of   207–212, 228–230
  See also: CGT; wage disputes; hierarchy,
    professional
Weber, Max   29, 158
Wieder, D.L. See "Telling the code"
wildcat strikes (see autonomous worker
  actions)
Wittgenstein, Ludwig   116, 287, 321
  See also: language games
worker councils   22, 26, 31, 68, 103, 189, 190,
  299–300
  See also: autonomous worker actions;
    Castoriadis, Cornelius; direct
    democracy; socialism, content of
worker experience
  at the point of production   6–7, 11, 13–17,
    19, 25, 43, 68, 75, 104–136, 188, 190–192,
    196–198
  of political action   95, 156–164
  and Correspondence   165–168, 173–175
  Mothé and the worker newspaper   188,
    190–192, 196, 199, 202
  and Tribune Ouvrière   202, 207, 212–213,
    215–216, 228–234

INDEX

worker management (of production, of society)   10, 13, 28, 47, 50, 75, 103, 191, 312
  See also: direct democracy; socialism, content of
worker newspaper   6–7, 17–18, 136, 165, 184, 190, 235, 244, 245, 247, 256, 281–282, 318–319, 324
  Correspondence   167–183
  Mothé on the worker newspaper project   196–202
  and *Tribune Ouvrière*   202–204, 206, 216–217, 219, 222, 224, 227, 232
  See also Correspondence, James, C.L.R., Mothé, Daniel, organization question, Tribune Ouvrière, worker writing
worker writing   4, 6–7, 15–18, 20, 23, 136, 165, 312
  Lefort and proletarian documentary literature   110, 113, 117, 121, 123, 127, 134, 136, 312
  Correspondence and   168, 170, 171–176, 179, 183, 282
  SB, *Tribune Ouvrière* and   184, 200, 202–214, 216
  and Daniel Mothé   235, 249, 255, 258, 260, 281
  proletarian literature and   265, 270–271, 273
  See also: Michelet, Jules; Poulaille, Henry; proletarian literature
  See also: Albert, Eric; Blachier, Pierre; Lefort, Claude, L'expérience prolétarienne; Mothé, Daniel; Romano, Paul
World War III   25–26, 61, 64, 69–71

Yugoslavia Communist Party   36–37

Zola, Emile   266, 270–272
Zupan, Johnny (editor, Correspondence)   170, 177–8